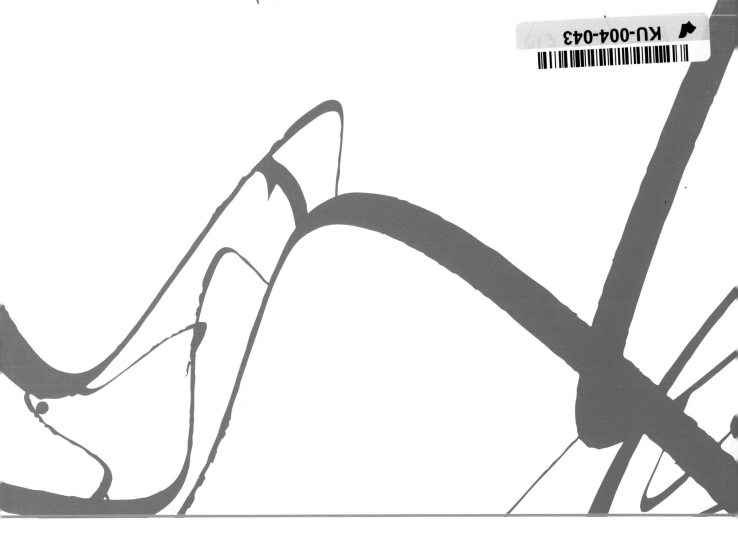

The Irish Study of Sexual Health and Relationships

Dr Richard Layte

Prof. Hannah McGee

Amanda Quail

Kay Rundle

Gráinne Cousins

Dr Claire Donnelly

Prof. Fiona Mulcahy

Dr Ronán Conroy

Published by the Crisis Pregnancy Agency and the Department of Health and Children

October 2006

ISBN 1-905199-08-2

30-01 10/06 (1,000) Brunswick Press Ltd. (17465)

Foreword by Minister for Health and Children, Mary Harney TD

I welcome the Report on the Irish Study of Sexual Health and Relationships (ISSHR).

The National AIDS Strategy Committee (NASC), in its report Aids Strategy 2000 recommended that a national survey be undertaken of sexual knowledge, attitudes and behaviours in Ireland. Such a survey is in line with research in other European countries. Its purpose is to provide useful information on attitudes and behaviours and to provide a benchmark for evaluating the impact of our policies and practices in relation to HIV and other STIs and in relation to our overall sexual health.

On foot of the NASC recommendation, my Department and the Crisis Pregnancy Agency commissioned the Irish Study of Sexual Health and Relationships in 2003. The results of that survey form the basis of this report. The survey was conducted by the Economic and Social Research Institute (ESRI) and the Royal College of Surgeons in Ireland (RCSI).

The ISSHR provides nationally representative statistical data describing levels of sexual knowledge, attitudes and behaviours of adults (18 years and over) in Ireland for the first time.

The data contributes to an informed understanding of the factors related to the broad spectrum of sexual behaviour and practice. It allows us to develop a greater insight into the contribution individual behaviours, appropriate service development and education and prevention activities can make to securing good sexual health and avoiding negative outcomes. The study underlines the need to develop appropriate responses in relation to sexual health inequalities, sexual practices and behaviours, sex education and life-long learning and service development and planning.

The Report provides detailed information and analysis of the responses received from 7,441 participants. I commend and congratulate all those involved in the survey and preparation of the Report, the participants who spoke candidly about this intimate, sensitive area of their lives, the 27 interviewers, the ESRI and the RCSI. The data it provides will inform the development of policies and services in the area of Sexual Health and Relationships in future years.

Mary Harney TD

Minister for Health & Children

Introduction

IT is a great pleasure for me to welcome the Irish Study of Sexual Health and Relationships (ISSHR). It is the largest nationally representative study on sexual knowledge, attitudes and behaviour ever undertaken in Ireland.

This study was commissioned by the Department of Health and Children and the Crisis Pregnancy Agency (CPA) in response to a recommendation of the National AIDS Strategy Committee.

The Crisis Pregnancy Agency became involved in the project in the light of international evidence showing that aspects of sexual health, such as contraception, crisis pregnancy and sexually transmitted infections, should be examined jointly.   The study builds upon the already extensive research conducted by the CPA since its establishment.

The CPA and the Department of Health and Children funded this research because the sexual health sector needs robust and comprehensive data to effectively plan sexual health policies and strategies and to inform effective approaches to promoting positive sexual health messages.

The findings of this report will be considered by various organisations and will inform the future development and strategic direction of the CPA's work in reducing the number of crisis pregnancies.

The report will also provide valuable and sought-after information for individuals, organisations and policymakers working to prevent and manage crisis pregnancy and sexually transmitted infections in Ireland. It will contribute to the development of a national sexual and reproductive health strategy.

I would like to thank the research teams, led by Dr Richard Layte of the ESRI and Professor Hannah McGee of the RCSI, and the team at Trinity College. I would also like to thank the people who gave of their time and expertise in steering and managing this project and in critiquing this report. A special word of thanks is due to the staff of the Crisis Pregnancy Agency and the Department of Health and Children for their strong commitment to completing this project.

Olive Braiden

Chair

Crisis Pregnancy Agency

About the authors:

Dr **Richard Layte** is a sociologist at the Economic and Social Research Institute. His work examines the way in which health and the use of health care services are influenced by socio-economic factors. Recent work includes papers on smoking and social class, contraceptive use and class, unemployment and mental health, and equity in health care utilisation in Ireland. He is the co-principal investigator on the ISSHR Study.

Professor **Hannah McGee** is a health psychologist and director of the Health Services Research Centre, Royal College of Surgeons in Ireland (RCSI). Her research addresses the psychological and social factors associated with health, illness and healthcare in Ireland. Ongoing work includes national studies of ageing, stroke care and population health behaviour. She is the co-principal investigator on the ISSHR Study.

Amanda Quail is a research fellow at the Economic and Social Research Institute. Her research centres on the psychological, educational, health and social development of children and young people. She is currently working on the National Longitudinal Study of Children in Ireland.

Kay Rundle is a research psychologist and researcher at the Health Services Research Centre, RCSI. Her research focus is on sexual health and patient experiences of healthcare. Recent work includes a national study of contraception and crisis pregnancy and a review of renal patient services.

Gráinne Cousins is a health psychologist and researcher at the Health Services Research Centre, RCSI. Her research focus is on sexual behaviour and alcohol. Recent work includes a national study on public perceptions of participation in biomedical research.

Dr **Claire Donnelly** is a consultant in infectious diseases at the Royal Victoria Hospital, Belfast. Her current research examines the distribution of behaviours which confer an increased risk of STI infection in the population and the implications this pattern has for the societal burden of STIs.

Professor **Fiona Mulcahy** is Medical Director of the Department of Genito Urinary Medicine and Infectious Diseases at St James's Hospital Dublin and is University Professor and Lecturer at Trinity College Dublin. Her research interests include antiretroviral management of marginalized groups including intravenous drug users and asylum seekers. She has conducted extensive research into the pharmacokinetics of antiretroviral therapy.

Dr **Ronán Conroy** is a senior lecturer and a statistical and research advisor at the RCSI. He has extensive experience in all areas of biostatistics and has worked in medico-social research since 1979. His own areas of research interest are in cardiovascular disease and low-technology solutions to major health problems in developing countries.

The views expressed in this report are those of the authors and do not necessarily reflect the views or policies of the sponsors.

Acknowledgements

THIS study was commissioned by the Department of Health and Children (DoHC) and the Crisis Pregnancy Agency (CPA).

The authors would like to acknowledge the role played by a large number of people outside of the study team who contributed to the completion of the study.

First, we wish to acknowledge the co-operation of the 7,441 individuals who gave their time to take part in the study and who discussed with us many extremely personal aspects of their lives. Without their generous assistance, this study could not have yielded the wealth of information that will be invaluable in developing locally informed policies and services in the coming years.

The ESRI Survey Division, and James Williams, Amanda Quail, Ita Condron and Pauline Needham in particular, not only contributed hugely to the design of the survey and its protocols, but also showed fine judgement and professionalism in guiding the fieldwork to successful completion.

The study team also wishes to acknowledge the hard work and commitment of the 27 interviewers who worked on the project: Miriam Ahern, Eimear Breheny, Delia Brownlee, Laura Callaghan, Claire Corcoran, Jessica Dempsey, Riona Donnelly, Frances Lyne, Phil Fitzsimons, Catherine Glennon, Kate Halligan, Kathleen Hyland, Hillary Heeney, Fiona Kane, Aoife Kearney, Ciara Lawless, Emer McDermott, Anne Marie McGirr, Charleen McGuane, Carmel McKenna, Katherine Norris, Marita O'Brien, Aideen O'Neill, Patricia O'Neill, Martine Taylor, Anne Toner and Eileen Vaughan.

A large number of other people contributed to the development of the methodology, protocols and data analysis of the ISSHR study. The research team acknowledges their contribution.

The following were members of either the Management and/or Steering Committee for part or all of the project: Bernie Hyland (HSE), Sharon Foley (CPA), Caroline Spillane (CPA), Dr Nazih Eldin (HSE), Dr Stephanie O'Keeffe (CPA), Olive McGovern (DoHC), Mary Smith (CPA), Frances Shearer (Department of Education & Science), Mick Quinlan (Gay Men's Health Project), Deirdre Seery (Alliance SHC), Madeleine O'Carroll (CPA), Ciara O'Shea (DoHC), David Moloney (DoHC), Brian Mullen (DoHC), Deirdre Sullivan (CPA), Deirdre McGrath (CPA), Paul Walsh (DoHC), Lucy Deegan Leirião (CPA), Prof. Linda Hogan (TCD), Paula Mullin (DoHC) and Chris Fitzgerald (DoHC).

Other people generously participated in reading groups for the research reports: Dr Máirín O'Sullivan (DoES), Maeve Foreman (TCD), Dr Fenton Howell (HSE), Geraldine Luddy (NWC), Shay McGovern (DoHC), Karen Griffin (IFPA), Teresa McElhinney (HSE), Ann Nolan (AIDS Alliance), Ciaran McKinney (GHS), Biddy O'Neill (DoHC) and Tim McCarthy (DoHC). Others contributed at important points in the overall process: Collette Leigh and Rebecca Garavan (Royal College of Surgeons in Ireland).

This study had a long gestation. Many groups and individuals encouraged and recommended the development of a robust evidence base on sexual health issues in Ireland. We thank all those who enabled this work. We hope that the ISSHR findings will help develop a better understanding of the interplay of sexual knowledge, attitudes and behaviours in contemporary Ireland, and inform the development of improved sexual health policy and services for all.

Contents

Recommendations 293

List of tables

List of figures

Abbreviations

AIDS	Acquired Immune Deficiency Syndrome
ASHR	Australian Study of Health and Relationships
CATI	Computer-aided telephone interview
CPA	Crisis Pregnancy Agency
DoHC	Department of Health and Children
ESRI	Economic and Social Research Institute
GMHP	Gay Men's Health Project
GUIDE clinic	Genito-urinary infectious disease clinic
GUM	Genito-urinary medicine
HIV	Human Immunodeficiency Virus
HPSC	Health Protection Surveillance Centre (formerly the NDSC)
HSE	Health Service Executive
ICCP	Irish Contraception and Crisis Pregnancy Study
IDU	Intravenous drug user (IVDU)
IFPA	Irish Family Planning Association
ISSHR	Irish Study of Sexual Health and Relationships
ISSP	International Social Survey Project
KABS	Knowledge, attitudes and behaviour surveys
MSM	Men having sex with men
NASC	National AIDS Strategy Committee
NATSAL	National Survey of Sexual Attitudes & Lifestyles
NDSC	National Disease Surveillance Centre
NHSLS	National Health and Social Life Survey
ONS	Office of National Statistics (UK)
RANSAM	Sample selection programme developed at the ESRI
RCSI	Royal College of Surgeons in Ireland
RDD	Random digit dialing
RSE	Relationship and Sexuality Education
SAVI	Sexual Abuse and Violence in Ireland Study
SILC	Survey of Income and Living Conditions
SPHE	Social, Personal and Health Education
STD	Sexually transmitted disease
STI	Sexually transmitted infection
WHO	World Health Organisation

Glossary

Cohort	A generational group.
Concurrency	Simultaneous occurrence (in ISSHR, of more than one sexual relationship).
Confidence interval	This provides an upper and lower bound within which we can be sure that true value will be found 95% of the time (derived from the 'standard error').
Cumulative distribution	A description of the population, once ranked by another factor. In ISSHR it is used in the construction of the 'median' statistic (eg, when assessing the median number of sexual partners). Individuals are ranked from those with the lowest number to those with the highest. The median value is that of the person who is half way up the ranked population (ie, at the 50% percentile).
Design effects	A measure of how much statistical uncertainty is introduced into a survey by the manner in which individuals are selected for interview.
Dichotomised	Separated into two parts or classifications.
Disaggregation	The separation of an aggregate body into its component parts. In statistics, categories may be split or disaggregated to reveal finer details.
Older women	This is a relative term used to make a distinction between different age groups in a study. The term 'older' is not used in a pejorative way for men or women.
Religiosity	The condition of being religious. The sociological use of this term has no pejorative connotation.
Sex and sexuality	Sex is used in this report to mean sexual activity. Sexuality encompasses sex, gender identities and roles, sexual orientation, pleasure, etc. It is affected by many factors and their interaction (biological, social, psychological, historical, cultural, economic, political, legal, religious and spiritual).
Sexual health	Sexual health is used to mean, not merely the absence of infection, disease, dysfunction or infirmity, but a state of general well-being (physical, emotional, mental and social) in the area of sexuality.
Standard errors	A quantification of the uncertainty in a measure. The smaller the absolute number of individuals interviewed and the less 'random' the selection procedure, the greater the standard error.
Survey instruments	The questionnaires used to interview individuals who agree to take part in the study.
Survivor curve	The generic name for a technique that examines the rate of change in a variable over time. A survivor curve usually plots the proportion of a population who have not yet experienced some outcome. It may also be used to plot a 'failure rate': the proportion who do not experience some outcome.

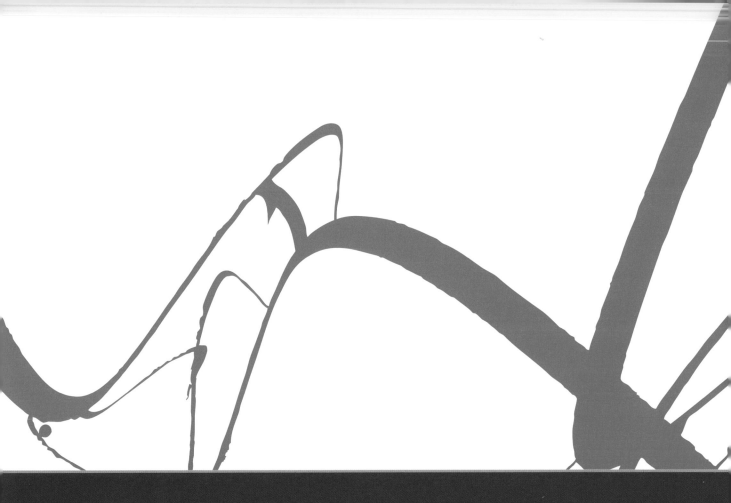

Chapter 1:

Introducing the Irish Study of Sexual Health and Relationships

1.1   Introduction

SEX and sexuality are core dimensions of the human experience and an important determinant of well-being. An individual's sexual behaviour and sexual health cannot be separated from their social and cultural context. This is brought out in the World Health Organisation's (WHO) definition of sexual health. It is concerned not just with the absence of disease or dysfunction but with a broad definition of health:

"Sexual health requires a positive and respectful approach to sexuality and sexual relationships, as well as the possibility of having pleasurable and safe sexual experiences, free of coercion, discrimination and violence." [1]

Nonetheless, sexual behaviour can have serious consequences for physical health. These have been the subject of growing concern: Rates of sexually transmitted infections have increased by over 250% in Ireland since the mid-1990s.[2] HIV notifications have increased by 243% between 1998 and 2003.

Research by the Crisis Pregnancy Agency[3] also shows that around a quarter of women who have been pregnant have experienced a 'crisis' pregnancy, a figure which rises to over half of all women under 26 who have been pregnant.

These worrying developments demand a coordinated policy response, yet in Ireland this response has been undermined by a lack of detailed information on sexual partnerships, practices and use of contraception and protection, and the manner in which these are related to sexual attitudes, knowledge and beliefs.

Research on sex in Ireland has been mainly confined to the study of sexual attitudes.[4][5][6][7] Representative sources of data on sexual behaviours include:

- a limited module on sexual behaviours in the 1994 International Social Survey Project[8][9]
- an analysis of contraceptive behaviour in the ICCP Survey[3]
- an analysis of general sexual activity, contraception and condom use using the 1998 and 2002 Slán surveys[10]

The availability or lack of representative and detailed data has an impact on the policy response. The Irish Study of Sexual Health and Relationships (ISSHR) was designed to fill the need for data. This report is one of four that detail the findings of the study.

This report provides a general overview of the main findings from the ISSHR Survey. **ISSHR Sub-Report 1: 'Learning About Sex and First Sexual Experiences'** provides more detailed findings on how individuals learn about sex and on their first sexual experiences.

ISSHR Sub-Report 2: 'Sexual Health Challenges and Related Service Provision' provides more in-depth analyses of sexual health challenges such as STIs and crisis pregnancy as well as examining associated service use.

ISSHR Sub-Report 3: 'Contemporary Sexual Knowledge, Attitudes and Behaviours in Ireland' provides a detailed examination of contemporary Irish sexual knowledge and attitudes, and the manner in which these are related to behaviours.

The ISSHR project and accompanying reports emerged from a series of developments over a number of years. In almost all countries where knowledge, attitude and behaviour (KAB) surveys have been carried out, public-health concerns have provided the impetus and legitimation for these. To a certain extent this has been true for Ireland. However, the ISSHR project, overall, emerged from a broader set of concerns and interests, such as:

- the development and findings of sexual knowledge, attitude and behaviour surveys (KABS) in other countries over the last two decades
- the deliberations and recommendations of the National AIDS Strategy Committee (NASC)
- a scoping study for an Irish KAB carried out in 2003
- the establishment, mandate and interests of the Crisis Pregnancy Agency in October 2001

These different influences together led to the commissioning in December 2003 of a national KAB survey for Ireland. These influences will be examined in more detail in the **second section** of this chapter.

The chapter's **third section** examines the importance of the Irish context for understanding the results of the ISSHR survey. Sexual knowledge, attitudes and behaviours can only be understood within the history and culture of an Ireland that has changed radically in recent decades.

The **fourth section** examines the issue of socio-economic differences in health and their role in shaping sexual knowledge, attitudes and behaviours.

The **fifth section** briefly discusses Irish legislation on sexual issues and, more importantly, how this has changed in recent decades.

The **sixth and last section** outlines the structure of the rest of the report and briefly summarises the issues examined in the next 11 chapters.

1.2   Context and rationale for the study

1.2.1   The development of sexual knowledge, attitude and behaviour surveys

STUDIES of sex have been carried out from the late 19th century onward. These include studies in the UK (see Hall 1999 for a review) and, in the USA, the renowned studies of Kinsey and Pomeroy in the 1930s and 1940s[11][12] and Masters and Johnson[13] in the 60s. However, modern survey methods and probability samples were not applied to sex research until the 1980s.

The earlier studies were general attempts to uncover the nature of human behaviour, largely from a biological perspective. Researchers felt it was not possible in the moral climate of the day to ask intimate questions of a broad swath of the population, using random probability sampling. Right up to Masters and Johnson, researchers of sexual behaviour were often regarded with suspicion and faced constraints on their work and even prosecution.[14]

It was only with the rise of the incurable virus HIV in the 1980s that large-scale surveys on sex were seen as legitimate and funding for them became available. Sex research was still regarded with suspicion in some, often powerful quarters, but a ground swell of support emerged for national KAB surveys in a number of countries once it was understood that HIV was, for the most part, a sexually transmitted disease and that the risk of infection was proportional to the number of both heterosexual and homosexual partners with whom unprotected sexual intercourse had taken place.[14][15] It became imperative to understand this, plus other risk factors such as intravenous drug use and the extent of mixing between higher- and lower-risk groups.[16][17]

1.2.2 Increases in HIV and STIs in Ireland and the role of the National AIDS Strategy Committee

THE level of new HIV infections in Ireland has been reasonably low compared to that in other countries.

The pattern remained fairly flat (see *Figure 1.1*) until the mid-1990s.[18] Since then, however, there has been a rise in infections. After 1998, there was a steeper increase. Between 1998 and 2003 infections rose by 243%, but this increase was not straightforward. First, it was from a comparatively low base; the rate of increase is misleading as the absolute number involved is relatively small. Secondly, the data show that most new infections occurred among heterosexuals of whom over 80% were recent immigrants from sub-Saharan Africa.[18] They would have acquired their infections outside the state.

The pattern of HIV infection in Ireland was not, then, one found in many other industrialised countries. After 1998, however, the rate of increase did suggest that HIV could be a substantial problem in time if conditions were conducive to its spread.

Figure 1.1: HIV incidence by transmission group and year of diagnosis – Ireland 1986-2004

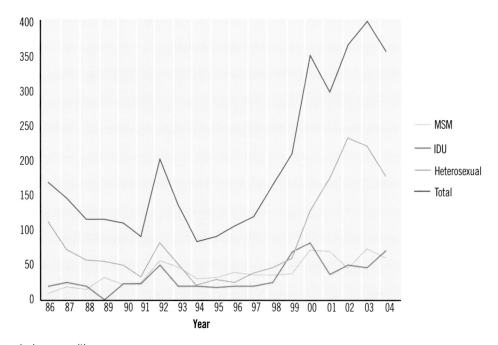

MSM: Men who have sex with men
IDU: Intravenous drug use

What is perhaps more striking in the Irish context is the steady increase in other sexually transmitted infections since 1989. This may be seen in *Figure 2.1*. It uses data from the reports from 2000 to 2003 of the Health Protection Surveillance Centre.[a] The data show that the number of new STI infections notified increased from 2,228 in 1989 to nearly 10,500 in 2003. Rates of genital warts, non-specific urethritis and Chlamydia trachomatis increased strongly, particularly after 1994.

---

[a] HPSC – formerly the National Disease Surveillance Centre.

Sexually transmitted infections (STIs) can have serious consequences for individuals and present a substantial burden for health-care services:

• If left untreated, Chlamydia can lead to pelvic inflammatory disease and be a cause of ectopic pregnancy and infertility.
• Genital warts and the virus which causes them can cause cervical and other genital cancers.
• Hepatitis C can cause chronic liver disease and liver cancer.

An increase in STIs is, therefore, a cause for deep concern in its own right, but infection with STIs also increases the risk of transmission of HIV during unprotected sex.

This means that the large increases in STIs in Ireland over the last 15 years and the rise in HIV infection among the heterosexual population, albeit from a low base, could lead to large increases in HIV infection in Ireland over the medium term. Whether or not there is a steep increase depends upon the extent and distribution of risky sexual behaviours in the population and the socio-sexual mixing of high- and low-risk groups.

Figure 1.2: Number of notified sexually transmitted infections 1989 to 2003 total & selected types

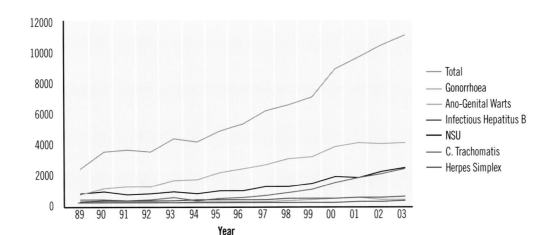

It was in the context of an increase in HIV and STI infections after the mid-1990s that the report of the National AIDS Strategy Committee (AIDS Strategy 2000) recommended that a National Survey of Sexual Knowledge, Attitudes and Behaviours in Ireland be carried out in line with those in other European countries. Such a study would provide:

• nationally representative information on knowledge and attitudes to sex, sexual health, sexual health services and sexual behaviour
• a benchmark for planning future sexual health promotion services and strategies

Both 'Quality and Fairness: A Health System for You' and 'The National Health Promotion Strategy 2000-2005' supported the full implementation of the AIDS Strategy 2000.

1.2.3   The scoping study for a national KAB survey

THE Education/Prevention Sub-Committee of the National AIDS Strategy Committee was responsible for ensuring the implementation of the recommendations from the report of the National AIDS Strategy Committee ('AIDS Strategy 2000') that a National Survey of Sexual Knowledge, Attitudes and Behaviours in Ireland be carried out.

In May 2002, it invited tenders for a Scoping Study for A National Survey of Sexual Knowledge, Attitudes and Behaviour. In September 2002, following an open competition, the Education and Prevention Sub-Committee commissioned a consortium from the Economic and Social Research Institute (ESRI), Royal College of Surgeons in Ireland (RCSI) and an independent research consultant to conduct a study to examine the practical and methodological issues involved in undertaking a new and separate national survey of sexual attitudes and behaviour.

The scoping study had four interlinked objectives:
- to review the issues that could feasibly be addressed in a national survey of sexual knowledge, attitudes, and behaviour in Ireland
- to review the operational and methodological procedures and cost implications relevant to a survey in this area
- to consult with relevant stakeholders
- to recommend terms of reference for a national survey of sexual KAB

The scoping study consulted widely with stakeholders in the area of sexual health and education. It brought forward a number of recommendations for a national KAB survey for Ireland.[9] As with such surveys in other countries, it was agreed that the survey would collect information on risky sexual practices and sexual attitudes, knowledge and beliefs as well as their socio-demographic correlates. But Layte *et al* (2003)[9] also reflected the strong view of stakeholders that considerable efforts be made to understand how people learned about sex throughout life and the nature and impact of early sexual experiences. There was also strong support for the view that risky sexual practices include those that contribute to crisis pregnancy and that these should form a substantial part of the final study.

One interesting feature of the development of a KAB survey for Ireland was the emergence early on of an intention to see sex as a positive and enjoyable behaviour rather than only as a pathological and risky pastime. The dominance of epidemiological concerns in KAB surveys means that sex and sexuality are often seen only through the prism of pathologies and problems. A major theme of the consultation process was that sex is also a positive and pleasurable experience that can contribute enormously to personal well-being.

On July 17th 2003, CPA and the Department of Health and Children published a tender document. It requested proposals for the first national sexual KAB survey. The primary aim of the project, as set out in the tender document, was the collection of reliable nationally representative baseline information that would:

- build a representative and reliable national picture of sex and sexual **behaviour** in Ireland
- measure levels of sexual **knowledge** among people in Ireland
- reliably assess national **attitudes** to important constructs related to sex, sexuality, service use, etc, to examine patterns (similarities and differences) among different cohorts and the patterns underlying these variations
- examine, explore and reliably describe the interrelationships between knowledge, attitudes and behaviours in the context of theory, sexual health promotion and policy development

The research objectives of the study were defined as:

- To establish baseline data that will enable key variables to be monitored, replicated and tracked over time.
- To provide nationally representative statistical data describing levels of sexual knowledge, attitudes and behaviours in Ireland, to better inform policy and practice.
- To understand the factors (behavioural, attitudinal and knowledge level) related to the broad spectrum of sexual behaviour and practice and to feed this information into policy and practice. Key sexual behaviours and practices of interest include risk-reductive behaviours, protective behaviours, positive and negative sexual health outcomes.
- To generate a better understanding of the factors that contribute to unplanned pregnancy, STIs and the interrelationships between these factors.
- To examine this data with respect to key variables (eg, urban/rural categories, gender, education levels) so as to assess any significant patterns with respect to behaviour, attitudes or service usage, for example.
- To compare findings with international data and with previous Irish data and to feed this information into policy and practice.

1.2.4   The role of the Crisis Pregnancy Agency

THE Crisis Pregnancy Agency was involved in the steering group of the Scoping Study for A National Survey of Sexual Knowledge, Attitudes and Behaviours. Since it has direct interest in the findings, it took part in both commissioning and joint-funding the first national KAB survey in Ireland from which the ISSHR study and this study report are derived.

Because of the interests of the Crisis Pregnancy Agency, and unlike in a number of other countries, the development of a national KAB survey in Ireland was substantially influenced by issues around reproductive health.

The CPA was established in October 2001 to act as the planning and co-ordinating body in the area of crisis pregnancy in Ireland. Its principal aim is to formulate and implement a strategy to address the issue of crisis pregnancy through:

- a reduction in the number of crisis pregnancies by the provision of education, advice and contraceptive services
- a reduction in the number of women with crisis pregnancies who opt for abortion by offering services and supports which make other options more attractive
- the provision of counselling and medical services after crisis pregnancy

The Irish Contraception and Crisis Pregnancy (ICCP) survey, which was commissioned by the CPA,[3] showed that significant numbers of Irish people still do not consistently use contraception even though they, or their partner, do not want to conceive at the time. Inconsistency was strongly related to the type of relationship which the person had with their partner. Sex in casual relationships or recently formed relationships was far more likely to occur without protection largely because respondents were not prepared, sex was unexpected or, more worryingly, because the individual had been drinking or taking drugs. Around 10% of respondents to the ICCP survey did not use contraception when they last had intercourse.

Inconsistent use of contraception is one of the main reasons why

- over a quarter of Irish women under 46 who have been pregnant have experienced a crisis pregnancy
- the number of women with Irish addresses visiting British abortion clinics increased strongly between the late 1980s and 2000

The establishment of CPA should help to change this picture, but its task was not helped by the lack of data linking sexual practices and partnerships with use of contraception, sexual attitudes and knowledge. For this reason CPA had a strong interest in seeing a national KAB survey being completed.

1.3 Influences on Irish sexual knowledge, attitudes and behaviours

SEXUAL behaviour is influenced by a wide range of factors, including the development of social attitudes and culture, public institutions and a country's regulatory/legal structure. In all these respects Ireland has changed dramatically in the last four decades.

Most Western industrial countries have experienced, in the decades after 1960, tremendous change in attitudes and behaviours in areas such as women's role in society and sexual freedom. In Ireland, however, these changes occurred in the context of the wider pressures of industrialisation and urbanisation that took place long after they happened in other countries in Europe.[20] The 1970s also brought closer integration of Ireland and Irish institutions with other European nations. This integration profoundly affected the nature of Irish society. Together these changes accelerated and intensified the extent and nature of change in attitudes and behaviours in Ireland in the last four decades.

Influences on Irish sexual culture have also come from outside the country. Although emigration was a constant in Irish society from the founding of the state in 1922 right up to the 1990s, particularly high numbers of Irish people left to find jobs elsewhere in the 1950s and 1980s. When economic fortunes changed in the 1990s, the experiences of these emigrants returned with them to Ireland. These may well have influenced national patterns of sexual attitudes and behaviours.

Lastly, the influence of the mass media in Ireland in stimulating attitudinal and behavioural change should not be underestimated. During the last three decades, media sources available in Ireland have proliferated; many of these originate outside Ireland's borders.

Such developments have had a substantial influence on the development of social attitudes.[7] The pace of change, particularly in the last 30 years, has been immense. Ireland has largely converged with other European countries in terms of living standards, demographic trends and legal frameworks. However, research shows that Irish people, both North and South, have significantly more conservative attitudes compared to populations in other European countries.

For example, Layte *et al* (2003)[9], using the European Values Survey 1999/2000, showed that, when asked on a scale of one to ten whether certain forms of behaviour are justified (1=never justified, 10=always justified)

- 70% of the Irish sample rated homosexuality at five or less
- 88% rated having casual sex at five or less
- 98% rated having sex under the legal age of consent at five or less

To put this in a European context, if the mean score of the Irish sample on these questions is used, the score on homosexuality in the Republic of Ireland is the lowest in Western Europe except for Portugal and Northern Ireland. On the issue of casual sex and sex under the age of consent, Ireland has the lowest score in Western Europe (ie, these behaviours are seen as less justified). Even among those under 30, people in the Republic are more conservative on these issues than all other Western European states except Portugal and Northern Ireland.

To understand the conservatism of current Irish sexual culture, present-day Ireland needs to be placed in the context of its recent history and the move from an agricultural/rural society which pursued protectionist and isolationist economic and social policies[21] to a highly globalised, mostly urban, post-industrial society.

It should also be remembered that, until comparatively recently, sexual discussion, public policy on sex and sexual behaviour itself all occurred within a cultural framework that was significantly influenced by Catholic social and moral teaching.[22] The Catholic ethical framework was the dominant framework in Ireland until the 1960s; concerns about sexual probity were part of daily life and were enforced, to various degrees, throughout Irish society.

Irish legislation and the Constitution also reflected Catholic moral teaching.[23] The foundation of the Irish state in 1922 was followed by a number of pieces of legislation that sought to bring Irish criminal law in line with Catholic thinking. The 1929 censorship law not only banned erotic literature but also defined as obscene any literature that provided information on or advocated 'unnatural' birth-control methods. Control of artificial contraceptives followed in 1935 (and remained in place until 1973) as did the Public Dance Halls Act in 1935 which sought to control the threat that unsupervised dancing supposedly posed to public morality.

The climate of repression in matters sexual shaped the imagery and language within which relationships and sex were experienced by the majority of Irish people. Most were brought up to associate sex with feelings of guilt, shame and embarrassment. This had a number of consequences.[24] First, it created an environment in which it was extremely difficult to find clear, factual information on sex and relationships. Secondly, the dominance of Irish Catholic moral teaching had the consequence of producing a state that simultaneously had the highest rate of non-marriage *and* fertility in Europe.[25] This pattern emerged from the strict sanction on sex outside marriage, widespread marriage avoidance and a ban by the Catholic Church on artificial forms of contraception within marriage. Marriage avoidance, a key pattern in Irish demography after the Famine, peaked in the first half of the 20th century. At that time it reached levels that were unprecedented either in Irish or broader European history.

Fahey[22] quotes figures showing that in the 1920s the average age at marriage rose to 35 for men and 29 for women. Among those aged 45 to 54, 29% of men and 24% of women had never married. This figure was far above the European norm of 10 to 15%. This high level of non-marriage may be one reason why Irish people born before 1960 are more likely than those born after to have never had sex. In a European context, this is a highly unusual pattern (see chapter seven).

Within marriage, Irish fertility rates were the highest in Western Europe and have remained so into the present, although they have decreased substantially in absolute terms. Marital fertility peaked in the 1880s and fell slowly thereafter until 1980 at which point it stabilised. After 1970 the growth in non-marital fertility balanced out the decline in marital fertility. Ireland's fertility rate thus remains comparatively high.[25]

The rise in non-marital fertility is a good indicator of the changes in sexual attitudes and behaviours that Ireland has experienced since the 1960s.

- Non-marital births represented just 1.6% of births in 1961.[25]
- By 2000, non-marital births represented around a third of all births (CSO 2005).

The bulk of this change occurred after 1980, at which point only 5% of births were outside marriage.

Marriage, clearly, has lost much of its previous importance as the gateway to sex and reproduction. This is underlined by changes in sexual attitudes on the subject.[b] Whereas, in 1973, 71% of the population felt that pre-marital sex was always wrong[4], by 1994 this proportion had fallen to 32%[22]. The ISSHR survey of 2005 found that just 6% of respondents thought that pre-marital sex was 'always wrong' (see chapter four).

Such changes suggest that the idea of sex before marriage has become increasingly normalised and that attitudes on the subject are no longer congruent with Catholic teaching. A softening of attitudes toward pre-marital sex has occurred across the age range, but the statistics suggest that it was particularly marked among younger age groups. In 1973, 44% of those under 30 thought sex before marriage 'always wrong' compared to 87% of those aged 51+ (a ratio of 2:1). This shows a deep difference between age groups even by the early 1970s. By 1994, this rift had substantially widened: only 8% of those under 30 thought sex before marriage 'always wrong' compared to 58% of those aged 51+ (a ratio of over 7:1). Even among older people, however, attitudes had changed substantially.

The relationship of these changing sexual attitudes to sexual behaviours is one of the major questions to be tackled in the ISSHR project. The increasingly secular framework through which sex is seen by Irish people means that the formal prescriptions and rules about acceptable behaviour advocated by the Catholic Church no longer have the force they once did to shape behaviour. What they have been replaced with is unclear. Inglis[24] has argued that a new secular moral framework based upon individual responsibility and rationality is becoming dominant in Ireland, with sex and sexuality increasingly seen as a dimension of general health and lifestyle. If so, this could have both positive and negative consequences for individuals and Irish society.

On the one hand, it may mean that discussion around sexual issues becomes easier and more rationally based; this could lead to improved knowledge of sexual issues and better sexual health behaviours. If so, this should eventually lead to lower levels of negative outcomes such as crisis pregnancy and STI infection.

On the other hand, fewer moral restrictions mean that individuals make choices based solely on whether they wish to have a particular experience and on its possible consequences. For most individuals this may present few problems; they will seek to balance their sexual expression with sufficient protection. However, if knowledge of sexual-risk factors is limited or risks are discounted, perhaps because sex takes place after the consumption of alcohol and other drugs, such an attitudinal framework could lead to problems.

1.4   The impact of socio-economic inequality

RESEARCH both in Ireland[26 27 28] and internationally[29] has shown that levels of both premature mortality and poor health vary across the socio-economic scale. People of lower income, education or social class are far more likely to suffer poor health. Living standards, life chances and the lifestyles of different socio-economic groups have a strong effect on general health. These differentials apply just as strongly in the area of sexual health.

Research internationally has shown that low levels of education and lower socio-economic position are associated with a higher probability of certain risk factors for sexual health such as sexual intercourse at a young age and poor or inconsistent use of contraception and protection. In fact, the English National Strategy for Sexual Health and HIV 2001[31] identifies poverty and social exclusion as

---

[b] It is important to emphasise that non-marital fertility does not necessarily imply single parenthood, simply that the mother was not married when the child was born.

the main determinants of sexual ill health in the English population. This is likely to be the case in Ireland as well.

For this reason, throughout this report there is an emphasis on the role of socio-economic factors such as education and social class in shaping sexual knowledge, attitudes and behaviours.

1.5 Key Legislative Developments

Contraception

Criminal Law (Amendment) Act, 1935	Prohibits the importation and sale of artificial methods of contraception.
McGee v. Attorney General [1974] IR 284	The Supreme Court decides that this prohibition is unconstitutional as it was an unjustified invasion of Mrs McGee's right to privacy in her marital affairs.
Health (Family Planning) Acts 1979, 1992 and 1993	Provides for the regulation and control of the sale, importation, manufacture, advertisement and display of contraceptive devices (excluding contraceptives with a medical dimension such as the contraceptive pill).
	Provides that Health Boards (as they then were) and other appropriate bodies may supply family-planning services.
	Deregulates the sale of condoms.
Health Acts 1947 onwards	Provides for the regulation and control of contraceptive pills and other contraception that has a medical dimension. Such contraceptives fall under the remit of medical legislation and are subject to the requirements of the National Drugs Advisory Board.

Abortion

Offences Against the Person Act, 1861	It is an offence to procure a miscarriage.
Eighth Amendment of the Constitution Act, 1983	Article 40.3.3° acknowledges the right to life of the unborn, with due regard to the equal right to life of the mother.
Attorney General v. X [1992] 1 IR 1	The Supreme Court, in interpreting this provision in the Constitution, held that the termination of pregnancy is unconstitutional unless there is a real and substantial risk to the life, as opposed to the health, of the mother, which risk includes the risk of suicide.

ECJ Case No. 375, 29.10.1992, Open Door and Dublin Well Woman Centre v. Ireland	The European Court of Justice ruled that it was legal for a pregnant woman to travel abroad to obtain a service in a European member state where that service was legally provided. The court also ruled that a state, in which abortion is illegal, is entitled to prohibit the distribution of information on the identity and location of clinics in another member state where abortions are legally carried out.
Twelfth Amendment of the Constitution Bill, 1992	In 1992 three proposals were put to the people - the Twelfth, Thirteenth and Fourteenth Amendments. The people rejected the Twelfth (which dealt with the right to life of the unborn) and approved the Thirteenth and Fourteenth (see below).
Thirteenth Amendment of the Constitution Act, 1992	Provided that Article 40.3.3° would not limit freedom to travel between Ireland and another state.
Fourteenth Amendment of the Constitution Act, 1992	Provided that Article 40.3.3° would not limit freedom to obtain or make available information relating to services lawfully available in another state.
Regulation of Information (Services outside the State for the Termination of Pregnancies) Act, 1995	Regulates the manner in which information on abortion services may be made available to the public generally and to individuals who request such information.
1996 - 2000	A constitutional review group (All-Party Oireachtas Committee on the Constitution: Fifth Progress Party Report – Abortion) and an Inter-departmental Working Group on Abortion were formed. A Green Paper was published. Another All-Party Oireachtas Committee was convened.
Twenty-Fifth Amendment of the Constitution (Protection of Human Life in Pregnancy) Bill, 2002	A referendum was held and the proposal was rejected.

Divorce

1937 Constitution of Ireland	Article 41.3.2° provided that no law could be enacted allowing for the dissolution of a marriage. The courts granted decrees of nullity and judicial separation and recognised some foreign divorces. In the case of a decree of nullity or a recognised foreign divorce spouses could lawfully remarry; in the case of a decree of judicial separation they could not.

1967 All Party Dáil Committee on the Constitution	Recommended that divorce should be legally granted in circumstances where it would be recognised by a person's religion.
1983 – 1985 - Joint Oireachtas Committee on Marriage Breakdown	Put forward arguments for and against divorce being made legal in Ireland and concluded that a referendum should be held on the issue.
Tenth Amendment of the Constitution Bill, 1986	Proposed that the prohibition on divorce in the Constitution be removed and that divorce be permitted in Ireland in specified circumstances. A referendum was held and the proposal was rejected.
Judicial Separation and Family Reform Act, 1989	Widened the grounds upon which a decree of judicial separation could be granted by the courts and enabled the courts to make a broad range of financial and property orders for the benefit of dependant spouses and children where a decree of judicial separation is granted. These are known as 'ancillary relief orders'.
1992 Government White Paper on Marital Breakdown: A Review and Proposed Changes	Considered the extent of marital breakdown in Ireland and discussed various proposals for reform. Noted that any change in the constitutional prohibition on divorce could only be decided by a Referendum. Various constitutional proposals were suggested.
Family Law and Social Welfare (No. 2) Act, 1995	Extended the court's powers in making ancillary relief orders in judicial separation, especially in the areas of life and pension policies and social-welfare entitlements.
Fifteenth Amendment of the Constitution Act, 1994	Provided for the dissolution of marriage in certain specified circumstances. A referendum was held and the proposal was accepted.
Family Law (Divorce) Act, 1996	Provide that a court may grant a decree of divorce if it is satisfied that the conditions in Article 41.3.2° of the Constitution are complied with. Divorce in Ireland is described as 'no fault' divorce in that proof of matrimonial misconduct, such as adultery or desertion, is not required.

Homosexual acts

Offences against the Person Act, 1861	Intercourse by penetration *per anum* (anal sex or buggery) upon a man, a woman or an animal was an offence at common law. Penalties were provided for in the 1861 Act.

Criminal Law Amendment Act, 1885	Provided that any act of 'gross indecency' between males was an offence.
	No legislation existed to deal specifically with sexual acts between females.
Norris v. Ireland [1988] EHRR	The European Court of Human Rights held that the existence of a law that penalised certain homosexual acts carried out in private by consenting male adults constituted a breach of rights under Article 8 of the European Convention on Human Rights.
Criminal Law (Sexual Offences) Act, 1993	Abolished the offence of buggery between consenting adults. Homosexual acts between consenting adults are not prohibited or regulated by law.
	It is an offence to commit or attempt to commit an act of buggery upon a person under 17 years of age or a person of any age who is mentally impaired (unless married to that person).
	It is also an offence to commit or attempt to commit an act of gross indecency with another male person under the age of 17 or a person of any age who is mentally impaired (unless married to that person). 'Gross indecency' is defined as an act of a gross nature and purpose between male persons which falls short of buggery. Soliciting or importuning for the purposes of gross indecency is also an offence.

Rape and Other Sexual Offences

Criminal Law Act, 1935	This Act raised the age of consent from 16 to 17 years of age.
	It provides that it is an offence to have 'unlawful carnal knowledge' of girls under 15 and 17 years of age respectively. The presence of consent is not a defence. It is not a defence for the accused to say that he believed the girl to be over the age of 15 or 17.
Criminal Law (Rape) Act, 1981	Rape is an offence at common law. It is defined in the 1981 Act as an offence committed by a man if he has unlawful sexual intercourse with a woman who at the time of the intercourse does not consent to it, and at that time he knows that she does not consent to the intercourse or he is reckless as to whether or not she consents.
	'Sexual intercourse' is defined as penetration of the vagina by the penis.

Criminal Law (Rape) (Amendment) Act, 1990	Extends the definition of rape to a sexual assault that includes a penetration (however slight) of the anus or mouth by the penis, or a penetration (however slight) of the vagina by any object held or manipulated by another person. This is known as 'section 4' rape as it is provided for by section 4 of the Act. Rape as defined by the 1981 Act is an act perpetrated by a man on a woman; however, section 4 rape is gender-neutral.

In common law a husband could not be found guilty of the rape of his wife. The 1990 Act abolishes this 'marital exemption'.

The Act also provides that the common law offence of indecent assault shall be known as "sexual assault".

It also defines the offence of 'aggravated sexual assault' as a sexual assault involving serious violence or the threat of serious violence or is such as to cause injury, humiliation or degradation of a grave nature to the person assaulted.

Criminal Law (Sexual Offences) Act, 1993	Provides for the following offences:

- Committing or attempting to commit buggery with a person under the age of 17 (unless married to that person);
- Having or attempting to have sexual intercourse with a person who is mentally impaired;
- Committing or attempting to commit an act of gross indecency with another male who is under the age of 17 or who is mentally impaired (unless married to that person);
- Soliciting or importuning for the purposes of committing a sexual offence; and,
- Offences in relation to prostitution – soliciting, loitering with intent, organising, living off the proceeds, brothel keeping.

Criminal Law (Sexual Offences) Act, 2006	This Act made significant changes to the Criminal Law Act, 1935 where it was an offence to have "unlawful carnal knowledge" with a girl under 15 and 17 years of age.

Under the 2006 Act it is an offence to engage or attempt to engage in a sexual act with a child under the age of 15. This is described in the Act as "defilement". Unlike the 1935 Act, the offence extends to any sexual act and is gender neutral. A "sexual act" is defined as sexual intercourse or buggery between persons who are not married to each other or an act of aggravated sexual assault or section 4 rape. A new defence of "honest belief" is provided for where it is open to the accused to argue that he or she honestly believed that the child was aged 15 or over. The Court will then consider if there are reasonable grounds for that belief. It can never be a defence to argue that the child consented to the sexual act as the age of consent for both heterosexual and homosexual activity is 17 years of age.

It is also an offence to defile or attempt to defile a child under 17 years of age. If the perpetrator is "a person in authority" they shall be subject to a higher penalty. The defence of "honest belief" may also be argued.

If the perpetrator is under the age of 17 the consent of the Director of Public Prosecutions is required before he or she may be prosecuted.

A girl under the age of 17 shall not be guilty of an offence by reason only of her engaging in an act of sexual intercourse.

Criminal Justice Act, 2006   Provides for the offence of reckless endangerment of children.

In response to the "C" Case ruling, which led to the introduction and passing of the Criminal Law (Sexual Offences) Act 2006, the Government established a Joint Committee of the Oireachtas on Child Protection which is due to report in November 2006. The terms of reference of this committee include the review of criminal law relating to sexual offences against children, the age of consent, and procedures relating to the evidence of children in abuse cases. The Government also appointed two specialists from the fields of civil and criminal law as special rapporteurs for child protection. They will review and audit legal developments and assess what impact litigation in national and international courts will have on child protection. They will be independent and accountable to the Oireachtas, to whom they will report annually.

1.6   A brief outline of the report

THIS report aims to give a general overview of the results of the first Irish national KAB survey and examine a number of key issues around sexual behaviour in Ireland. Because of the range and depth of data gathered, this report has to be selective in the issues addressed. It cannot examine these issues in the depth that a more specialised report would. That is the task of the three sub-reports.

The content of chapters is as follows:

Chapter two examines the design and methodology of the ISSHR survey.

Chapter three analyses data from the ISSHR survey on the ways in which Irish people learnt about sex and their views on what should be taught to children now. Results show that the proportion of Irish people who received sex education increases steadily as their age decreases. The ISSHR survey included questions on the form that this sex education took and whether it was received from school, parents or another source. The results for these questions are analysed in detail. Chapter three also examines the important issue of the extent to which respondents could speak to their parents about sex when they were younger.

Chapter four undertakes an analysis of sexual attitudes, beliefs and knowledge in Ireland (following chapter one's general discussion of the enormous change in these attitudes over the last three decades or so). Using data from previous surveys and the ISSHR data, it examines in detail how attitudes to premarital sex, casual sex and abortion have changed over time and are currently distributed across the population. It also examines attitudes toward emergency contraception. Using a range of characteristics, chapter four presents evidence of intense change in attitudes across Irish people of all age groups over the last three decades, but a particularly pronounced change in attitudes among young people. It is clear that the gap in levels of sexual liberalism in attitudes between age groups has grown substantially over time. Attitudes are also related to many other characteristics such as level of education and social class. These are examined in detail.

Chapter five examines the relationship between sexual attraction, sexual identity and sexual experience. It analyses the extent of same-sex attraction among the Irish population, the distribution of sexual identity and the relationship of both to same- and opposite-sex experience. Many people tend to think of sexual orientation in an essentialist fashion, seeing individuals as either heterosexual or homosexual, but results show that sexual orientation should be seen more as a spectrum than a dichotomy; even if analyses are restricted to examining current relationships, it is apparent that most individuals with same-sex experience also have opposite-sex experiences.

Chapter six analyses people's first heterosexual intercourse. First sexual intercourse is a highly significant event in all societies and most people recollect the event clearly for a long time. Drawing on this clarity of memory, the chapter analyses how the event has changed across the age groups, particularly the age of first occurrence, and examines the role of other factors such as social class and education. One of the most important issues around early sexual experience is the use of contraception; this is examined in detail. The chapter finishes by examining the extent to which first vaginal sex was planned, the willingness of the partners and the degree of regret that it happened when it did.

Chapter seven focuses on the number of heterosexual partnerships which ISSHR respondents had experienced over three periods: over their lifetime so far, over the last five years and over the last year. The number of partners is a major determinant of the risk of sexually transmitted infections. The main aim of the chapter is to examine how this number has changed across age groups, the patterns in Ireland compared to other countries and the influence of other factors such as highest education, religiosity and relationship status. The chapter's final section also examines the extent to which Irish men pay for sex.

Chapter eight examines the sexual practices and frequency of sex among opposite-sex partners. Research from other countries[14] [30] shows not only that the pattern of vaginal, oral and anal sex varies significantly across age groups, but also that there has been a long-term change in the experience of oral sex through time. The chapter examines these issues as well as analysing the frequency of sex among heterosexual partners.

Chapter nine examines the pattern of homosexual partnerships and practices (much as heterosexual partnerships and practices were examined in chapters seven and eight). It looks at the number of same-sex partners that individuals have experienced over different time periods and compares our findings with those of other Irish and international studies. It also examines the frequency of specific sexual practices in same-sex relationships, including the reciprocity of these practices.

Chapter 10 analyses the patterns in use of contraception and condoms and the extent to which this varies across different groups. Along with sexual practices and partnerships, use of contraception and protection are major determinants of the risks of STI infection and crisis pregnancy. This chapter also examines the reasons that respondents gave for not using contraception and protection.

Chapter 11, the final substantive chapter, examines the experience of crisis pregnancy and sexually transmitted infections (STIs) as found in the ISSHR survey. In its first section, it looks at the prevalence of crisis pregnancy according to a large number of factors, changes in the age at which women have experienced their crisis pregnancies, and the outcomes of these pregnancies. It analyses the determinants of a woman experiencing an abortion and how this risk varies among groups with different characteristics. The chapter then examines the prevalence of reported STIs in the ISSHR survey and the socio-demographic predictors of this. Lastly, it looks at the extent to which individuals have sought advice on STIs, where they went for this advice and where they would prefer to go.

The final, **12th chapter** summarises the material presented in the other chapters and attempts to draw this together to present some important conclusions that emerge from the study and their implications for policy.

1.7   Reference list

1   WHO. *Progress in Reproductive Health Research*, p67. Geneva: WHO, 2004.

2   NDSC. *National Disease Surveillance Centre Annual Report 2003*. Dublin: National Disease Surveillance Centre, 2004.

3   Rundle K, Leigh C, McGee H, Layte R. *Irish Contraception and Crisis Pregnancy (ICCP) Study: A Survey of the General Population*. Dublin: Crisis Pregnancy Agency, 2004.

4   Nic Ghiolla Phadraig M. *Survey of Religious Beliefs and Practices in Ireland*. Moral Attitudes [3]. Dublin: Research and Development Commission, 1976.

5   Hornsby-Smith MP, Whelan CT. 'Religion and Moral Values'. In: Whelan CT, editor. *Values and Social Change in Ireland, pp7-44*. Dublin: Gill and Macmillan. 1994.

6   Mac Gréil M. *Prejudice in Ireland Revisited*. Maynooth: St Patrick's College, 1996.

7   Fahey T, Hayes BC, Sinnott R. *Conflict and Consensus: A Study of Values and Attitudes in the Republic of Ireland and Northern Ireland*. Dublin: Institute of Public Administration, 2005.

8   Heffernan C. *Sexually Transmitted Infections, Sex and the Irish*. Maynooth: Department of Sociology, NUI Maynooth, 2004.

9   Layte R, Fullerton D, McGee H. *Scoping Study for a Survey of Sexual Knowledge, Attitudes and Behaviour*. Dublin: Crisis Pregnancy Agency, 2003.

10 Shiely F, Kelleher C, Galvin M. *Sexual Health and the Irish Adult Population: Findings from Slán*. p11. Dublin: Crisis Pregnancy Agency, 2004.

11 Kinsey AC, Pomeroy WB, Martin CE. *Sexual Behavior in the Human Male*. Philadelphia: Saunders, 1948.

12 Kinsey AC, Pomeroy WB, Martin CE, Gebhard PH. *Sexual Behavior in the Human Female*. Philadelphia: Saunders, 1953.

13 Masters WH, Johnson VE. *Human Sexual Response*. Boston: Little, Brown, 1966.

14 Johnson A, Wadsworth J., Wellings K, Field J. *Sexual Attitudes and Lifestyles*. Oxford: Basil Blackwell, 1994.

15 Liljeros F, Edling CR, Nunes Amaral LA, Stanley HE, Aberg Y. 'The Web of Human Sexual Contacts'. *Nature* 2001, 411:907-914.

16 Anderson RM. 'A Preliminary Study of the Transmission Dynamics of the Human Immunodeficiency Virus (HIV), the Causative Agent of AIDS'. *Journal of Maths, Applied Medicine and Biology* 1986; 3:229-263.

17 Bound J, Johnson G. 'Changes in the Structure of Wages During the 1980s: An Evaluation of Alternative Explanations'. *American Economic Review* 1992; 82:371-392.

18 NDSC. 'Newly Diagnosed HIV Infections in Ireland'. Quarter 3 and 4, 2003 and 2003 Annual Report. 2004. Dublin: National Disease Surveillance Centre.

19 NASC. *AIDS Strategy 2000: Report of the National AIDS Strategy Committee*. Dublin: Stationery Office, 2000.

20 Layte R, Whelan CT. 'Class Transformation and Trends in Social Fluidity in the Republic of Ireland 1973 to 1994'. In: Breen R, editor. *Social Mobility in Europe*. Oxford: Oxford University Press, 2004.

21 Layte R, O'Connell PJ, Fahey T, McCoy S. 'Ireland and Economic Globalisation: the Experiences of a Small Open Economy'. In: Blossfeld H-P, Klijzing E, Mills M, Kurz K, editors. *Globalisation, Uncertainty and Youth in Society.* London: Routledge, 2005.

22 Fahey T. 'Religion and Sexual Culture in Ireland'. In: Eder FX, Hall L, Hekma G, editors. *Sexual Cultures in Europe: National Histories, pp53-70.* Manchester: Manchester University Press, 1999:

23 Hug C. *The Politics of Sexual Morality in Ireland.* Basingstoke: Macmillan, 1999.

24 Inglis T. *Lessons in Irish Sexuality.* Dublin: University College Dublin Press, 1998.

23 Coleman D. 'Demography and Migration in Ireland, North and South'. In: Heath AF, Breen R, Whelan CT, editors. *Ireland North and South: Perspectives from Social Science, pp69-116.* Oxford: Oxford University Press, 1999.

26 Department of Health and Children. *Quality and Fairness: A Health System for You.* Dublin: Department of Health and Children, 2001.

27 Balanda KP, Wilde J. *Inequalities in Mortality 1989-1998: A Report on All-Ireland Mortality Data.* Dublin: Institute of Public Health in Ireland, 2001.

28 Barry J, Sinclair H, Kelly A, O'Loughlin R, Handy D, O'Dowd T. *Inequalities in Health in Ireland - Hard Facts.* Dublin: Department of Community Health and General Practice, Trinity College, 2001.

29 Mackenbach JP, Bakker M. *Reducing Inequalities in Health: A European Perspective.* London: Routledge, 2002.

30 De Visser R, Smith AM, Rissel CE, Richters J, Grulich AE. 'Sex in Australia: heterosexual experience and recent heterosexual encounters among a representative sample of adults'. Australian and New Zealand Journal of Public Health 2003; 27(2):146-154.

31 Department of Health. *National Strategy for Sexual Health and HIV 2001.*

Chapter 2:

Designing the ISSHR

2.1   Introduction

THE core aims of the ISSHR were to generate a nationally representative and reliable picture of the sexual knowledge, attitudes and behaviours of the Irish population and to describe the interrelationships between knowledge, attitudes and behaviours in the context of theory, sexual health promotion and policy development (CPA and Department of Health and Children tender documentation 17th July 2003).

From the beginning of the project, a series of decisions had to be taken on how these objectives could be achieved and a balance struck between the competing requirements. A nationally representative survey demands a national sampling strategy that takes account of the geographical and socio-demographic diversity of the country. However, the sampling frame used is influenced by the mode of data collection and this in turn influences the nature of the survey instrument that can be used.

Balancing these requirements is a difficult process, but other important issues also need to be considered. Sexuality and sexual behaviour are sensitive subjects; the methodological approach adopted needs to recognise this if it is to be successful and protect the privacy of respondents. Similarly, many of the issues addressed within a knowledge, attitudes and behaviour (KAB) survey can provoke a strong emotional reaction. Thus, the welfare of respondents is of major concern when the methodology for the study is being designed. Fortunately, the Irish Contraception and Crisis Pregnancy Study,[1] carried out the year before development work on ISSHR began, had tested ways of dealing with issues of sensitivity and privacy. This contributed greatly to the development of the ISSHR project.

In this chapter, we examine the range of methodological questions addressed before the study could begin. In the **second section**, we begin by examining whether a KAB survey among Irish people is feasible and will return valid, reliable results.

In the **third section**, we consider the question of the target population for the study in terms of the minimum and maximum ages of respondents and other population groups that should be included.

In the **fourth section**, we examine the issue of how the questionnaire should be administered. Administration is a crucial issue in a survey of such sensitive information, but the choice of method also has implications for the sampling strategy. This is examined in **section five**.

In **section six**, we detail the development of the questionnaire and how this was shaped by the aims and objectives of the study and influenced by previous KAB surveys in other countries.

In the **seventh section**, we outline the pilot survey for the project. In **section eight**, we turn to the recruitment and training of interviewers; in **section nine**, to the issue of ethical clearance.

In **section 10**, we examine the interviews carried out and the response rate achieved. Finally, in **section 11**, we assess the representativeness and demographic profile of the final data file. This last section also details the weighting strategy adopted to ensure that the data were representative.

2.2   Asking questions about sex and sexuality

SEX is a sensitive subject in almost all cultures.[2] Irish society is no different. Thus the question arises as to whether it is feasible to ask people such sensitive questions and expect an honest answer. This concern was one of the primary reasons why, until the mid-1980s, research into sex around the world was confined to convenience samples and sub-groups of the population. However, since then it has been shown in a number of countries that people will answer deeply sensitive questions as long as they feel that these are part of a legitimate and socially valuable research project and they are guaranteed that their information will be treated in the strictest confidence. In this sense, survey research on sex faces many of the same problems that all survey research faces.

The techniques for gaining cooperation are essentially the same as those used when investigating other subjects. For example, within 20 or so seconds of contact being established, the interviewer needs to convince the respondent that the research is being conducted for a legitimate purpose and that its findings will be used to improve the health and welfare of the population. Establishing this may require verification of the project and/or interviewer. The ISSHR project used a system whereby respondents could call back to the ESRI directly and speak to a researcher, or, if need be, the researchers could fax the details of the project to a local garda station. Using these procedures, previous Irish researchers had found that most fears over participation could be dealt with and cooperation obtained.

Although people may answer the questions, the fear of social judgement may motivate them to conceal their true sexual behaviour. Where behaviours are socially disapproved of, or do not reflect well on the individual reporting them, there is always an incentive to not report or to under-report. Similarly, others may embellish the accounts they present of their sexual behaviour, over-reporting the frequency of a particular behaviour or reporting behaviours they have not in fact experienced. Added to these issues are the more mundane problems of survey research such as inaccurate recall of past events or the fact that respondents may reconstruct their experiences in a manner that they perceive the interviewer would like them to.

A number of studies have examined the reliability of self-reported sexual behaviour. In general, these are quite positive in their findings. One route has been to compare the data given by sexual partners independent of each other to examine the extent to which these present a coherent picture.[3][4][5] These data have generally shown a high level of agreement. A number of studies have used a test-retest approach to check the reliability of self-reported sexual behaviour[6][4][7] and have found high levels of reliability even where the tests were carried out up to 18 months apart.

Another test of the extent to which survey data present a reliable picture of actual behaviours is to compare self-reported behaviours with outcomes measured in other statistical sources. A good example of this is the results for the British NATSAL survey.[8] This showed a pattern of sexual-risk behaviour across different age groups that is highly consistent with the patterns observed across age groups in statistics on STIs and abortions gathered through surveillance centres in the UK.

2.3   The target population

THE overall aim of the ISSHR project was to collect representative data on KAB issues for the Irish population. This presents several problems. First, interviewing all groups, even where they reside in institutions (say prisons or care homes) would entail creating a complicated sampling frame of those who could be interviewed. There would be serious doubt as to whether the samples attained would be useful for analysis because of the particular circumstances in which they live. For this reason, in a consultation process with a panel of interested stakeholders in the area of sexual health and education, it was decided early on[9] that the sampling frame for the project would be drawn from the non-institutional population in private residential housing.

This choice simplifies the sampling frame required, but there is a second problem. There are many groups that it would be beneficial to have in the sample if it is to be representative of the population. If analysis is to be performed of issues specific to a group (such as Travellers or refugees), that group must, of course, be included. However, if such groups make up a small part of the population,[c] the number who would be found in the final sample would not be useful for analysis unless a very large sample was drawn, or a 'booster' sample of that group was collected.

These issues, too, were discussed in the consultation with stakeholders. It was decided that the survey would not attempt to over-sample specific sub-groups, although individuals from these groups might find their way into the sample on a *pro rata* basis. In other words, no specific measures should be taken to increase the representation of specific sub-groups beyond the proportions that would be found by sampling the national, non-institutional population in a representative fashion. Such a national study could then provide the contextual data required for smaller studies of specific populations.

2.3.1   The age range

A THIRD issue was the age range of the respondents to be interviewed. Sensitivity to the well-being of minors means that the bottom age cut-off was set at 18 (the age range to be interviewed was another question addressed during the consultation process).[9]

A more difficult question was the maximum age. Initially we aimed, and most groups consulted agreed, that all those aged 18 or more should in principle be able to be selected for inclusion. However, resources were limited and evidence from elsewhere suggested that those aged 65 or more were less likely to engage in behaviour that would put them at risk of contracting an STI or HIV. The risk for younger groups has been shown in other country studies and Irish HPSC reports to be much higher. If those over 64 were included in the study, there would not be sufficient resources to collect a large enough sample of this group to make accurate estimates. Such concerns led us to adopt a maximum age of 64 and to use the extra resources to interview a larger proportion of younger respondents.

2.4   Mode of administration

THE sensitivity of the content of KAB surveys means that the quality of data is highly influenced by the manner in which it is collected. Interviewer bias, where the characteristics of the interviewer influence the response, is a constant problem. Because of this, previous studies, notably the National Survey of Sexual Attitudes and Lifestyles (NATSAL 1990 and 2000) carried out in Britain and the National Health and Social Life Survey (NHSLS 1992) carried out in the US, used face-to-face interviews supplemented with a self-completion survey.

This combination of methods has a number of advantages. First, face-to-face surveys generally lead to higher quality of data as the interviewer can clarify issues with the respondent and monitor data quality.[10] Secondly, the instrument can be longer, as the method requires less dedication from the respondent, and more complex, since the interviewer can clarify issues and use visual aids. Thirdly, the self-completion element means that the respondent can provide information anonymously.

However, all methodologies have their problems. Face-to-face interviews are more expensive than telephone or mail surveys as the interviewer has to travel to the home of the respondent, often several times, before an interview can be carried out. To minimise this cost, interviews may be

---

[c] For example, if a group make up 2% of the population, as do Travellers, it is likely that just 200 individuals will be contacted in a sample of 10,000 people, although this number may vary because of sampling error. There is also the issue of having a sampling frame that contains such groups.

clustered in geographical areas. This, however, has a cost in terms of increasing sample errors through 'design effects' (that is, the sample is no longer a simple random sample of the population, but rather a random sample within each 'cluster'). Face-to-face interviews are also inherently riskier for field staff who must travel to respondents' homes. This is a concern in a survey on sexual issues.

Self-completion surveys put greater demands on the respondent in terms of literacy, motivation and time. The people who complete a survey may be different from the people who do not. This can lead to biased samples. For example, Copas *et al* (1997)[11] have shown that people with poorer literacy skills were less likely to complete a self-completion survey. This makes it difficult to generalise from the results to the general population.

The alternative to these two methods is the phone survey. Unlike face-to-face methods, phone surveys allow interviewers to make calls from a centralised call centre, thus saving on travel costs. At the centre they can be monitored and given appropriate support. This is less risky than face-to-face interviews in the respondents' home when discussing sexual subjects. Also, when faced with difficult issues, the interviewer can be given advice directly by other team members. Since no travel is required, phone surveys are substantially cheaper than face-to-face surveys. They allow a higher number of interviews to be completed for a given budget. Finally, phone surveys offer a high degree of anonymity and respondents may be reassured when told that their phone number was randomly generated and their name and address is unknown.

As with face-to-face and self-completion surveys, however, phone surveys also have their drawbacks. First, phone interviews are shorter than face-to-face interviews. Average effective phone interviews last no more than 30 minutes whereas face-to-face interviews may last 60 minutes or more with few problems. This limitation means that the time spent phone-interviewing must be maximised. Secondly, the questions must be less complex than when in face-to-face interviews since visual aids cannot be used and, when answering questions, respondents can retain only a limited number of options in their heads. This restriction can present particular problems when questions used previously in face-to-face surveys are replicated.

After these costs and benefits were weighed up, the phone interview was chosen as the method for data collection. The phone interview has been used successfully in KAB surveys outside Ireland, notably in Australia[12] and France.[13] It has also been used successfully in Ireland for surveys on sensitive issues.[d] To minimise the problems of a short interview time, the research team chose to use Computer-Aided Telephone Interviewing (CATI). This had the added benefit of improving data quality as data do not have to be coded from paper questionnaires. In CATI interviews, questions are selected and answers coded directly into a computer. This allows far more complicated routing and filtering than is possible using a paper questionnaire.

2.5 The sample design

TO be nationally representative, the sample for the ISSHR survey would have to be systematically selected from a national sampling frame. This could be achieved by using the electoral register or the An Post GEO directory of residential addresses.

---

[d] For example, the Irish Contraception and Crisis Pregnancy Survey 2004 [ICCP][1] and the Sexual Abuse and Violence in Ireland [SAVI] Study.[22]

2.5.1   Random digit dialing

THE choice of phone interview opened up another possibility: random digit dialing (RDD). This can be used to create a sample of phone numbers from the national population. It has the advantage that numbers are generated without recourse to a number directory; thus ex-directory numbers or recent numbers not yet in the directory are also listed. This approach means, however, that letters to households cannot be sent prior to the interview call (as used in the French and Australian phone surveys). The method has been shown to increase response rates.[14] However, we were concerned that using address matching and notification letters might lead to a biased sample (only registered numbers would be sampled) and felt that, in the Irish context, better responses might be obtained by cold-calling households. Indeed, during the pilot process, cold-calling produced a response rate comparable to Irish face-to-face surveys with notification letters.

2.5.2   Mobile-phone use

IT is not possible to randomly sample from mobile phone numbers at present in Ireland. This is a concern, given the increasing penetration of mobiles in the Irish population and anecdotal evidence that some households may only use a mobile phone. Although 'random digit dialing' can be used with mobile phones as with landlines, it is not possible to 'stratify' the sample so as to represent the population geographically, since mobile phones have no geographical prefix. This would seriously increase the sample error in any survey. As well, phone surveys using mobile phones face the problem that individuals are likely to be in a public space when called. This is likely to inhibit an interview on a sensitive subject such as sex. However, because of the growing penetration of mobiles, particular groups such as young and single people and those living in rented accommodation are less likely to be reached by a landline survey. It is important to clarify the extent of this challenge.

Most analysts of mobile phone penetration quote the COMREG Trends Survey, the most recent of which was carried out in 2005.[15] This indicated that 76% of households have a landline and, perhaps more importantly, that 24% of households have only a mobile phone. However, this survey included just 1,000 individuals and was not a national probability sample.

The CSO's Survey of Income and Living Conditions (SILC) from late 2004, a more robust survey, showed a much lower proportion of households with no landline. SILC is a weighted, clustered, two-stage probability sample of over 14,000 individuals and 5,000 households and is the main source of official statistics on income and living conditions. It showed that 88% of individuals lived in households with a landline, a significantly higher proportion than found in the COMREG survey. Interestingly, of the 12% of individuals who did not have a landline in their home, about 2% did not have a mobile either.

SILC also showed which population groups were less likely to have a landline. Over 90% of men and women over 35 lived in households with a landline, but this fell to 86% among men and 74% among women aged 18 to 24. This confirms the view that younger individuals are the most likely to live in mobile-only households. This indicates that a landline survey would suffer from sample error among the young and particularly among younger women.

Concern about potential exclusions from the survey due to reduced landline coverage within various groups (such as younger people) was balanced in the survey by the use of a sophisticated re-weighting or statistical-adjustment procedure, This was to ensure that the data collected were balanced by population characteristics such as age and gender. This adjustment was implemented prior to data analysis. The study used a 'minimum information loss' algorithm to implement the re-weighting adjustment. This adjusted the data on the basis of gender, age cohort, educational attainment level, marital status, current employment status and region. Thus, the data are fully representative of the population that fall within the scope of the survey (18-64 years). Such re-weighting of survey data is a standard aspect of sample surveying and allows conclusions of a wide generalisability.

2.5.3 RDD stratification – the 'hundred banks' method

RDD phone interviewing allows researchers to stratify numbers within the population so that full coverage of different geographical areas can be achieved. This guaranteed that all areas in Ireland would be represented in the final data set, rather than this depending on statistical probability. The ESRI's RANSAM system was used to perform this stratification of areas (selected through their area code) and number 'stem' selection.

The 'hundreds bank' method was then used to create a sample of numbers for calling. In this method, the number 'stem' is generated and the last two digits varied from '00' to '99'. This creates a full set of 100 numbers to be called. Some of the numbers may not exist or may not be residential numbers, but by calling numbers in this manner a full probability sample of all Irish numbers can be built up.

If respondents did not wish to be interviewed at this first call and did not arrange for the interviewer to call back, a 'conversion' call was placed after a suitable time (usually around two weeks). The 'conversion call' provides an opportunity to reconsider for those who have declined participation in an unsolicited ('cold call') contact by a researcher. Conversion calls were made to all those who had refused participation on the first call. The reasons for re-contact ("It provides us and you with the possibility to reconsider your decision to participate") were provided, with an assurance that this would be the only re-contact.

2.5.4 Sample size

THE feasibility study for the ISSHR project[9] argued that a sample of 10,000 respondents would be enough to allow the necessary level of sample disaggregation. Assuming five age groups of roughly equal size, a cross-tabulation of age and sex groups would produce sub-samples of around 1,000 respondents each, where the confidence interval including design effects is +/-3.92%. A power to detect differences of +/-3.92% between groups was deemed sufficient for the project overall.

Budget constraints meant that the final sample was approximately 7,668 cases. This produced an average age/sex cell size of 744 individuals, with a power to detect differences of 5.39%. This power was not deemed acceptable for the analysis of important high-risk groups among people under 30. To improve statistical power for the younger age group, those aged less than 30 were 'over-sampled' in the final data file. This means that this group make up 4.9% more of the final data file than they represent in the Irish population (36.4% rather than 31.5%). This allows greater disaggregation in specific analyses of this age group but, by weighting down this group, representativeness is preserved in analyses of the total sample. A separate weight just for the analysis of those under 30 was generated (see section 2.11 for details of the weighting procedures employed).

2.6 Questionnaire development

THE design of the questionnaire is possibly the most important issue in the development of the research project, since it determines the nature and quality of information collected. Fortunately, the development of the questionnaire for the ISSHR study occurred at a time when a number of other national KAB studies had been carried out. Both their research instruments and results were available. This was crucial as development time was to be extremely compressed; questionnaire development occurred within a five-month period.

Questionnaire development is a difficult task. As well as choosing the areas that must be covered to fulfil the study objectives, research needs to be carried out on the exact nature of the questions and what impact these might have on the response. The ordering of questions and sections is also crucial. The sequence of questions has a considerable impact on the nature and reliability of answers received. For example, the early stages of the questionnaire need to establish a rapport between interviewer and respondent; particularly sensitive or intrusive questions should be avoided at this stage. Similarly, it is advisable to ask questions about beliefs and attitudes early on; doing so later may lead to contamination if they follow behavioural questions, as these might prompt respondents to reflect on their sexual beliefs and lifestyle.

These are just simple examples of a more complex developmental process which requires that each question be tested to ensure that it is a worthwhile addition. This development would not have been possible in the time available if much of the ground work had not already been carried out and discussed in the documents describing the ASHR (Australia), NATSAL (Britain), NHSLS (USA) and ACSF (France) surveys.

Some developmental work on new questions was also carried out. Questions were selected in discussions with the project steering committee and, after initial work within the research group on question formats, the questions were tested in a pilot survey. The limit on time and resources meant that only this single pilot was possible and different forms of the same question could not be tested.

A large collection of possible questions drawn from a range of surveys was distilled to a first-draft questionnaire that would take only 10 minutes longer than the required 30-minute average interview. This first draft was tested in mock interviews and improved. It was also shortened in editorial meetings with the steering committee. From this process a final draft questionnaire was arrived at for CATI development and testing. The question domains established remained intact for the main fieldwork, although many individual items changed. The 12 question domains of the survey were:

SECTION A: Introduction and respondent agreement
This section provided a standardised introduction to the study, detailing who was carrying out the survey, its confidential nature and how the phone numbers had been randomly selected. Following agreement to participate, information on study-verification procedures was offered, and interviewers confirmed that the respondent was over 18 and younger than 65 before proceeding. The section also collected information on marital status and number of children.

SECTION B: Learning about sex
Section B provided a non-contentious opening to the questioning centred on sex education experienced both at home and in school, the helpfulness of this education and whether children should receive sex education and, if so, from whom.

SECTION C: Knowledge, attitudes and beliefs
Section C investigated the sexual knowledge, attitudes and beliefs of respondents, using a series of multi-item instruments. Questions were included on sexual morality, beliefs about contraception and knowledge of STIs, a woman's fertility and emergency contraception, as well as on a subjective analysis of the person's risk of contracting HIV.

SECTION D: First sexual experience

This section investigated the range of sexual behaviours experienced and when these first occurred, before examining in detail the first occasion of penetrative sex (vaginal or anal).

SECTION E: Attraction

Section E contained a single item asking respondents to indicate the extent to which they had been attracted to the opposite gender alone, their own gender alone, or some mix of the two.

SECTION F: Heterosexual partnerships and practices

This section quantified when the respondent last experienced different types of sexual behaviours (vaginal, oral and anal sex) with members of the opposite gender and the number of sexual partners they had had over different periods (life, last five years, last year). The section also examined the number of partners which the respondent had paid to have sex with over their life so far, and use of condoms with these partners. Lastly, it examined use of condoms 'in the last year' and the perceived risk of conception given the respondent's current lifestyle.

SECTION G: Homosexual partnerships and practices

This section examined the same subjects as section F, except that here the questions were asked of sexual partners of the same gender.

SECTION H: Most recent event

Whereas sections F and G examined total sexual experience, section H examined the last sexual event (with the opposite or same gender). 'Sexual event' is broadly defined, but actual experiences were then examined (vaginal, oral and anal sex). Emphasis was placed on contraception (whether used or not, and which type) and protection from STIs. This section also examined the expectations the respondent and partner had of their relationship at last event, sexual and emotional satisfaction and number of sexual events in the last four weeks, as well as preferences for frequency of sex.

SECTION I: Sexual problems

Section I asked whether the respondent had experienced a range of sexual problems and if so whether they had sought professional help with these and what form this took. Preferences for sexual health-care services were also examined. The section also examined lifetime fertility and infertility, with a particular emphasis on 'crisis pregnancies' and their outcomes.

SECTION J: Sex outside Ireland and the UK

This section examined sex outside Ireland and the UK 'in the last five years' with a new partner met whilst abroad. Prime focus was on vaginal or anal sex without a condom. Information was sought on the number of partners concerned.

SECTION K: STIs and use of health-care services

This substantial section examined use of sexual health and contraceptive services. Questions included what types of service were used, whether payment was involved, impediments to service use and preferences for future use. The section also examined whether the respondent had ever been diagnosed with an STI, which type, and details of treatment. It finished with questions on AIDS and HIV, examining knowledge on the subject, experience of testing and history of injecting drug use.

SECTION L: Demographics and personal characteristics

The final section gathered basic information on education, nationality, employment status and occupation, and place of residence (urban v rural). It also examined health status and consumption of alcohol.

2.6.1   Question order

THE questionnaire began with a section on sex education so that the interview would start in a relatively uncontentious and sensitive way. As noted earlier, we also placed questions on attitudes and beliefs early so that responses would not be contaminated by the information on behaviour given later.

2.6.2   Survey length

THE overall length of the interview was a concern. Previous experience indicated that an average phone interview should be around 30 minutes as after this point lack of response to questions becomes a serious issue. In some cases, informing the respondent beforehand that the survey might take longer than 30 minutes impaired response to the overall questionnaire.

One option was to follow the French ACSF survey and use a combination of short and long survey instruments. In that survey, 24% of the sample were administered a long instrument (45 minutes) and 76% a short (15 minutes). The large size of the French sample (20,055) meant that the 4,820 respondents doing the long version still represented a significant sample. However, confidence intervals around questions demanding detailed information were higher than we thought acceptable.

For the above reason, we used a method similar to that in the ASHR survey (Smith 2003). In that survey, all those with two or more partners in the year prior to the survey were asked a long form of questionnaire and those with one partner a short version (although a random selection of the 20% with one partner also completed a long form of questionnaire).

The ISSHR survey used the filtering facilities of the Computer-Aided Telephone Interviewing (CATI) system to identify questions in the survey already completely determined by earlier answers. The CATI system was used to skip these questions in the case of individual respondents and to insert the appropriate answer. CATI was also used to reduce the number of questions to which people were exposed. For example, if a respondent indicated in section D that they had never experienced oral sex, any further questions on oral sex were skipped and coded as 'not applicable'.

2.6.3   Questionnaire language

THE type of language used in a survey can have major implications for results. Since interviewers are trying to establish a rapport with respondents, it is possible that tailoring language to the respondent may improve response. Kinsey[16][17] advised against using scientific terms in interviews. The use of vernacular language has been adopted in a number of surveys on sex, some of which have been carried out in Ireland. The All-Ireland Gay Men's Sex Survey (2000), for instance, used vernacular terms throughout, with some success.[18] Tailoring language, however, can increase the chance that the respondent will have a different understanding of the subject matter, even though this difference may be extremely subtle. This is a particular problem in broad population surveys. We therefore chose to follow the practice of the majority of KAB surveys and used scientific/anatomical language within questions.

2.7 The pilot survey

TESTING the instrument to be used in a survey and the interview protocols is an essential element of a project. After a substantial period of questionnaire development, CATI programming and testing, the pilot survey for the ISSHR project was carried out in the first two weeks of June 2004. As with the main fieldwork, the ESRI's RANSAM system was used to draw a sample of number stems to which the 'hundreds bank' method was applied to generate the sample numbers. Before pilot interviewing, six experienced interviewers were given in-depth training, which included:

- the background to the survey and survey content
- sensitivity-and-awareness training related to issues around sex, sexuality and sexual abuse
- procedures for legitimising the research should respondents have doubts about the authenticity of calls

The latter procedure was that, first, the respondent could call back directly to the ESRI and talk to a senior researcher or interviewer supervisor; if more assurance was needed, the interviewer could fax the credentials of the project to a garda station nominated by the respondent.

In all, 1,529 calls were placed, yielding 354 valid households (ie, a private residential address where a member of the household was aged 18-64). Of these 354 households, full interviews were completed with 205 respondents, 101 refused, 34 appointments were made for a later date and time, and 13 were partially completed.

Counting the appointments made as refusals gives a crude response rate of 61.8% without any attempt at conversion. Conservative estimates of conversion rates (where refusals are recalled and an attempt made to 'convert' these households to answering a questionnaire) led us to expect a final response rate of at least 65%. This would be similar to that obtained in the NATSAL surveys in Britain, though lower than that obtained in Australia, France and the US. Previous experience has shown that Irish response rates tend to be lower than those in other comparable countries (response rates for the Australian, French and US samples are not available and are not applicable to the NATSAL surveys).

Figure 2.1: Profile of unique phone numbers called and outcome classifications for survey

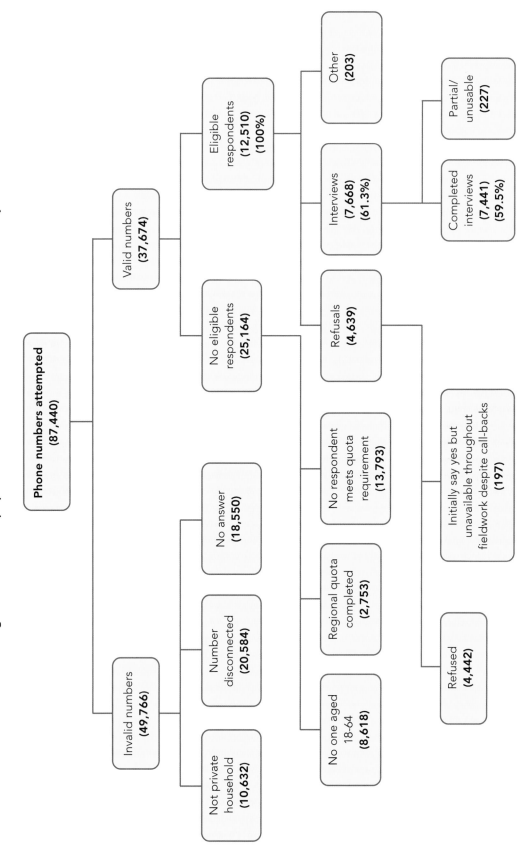

The pilot was particularly useful for identifying aspects of the questionnaire that needed to be changed. Some substantial alterations were made before the instrument re-entered CATI development and testing.

2.8   Recruitment and training of interviewers

INTERVIEWER training is extremely important in all areas of survey research, but especially in such a sensitive area as sex. The interviewer's ability to contextualise the research and answer questions is crucial in getting a respondent to commit to taking part in an interview. Interviewers also need to be aware that the subject matter of KAB surveys can touch on areas in the respondent's life and past that they may find hard to talk about and that might, in a small number of cases, lead to distress.

The first requirement of social-survey research is that the respondent should not be harmed by the research. This puts a particular onus on those carrying out a KAB survey to make sure that research protocols are well developed and that interviewers are well skilled in dealing with sensitive issues.

Along with recruiting experienced interviewers and others with relevant professional experience, the research team designed a six-day training schedule which prepared the interviewers for fieldwork. As well as covering the issues noted above (see section 2.7), the training worked through the protocols for dealing with distress.

It was particularly important for interviewers to understand that, in cases of distress, their role was not to be counsellors but to provide useful information using a standard national list of phone numbers of support agencies which was developed for the study.

Strategies for interviewer debriefing were established to protect interviewer well-being in a potentially sensitive research setting. One important part of developing good interview and support skills among interviewers was role-playing, where interviewers had to deal with a number of situations. In the final part of training, interviewers carried out a number of mock interviews with members of the research team who varied the type of interview to assist training.

2.9   Ethical clearance

THE full set of instruments and protocols for the study and the training and back-up procedures to be used were submitted for consideration by the Research Ethics Committee of the Royal College of Surgeons in Ireland. It provided ethical approval.

2.10 Total interviews and response rates

IN total, 87,440 unique phone numbers were called as part of the main fieldwork of the ISSHR study. Of these, 37,674 were to valid numbers, that is, to private residential households. *Figure 2.1* summarises the call outcomes for the survey in total.

Of the 37,674 households, 12,510 contained a person within the required age range (18 to 64). Out of this total, 7,441 completed interviews were obtained and 227 partial interviews. This is a final response rate of 61.3% including partial interviews and 59.5% excluding these interviews. All analyses in this report and the three accompanying sub-reports are based on the 7,441 completed interviews.

This response rate is close to that obtained by the Irish Contraception and Crisis Pregnancy Survey (63.8%) and the 2000 British National Survey of Sexual Attitudes and Lifestyles (65% after regional reweighing). The result is also substantially higher than that of many of the face-to-face surveys carried out in Ireland, such as the Quarterly National Household Survey or Household Budget Survey (undertaken by the Central Statistics Agency) which achieve response rates in the low 50s.

Although a successful rate in the Irish context, especially given the sensitive nature of the subject matter, the rate is below that achieved in other countries such as Australia, which achieved the very high response rate of 73%. On the other hand, it is substantially higher than that achieved by other Irish surveys on sexuality that used self-completion mail surveys. For instance, the 1994 ISSP module achieved a response rate of 53%.

The response rate was achieved by using multiple strategies, as is standard in international phone research protocols, to facilitate participation.

First:
• Interviewers let each number ring ten times before halting.
• This was done a further 10 times at other times across the day and the following week to try to achieve contact.
• If there was an answering machine, no message was left (previous experience showed that messages caused confusion or concern).
• If no contact was achieved after 10 separate attempts, the number was logged as 'no answer'.

Secondly:
• To facilitate respondents who could not participate during the day on a weekday, calls were made in the evenings up to 9pm and on Saturdays up to 4pm.

Thirdly:
• Interviewers were given training in first-contact procedures and attaining participation. This was augmented by regular meetings between interviewers, supervisors and fieldwork managers where the best approach was discussed and successful methods shared.

Fourthly:
• Respondents who refused the first time were offered – in a 'conversion call' – another opportunity to take part in the survey about two weeks after the first call.

2.11 Demographic profile and representativeness

TABLE 2.1 indicates the representativeness of the ISSHR data by comparing the distribution of cases across a number of different characteristics with that found in the 2002 Census of Population.

We give the distribution of cases in the ISSHR data separately for men and women: first by the 'unweighted' proportion and then by the 'weighted'. Data from the Census of Population (2002) are displayed in the third column so that the ISSHR distributions can be compared.[e]

---

[e] The social-class distribution is compared to results from the Living in Ireland Survey (2001) as data on this class measure were not available from the CSO.

In population surveys it is standard practice, prior to analysis, to adjust statistically or 'reweight' the information collected from the questionnaire so that it is representative of the population. For example, *Table 2.1* shows that the 'unweighted' sample comprises 42.8% men and 57.2% women. The national pattern, indicated by the 2002 Census, suggests the proportion should be about 50/50, so reweighting is used to achieve such a proportion in the sample.

Statistically adjusting data addresses any potential bias that may arise from issues related to sample design and also to differential non-response within sub-groups of the population. The reweighting procedure used is based on a 'minimum information loss' algorithm, which adjusts an initial weight to ensure that the distributional characteristics of the sample match those of the population, according to a set of externally determined controls.[f] The variables used in the statistical adjustment or reweighting procedure were: gender, age cohort, marital status, level of educational attainment and region. The interaction of these variables was also incorporated into the reweighting scheme.

As mentioned (section 2.5), the ISSHR sample included an 'over-sample' of the population aged under 30 so that more disaggregated analyses could be made of a population that, as previous research suggests, engages in riskier behaviours. Two weights were needed for the data:

* The first or 'total population weight' reweighted the data to represent the population and thus 'weighted down' the proportion of respondents under 30.
* The second or 'young persons' weight, applied only to those under 30, reweighted this group to represent the population under 30, and included a disaggregation into three sub-age groups.

All analyses in this report after *Table 2.1* were carried out using data weighted using the first of these weights, the total population weight. Analyses in the three ISSHR sub-reports were carried out using whichever weight was most appropriate to the particular analyses. Where the number of individuals included in an analysis is given, this is always the unweighted number of cases. (In section 2.12, we describe how the analyses were carried out and how the tables in this report should be interpreted.)

The categories used in *Table 2.1* are those used by the Census of Population (2002) from the CSO. They are purely for reweighting purposes and for comparisons with population data and are not used for analysis in the report. We will examine shortly the distribution of variables used in the analyses.

Table 2.1 shows that, although there are some differences between the unweighted proportions of some groups in the ISSHR data compared to the census data, the weighted data are very close to those of the population as measured by exterior data sources. The weighted proportions will not exactly match the census totals as some weights are adjusted so that undue weight is not placed on a small number of individuals. The unweighted differential stems in part from the intentional over-sampling of younger respondents. Thus:

* whereas those under 30 make up 35.2% of the ISSHR sample when unweighted compared to 31.2% in the census population, this figure falls to 31.8% when weighted.

---

[f] These are based on independent national sources such as the Census of Population 2002 and the Quarterly National Household Survey (both undertaken by the Central Statistics Office).

Table 2.1: Unweighted, weighted and population proportions of selected characteristics: by gender (%)

Demographic Characteristics	Men (n=3,188)			Women (N=4,253)		
	Un-weighted Sample	Weighted Sample	General Population	Un-weighted Sample	Weighted Sample	General Population
All*	42.8	50.1	50.1	57.2	49.9	49.9
Age*						
18-29	38.1	31.1	30.7	35.2	31.8	31.2
30-39	17.2	23.9	24.3	22.4	23.6	23.8
40-49	20.6	21.1	21.5	19.5	21.3	21.2
50-59	17.8	17.6	17.3	17.3	17.1	17.6
60-64	6.4	6.3	6.2	5.7	6.2	6.2
Relationship status*						
Single	45.4	44.7	45.0	38.1	41.8	42.2
Married	47.1	49.0	48.7	55.5	51.8	51.5
Cohabiting	7.5	6.3	6.3	6.4	6.4	6.3
Highest education*						
Primary or less	9.2	17.4	17.5	8.0	14.4	14.4
Lower secondary	18.5	24.4	24.4	16.8	22.0	22.0
Upper secondary	25.7	31.0	30.9	25.9	32.7	32.7
Post Leaving Certificate	11.2	10.5	10.5	15.2	12.5	12.5
Third level	35.5	16.8	16.8	34.1	18.5	18.4
Region*						
Dublin	30.6	29.4	29.4	26.7	31.1	31.1
Border, Midlands & West	25.4	25.9	25.8	28.2	24.9	24.9
Rest of country	44.0	44.7	44.8	45.1	44.0	43.9
Social class#						
Higher prof. & managerial	22.3	17.9	19.5	11.1	9.2	11.4
Lower prof. & managerial	21.9	19.1	13.9	29.6	22.9	20.9
Clerical/administrative	13.5	13.3	15.1	29.5	30.5	34.8
Skilled manual	22.8	27.2	28.4	1.8	2.1	1.7
Semi-skilled manual	12.3	13.1	13.3	19.3	23.2	21.8
Unskilled manual	7.4	9.4	9.6	8.8	12.1	9.4

*Central Statistics Office (2004)
Living in Ireland Survey (2001)

The satisfactory response rate and effective re-weighting mean that results are very representative of the general population.

In the following sections we examine the distribution of cases in the ISSHR data across the various socio-demographic categories used in the later chapters. We have seen in Table 2.1 the distribution of educational and relationship status categories in the data. In the following sections we examine a range of other factors.

2.11.1 Social classification

AS the last chapter made clear, socio-economic differences are a key interest of this study. We needed measures that would allow us to examine these differences. The term 'socio-economic' covers a range of different measures of a person's relationship to the labour market, their level of resources (and power) and the manner in which these are translated into social status.

Although it would be ideal to have measures of all the constituent factors (ie, education, income, social class and social status), this was not practical within the confines of a 30-minute KAB survey. Instead we chose to measure education and social class. Education was measured because it is a major determinant of other socio-economic factors such as income and status, and social class because it is a useful summary measure of occupational success and income level.

A number of social-class measures have been developed, both in Ireland and internationally. One of the best known and most frequently used is the Erikson/Goldthorpe or EG class measure. It is based on the employment relationship of an individual. It has informed the development of other national class measures such as the current Office of National Statistics (ONS) measure in the UK and the current CSO (1996) measure in Ireland.

Operating the EG, ONS or CSO measures requires detailed information on the number of individuals that a person supervises or manages as well as information on the person's occupation and employment status. Space and time pressures in the KAB questionnaire made this impractical. We chose instead to use the social-class measure used by the Central Statistics Office from 1986 to 1996 and known as the 1986 class schema. Although since superseded by the 1996 measure in Ireland, the 1986 measure remains a robust and valid class measure that is still used for research even by the CSO itself.

Table 2.2 provides an overview of the distribution of social class in the ISSHR sample. The largest grouping among social classes is social class III (other non-manual) at 21.4%, followed by social class II (lower professional) at 20.9%. These proportions are close to those of the general population as measured in a recent national sample.

It should be remembered when examining the distribution of classes in *Table 2.2* that the age distribution of the population is truncated to those aged between 18 and 64. This means that there is a higher proportion of non-manual occupations in ISSHR than in the general population (it is also true that Ireland has a higher proportion of non-manual occupations in the population generally).

Table 2.2: Social class of study sample: by gender	Men n=3,188 %	Women n=4,253 %	Total n=7,441 %
Higher prof. & managerial (social class I)	17.9	9.2	13.8
Lower prof. & managerial (social class II)	19.1	22.9	20.9
Clerical/administrative (social class III)	13.3	30.5	21.4
Skilled manual (social class IV)	27.2	2.1	15.4
Semi-skilled manual (social class V)	13.1	23.2	17.8
Unskilled manual (social class VI)	9.4	12.1	10.7

The above are weighted proportions

2.11.2 Relationship status

WHILE marital status was used in weighting the sample to match the general population profile (*Table 2.3*), for the purposes of analysis the data were re-categorised by current relationship status. Current relationship status was considered to be a more useful variable in terms of current sexual and contraceptive behaviour. In total, 50% of participants were married, 6% were living with a partner, and 11% were in a steady relationship.

Table 2.3: Relationship status of study sample: by gender

	Men n=3,188 %	Women n=4,253 %	Total n=7,441 %
Not in a relationship	27.3	26.1	26.7
Married and living with spouse*	49.0	51.8	50.4
Not married and living with a partner	6.3	6.4	6.4
In a steady relationship	10.1	12.4	11.2
In a casual relationship	7.4	3.4	5.4

* If married, participants were asked if they were currently living with their husband/wife. If not, their current relationship status was ascertained.
The above are weighted proportions.

2.11.3 Religious beliefs

ISSHR respondents were asked whether they would describe themselves as a religious or spiritual person. Responses were coded from 'not at all' to 'extremely religious'. The weighted responses show (*Table 2.4*) that those who responded that they were 'a little religious' (38%) were the largest grouping, followed by those who were 'quite religious' (30%).

Table 2.4: Level of religiosity of study sample: by gender

	Men n=3,188 %	Women n=4,253 %	Total n=7,441 %
Not at all religious	24.4	17.0	20.7
A little religious	38.1	38.0	38.1
Quite religious	27.1	32.2	29.7
Very religious	9.3	11.1	10.2
Extremely religious	1.1	1.6	1.4

Weighted proportions

2.11.4 Country of birth

In the last decade, inward migration to Ireland has substantially increased. Much of this migration has been of returning Irish people, but the numbers of people moving to Ireland from other EU states and further afield have also risen greatly. *Table 2.5* gives the proportion of the ISSHR sample who were born in Ireland (Republic and Northern Ireland), Britain, another EU country or elsewhere.

Table 2.5: Country of birth of study sample: by gender	Men n=3,186 %	Women n=4,251 %	Total n=7,437 %
Ireland	91.8	89.7	90.8
Britain	5.5	6.9	6.2
Other EU	0.9	1.2	1.1
Elsewhere	1.8	2.1	2.0

Weighted proportions

This table shows that the vast majority of ISSHR respondents were born in Ireland and that the largest group of non-Irish-born respondents were born in Britain. Around 3% of respondents were born elsewhere.

2.11.5 Type of geographic location

AS a representative sample of the population of Ireland, the ISSHR data include geographical breakdown. Geographic location could be associated with sexual attitudes and behaviours and this is one of the dimensions investigated in this report. This table shows that the sample breaks down relatively evenly across types of location:

* The largest grouping (30%) live in a rural ('open country') location, 24% in a town and 35% in a city (most in Dublin city or county). A total of 59% live in either a town or a city.

Table 2.6: Current location of residence: by gender	Men n=3,187 %	Women n=4,249 %	Total n=7,436 %
Rural (open country)	30.3	28.9	29.6
Village	9.9	12.7	11.3
Town (1500+)	24.7	23.0	23.9
City	11.6	11.5	11.6
Dublin city or county	23.6	23.9	23.7

Weighted proportions

2.11.6 Employment status

EMPLOYMENT status is an important socio-economic indicator. *Table 2.7* shows that the employed make up the largest grouping, with 40% of all respondents employed full-time and 12% employed part-time. A smaller proportion of women are employed compared to men, and women are more likely to be employed part-time (19% compared to 6% of men). The small proportion of unemployed respondents (4%) reflects the generally buoyant economic environment in which the survey was carried out.

Table 2.7: Employment status: by gender

	Men n=3,188 %	Women n=4,253 %	Total n=7,441 %
Full-time employment	52.0	27.1	39.6
Part-time employment	5.6	19.1	12.3
Self-emp./farming	17.6	2.8	10.2
Full-time student	9.5	13.4	11.5
Govt. training scheme	0.1	0.3	0.2
Unemployed	5.8	2.7	4.3
Sick/disabled	2.8	2.2	2.5
Full-time carer	0.4	29.8	15.1
Retired (before 65)	5.8	2.5	4.1
Other	0.3	0.2	0.2

Weighted proportions

2.11.7 Age group

IN *Table 2.1* we showed that the age distribution of the ISSHR sample is very representative of the Irish population. The categories were used for comparison because they matched the data available from the CSO. In the rest of this report, we use a different set of age categories. These allow us to differentiate more finely between age groups, particularly at the younger end of the age spectrum. Two age categories will be used: a nine-category age group (as displayed in *Table 2.8*) and a collapsed five-category version which retains those under 25 as one group but thereafter collapses all other five-year age groups into 10-year groups.

Table 2.8: Age groups: by gender

	Men n=3,188 %	Women n=4,253 %	Total n=7,441 %
18-24	20.8	20.9	20.8
25-29	10.3	11.0	10.7
30-34	10.7	9.4	10.0
35-39	13.2	14.2	13.7
40-44	11.0	11.0	11.0
45-49	10.1	10.2	10.2
50-54	7.9	8.4	8.1
55-59	9.7	8.7	9.2
60-64	6.3	6.2	6.2

Weighted proportions

This table shows that the largest age group is those under 25 who make up 21% of the population. The next largest group is those between 35 and 39 and the smallest age group those aged 60 to 64.

2.12 The relationship between age group and social class, education and relationship status

2.12.1 Age and highest educational level

THE last section gives a breakdown of the main socio-demographic predictors used in this study. It is important to understand the relationship between these variables. In this section, we cross-tabulate four of these variables – age group, social class, education group and relationship status – to show the relationships between them. The five-category age version uses 10-year age groups.

The first important pattern is that between age and level of education. Since the introduction of free secondary education in 1967, the level of education in the population has risen steadily. Younger age groups are now far more likely to complete secondary education and go on to third level. This is shown clearly in *Table 2.9*, which gives the distribution across age groups of highest educational qualification.

Table 2.9: Highest educational level attained: by age group (%)

	<25	25-34	35-44	45-54	55-64
Primary only	2.2	4.6	9.0	21.5	42.9
Lower secondary	11.0	20.0	27.0	27.3	19.4
Upper secondary	57.0	46.1	45.2	35.1	27.6
Third level	29.8	29.3	18.8	16.1	10.2

Weighted proportions

This table shows that the average level of highest education increases as age decreases. Those under 35 are much more likely to have third-level education than those aged 35 or more. The effect of free secondary education from 1967 on is clear:

- A large proportion (43%) of those in the oldest age group have primary-level education alone.
- Among those aged 45 to 54, this proportion falls to 22% and to just 2% among those under 25.

It will be important in the analyses to come to bear in mind the structured relationship between education and age group when examining patterns of sexual knowledge, attitudes and behaviours across education groups, since results that do not control for age may largely reflect the average age of the people in the education groups rather than the impact of education *per se*.

2.12.2 Age and social class

THE rising educational profile of younger Irish people is reflected in their occupational and social-class status. Ireland's move from a predominantly agricultural economy in the 1950s to one of the most 'post-industrial' economies in the world by the end of the century has increased the proportion of the population working in professional and 'white-collar' occupations. This is particularly the case among younger cohorts who have the higher levels of education required.[19]

Table 2.10 shows that the lowest proportion in semi-skilled or unskilled occupations is found among the youngest age group. This group also have the highest proportion in professional and managerial occupations.

Table 2.10: Highest professional level attained: by age group (%)

	<25	25-34	35-44	45-54	55-64
Higher prof. & managerial	25.0	17.6	17.2	16.0	14.2
Lower prof. & managerial	23.7	22.0	22.3	22.6	21.4
Clerical/administrative	15.6	19.5	22.4	20.3	20.4
Skilled manual	17.5	16.5	13.0	15.6	18.5
Semi/unskilled manual	18.1	24.4	25.1	25.5	25.5

Weighted proportions

As with education, it is important to bear this distribution in mind when examining the patterns of sexual knowledge, attitudes and behaviours where age is not controlled statistically.

2.12.3 Education and social class

THE influence of higher levels of education among younger age groups on their social-class attainment has been found across all industrial societies studied in social mobility research. It results from the role which education plays in the allocation of occupations in industrial economies.[20][21] This relationship can be seen clearly in *Table 2.11* which shows that those with higher levels of education are far more likely to have a higher occupational position. For example:

* Among those with primary education alone, 22% are in professional and managerial positions compared to 66% among those with third-level qualifications.
* Whereas 41% of those with primary education alone are in the unskilled manual class, this is true of just 11% of those with a third-level qualification.

Table 2.11: Social class position: by highest educational level attained (%)				
	Primary	**Lower secondary**	**Higher secondary**	**Third level**
Higher prof. & managerial	8.6	13.3	17.3	31.0
Lower prof. & managerial	13.4	13.5	23.5	34.9
Clerical/administrative	13.1	20.2	23.9	15.0
Skilled manual	23.7	21.3	14.8	8.4
Semi/unskilled manual	41.1	31.8	20.6	10.7

Weighted proportions

This structured relationship between education and social class has implications for the analyses in this report. When testing the impact of education on a person's level of knowledge or their likelihood of having a certain attitude, we need to control for factors such as age and social class. However, because social class and education are often closely related in their effects, controlling for both simultaneously can lead to the effects of both being cancelled out. In the analyses, we thus explain where this effect is an issue and test the variables separately.

2.12.4 Age group and relationship status

THROUGHOUT this report we examine the patterns of sexual knowledge, attitudes and behaviours according to a person's relationship status. As explained in section 2.11.2, relationship status is a more powerful predictor of sexual behaviours than marital status since those who are legally married, divorced, separated or widowed may or may not have a sexual partner. We assume that the latter factor is more important for many outcomes than the legal status itself.

Table 2.12: Relationship status: by age group (%)

	<25	25-34	35-44	45-54	55-64
Not in a relationship	51.1	26.8	16.6	14.6	21.3
Married (and living with spouse)	1.5	36.4	71.6	76.4	72.8
Cohabiting	5.0	15.9	5.5	2.6	1.5
Steady relationship	30.3	14.4	3.5	3.5	2.2
Casual relationship	12.1	6.5	2.8	2.9	2.2

Weighted proportions

Relationship status, however, varies significantly by age group. This influences the patterns seen in analyses. For example, as shown by *Table 2.12*, younger individuals are far less likely to be in a committed relationship:

- Over half (51%) of under-25s are single (not currently in a relationship), compared to 27% of those aged 25 to 34 and just 15% of those aged 45 to 54.

The corollary of this is that older age groups are far more likely to be married:

- 76% of those aged 45 to 54 are married and living with their spouse compared to just 2% of under-25s.

2.13 Methodology and presentation of findings

THE style of the main ISSHR report is intended to be accessible to a broad readership. This is reflected in the presentation of analyses. For the most part, these are presented graphically, with an emphasis on bringing out differences in the knowledge, attitudes and behaviours of groups defined according to particular characteristics. Almost all analyses presented are therefore 'bivariate' in the sense that they present the proportion of a group defined by education, age, social class, etc, who show a particular attitude or behave in a particular fashion.

A large number of more complex analyses lies behind these bivariate analyses, however. These are discussed in the text where the findings are noteworthy or important. Details of these more elaborate analyses are available in Appendices one to nine, in the form of tables.

The tables in Appendices one to nine present the results of multivariate analyses that were carried out to test the relationship of particular variables to the outcome of interest, controlling for other factors. For example, section 2.12.1 shows that younger individuals are far more likely to have higher levels of education. This is reflected in the ISSHR sample. When examining the relationship between education and some variables such as attitudes to contraception, we thus need to be aware that the relationships that we find with education may actually result from the fact that different age groups are unevenly distributed across the education categories. However, when examining the influence of education, it is possible to control for the influence of age by using a multivariate statistical model. The results for these models are listed in Appendices one to nine alongside the results for bivariate analyses. An example of such a table is given in *Table 2.13*.

Table 2.13: Proportion believing that the cost of condoms would discourage their use of them: by gender

	Men		Women	
	%	N	%	N
All	16.5	2,933	16.9	3,584
Age group				
<25 years	19.5**	754	17.7*	866
25-34 years	19.0**	679	20.8*	894
35-44 years	17.7**	596	13.9 ns	858
45-54 years	12.1 ns	502	14.7 ns	572
55-64 years	11.2 c	402	17.8 c	394
Education (highest level attained)				
Primary	19.0c	227	23.0 c	217
Lower secondary	18.3 *ns*	491	18.9 ns	513
Upper secondary	16.2*	1,107	16.1*	1,521
Third level	13.5**	1,108	14.4*	1,333

Significance key: ns = not significant; *= P<0.05; ** = P<0.01; *** = P<0.001
c = reference group to which all other groups are compared.
NOTE: Significance given after adjusting for all variables in the table. This table is provided here for illustrative purposes.

Reading from the top line, *Table 2.13* gives the overall proportion of men and women ('All') who believe that the cost of condoms would discourage them from using them: 16.5% of men and 16.9% of women. Beside this proportion, the actual number of men or women involved in the analysis (the 'N') is given, eg, 2,933 men. The proportions given here are 'bivariate' statistics.

Below the top line, we find the proportion of men or women in different age groups who believe that the cost of condoms would discourage them from using condoms and the actual number involved in the analysis. These proportions by age group are not connected to those in the top line. For example, 19.5% of *all* men aged under 25 believed that the cost of condoms would discourage them from using them, *not* 19.5% of the 16.5% in the top line. Each line can thus be read independently of all others to give the simple probability of some belief, attitude or behaviour being true or occurring.

While it was statistically possible to present the results of multivariate analyses next to the bivariate statistics, it was agreed that this format could be confusing. Instead the report presents the statistical significance of differences between groups, after controlling for all other variables in the table. This significance is represented using asterisks (see key at bottom of each table). The more asterisks next to a proportion, the more significant is the difference after controlling for other factors in a multivariate model.

Several cautions are needed about this method of presentation. First, statistical differences between groups may not be reflected in the actual proportions in the table. Thus, what appears to be a large difference on one variable might not be significant, whilst a small difference on another could be. This is because statistical significance depends not only on the difference between groups in outcome but also on the size of the groups involved and the distribution of other variables in the analysis.

Secondly, controlling for other factors in a multivariate model can mean that the difference between groups is reversed. In this situation a bivariate difference in one direction can be replaced by a statistically significant difference in the other direction once we control for other factors. This is not shown in the table. It is a rare occurrence and will be commented on in the text where appropriate.

Thirdly, evaluating the significance of differences across groups requires a reference category. This is identified in tables using the letter 'c' (constant) which is another term for the reference category. The asterisks in the table thus indicate whether a group is statistically different from the reference category and not necessarily all other categories. For instance, in *Table 2.13*, the reference age is 55-64, with 11.2% of men in this age group believing cost would discourage use. Compared to this reference group, there was no difference (*ns.: not significant*) in views of men aged 45-54.

However, a significantly smaller proportion of men aged 55-64 believed that cost would discourage condom use than did men in age categories 35-44, 25-34 and under 25. Each of these differences was significant; for example, the oldest age group at the p<.01 statistical level (meaning that a significant difference was assumed with a 1% chance of being incorrect). Where possible the reference category in analyses is consistent across analyses. It changes in some instances to aid presentation.

2.14 Reference list

1   Rundle K, Leigh C, McGee H, Layte R. *Irish Contraception and Crisis Pregnancy (ICCP) Study: A Survey of the General Population*. Dublin, Crisis Pregnancy Agency, 2004.

2   Weeks J. *Sex, Politics and Society: The Regulation of Sexuality Since 1800*. London: Longman, 1981.

3   Padian NS, Aral S, Vranizan K, Bolan G. 'Reliability of Sexual Histories in Heterosexual Couples'. *Sexually Transmitted Diseases* 1995; 22:169-172.

4   Van Duynhoven YT, Nagelkerke NJ, Van De Laar MJ. 'Reliability of Self-Reported Sexual Histories: Test-Retest and Inter-partner Comparison in a Sexually Transmitted Diseases Clinic'. *Sex Transm Dis* 1999; 26:33-42.

5   Mathias SD, O'Leary MP, Henning JM, Pasta DJ, Fromm S, Rosen RC. 'A Comparison of Patient and Partner Responses to a Brief Sexual Function Questionnaire'. *Journal of Urology* 1999; 162:1999-2002.

6   Jeannin A, Konings E, Dubois-Arber F, Landert C, Van Melle G. 'Validity and Reliability in Reporting Sexual Partners and Condom Use in a Swiss Population Survey'. *European Journal of Epidemiology* 1998; 14:139-146.

7   De Irala J, Bigelow C, McCusker J, Hindin R, Zheng L. 'Reliability of self-reported human immunodeficiency virus risk behaviors in a residential drug treatment population. *American Journal of Epidemiology* 1996; 143:725-732.

8   Johnson A, Mercer C, Erens B, Copas A. 'Sexual behaviour in Britain: partnerships, practices and HIV risk behaviours'. *Lancet* 2001; 358:1835-1842.

9   Layte R, Fullerton D, McGee H. *Scoping study for national survey of sexual attitudes and behaviours*. Crisis Pregnancy Agency, 2003.

10 Laumann EO, Gagnon JH, Michael TM, Michaels S. *The Social Organisation of Sexuality: Sexual Practices in the United States*. Chicago: University of Chicago Press, 1994.

11 Copas A, Johnson A, Wadsworth J. 'Assessing participation bias in a sexual behaviour survey: implications for measuring HIV risk'. *AIDS* 1997; 11:783-790.

12 Smith AMA, Rissel CE, Richters J, Grulich AE, de Visser RO. 'Sex in Australia: the rationale and methods of the Australian Study of Health and Relationships'. *Australian and New Zealand Journal of Public Health* 2003; 27(2):106-117.

13 Spira A. *Sexual Behaviour and AIDS*. Aldershot: Averbury, 1994.

14 ACSF investigators. 'What Kind of Advance Letter Increases the Acceptance Rate in a Telephone Survey on Sexual Behaviour?' Bulletin de Methodologie Sociologique 1992; 35:46-54.

15 COMREG. *Residential Telecommunications and Broadcasting Survey Report 2005*. 2005: Dublin, Commission for Communications Regulation. Trends Survey Series.

16 Kinsey AC, Pomeroy WB, Martin CE. *Sexual Behavior in the Human Male*. Philadelphia: Saunders, 1948.

17 Kinsey AC, Pomeroy WB, Martin CE, Gebhard PH. *Sexual Behaviour in the Human Female*. Philadelphia: Saunders, 1953.

18 Carroll D, Foley B, Hickson F, O'Connor J, Quinlan M, Sheehan B *et al. Vital Statistics Ireland: Findings from the All-Ireland Gay Men's Sex Survey, 2000*. Dublin: Gay Health Network, 2002.

19 Whelan CT, Layte R. 'Late Industrialisation and the Increased Merit Selection Hypothesis: Ireland as a Test Case'. *European Sociological Review* 2002.

20 Erikson R, Goldthorpe JH. *The Constant Flux: A Study of Class Mobility in Industrial Societies*. Oxford: Oxford University Press, 1992.

21 Shavit Y, Müller W. *From School to Work*. Oxford: Oxford University Press, 1998.

22 McGee H, Garavan R, de Barra M, Byrne J, Conroy R. *The SAVI Report: Sexual Abuse and Violence in Ireland*. Dublin: The Liffey Press, 2002.

Chapter 3:

Learning About Sex

3.1 Introduction

PEOPLE learn about sex from a multitude of sources, both formal and informal. Sex education should be seen as a life-long process rather than one confined to childhood or teenage years. However, little good evidence is available about the extent of sex education among the current adult population of Ireland, where it was received or its impact on subsequent behaviour. The ISSHR survey was designed to collect data on these issues. The results are reported in this chapter.

A number of studies have found that many Irish adults have a less than adequate understanding of the basic facts of life.[1][2][3][4] Research among young Irish mothers and pregnant women has found an inability to link sexual activity with the risk of pregnancy.[5][6] The Irish Family Planning Association has reported that it "continues to see clients who lack an understanding of bodily functions and the risks posed by casual, unprotected sex".[7] The ISSHR survey also investigated the level of sexual knowledge among participants. The results are presented in the next chapter.

One of the main sources of information and education about sex is parents and the home environment. Parents can communicate to their children a wide variety of messages about sexual behaviour and sexuality, both intentionally and unintentionally.

International research on the intentional messages is largely inconclusive as to their impact on children's subsequent behaviour. Some studies have found that open and positive parental communication about sex is related to an older age of sexual initiation,[8][9] but a similar number of studies have found little or no effect.[10][11] Such mixed results may stem from the varied methods and approaches adopted in different studies.

Research has found, however, that there is a strong association between parental attitudes and values and the age of onset of sexual activity.[8] The unintentional messages that parents transmit to their children may have more influence on their behaviour than their explicit attempts to influence their children's thinking.

It is also important to remember that the home environment, as measured by factors such as socio-economic group and parental education, plus the nature of the local community, can also have a profound influence on adolescent sexual behaviour in a number of ways.

One of the other main sources of sex education is the school, but in Ireland formal sex education in schools was introduced only in the late 1990s, in the form of the Relationships and Sexuality Education programme (RSE). RSE aims to provide young people with a holistic understanding of sexuality in the context of relationships; it includes:

- lessons on self-esteem, understanding feelings, communication skills, decision-making, conflict resolution and personal safety
- biological information on puberty, the reproductive system, sexual intercourse, sexual orientation, fertility, family planning and sexually transmitted infections

Each school is required to develop a policy for RSE in consultation with the whole school community. The policy provides a framework within which the RSE programme, as laid out in the National Council for Curriculum and Assessment guidelines, is taught.

Little is known about the extent to which the current Irish adult population received sex education in school. An evaluation in 2000 of sex education in Irish schools found that:

- 42% of primary and 34% of post-primary schools had not drafted an RSE policy document
- around a quarter of both primary (26%) and post-primary (28%) schools had not established an RSE policy committee

The author concluded that many children were not receiving adequate sex education at school or at home. The evaluation did find an increase in the number of schools establishing committees and drafting policy documents between 1999 and 2000. Additionally,

- 36% of primary schools and 64% of post-primary schools had drawn up an RSE programme by the year 2000
- 19% of primary and 42% of post-primary schools had implemented RSE in all classes

Again, an increase in schools drawing up and implementing RSE programmes was seen between 1999 and 2000, and 59% of primary and 42% of post-primary schools stated that they intended to implement an RSE programme in all classes in the following year (Morgan 2000).

A national survey of implementation of Social, Personal and Health Education (SPHE) at Junior Cycle,[9] carried out by the University of Limerick, asked school principals to outline the availability of RSE programmes (response rate 48%). Results showed that an RSE programme was available to 73% of first-year pupils, 69% of second-year and 63% of third-year. The authors suggested that, while fewer students received RSE as they moved into adolescence, their need for such education was likely to increase at that stage.[12]

Another evaluation of RSE implementation across primary schools carried out in 2002 found that 69% had established an RSE policy committee, 65% had drafted an RSE policy document and 50% had implemented the policy through an RSE programme (response rate 50%). However, many schools reported an intention to implement an RSE programme in the coming years.

Young people in Ireland today are receiving more comprehensive sex education than previous generations. The experience of school sex education in the current adult population is assumed to be considerably more varied in both the extent received and the depth to which it was provided. In the few small-scale Irish studies available, reports of inadequate sex education[12] and dissatisfaction with sex education[13] were found among those who finished school prior to formal RSE introduction.

In the **next section**, we examine the extent of sex education received by the current adult population aged 18 to 64 while they were growing up, and from whom this education was received.

The **third section** analyses the level of communication between survey respondents and their parents, as indicated by the ease with which they could talk to them about sexual matters. Ease of talking to mother and father are looked at separately, and patterns across gender, age and education groups are examined.

The **fourth section** examines the extent to which individuals perceived as useful the sex education received from all sources and how this varies by sex and age. The **fifth section** looks at opinions on what sex education should be given to young people today. The **sixth section** analyses whether respondents have information deficits on particular issues. Finally, the **seventh section** summarises the results found and their implications.

---

[9] SPHE is the curriculum within which other specific programmes are delivered, including RSE. All second-level schools have had to timetable SPHE as part of the Junior Cycle core curriculum from September 2003.

3.2 Experience of sex education, its source and type

SUMMARY

ONLY 53% of men and 60% of women reported having received sex education. This is largely due to the fact that the Relationships and Sexuality Education (RSE) programme was only introduced into Irish schools in 1997.

The introduction of RSE is the primary reason why the proportion who have received sex education is highest among under-25s.

■ Most under-35s have received sex education to some degree.

■ 88% of men and 93% of women under 25 have received some sex education.

■ People with lower levels of education and/or of lower social class are less likely to have received sex education. Sex education is received less often at home in working-class households.

■ Respondents were most likely to be taught about biological aspects of sex and sexual intercourse (51%) and least likely to receive information on sexual feelings, relationships and emotions (27%).

■ Sex education received by younger age groups is much more likely to have included information on contraception and safe sex than that received by older age groups.

■ Most individuals who received sex education did so in school. School has become the predominant source among younger age groups.

THE extent to which people received sex education when growing up, what topics they received it on and from whom they received it are of interest when their level of knowledge about sexual issues in adult life is being examined. In the past in Ireland, sex education was set within either a religious ethical or a natural scientific perspective. Children were taught moral stances on appropriate and inappropriate sexual behaviour, on the one hand, and, on the other, the facts about reproduction.[14]

The Relationships and Sexuality Education (RSE) programme, introduced in secondary schools in 1997, is part of the broader programme of Social, Personal and Health Education (SPHE). Prior to this, primary schools introduced the Stay Safe Programme (SSP) in the early 1990s. A response to the increase of reported child sex abuse, it aimed to teach children about appropriate and inappropriate touching. The RSE programme consists of a set of procedures and guidelines, but each school develops its own policies, programmes, resources and materials.

The RSE and SSP programmes represent a relatively progressive view of sex education which, instead of providing merely basic biological information and/or teaching abstinence, aims to develop in children specific skills and competencies. They mirror the shift in control of sexual discourse and education away from the Catholic Church to the state. Censorship laws were eased in the 1960s and the laws on contraception were changed in the 1970s and 1980s, but changes in sex education were introduced later, mainly because of the major role of the Catholic Church in the field of education. The reasons put forward for the necessity of an RSE programme were:

• earlier physical maturation of children
• increased evidence of earlier sexual relationships among young people
• conflicting and confusing messages about sexuality from teenage magazines and the media in general

- increased health risks in the AIDS/HIV era

Wiley and Merriman's 1996 survey[4] of 3,000 women found that only 49% had received any form of sex education, though this percentage was much higher for the younger age cohorts: 88% of 18 to 24-year-olds had received sex education compared to only 15% of those aged 55 to 60.

They found a link between poorer knowledge and births outside marriage. A total of 69% of those who did not get sex education agreed that a woman could not get pregnant during first sexual intercourse, compared to 31% of those who did get sex education.

3.2.1   Receipt of sex education

IN the ISSHR survey, respondents were asked whether or not they had received sex education on four topics when they were growing up. The topics were:

- sex and sexual intercourse
- sexual feelings, relationships and emotions
- contraception
- safer sex and STIs

Figure 3.1 shows that 44% of individuals interviewed had received no sex education at all, while 56% had received at least some sex education on one or more of the above topics.

Women are more likely than men to have received some form of formal sex education: 60% as opposed to 53%.

Figure 3.1: Proportion who received sex education: by gender

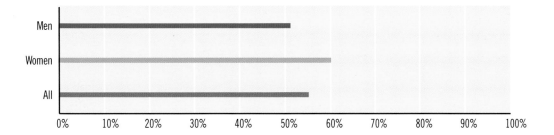

Since guidelines on formal sex education in Irish schools were introduced only in the late 1990s, it would be surprising if older Irish people were not significantly less likely to have received sex education. *Figure 3.2* shows that younger individuals are much more likely to have received at least some form of sex education. There is a graduated relationship between age and probability of sex education for both men and women:

- 88% of men aged 18 to 24 received some form of sex education compared to 12% of those aged 55 to 64
- 93% of women aged 18 to 24 received sex education compared to 19% of those aged 55 to 64

Given the recent introduction of the RSE programme, it is surprising that there is a graduated relationship between the proportion receiving sex education and age. The *a priori* assumption would be that all age groups other than the youngest would report uniformly low levels of sex education. However, it is likely that the liberalising trend of the last three or four decades provided an increasingly positive environment for sex education both in the home and at school. This would have led to a gradual increase in provision, albeit on a nationally inconsistent basis. More evidence on this issue is presented below.

Figure 3.2: Proportion receiving sex education: by gender and age group

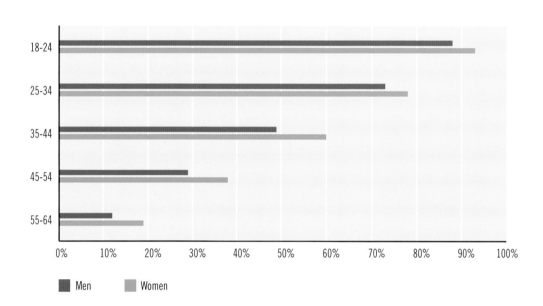

Highest level of education received is also strongly related to whether or not men and women report having received sex education. *Figure 3.3* shows that people with higher levels of education are much more likely to have received it:

- 71% of men with tertiary education compared to 15% of those with only primary education had received sex education
- 77% of women with tertiary education compared to 21% of those with only primary education had received sex education

This difference in the probability of having received sex education across education groups occurs across age groups, but the difference between education groups is far smaller in the youngest age group than in all older groups.

The significant difference across educational groups is replicated in differentials across social-class groups:

- 57% of men and 71% of women in professional and managerial occupations have received sex education, compared to 49% of men and 53% of women from semi-skilled and unskilled groups

Figure 3.3: Proportion receiving sex education: by gender and highest level of education

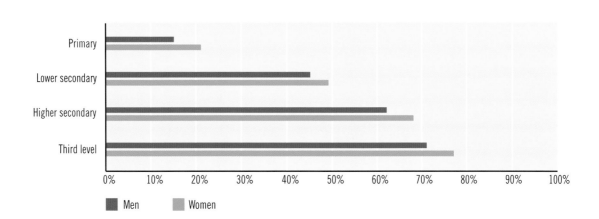

Sex education in schools has been policy in Ireland since the mid-1990s. People with lower levels of education are now more likely to receive sex education than they were in the past. The reasons for the differential across education groups are complex but are linked largely to the social background of those with low levels of education.

ISSHR Sub-Report 1: 'Learning About Sex and First Sexual Experiences' shows that the differential in total sex education across social class and educational groups is explained by lower levels of sex education at home for those with a lower education and/or social class. Individuals with lower levels of educational attainment are likely to have come from working-class backgrounds and have had parents with lower educational attainment. As we will see in the next chapter, working-class groups are less likely to report liberal attitudes toward sex. Such attitudes may inhibit their willingness to give, or their comfort in giving, sex education. This may be reflected in the patterns found in this section.

Introducing sex education in schools in the recent period may have gone a long way toward decreasing the sex-education inequalities across social groups.

3.2.2 Type of sex education received

THE most common topic of sex education received is basic biological information on sexual intercourse. Education about sexual feelings, relationships and emotions is the least likely topic to be received. *Figure 3.4* shows that:

- 51% of all respondents received education on sex and sexual intercourse
- 27% on sexual feelings, relationships and emotions
- 34% on contraception
- 30% on safer sex and STIs

Where sex education was received, it was more likely to be on the technical aspects of sex rather than on how to deal with sexual relationships and on safer sex and contraception.

Figure 3.4: Proportion receiving sex education on four topics

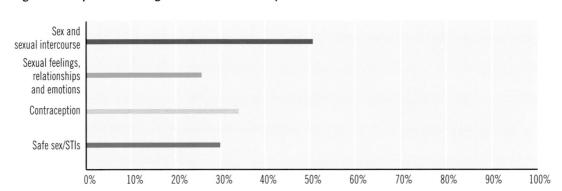

We have seen that older age groups were far less likely to have received any sex education. Older and younger groups may also have received different types of sex education. *Figure 3.5* gives the distribution of different types of sex education across age groups. It shows a change in the content of sex education across time (assuming that this sex education was received in childhood or adolescence). The pattern of increasing sex education with younger age is clear for all four topics.

Figure 3.5: Proportion receiving sex education on four topics: by age group

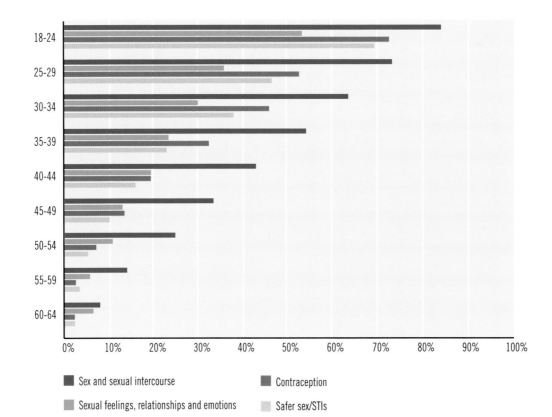

Figure 3.5 shows that where sex education was received among older age groups, it was more likely to be on sex and sexual intercourse or sexual feelings, relationships and emotions rather than contraception and safe sex (2.2% of 60 to 64-year-olds received sex education on both these topics).

A shift in the content of sex education is noticeable in those aged under 40. Whereas sex and sexual intercourse remain the most likely topics covered, respondents under 40 are more likely to have received education on contraception and safe sex than on sexual feelings, relationships and emotions. This may reflect a change in priorities in society and a greater acceptance of the need for contraception and protection, but may also suggest a lack of attention to the relational and contextual aspects of sex.

Respondents who had received sex education were asked from whom they had received it. The most common source was school:

- 86% reported receiving at least some of their sex education from school
- 29% reported some sex education at home
- 10% reported another source, the most common being books, magazines and friends[h]

Figures 3.6 and 3.7 show the relationship between source of sex education and age for men and women respectively.

Figure 3.6: Men who had received sex education from school, home or other source: by current age

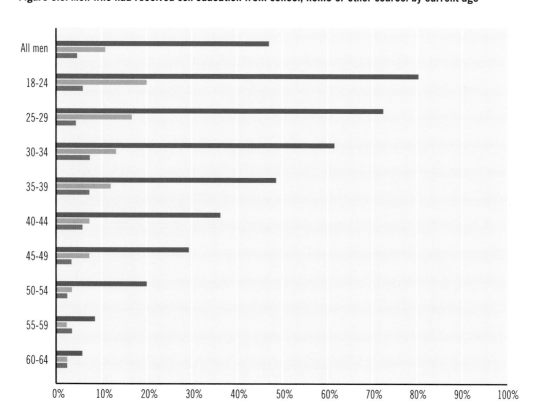

---

[h] Because respondents were given the opportunity to answer 'more than one source', the percentages do not add up to 100.

The increase in receipt of school sex education with younger age is clear in both *Figure 3.6* and *Figure 3.7*.

- 81% of men and 85% of women aged 18-24 received sex education at school
- 6% of men and 7% of women aged 60-64 received sex education at school

Just 21% of men aged 18-24 have received sex education at home. However, this proportion has increased substantially over time: from just 3% of men aged 60-64. Among women, the same pattern is evident. Whereas just 6% of women aged 60-64 received sex education at home, this figure increases to 38% of 18-24 year-olds.

Figure 3.7: Women who had received sex education from school, home or other source: by current age

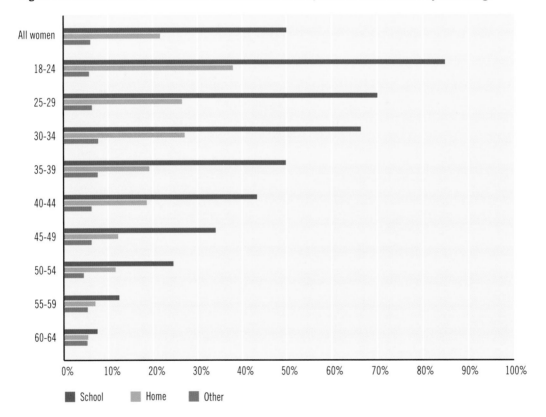

ISSHR Sub-Report 1: 'Learning About Sex and First Sexual Experiences' investigates in depth the distribution of sex education from different sources. This shows that lower levels of education are associated with a lower likelihood of receiving sex education in school. Analyses show that this pattern is strongly associated with age (since older age groups are both more likely to have lower educational qualifications and less likely to have received sex education). If we confine analysis to respondents under 30, we find that only those with primary education alone report lower levels of sex education in school. These are a small group among younger Irish people.

Sub-Report 1 found that not only are men and women in lower educational groups significantly less likely to receive sex education at school, they are also less likely to receive it at home. This differential largely explains the gap between education groups in their probability of receiving sex education overall.

For more detail on the analyses in this section, see Appendix *Table 1.1.*

3.3 Ease of talking openly with parents about sex

SUMMARY

THIS section examines how easy or difficult respondents found talking to their parents about sex. It looks at the overall pattern of responses as well as differences across sex, age group and level of education.

Overall, for most respondents, either sexual matters never came up or when they did discussion was 'difficult'. Both men and women were more likely to find talking to their mother easier than talking to their father.

The results strongly suggest that communication between parents and children on sexual matters has improved significantly over time.

■ 46% reported that talking to their mother about sexual matters was 'difficult' and 45% that talking to their father was 'difficult'.

■ A minority found talking to either parent 'easy'.

■ 25% said sexual matters 'never came up' with their mother and 36% that they 'never came up' with their father.

■ Both men and women found it easier to talk about sexual issues to their mother than their father.

■ Women (29%) were more likely than men (17%) to find it easier to talk to their mother.

■ Men (13%) were more likely than women (9%) to find it easy to talk to their father.

■ Younger people are more likely to report that talking to their mother and father about sex was 'easy'.

■ There were no differences across educational levels in the ease with which women spoke to their parents about sex.

■ Men with higher levels of education found it easier to talk to their parents about sexual issues.

THIS section looks at how easy or difficult respondents found it to talk to their parents openly about sex when they were growing up. Parents' attitudes towards sex and the general atmosphere surrounding the issue may have an influence on an individual's own opinions about sex and sexual issues. If parents are reluctant to talk about sex with their children or treat it as a taboo topic, this may have an impact on how the young person views sex and sexual issues.

The results of studies on the impact of parental sex education on age of first sex are mixed. Previous research, however, has found that parental factors can have a significant impact on contraceptive use.[15][10][16] In particular, parents' manner and style of communication about sexual behaviour and contraceptive use is important.

Figure 3.8: Ease of discussing sexual matters with mother – all respondents

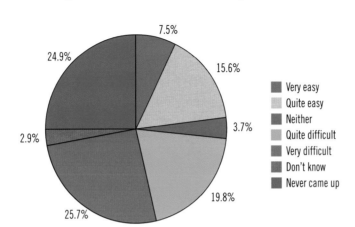

The Mueller and Powers (1990)[17] study of 234 college students found that those who perceived their parents' style of communication about sexual behaviour and contraception as friendly, attentive and open were more likely to use contraceptives.

Figures 3.8 and *3.9* show that respondents found it difficult to talk to both their mother and father about sex:

- 46% found it 'quite difficult' or 'very difficult' to talk to their mother about sex matters when they were growing up.
- 45% had similar difficulties talking to their father.

These results suggest that most people found talking to their mother just as difficult as talking to their father. However, there are substantial differences in the proportion of individuals stating that sexual matters 'never came up' with fathers compared to mothers. In piloting for the ISSHR survey, some respondents requested the category of 'never came up' as an option when answering these questions.

Figures 3.8 and *3.9* show that 25% of respondents in the ISSHR survey said sexual issues never came up with their mother and 36%, the largest single category, that it never came up with their father. This may suggest that parents were not comfortable with sexual issues. If so, the higher proportion stating that sex never came up with fathers would imply that fathers found talking about sex more difficult or felt this was not their role. Analysis by the respondents' gender shows that men are more likely to report sex not coming up with mothers (33% of men compared to 17% of women), but both men and women are equally unlikely to discuss sex with fathers (36%).

The degree of difficulty with which respondents talked with their parents about sex is shown well in *Figures 3.8* and *3.9*: 26% of respondents found it 'very difficult' when growing up to speak about sexual matters with their mother; 30% had the same level of difficulty with their father.

Figure 3.9: Ease of discussing sexual matters with father – all respondents

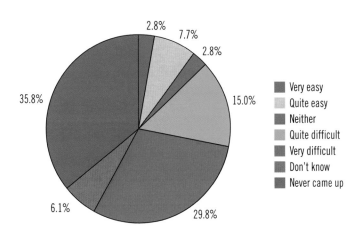

■ Very easy
■ Quite easy
■ Neither
■ Quite difficult
■ Very difficult
■ Don't know
■ Never came up

The survey shows wide variation across the population in the extent of difficulty that individuals had in speaking to parents about sex. Gender, age and educational level of the respondent were particularly important factors.

The pattern by age group and gender is shown in *Figures 3.10* and *3.11*:

• Women were more likely than men to find it easy to talk to their mother about sex: 29% of women, 17% of men.

• Men were more likely than women to find it easy to talk to their father about sex: 13% of men, 9% of women.

This suggests a definite gender effect that has implications for messages seeking to improve the extent and quality of sex education in Irish homes.

Figure 3.10: Proportion finding it 'easy' to talk to their mother about sexual matters: by gender and age group

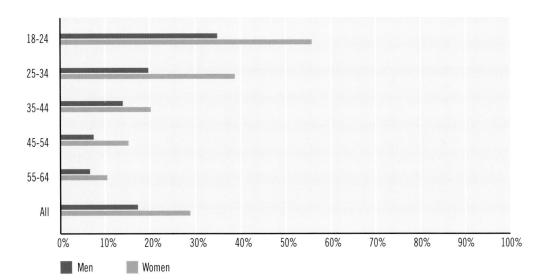

■ Men   ■ Women

Figure *3.10* shows that younger people are more likely to report that they found it easy to talk to their mothers about sex, but the difference between men and women is still apparent across age groups. As well, the gap between men and women is larger among younger age groups.

A total of 35% of men and 56% of women aged 18 to 24 found it easy to speak to their mother about sex, compared to 6% of men and 11% of women aged 55 to 64. This perhaps reflects a shift in society towards a more relaxed attitude towards sex and talking about sexual issues. Sex would not have been discussed openly or in the media when the older people were growing up. Today, depictions of sex and sexual content are far more common in all areas of the media.[18] This is part of a general liberalising trend toward sex that may make it an easier topic for parents to broach with their children.

Figure 3.11: Proportion finding it 'easy' to talk to their father about sexual matters: by gender and age group

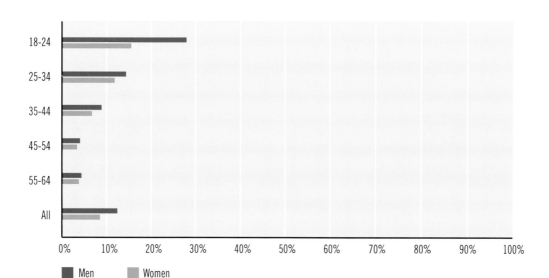

Figure 3.11 shows that the pattern by gender is reversed in terms of ease of speaking to fathers about sex:

- Men are more likely than women to report finding it easy when growing up to discuss sex with their father: 13% of men, 9% of women.

Age group, again, is a very important factor: younger individuals are much more likely than older people to report discussion being easy. The differential between men and women is particularly pronounced among the youngest age group (18 to 24): 28% of men report 'easy' discussion with their father compared to 15% of women. This suggests an improvement in the recent period in the ability of young men to speak to their fathers about sexual matters. Highest level of education achieved is also related to whether or not a respondent found it easy or not to talk to their mother and father about sex.

Figure 3.12: Proportion finding it 'easy' to talk to their mother about sexual matters: by gender and highest education

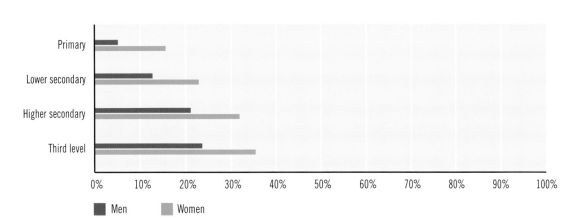

Figure 3.12 shows that, for both men and women, the higher the level of education achieved the more likely the respondent was to find it easy to talk to their mother about sex. Further analysis showed that, for women, the impact of education was almost entirely due to the fact that those women with higher qualifications were also younger (see section 2.12.1). Among men, however, higher levels of education were associated with greater ease in discussing sexual subjects with their mother. This greater ease may largely reflect the education level of parents rather than that of the sons, since individuals with higher levels of education are more likely to have parents with more education.

Figure 3.13: Proportion finding it 'easy' to talk to their father about sexual matters: by gender and highest education

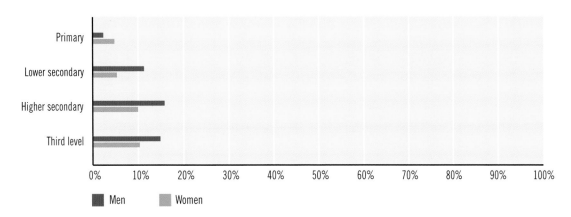

The same sorts of patterns emerge in respondents' ease of talking about sex with their father, by level of education. For both men and women, a higher level of education is associated with greater ease in talking about sex with their father. As with talking to mothers, further analysis showed that the difference across education groups for women was largely due to the younger average age of women with higher levels of education.

For more detail on the analyses in this section, see Appendix *Tables 1.2* and *1.3*. ISSHR Sub-Report 1: 'Learning About Sex and First Sexual Experiences' includes additional analyses.

3.4   Relationship between sex education received and its helpfulness

SUMMARY

JUST over half of individuals who reported receiving sex education said this was 'helpful' or 'very helpful' in preparing them for adult relationships.

Men and women were just as likely to report that their sex education was 'unhelpful', but women were more likely to report that it was 'helpful' and men that it was 'neither helpful nor unhelpful'.

Younger age groups were significantly more likely to report that the sex education they received was 'helpful'.

- More women (54%) than men (49%) who had received sex education reported that this was 'helpful'.

- Under-25s were significantly more likely than all older groups to report that their sex education was 'helpful'.

- Even among the youngest age group, 42% of men and 34% of women found their sex education 'unhelpful'.

OVERALL, 56% of respondents and up to 91% of those aged 18 to 24 reported receiving some form of sex education. This section examines the extent to which respondents found that the sex education they received was helpful in preparing them for adult relationships.

Wiley and Merriman's 1996 survey[4] of 3,000 women found that 63% of those interviewed reported thinking that the sex education they had received was adequate. In the ISSHR survey, if a respondent answered that they had received sex education on any of the four topics (listed in section 3.3), they were asked how helpful they thought the sex education they had received was in preparing them for adult relationships. As this question was not asked separately for each topic, we cannot assess the relative helpfulness of any one topic. However, we can look at those who received sex education on at least one of the topics and the perceived helpfulness of this education.

Figure 3.14: Perceived helpfulness of having received sex education while growing up: by gender

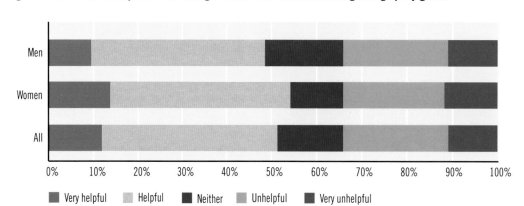

Figure 3.14 shows that 52% of those who received at least some sex education felt it had been 'helpful' or 'very helpful' in preparing them for adult relationships. A total of 23% found it 'unhelpful' and 11% 'very unhelpful'.

Men and women were equally likely to find their sex education 'unhelpful', but women were significantly more likely than men to report that it had been 'helpful'. A smaller proportion of women said it was 'neither helpful nor unhelpful'.

Figure 3.15: Proportion responding that the sex education they received was 'helpful': by gender and age group

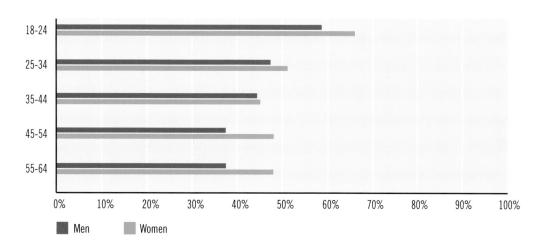

The last section showed that both the extent and type of sex education received has changed through time. This is reflected in the sex education reported by different age groups. The current age of the individual may also be related to the perceived helpfulness of the sex education received.

Figure 3.15 shows that younger age groups are more likely to have found the sex education they received 'helpful' in preparing them for adult relationships:

* Of men, 58% of those aged 18 to 24 found it helpful, compared to 38% of those aged 55 to 64.
* Of women, 66% of those aged 18 to 24 found it helpful, compared to 48% of those aged 55 to 64.

This difference may be related to the fact that the younger age group were the first to be covered by the national guidelines on sex education.

For more detail on the analyses in this section, see Appendix *Table 1.4*.

3.5 Views on the sex education that young people should receive

SUMMARY

THE overwhelming majority of individuals believed that young people today should receive sex education on the five topics that were presented to them.

The proportion was higher among women than men, but even among men over 92% supported education on each topic.

Younger respondents were more likely to support sex education on all the topics, except in the case of young men among whom the proportion supporting education on homosexuality is lowest of all groups.

■ At least 92% supported sex education for young people on the subject of sexual intercourse, sexual feelings, contraception, safer sex and homosexuality.

■ Support for sex education on homosexuality was lowest, but even here 92% of men and 96% of women supported it.

■ Individuals with higher levels of education or who are less religious are more likely to support sex education.

THE content and effectiveness of sex-education programmes and the extent to which education itself encourages young people to enter into sexual relationships has been much debated.[19] [20] However, most research has found that sex education does not increase sexual activity and that some programmes can actually decrease sexual activity among young people or encourage them to delay first intercourse.

Some sex-education programmes, including the Irish Relationships and Sexuality Education (RSE) guidelines, have begun to incorporate teaching of interpersonal skills such as negotiation and assertiveness, in an attempt to provide adolescents with the skills to avoid unwanted sexual interactions and to secure the use of contraception. Such programmes may be effective in delaying the onset of sexual activity and in increasing contraceptive use among adolescents.[19] [21]

In a review of sexual health policy, Hosie (2002)[22] described one stance on sex education, which envisages it as being about learning how to conduct healthy sexual relationships, about personal and social skills and about increasing knowledge about sexuality and sexual health, rather than being focused just on the mechanics of sex. This view is supported by a number of organisations including the British Medical Association and the Sex Education Forum.[22] International reviews of research to date suggest variations in the effectiveness of sex-education programmes internationally,[19] [20] with many key areas not being covered.[23]

In the ISSHR survey, respondents were asked their opinion on whether or not young people today should receive sex education on five topics:

- sex and sexual intercourse
- sexual feelings, relationships and emotions
- contraception
- safer sex and STIs
- homosexuality

The results show varying but extremely high levels of support across all population groups for sex education on all five topics.

Almost all (99.4%) individuals surveyed believed that young people today should receive sex education on at least one of the topics. There is little variation between topics: most people supported education on contraception (98%) and safer sex and STIs (99%), followed by sex and sexual intercourse (96%) and sexual feelings, relationships and emotions (96%). Homosexuality was the least supported topic, at 94.2%. For some of the topics, however, the gender of the respondent has a significant effect, as is shown in *Figure 3.16*.

Figure 3.16: Support for sex education on different subjects: by gender

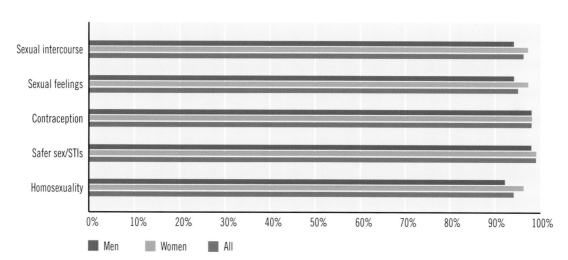

Men and women do not differ in their opinions on whether or not young people should receive sex education on contraception and safer sex. Most supported education on these topics. However, there are significant differences between men and women regarding the other topics. The most notable one is homosexuality, about which 92% of men compared to 96% of women believed young people should receive education. For this reason results for men and women have been displayed separately below.

Figures 3.17 and *3.18* below show the proportions of men and women, by age group, who think young people should receive sex education on the five topics.
In general, and for most of the topics, younger men are more likely than older men to think young people should receive sex education. For example, 97% of men aged 18 to 24, compared to 89% of those aged 55 to 64 think young people should receive sex education on sex and sexual intercourse.

There is a lot more fluctuation when it comes to views on whether young people should receive education about homosexuality. Young men aged 18 to 24 are least likely (91%) to support this, along with men aged 55 to 64.

Figure 3.17: Support for sex education on different subjects among men: by age group

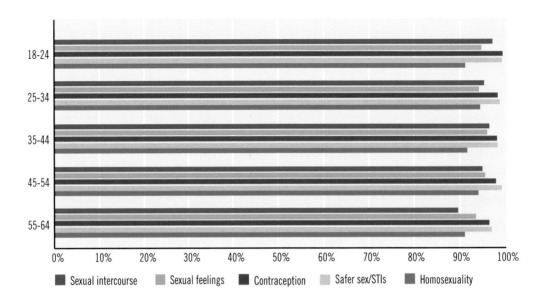

For women, age is also related to whether they think young people should receive sex education on all topics, including homosexuality. As shown in *Figure 3.17*, the same proportion of men aged 18 to 24 as men aged 55 to 64 years, thought young people should receive sex education on homosexuality. This was contrary to the trend in the other topics of young people being more supportive of sex education. This trend was, however, found among women, where 97% of the youngest group support sex education on homosexuality, compared to 92% of the oldest age group. This suggests a more accepting attitude toward sexuality among women than among men overall and an increasing acceptance across age cohorts.

Among both men and women, higher levels of education are related to greater support for the provision of education on all five topics.

More religious respondents are less likely to support sex education generally, but the impact of religiosity is particularly marked for education on contraception and homosexuality. This relationship is not unexpected, given the stated views of the Catholic Church on contraception and homosexuality (research by Fahey *et al* 2005[24] shows that 88% of the population of the Republic of Ireland still identify as Roman Catholic). However, almost 90% of those who report being 'extremely religious' also support teaching children about contraception, and three-quarters support teaching them about homosexuality. This suggests an increasing openness among Irish Catholics to these issues. (This assumes that these respondents were supporting teaching children that tolerance of homosexuality and use of contraception are acceptable.)

For more detailed figures on the role of different factors in attitudes toward sex education, see Appendix *Tables 1.5* and *1.6*.

Figure 3.18: Support for sex education on different subjects among women: by age group

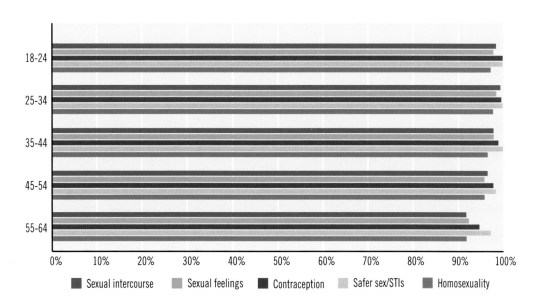

3.6 Views on where sex education should be provided to young people

SUMMARY

RESPONDENTS were first asked if young people today should receive sex education. If they said yes, they were asked where sex education should be provided – the home, school or 'other location'.

■ Approximately 90% of people who supported sex education favoured it being taught in school. Approximately 80% of those who supported sex education believed it should be provided in the home.

■ 66% of men and women advocated that sex education be given both at home and in school. This view was more prevalent among women, those with higher levels of education and those aged between 35 and 54.

■ Men, young people and the lower-educated were more likely to support sex education in the school only.

THE overwhelming majority of respondents believed that young people should receive sex education on at least one of the five topics. At least 92% supported providing young people with education on each subject. The proportion was 99% in the case of safer-sex education.

This overwhelming support leaves open the question of what form this education should take and who should provide it. The ISSHR survey could not accommodate the detailed questions needed to address the issue of the content of sex education. It did contain questions on who should provide education on each of the five topics, if the respondent supported sex education on that topic.

In particular, the questionnaire asked whether the sex education should be provided in the home, at school or at another location. In this section we examine the responses to these questions.

Figure 3.19: Proportion supporting provision of sex education in the home, school or other: by topic

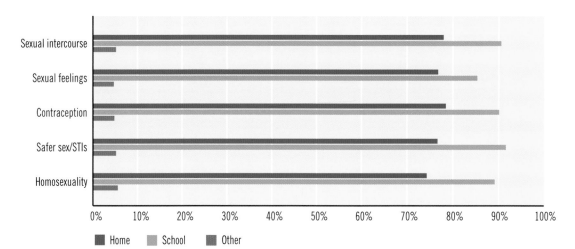

Figure 3.19 gives the proportions of people (of those who supported sex education on each of the five topics) who support sex education in the home, at school and at 'other' locations. A majority of people supported sex education in both the home and school (since individuals could choose three locations, the proportions add up to more than 100%).

A higher proportion supported sex education in schools than in the home. For example, on the subject of sex and sexual intercourse, 78% supported sex education in the home, 91% in school and 5% in another location that they were then asked to specify. These proportions vary only marginally across the five topics. Around 5% said sex education should be provided in 'other' locations. The suggestions for location were many and varied. A large proportion suggested some form of sex-education 'expert' or a professional counsellor. Some suggested that this professional be independent in the sense of not being attached to the school.

Figure 3.20: Proportion supporting sex education in school alone: by topic and gender

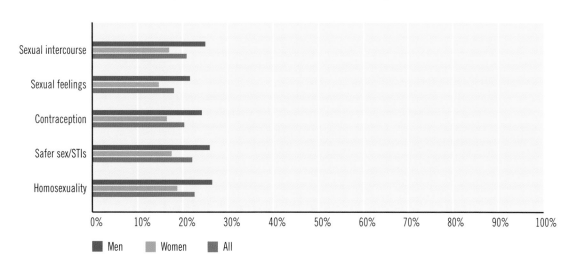

A substantial minority said sex education should be provided at school only. This proportion varied substantially across groups. *Figure 3.20* shows that men were significantly more likely than women to advocate that each of the topics be provided in school only.

Figure 3.21: Proportion supporting sex education in school alone: by topic and age group

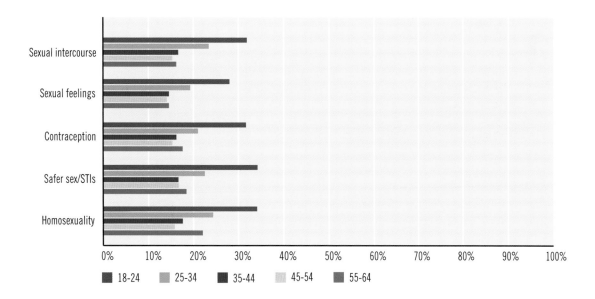

Younger age groups were also more likely to hold this opinion (see *Figure 3.21*). The two youngest age groups are significantly more likely than all older groups to advocate sex education at school only, rather than both at school and in the home.

Individuals with lower levels of education were also more likely to advocate sex education in school only. This may be one reason why these individuals were less likely to report having received sex education in the home. The tendency among lower-educated groups to support sex education in schools alone was more pronounced for 'technical' areas, such as sexual intercourse, contraception and safer sex, than for subjects such as relationships/emotions and homosexuality. One interpretation is that those with lower levels of education feel less competent on these subjects and thus defer to those they regard as 'experts' in schools.

Women, people with higher levels of education and those aged 35 to 54 were most likely to support sex education in both the home and school. This underlines the greater confidence of women and the more educated in feeling able to deliver this education, particularly those who most likely currently have children.

3.7 Extent of satisfaction with current knowledge

SUMMARY

MOST respondents reported being satisfied with their level of knowledge on contraception, on how to have a satisfying sex life and on safe sex/STIs.

Around 20%, however, would like more information on how to have a satisfying sex life and on safe sex/STIs. Among women there are pronounced differences across age groups concerning desire for more information: younger women are more likely to want more information.

- Around 9% of respondents would like more information on contraception, 19% on having a satisfying sex life and 22% on safe sex.

- A significantly higher proportion of women aged 18 to 24 (15%) would like more information on contraception, compared to older age groups.

- Younger respondents, and particularly younger women, would like more information on how to have a satisfying sex life and on having safer sex.

- There is little age variation among men except on the subject of safe sex/STIs: younger men are more likely to report a desire for more information.

A NUMBER of studies have identified a lack of basic sexual knowledge among Irish adults and young adults.[25][14][2] This survey shows that many adults report never having received any form of sex education while growing up. This may indicate that a need among the adult population for education about sexual matters.

Respondents to the ISSHR survey were asked about the extent of their satisfaction with their current knowledge of three areas related to sex. They were asked if they knew enough or would like more information on: contraception; how to have a satisfying sex life; and safer sex and STIs.

Figure 3.22 shows the results. Contraception was the area where most people were satisfied with their current knowledge: 92% of men and 91% of women reported that they already know enough. Just over one-fifth of both men and women (21% and 22% respectively) said they would like more information on safer sex. Respondents were satisfied that they knew how to protect themselves against pregnancy but were not so confident about protection against STIs. This shows a clear need for more information to be made available on safer sex and STIs.

A similar proportion (20% of men and 18% of women) also reported that they would like to have more information on how to have a satisfying sex life. Once again this suggests a substantial need for such information. A slightly higher proportion of women reported knowing enough about how to have a satisfying sex life than men (82% compared to 80%). This is a small but statistically significant difference.

Figure 3.22: Proportion reporting that they would like to know more: by subject and gender

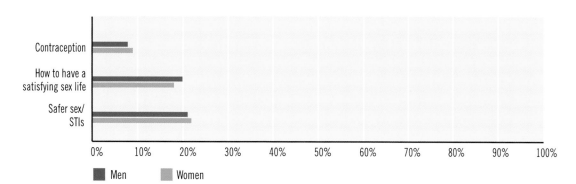

It is useful to find out whether respondents with lower levels of knowledge were more likely to report that they would like more information. Among both men and women, those who could not correctly identify the correct time limit for the use of emergency contraception were just as likely to report that they knew enough about contraception. On the other hand, those who had poor knowledge of Chlamydia were more likely to report that they would like to know more about 'safer sex/STIs/VD', as were respondents who had a poor knowledge of HIV/AIDS. This suggests that those with knowledge deficits were aware that they have them, although the differences between groups should not be overstated. Only 22% of men and 25% of women with poor knowledge of Chlamydia wanted more information (compared to 19% and 21% with good knowledge).

It is likely that desire for more information on different subjects varies across the population. For instance, post-menopausal women or their partners might be less concerned to learn more about contraception since this has less relevance to their current life. Similarly, older respondents or those in settled long-term relationships might be less concerned to learn about STIs since they may feel they are no longer at significant risk. On the other hand, those in older age groups, who are less likely to have received sex education in the past, might be anxious to learn more about subjects such as STIs or how to have a satisfying sex life.

Analyses showed little variation across the population in reported desire for more information about the subjects presented, except across age groups. Age was a significant predictor for all three subjects. The main exception was the greater desire of men with lower levels of education for information about STIs. We examine below the results across age groups for the three subjects and discuss the pattern by education for men on the subject of STIs.

3.7.1 Desire for information on contraception

FIGURE 3.23 shows by sex and age group the proportion of people who would like more information about contraception. Although men aged 18-24 and 35-44 have the highest proportions reporting such an interest, statistical tests show that the difference across age groups is not significant among men.

Among women, however, there is a clear trend among *young* women: they are far more interested in learning more about contraception, while the oldest age group is least interested. Young women are more likely to be experimenting with methods of contraception than older women, who are more likely to be in long-term relationships, have settled methods of contraception or have no need of contraception.

Figure 3.23: Proportion stating that they would like more information about contraception: by gender and age group

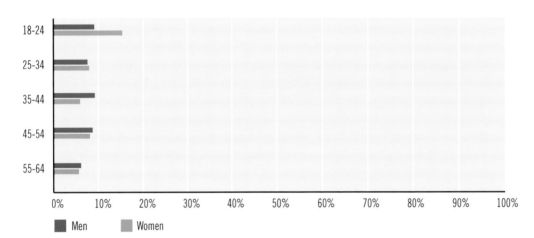

3.7.2   Desire for information on how to have a satisfying sex life

FIGURE 3.24 shows by gender and age group the proportions of men and women who would like more information about how to have a satisfying sex life. Among men, the pattern is indistinct: only the oldest age group is significantly less likely to desire more information than the other age groups (13% compared to proportions almost or greater than 20% for other age groups).

Among women we see a similar pattern as with contraception. Those aged 18 to 24 are most likely (27%) to want more information on how to have a satisfying sex life, and women aged 55 to 64 least likely (12%). Between these two groups the proportion steps down from 20% for women aged 25 to 34 to 13% for women aged 35 to 44, and 16% for those aged 45 to 54.

Figure 3.24: Proportion stating that they would like more information about how to have a satisfying sex life: by gender and age group

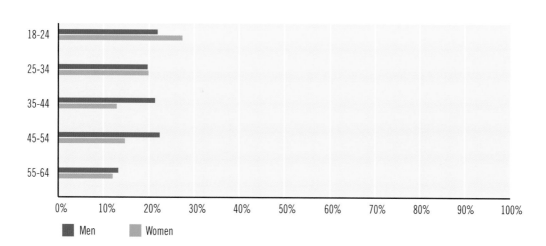

3.7.3 Desire for information on safe sex

FIGURE 3.25 shows by gender and age groups the proportion of respondents who would like more information on safe sex/STIs/VD. This shows that there is a high demand among the adult population for further information on safe sex: over a fifth said they would like this.

Figure 3.25: Proportion stating that they would like more information about safe sex, STIs: by gender and age group

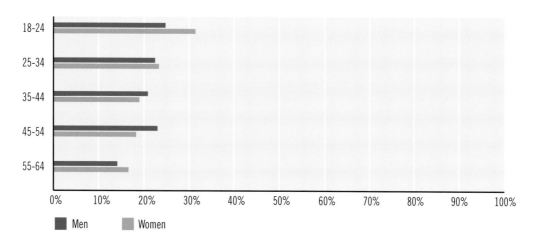

The figure also suggests a relationship between age and the need for more information on this subject, but there is a strong pattern by age for both men and women:

- 25% of men and 32% of women aged 18 to 24 said they would like more information on safe sex.
- The proportion drops gradually among women as age increases but stays relatively high among men until the group aged 55 to 64.

Apart from age, there is little variation across other dimensions in reported desire for more information, but there are interesting differences between men with different levels of education (see tables in Appendix). Men with lower and higher secondary education were significantly more likely to report wanting more information on STIs than men with third-level qualifications. As noted earlier in this chapter, lower levels of education were associated with a lower likelihood of sex education. This may be reflected here in a desire for more information in adulthood. However, analysis of whether or not a man received sex education on STIs and safer sex showed no relationship to wanting more information. Among women, on the other hand, not having had education on this subject was a significant predictor of wanting more information.

For more details on the analyses in this section, see Appendix *Tables 1.7*, *1.8* and *1.9* as well as ISSHR Sub-Report 1: 'Learning About Sex and First Sexual Experiences'.

3.8 Summary of chapter

THIS chapter has examined:

- the extent to which the current adult Irish population has received sex education
- the sources of sex information and its perceived helpfulness
- views on what sex education should be provided to young people today
- perceived need for more information among Irish people

Sex education occurs across a number of contexts, both formal and informal. One of the most important is the home. The ability and ease with which young people can discuss sexual issues with their parents is likely to be an important predictor of better knowledge and less risky behaviour.

The study found that most Irish people surveyed did not find it easy to talk to their parents about sex. In general, people reported greater difficulties talking to fathers than to mothers. Both men and women were more likely to report that they found it easier to talk to their mother, but men were more likely to report that it was easy to talk to their father, and women that it was easy to talk to their mother. This shows a gender preference when it comes to discussing sexual issues with parents; respondents reported being more comfortable discussing sex with the parent of the same gender. As might be expected, the individual's age has a substantial bearing on the reported ease with which they could talk to their parents about sex when they were growing up.

As the next chapter will show, attitudes toward sex have substantially softened in Irish society over the last three decades. This liberalising trend also seems to have made discussion between parents and their children more common and easier. This positive trend suggests that the home is an increasingly important environment in which sex is discussed, although, as we discuss below, this is from a low starting point.

Education is also related to level of ease on this subject, but only for men. Level of education received has no impact on how easy women found it to talk to their parents, but men with higher levels of education were more likely to report that they found it easy to talk to both their mothers and fathers about sex. This result for women may be seen in a positive light, ie, that women of different educational backgrounds found it equally easy to talk to their parents whereas, among men, the higher educated had an advantage.

The differential among men could be related to the difference in attitudes across social classes whereby the less educated and those from manual social classes, and particularly the unskilled manual class, are less permissive in the sense that they are more likely to disagree with developments such as non-marital, casual and homosexual sex (children's educational attainment is strongly related to that of their parents). We present more details on this in the following chapter. The lack of difference between women of different education and social class groups, however, tends to militate against this explanation. Whatever the explanation, the pattern underlines a general trend of pronounced socio-economic differences found in relation to sexual knowledge, attitudes and behaviours.

In terms of having received sex education, women were more likely than men to have received some form while growing up. Overall however, 44% of respondents reported that they had received no sex education at all. This means that almost half of the adult Irish population, most of whom will be in sexual relationships, never received any education on sex from any source. Whatever knowledge this 50% of the population have, it must be assumed that it was gathered *ad hoc* from random sources and is likely to be incomplete and perhaps flawed.

The probability of having received sex education increases dramatically among younger age groups. Most people aged 18 to 24 have received some education on sex (as expected, given developments in sex education in Ireland since the mid-1990s). Those with higher levels of education are also more likely to have received some sex education; this is particularly true for men. Although most young people now receive sex education, there is a significant difference in the likelihood of receiving sex education between those with higher and those with lower educational qualifications. There is insufficient information in the ISSHR survey to fully explain this differential, but further analysis in the ISSHR Sub-Report 1: 'Learning About Sex and First Sexual Experiences' shows that, among under-30s, the absence of sex education at home largely explains the difference across educational groups. This suggests that urgent attention should be given to helping parents in lower socio-economic groups with the sex education of their children, who are most likely to leave school with lower educational qualifications.

In terms of the content of sex education, over half of respondents had received education on sex and sexual intercourse, but only a third had been educated about contraception and safer sex and less again (about a quarter) for sexual feelings and relationships.

School was reported to be the most common source of sex education, especially among young people. Few people, even in the younger age groups, reported home as a source of information about sex. This reflects the unease that respondents reported in talking about sex with their parents. This issue is perhaps more difficult to deal with than school-based sex education, but more information and resources directed at parents might help them become more comfortable and give them the skills necessary to talk to their children about sex.

Provision of sex education alone is not enough, however. What is important is the helpfulness of this education in preparing the young person for adult relationships. Just over half of those who had received any sex education reported that they had found the information received useful in preparing them for adult relationships. There was no relationship between level of education and respondents' perception of the helpfulness of their sex education, but there was a relationship between this and the age of the respondent.

The vast majority (>92%) of both men and women favour providing sex education. Individuals were asked whether they favoured education on five topics: sex and sexual intercourse; sexual feelings, relationships and emotions; contraception; safer sex and STIs; and homosexuality. There is very little variation across age and education levels in terms of support for these topics, but a higher level of religiosity is associated with lower support for teaching about contraception and homosexuality. However, even among the 'extremely religious', 90% support teaching about contraception and 75% support education on homosexuality.

Of those respondents who supported sex education for young people today, around 80% supported this being delivered in the home and 90% in the school. Around 66% supported sex education being delivered in both the home and school; this two-thirds were more likely to be female, more educated and have children themselves. Those supporting sex education in the school only were more likely to be young (aged less than 35), male and less educated. This pattern is likely to be linked to the fact that those with lower levels of education are also less likely to have received sex education in the home.

As stated earlier, many adults in the Irish population have not received any formal sex education and thus may not be fully informed about sexual issues. Respondents were asked if they knew enough about or would like more information on contraception, how to have a satisfying sex life and safer sex and STIs. Respondents had a dearth of knowledge about safer sex and STIs: around one-fifth of both men and women said they would like more information about these.

ISSHR Sub-Report 1: 'Learning About Sex and First Sexual Experiences' shows that women who had received sex education on safe sex and STIs were almost 40% less likely to say they would like more information on this subject in adulthood than those who had not received education on this subject. This lack of knowledge is further evidence that, in the debate about providing sex education, focus needs to be placed not just on young people currently at school but also on adults whose level of knowledge may be low.

3.9   Reference list

1   Dempsey M, Heslin J, Bradley C. *The Experience of Teenage Pregnancy*. Waterford: South-Eastern Health Board, 2000.

2   Mahon E, Conlon C, Dillon L. *Women and Crisis Pregnancy*. Dublin: The Stationery Office, 1998.

3   Rundle K, Leigh C, McGee H, Layte R. *Irish Contraception and Crisis Pregnancy (ICCP) Study. A Survey of the General Population*. Crisis Pregnancy Agency Report no. 7, 2004.

4   Wiley M, Merriman B. *Women and Health Care in Ireland*. Dublin: Oak Tree Press, 1996.

5   Richardson V. *Young Mothers: A Study of Young Single Mothers In Two Communities*. Dublin: University College Dublin, 2000.

6   Hyde A. 'Unmarried Pregnant Women's Accounts of Their Contraceptive Practices: A Qualitative Analysis'. *Irish Journal of Sociology* 1996; 6:179-211.

7   IFP Association. IFPA submission to the Crisis Pregnancy Agency. 2002.

8   Miller BC, Benson B, Galbraith KA. 'Family relationships and adolescent pregnancy risk: a research synthesis'. *Developmental Review* 2001; 21(1):1-38.

9   Stanton B, Li X, Pack R, Cottrell L, Harris C, Burns J. 'Longitudinal influences of perceptions of peer and parental factors on African American adolescent risk involvement'. *Journal of Urban Health* 2002; 79(4):536-548.

10   Casper LM. 'Does family interaction prevent adolescent pregnancy?' *Family Planning Perspectives* 1990; 22(3):109-14.

11   Huebner AJ, Howell LW. 'Examining the relationship between adolescent sexual risk-taking and perceptions of monitoring, communication, and parenting styles'. *Journal of Adolescent Health* 2003; 33(2):71-8.

12   Geary T, McNamara PM. *Implementation of Social, Personal and Health Education at Junior Cycle: National Survey Report*. Limerick: University of Limerick, 2002.

13   Mason C. 'A Needs Assessment for Contraceptive Services in the North Western Health Board'. Faculty of Public Health Medicine, Royal College of Physicians of Ireland, 2003.

14   Inglis T. *Lessons in Irish Sexuality*. Dublin: University College Dublin Press, 1998.

15   Nguyen MN, Saucier JF, Pica LA. 'Influence of attitudes on the intention to use condoms in Quebec sexually active male adolescents'. *Journal of Adolescent Health* 1994; 15(3):269-74.

16   Baker SA, Thalberg SP, Morrison DM. 'Parents' behavioral norms as predictors of adolescent sexual activity and contraceptive use'. *Adolescence* 1988; 23(90):265-82.

17   Mueller KE, Powers WG. 'Parent-child sexual discussion: perceived communicator style and subsequent behavior'. *Adolescence* 1990; 25(98):469-82.

18   MacKeogh C. *Teenagers and the Media: A Media Analysis of Sexual Content on Television*. 10. Dublin, Crisis Pregnancy Agency, 2005.

19   Kirby D. 'Sex and HIV/AIDS education in schools'. *BMJ* 1995; 311(7002): 403.

20   Kirby D, Short L, Collins J, Rugg D, Kolbe L, Howard M *et al*. 'School-based programs to reduce sexual risk behaviors: a review of effectiveness'. Public Health Rep 1994; 109(3): 339-60.

21   Mellanby AR, Phelps FA, Crichton NJ, Tripp JH. 'School sex education: an experimental programme with educational and medical benefit'. *BMJ* 1995; 311(7002):414-7.

22   Hosie A. *Sexual health policy analysis in selected European countries*. Edinburgh, Health Education Board for Scotland, 2002.

23   Kirby D. 'Effective approaches to reducing adolescent unprotected sex, pregnancy, and childbearing'. J *Sex Res* 2002; 39 (1): 51-7.

24   Fahey T, Hayes BC, Sinnott R. *Conflict and Consensus: A Study of Values and Attitudes in the Republic of Ireland and Northern Ireland*. Dublin: Institute of Public Administration, 2005.

25   Rundle K, Leigh C, McGee H, Layte R. Irish Contraception and Crisis Pregnancy (ICCP) Study: A Survey of the General Population. Dublin, Crisis Pregnancy Agency, 2004.

Chapter 4:

Sexual Knowledge, Attitudes and Beliefs

4.1   Introduction

THE study of sexual attitudes, knowledge and beliefs is central to understanding the patterning of sexual behaviours. Sexual behaviour, like any other human behaviour, is the outcome of a complex mixture of rationality, social attitudes, beliefs about the world and level of knowledge, plus a large component of situational factors, emotions and desires.

In this chapter the focus is on three of these factors: sexual knowledge, attitudes and beliefs. An examination of these will allow better understanding of the patterning of sexual behaviours, particularly where these place individuals at risk of unplanned conception or infection from STIs and HIV. However, there are broader reasons for studying these subjects.

Social scientists are interested in social attitudes and beliefs because of their role in explaining social change. Sex and sexuality are strongly regulated across all societies; this (as chapter one argued) was particularly true of Ireland during the late 19th and 20th centuries. A strong variant of the Judaeo-Christian attitude to sex prospered under the auspices of the Catholic Church.[1]

Since the 1960s however, attitudes have changed quite dramatically. Sex is increasingly seen as an aspect of personal choice and conscience. This has led to a growing separation of sex from its procreative function (still a central tenet of Catholic teaching), a growing acceptance of sexual diversity, support for contraception and a generally more open attitude to sex.

The last four decades or so have also seen dramatic changes in behaviour, such as the increase in non-marital births and cohabitation. Irish research has plotted these trends against quickly changing attitudes. It has not, however, examined the relationship between attitudes and sexual practices and partnership patterns at an individual level. This is one of the central aims of the ISSHR project.

Social scientists tend to focus on the impact of changing attitudes on aggregate patterns in society. Policy practitioners tend to focus in particular on the relationship between behaviour, knowledge, attitudes and beliefs at the individual level, with a view to changing the behaviours themselves. This is usually where the behaviour impacts negatively on the individual and society at large. The chief aim of policy practitioners is to understand the determinants of behaviour so that policies can be developed to change it.

Research in social psychology since the 1930s has shown that the relationship between attitudes and behaviour is complex. As far back as the late 1960s, Wicker (1969)[2] showed that only a minority of attitude studies found a close relationship between verbally expressed attitudes and overt behaviour. Subsequent research has shown that some of this weak relationship is explained by the 'subjective norms'[3] of the person, or beliefs that an individual holds about what others will think of their behaviour. This means that, in attempting to explain behaviour, we need to understand not only the attitudes that the person holds and their beliefs and knowledge of the situation, but also the situational factors and context within which behaviour occurs.

King (1996)[4] has put forward a more complex model of behaviour which takes account of these situational factors, arguing that attitudes and intentions to act often conflict directly with other motivations to behaviour, such as high sexual arousal and alcohol intoxication. Thus, decisions to engage in unsafe practices may well occur with less–than–perfect rational deliberation. In the area of sexual health, the problem may also be exacerbated by a lack of preparedness on the part of the individual. Even where thought is given to protection, if a condom is not immediately available, the incentive to begin intercourse without protection may outweigh the risks of unsafe sex as perceived at that moment.[5]

In this chapter we examine the knowledge, attitudes and beliefs of the Irish population about sex and sexuality and how they vary across socio-demographic groups. In the next, **second section**, we examine levels of knowledge in the population, including knowledge of a woman's fertility, emergency contraception (EC), the sexually transmitted infection Chlamydia, and HIV/AIDS.

In the **third section**, we examine sexual attitudes, in particular attitudes toward pre-marital sex, casual sex, homosexual sex, abortion and EC. In the **fourth section**, we examine beliefs about contraception, specifically condoms, the contraceptive pill and EC (the 'morning-after pill'). In the final, **fifth section**, we summarise the results and extract some implications from them.

4.2 Sexual knowledge

SUMMARY

THIS section reports the results of the ISSHR survey questions on the level of knowledge of fertility, emergency contraception (EC), Chlamydia and HIV/AIDS.

Findings show that a majority of men and a substantial minority of women do not know when the most fertile period of a woman's cycle occurs. The level of incorrect knowledge increases across all age groups over time (shown by comparisons with previous surveys).

Levels of knowledge do not vary by age for men, but younger women are significantly less likely to have accurate knowledge about fertility.

Very high proportions of both men and women have incorrect knowledge of the time limit for the effective use of EC (the morning-after pill). Knowledge is worse among men and older individuals.

Higher proportions had correct knowledge of the STI Chlamydia and HIV/AIDS, but older individuals and men were less likely to have such knowledge.

Across all the areas of knowledge examined, those with lower levels of education were less likely to have accurate knowledge.

- Compared to women, men have significantly worse knowledge of when a woman is most fertile.

- Among women, 56% of under-25s cannot correctly identify a woman's most fertile period.

- Lower levels of education and being single or in a casual relationship are related to low levels of knowledge about fertility.

- 21% of men and 42% of women know the correct time limit for the use of EC.

- Younger and better-educated respondents are more likely to know the correct EC time limit.

- 54% of men and 73% of women have heard of Chlamydia.

- 37% of men and 60% of women have correct knowledge of Chlamydia.

- Higher levels of education among women and belonging to the professional social class among men are associated with higher levels of knowledge.

- 71% of men and 69% of women can correctly answer three questions about HIV/AIDS. Younger and better-educated respondents are more likely to give correct answers to all questions.

AN individual's level of specific knowledge about a subject is an important component in all models of human behaviour and decision-making. Knowledge is a particularly important determinant of an individual's ability to take informed protective action.[6] It is thus a focus of much of the research in health-promotion science. In many cases, increasing an individual's level of accurate knowledge forms the central aim of health-promotion interventions and is the prime indicator used in the evaluation of effectiveness.

In this section, we focus on the measures of sexual knowledge used in the ISSHR questionnaire. We then examine individual levels of knowledge associated with four important subject areas:

- fertility
- time limit for the effectiveness of the emergency contraceptive pill
- Chlamydia
- HIV and AIDS

The topics selected represent a balance and a choice: questions asked are intended to achieve a balance across a wide range of disparate themes. Thus, typically, instead of in-depth evaluations of a few topics, a few questions are asked about a wide range of topics. This choice provides more coverage but less depth. The consensus across the research team and the steering group was that this approach was necessary given the wide-ranging coverage of the survey, the limited national evidence on sexual health matters and the need to provide useful information to a diverse policy and service constituency.

Knowledge is difficult to assess in surveys. Questions evaluating knowledge may cause offence; participants may feel they are being 'tested' and consequently feel threatened. In parallel, it is difficult to ask many knowledge-type questions without prompting the answer. For example, several questions about Chlamydia signal the importance of this issue, which may not have been previously evident to the participant. The questions used in the ISSHR project were based on those used in previous research concerning key targets for health-promotion campaigns.

4.2.1   Knowledge of a woman's fertility

READY access to contraceptives means that knowledge of female fertility is not essential for effective contraceptive and protective practices. When contraception such as condoms or the contraceptive pill is not an option, as in Ireland before the change in legislation on contraception, knowledge of cycles of fertility provides the only contraception available. It is interesting, thus, to examine how levels of knowledge about a woman's fertility may have changed in Ireland since the greater availability of contraception.

Accurate knowledge of a woman's fertility cycle is also important in terms of achieving, as well as avoiding, pregnancy. Knowing the most fertile period in a woman's menstrual cycle can assist in both aspects of fertility management. However, it appears that levels of knowledge about female fertility in Ireland are poor. The Irish Family Planning Association (IFPA) reported that it "continues to see clients who lack an understanding of bodily functions and the risks posed by casual, unprotected sex".[7] Research findings have supported this anecdotal evidence. For example, Richardson (2000)[8] noted that young Irish mothers had a limited ability to link sexual activity with the risk of pregnancy.

The ISSHR study measured knowledge of a woman's fertility using a question (used in past surveys[9]) that asks: "At what time of the month do you think a woman is most likely to become pregnant?" The choice of answers available was: during her period; just before her period; just after her period; halfway between periods; anytime during the cycle; don't know. The correct answer is 'about half way between periods'.

Figure 4.1 shows the answers chosen by men and women to this question. A minority of men (31%) knew the most fertile period of a woman's cycle. The level of knowledge was higher among women, but 44% did not give the correct answer.

Figure 4.1: Answers to "when during the menstrual cycle is a woman most likely to conceive?": by gender

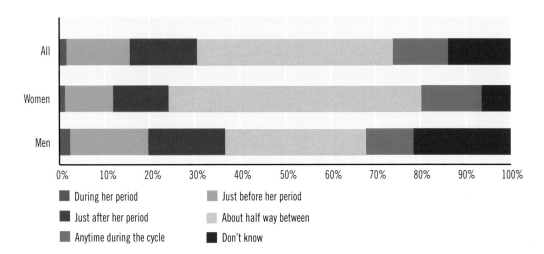

Three nationally representative studies to date, including the ISSHR study, have included questions on fertility knowledge. We can use their results to compare trends in knowledge on this issue. Of the two earlier studies:

- Wiley and Merriman (1996)[10] found in their 1993 study that between one-third and one-quarter of women across different age groups did not know that a woman is most likely to get pregnant in the middle of her menstrual cycle.
- The ICCP survey (2004)[9] found higher levels of inaccuracy: only 54% correctly identified the most fertile period in a woman's cycle. The Rundle *et al* study found that women were significantly more likely (65%) to report higher levels of knowledge than men (42%).

Figure 4.2 shows the proportion of women across three age groups who answered incorrectly the question on a woman's most fertile period, across the three surveys from 1996 to 2005. It shows an increase in the proportion with incorrect knowledge, although the large difference between the last two surveys, carried out less than a year apart, is difficult to explain. There is also a clear differential by age group across all three surveys in the level of incorrect knowledge.

Figure 4.2 shows a large difference in the level of incorrect knowledge across three age groups. *Figure 4.3*, using the results from the ISSHR survey, examines this in more detail, showing the level of incorrect knowledge by five age groups and by gender.

Figure 4.2: Proportion incorrectly identifying a woman's most fertile period

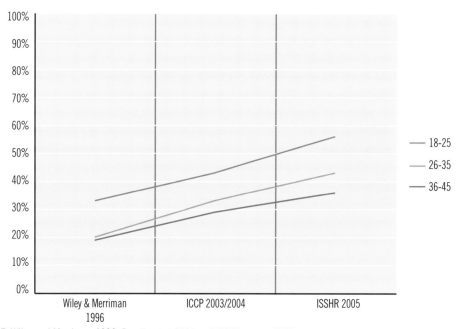

SOURCE: Wiley and Merriman 1996; Rundle et al 2004 and ISSHR survey 2005

Figure 4.3: Proportion with incorrect fertility knowledge: by gender and age group

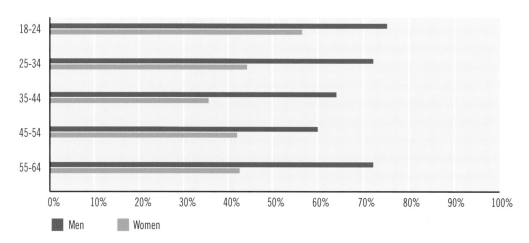

The figure shows higher levels of incorrect knowledge among men generally and a pattern of increasing incorrect knowledge among the three younger age groups (the younger the group, the more incorrect the knowledge). These results and those from previous surveys suggest that levels of fertility knowledge have been falling over time across all age groups, and that they are lowest among the youngest age groups.

Both Wiley and Merriman (1996)[10] and Rundle *et al* (2004)[9] found that women with higher educational attainment were more likely to correctly identify the most fertile period of a woman's cycle. This finding is replicated in the ISSHR study, as shown in *Figure 4.4*.

Figure 4.4: Proportion with incorrect fertility knowledge: by gender and highest education

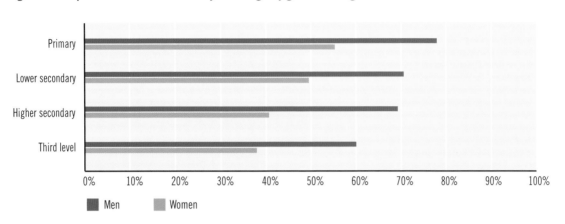

The figure shows a significantly higher level of fertility knowledge among both men and women with higher levels of education. Further analyses showed social-class differentials in levels of fertility knowledge also, but only among women. Women in manual social classes are more likely to have inaccurate knowledge than women in non-manual occupations. Further detail on the analyses in this section can be found in Appendix *Table 2.1*.

4.2.2 Knowledge of the emergency contraceptive pill

RESEARCH carried out in Ireland suggests that knowledge of emergency contraception (EC) is less than perfect among a large proportion of the population. For instance, the ICCP survey in 2004[9] found that almost all individuals surveyed had heard of the EC (morning-after) pill, but less than two-fifths could identify the correct period of 72 hours within which it could be used after intercourse. Almost half believed the limit to be substantially less than the true maximum limit. Inaccurate knowledge was most common among men (74%), but a substantial 49% of women also incorrectly identified the true time limit.

Contrary to its findings on fertility knowledge, the ICCP survey found that knowledge of EC is better among younger age groups. This knowledge seemed to be related to level of education.

The item used in the ISSHR survey to measure the individual's level of knowledge on the effective time limit of the EC pill was identical to that used in the ICCP report, thus allowing for comparisons across studies. Respondents were asked how long after sexual intercourse the morning-after pill can be effectively used. Five response options were suggested: up to 12 hours, up to 24 hours, up to 72 hours, up to five days or over five days. A 'don't know' option was also included.

The proportion of men and women who endorsed each of the various options is displayed in *Figure 4.5*. This shows results similar to those of the ICCP survey: more women (42%) than men (21%) could identify the correct time limit for taking EC.

Figure 4.5: Answers to "how long after intercourse is the emergency contraceptive pill effective?": by gender

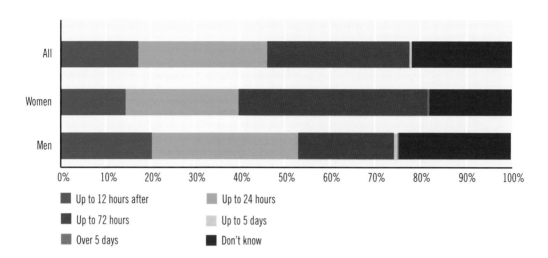

Interestingly, the respondents – and men in particular – were more likely to underestimate than overestimate the period in which EC can be taken effectively: 53% of men and 39% of women under-estimate this period. This may mean that EC is not used in some instances because individuals believe the window of opportunity has passed.

Results from the ICCP survey indicated that age is an important factor in relation to correct knowledge of emergency contraception. This is supported by the results in *Figure 4.6*. This shows a very pronounced age pattern: younger respondents are far more likely to know the correct time period of 72 hours. Women in the youngest age group are four times more likely to have correct knowledge of EC than women in the oldest age group. This difference by age among women may be partly explained by the fact that, since EC has been generally available only relatively recently in Ireland, and older women may not have any experience of it.

The results also show that the difference in levels of knowledge between men and women increases as age decreases: the differential between young men and young women is far larger than that between men and women in older age groups.

Figure 4.6: Proportion who correctly identified the 72-hour time limit for emergency contraception: by gender and age group

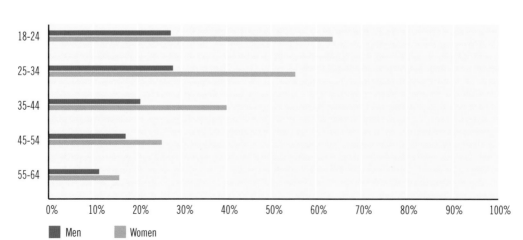

The ICCP survey found that educational attainment is an important factor in the level of knowledge of EC. This finding, too, is replicated in the ISSHR study, as shown in *Figure 4.7*. This indicates a pronounced gradient by highest educational qualification. Women with third-level qualifications are over twice as likely as those women with primary education alone to know the correct answer. These results partly reflect the fact that men and women with primary education alone are more likely to be older (and older people have worse knowledge of EC), but analyses show that, within age groups, those with lower levels of education are less likely to know the correct time limit.

Figure 4.7: Proportion who correctly identified the 72-hour time limit for emergency contraception: by gender and highest education

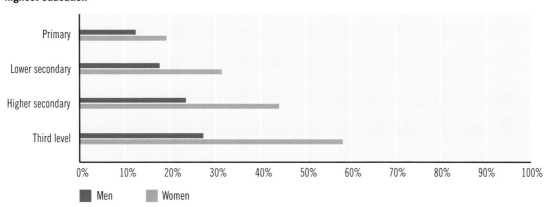

Lastly, analyses indicate that those in a steady relationship or who are cohabiting are most likely to have accurate knowledge. More details on the analyses in this section can be found in Appendix *Table 2.2*.

4.2.3   Knowledge of Chlamydia

UNPROTECTED sex carries an increased risk of exposure to sexually transmitted infections. In this section we examine knowledge of Chlamydia, chosen partially because it is the most commonly diagnosed bacterial STI, but also because knowledge of Chlamydia is a useful marker for an individual's wider knowledge of STIs. Despite being the most commonly diagnosed STI, Chlamydia often goes undiagnosed as it is asymptomatic in about 70% of women and 50% of men. It can have serious long-term consequences, especially in women. It is a cause of pelvic inflammatory disease, ectopic pregnancy and infertility. In men, Chlamydia causes 30-50% of non-gonococcal urethritis, and can cause epididymitis, prostatitis and proctocolitis. Less common manifestations include a reactive arthritis.

Ireland has witnessed an increasing number of cases of Chlamydia each year since 1995 (see chapter one). In cases reported between 1995 and 2002, there was a 684% increase.

In keeping with international prevalence studies, young adults have the highest levels of Chlamydia infection. In Ireland, 84% of infections occur among under-30s. Women account for 53% of reported cases. These figures represent cases mainly reported by STI clinics. However, many cases are managed in other health-care facilities, such as GP practices and family planning clinics, and may not be reported to infection-monitoring groups. Although the increasing figures may be partly explained by improved diagnostic tests and higher levels of testing in recent years, they are likely to reflect a real increase in overall incidence of Chlamydia. These figures almost certainly underestimate the levels of Chlamydia infection, as a significant proportion of asymptomatic infection in men and women will not have been diagnosed.

Given the rising levels of Chlamydia in Ireland and the serious consequences of an untreated case, it is important to measure the level of knowledge of this subject in the population. In relation to awareness, research has found that Chlamydia is one of the least well-known STIs.[11][12][13] However, Dawe & Rainford found in their national study in the UK (2003)[11] that the proportion of men and women who recognised Chlamydia as an STI had increased significantly. Among men, the level of recognition almost doubled: 35% recognised it in 2000/01, and 67% in 2003/04. Among women the proportion rose from 65% to 87% during the same period.

Women continue to be more likely than men to know that Chlamydia is an STI.[11][12][13] The likelihood of knowing this appears to be lower with increasing age. [11] Men under 30 were more likely than those aged 40 and over to recognise Chlamydia as an STI. This awareness continued to decrease with age after 40: 71% of men aged 40-44, dropping to 60% among those aged 45-49, and to 52% among men aged 50-69. Similar trends were observed among women.

Figure 4.8: Proportion who have heard of Chlamydia: by gender

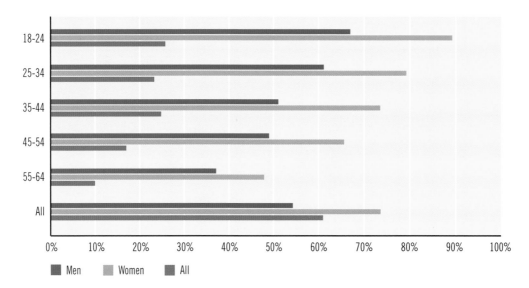

The ISSHR survey used two questions to examine knowledge of Chlamydia. Respondents were asked first whether they had ever heard of Chlamydia. *Figure 4.8* shows that just over half of men (54%) had heard of Chlamydia, compared to 73% of women. Analyses also show that knowledge of Chlamydia is related to level of education and social class: those with higher levels of education were significantly more likely to have heard of it, as were those in higher social-class positions. Having received education on sex and sexually transmitted infections also seemed to contribute to higher levels of recognition. Analyses on this issue can be found in ISSHR Sub-Report 3: 'Contemporary Sexual Knowledge, Attitudes and Behaviours in Ireland'.

Having heard of an STI does not guarantee specific knowledge of its symptoms or treatment. The ISSHR survey thus also gave respondents five statements about Chlamydia and asked them to state whether they were true or false:

- "Chlamydia only affects men" [FALSE]
- "Chlamydia can cause infertility if untreated" [TRUE]
- "Chlamydia has no serious side-effects" [FALSE]
- "Chlamydia is easily treated with antibiotics" [TRUE]
- "Chlamydia does not always cause symptoms" [TRUE]

Figure 4.9 gives the proportion of those respondents who had heard of Chlamydia and correctly answered each of these five questions.

Figure 4.9: Proportion who had heard of Chlamydia and correctly answered specific questions on Chlamydia: by gender

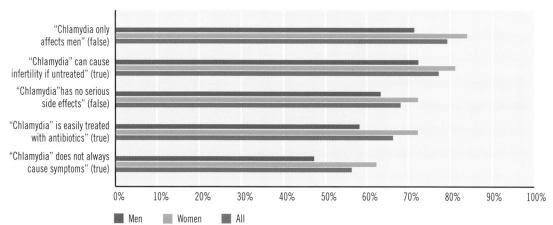

The figure shows that, among those who had heard of Chlamydia, substantial proportions answered the questions incorrectly. These proportions vary across questions. Whereas 21% incorrectly believed that Chlamydia only affects men, 44% believed that Chlamydia always has symptoms. To all questions, women are significantly more likely than men to know the correct answer. It appears that women are more likely to have higher levels of knowledge of STIs such as Chlamydia, just as they had more knowledge of issues around fertility and contraception.

To aid the analysis of how levels of knowledge of Chlamydia vary across population groups, individuals were given a score of one for each correct answer and divided between those with 'correct' knowledge who scored three or more and those without correct knowledge who scored one or two. The proportions scoring three plus are shown in *Figure 4.11*. Those who had not heard of Chlamydia were taken to have 'incorrect knowledge' and are thus included in the analyses.

Figure 4.10 confirms the finding that women are more likely than men to have 'correct' knowledge of Chlamydia (score of 3+). The graph also shows that age is an important factor: younger age groups are more likely to have correct knowledge. For example, 49% of men and 76% of women aged 18 to 24 have correct knowledge of Chlamydia, compared to 26% of men and 34% of women aged 55 to 64.

Figure 4.10: Proportion with 'correct knowledge' (score 3+) of Chlamydia: by gender and age group

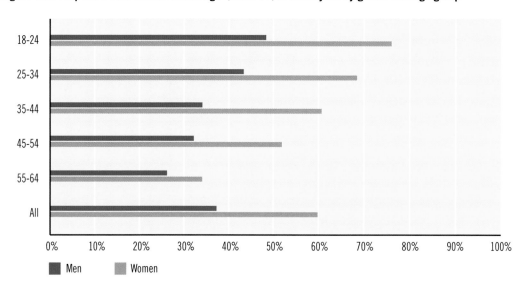

Highest level of education was an important predictor among both men and women of level of knowledge around fertility issues. This pattern is repeated again here. *Figure 4.11* shows a pronounced gradient across education groups: those with higher levels of education are more likely to have 'correct knowledge' of Chlamydia. Correct knowledge was also more likely among those in the professional and managerial social class, and less likely among those in the manual-class groups (analyses not shown here).

Figure 4.11: Proportion with 'correct knowledge' (score 3+) of Chlamydia: by gender and highest education

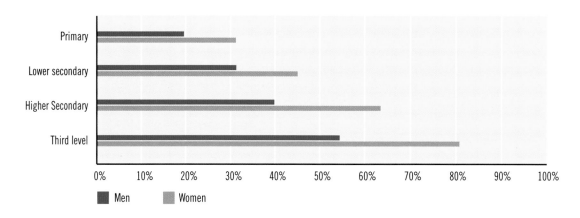

For further details on the analyses in this section, see Appendix *Table 2.3*.

4.2.4   Knowledge of HIV/AIDS

THE discovery of HIV in the early 1980s has had immense ramifications for investment and practice in sexual health promotion. It was largely due to the advent of HIV that KAB surveys were undertaken in Western countries after 1985. Since then, knowledge of HIV and the behaviours that lead to its spread have increased dramatically.

Research since the mid-1990s has generally found high levels of knowledge regarding HIV transmission routes and prevention.[5][14][15][16] This is largely due to the widespread public-education campaigns that were run in many countries after the facts about HIV transmission were established. However, certain misconceptions persist, including the idea that withdrawal of the penis before ejaculation (coitus interruptus) is an effective means of protecting against HIV. Developments in drug therapies to delay the onset of AIDS may also have led to the misconception that there is a vaccine for HIV or a cure for AIDS.[17]

National studies, conducted in France in 1992 and Belgium in 1993, examined perceptions of the effectiveness of withdrawal as a means of preventing the transmission of HIV. Over 30% of Belgian and 39% of French respondents believed that withdrawal was effective in preventing HIV. Although most respondents in both countries were aware of the ineffectiveness of withdrawal, a significant minority held the misconception of it being effective.[17][i]

In relation to age, studies[17] have found that the proportion of respondents thinking that withdrawal is totally ineffective against HIV is significantly smaller among those aged 18-19 than among those aged 20-24 and all the other age groups combined. The most highly educated respondents are also less likely to consider withdrawal as an effective protection method.

In relation to AIDS, early studies conducted in the Netherlands and Portugal found that 88% and 75% of respondents respectively rejected the statement that there is a cure for AIDS. No gender differences were found in either study, but those with higher levels of education were more likely to report, in both studies, that there is no cure for AIDS.[17]

Studies conducted in France and Belgium (1993) investigated a similar misconception regarding the existence of a vaccine for HIV. Although a vaccine against HIV is distinct from a cure for AIDS, both imply the role of medicine as a partial solution for HIV and AIDS. Higher proportions of respondents rejected the idea of a vaccine: 96% of Belgian and 91% of French respondents said there was no effective vaccine against HIV. Both studies found that the highly educated were most likely to believe that there is no vaccine for HIV.[17]

Holding the belief that withdrawal is an effective means of preventing HIV and that there is a cure for HIV may result in unsafe sexual practices due to a false sense of security. Therefore, it is important to identify if respondents in an Irish context hold these beliefs. It is accepted that improved knowledge does not automatically lead to the adoption of risk-reduction behaviour. However, safe-sex practices are highly improbable in the presence of ignorance or misconceptions.

Levels of knowledge about the transmission and consequence of HIV may also influence a person's view regarding their susceptibility to infection. Perceived susceptibility refers to the extent to which one feels personally at risk of infection.[5] Brien *et al* (1994)[20] argue that people may be aware of the transmission routes and consequences of HIV but do not feel personally at risk as many do not personalise the risk of HIV and perceive themselves to be invulnerable.[21] It is unclear whether such judgements are based on realistic appraisals of relevant past behaviour or optimistic bias. Again it is important to identify those respondents who do not consider themselves at risk of infection.

Knowledge of HIV was examined by asking participants to indicate the veracity of three statements:

- "There is a cure for AIDS" [FALSE]
- "A person can be infected with HIV for years without getting AIDS" [TRUE]
- "Withdrawing the penis before a man climaxes or ejaculates prevents his partner from getting HIV during sex" [FALSE]

---

[i] Although withdrawal prior to ejaculation reduces the potential viral dose of HIV transmission, withdrawal cannot be considered an effective means of protection, as pre-ejaculatory fluid may be a vector for the transmission of HIV.[18][19]

Figure 4.12: Proportion correctly answering each of three questions about HIV/AIDS: by gender

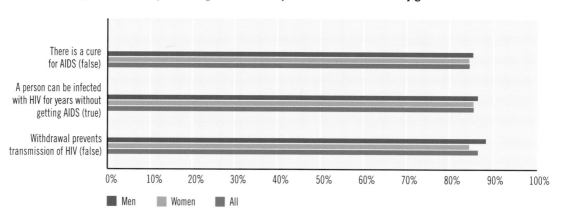

Men ■   Women ■   All ■

Figure 4.12 shows high levels of knowledge across all three questions: over 85% of respondents answered each correctly. The proportion with incorrect knowledge about the efficacy of withdrawal in preventing infection is less than half the rates found in France and Belgium in the early 1990s (we do not have more recent data to compare with). Although men appear from *Figure 4.12* to be more likely to give a correct answer, analyses show that the difference between genders is significant for only the final question on the efficacy of withdrawal in preventing infection. Here women were significantly less likely than men to give the correct answer.

Figure 4.13 shows variations in knowledge of HIV by age group. Having correct answers to all three questions is measured as correct knowledge.

Figure 4.13: Proportion with correct knowledge (score = 3) of HIV/AIDS: by gender and age group

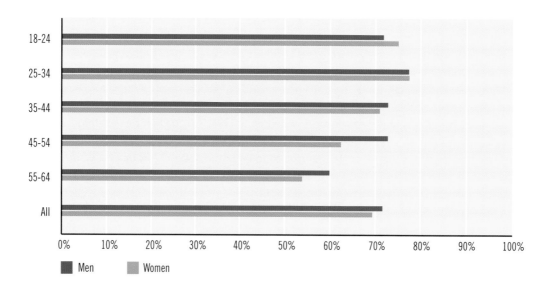

Men ■   Women ■

Figure 4.13 shows that although over 85% of respondents answered correctly each of the questions *individually*, the proportion answering all correctly is lower, at 71% of men and 69% of women. This means that, on basic questions concerning HIV and AIDS, around 30% of Irish men and women get at least one answer incorrect. The table shows that younger respondents are more likely to have correct knowledge about the subject. The main difference is that between men aged 55-64 and the other groups.

Figure 4.14: Proportion with correct knowledge (score = 3) of HIV/AIDS: by gender and highest education

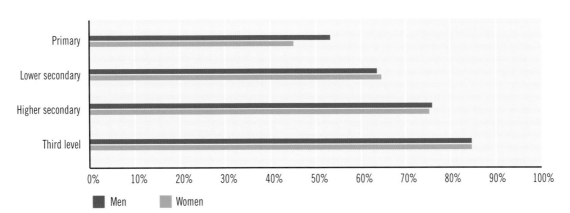

Figure 4.14 shows that individuals with higher levels of education are more likely to have correct knowledge of HIV/AIDS. It is worrying that over two-fifths of men and around half of women with primary education alone do not have accurate knowledge about the risks of HIV.

If analyses are confined to under-35s, the level of incorrect knowledge actually increases among those with low educational attainment.

Among under-35s, just 53% of men and 45% of women with primary education alone correctly answered all three questions. Analyses by relationship status (see Appendix *Table 2.4*) show that men in casual relationships and women who are not in a relationship are less likely to have correct knowledge. This, too, is a worrying pattern as these groups are more likely to have a higher number of partners over any recent period.

Both men and women in non-manual classes are more likely to have correct knowledge compared to those in unskilled manual classes. Higher professional classes have the highest level of correct knowledge among men and lower professionals the highest level among women.

4.3 Sexual attitudes

SUMMARY

THIS section examines the patterning of attitudes in the population towards:

- sex before marriage
- casual sex in the form of 'one-night stands'
- homosexual sex
- abortion
- use of the emergency contraceptive pill (EC)

Irish sexual attitudes have changed substantially over the last three decades. People are now more accepting of behaviours previously seen as wrong.

The rate of change has been fastest among younger age groups. There is an increasing gap between the attitudes of younger and older individuals. Young people now tend to see sex as a matter of individual conscience, or even as a lifestyle choice, whereas older respondents still tend to view sex within a more traditional moral framework.

■ Between 1973 and 2005, the proportion of Irish people agreeing that sex before marriage is 'always wrong' fell from 71% to 6%.

■ Attitudes among younger Irish people have become more liberal at a faster pace than those of older Irish people.

■ People with higher levels of education and in higher social classes are more likely to report more liberal attitudes.

■ People with lower levels of education are more likely to see homosexual sex, casual sex and abortion as 'wrong'.

■ 31% of men and 50% of women see casual sex as 'always wrong'. Among under-25s these proportions fall to 15% and 29%.

■ 47% of men and 59% of women believe that homosexual sex is 'never wrong'. These proportions increase to 57% and 77% among under-25s.

■ 35% of men and 37% of women see abortion as 'always wrong'.

■ 53% of men and 48% of women agree that using emergency contraception is 'never wrong'.

THE introduction to this report argued that the current pattern of sexual attitudes in Ireland can only be understood in the context of Irish history and economic and social development over the last forty years. Most Irish adults would have learnt about and experienced sex and sexual relations in a society still deeply influenced by a Catholic moral framework, but this influence has weakened considerably over the last three decades. There is a great deal of evidence from research that sexual culture in Ireland is undergoing immense change and moving closer to that of the UK and continental Europe.[22][23][24][25][26]

Sexual attitudes are still more conservative in Ireland (both north and south of the Border) than in other Western European states, but research shows substantial change in attitudes around sex and the family in recent decades. Recent change has seen the rise of a more secular attitude toward sexual behaviours, based on individual choice and personal conscience.[27] Part of this trend, as Inglis (1998)[28] has argued, is the absorption of sexual culture into the wider consumer culture based on lifestyle choice. The speed of this change has led to a widening gap between Irish people of different generations.

In this section, we examine answers to five questions from the ISSHR survey that encapsulate this change in attitudes. The **first question** elicited respondents' attitudes on sex before marriage. This issue is a key indicator of the change in sexual attitudes, from being influenced by Catholic teaching toward an ethos of individual choice and conscience. The dealignment of sex and marriage has been reflected in increasing rates of cohabitation in Ireland,[29] which changed from being a hidden form of partnership practised by a minority of younger people to an almost completely accepted practice by the late 1990s.

The **second question** examines attitudes toward the separation of sex from the context of an on-going relationship; it asks about the acceptability of casual sex in the form of 'one-night stands'. If sex is increasingly seen as part of an individual's 'lifestyle' choices, this may be reflected in the decoupling of sex from stable relationships.

The **third question** examines the issue of sex between two people of the same gender. Homosexual acts were decriminalised in the Republic of Ireland in 1993. This late development indicates the strength of conservative thinking on same-sex relationships up until recent decades.

The **fourth question** concerns the still highly contentious issue of abortion. The current legal position is that constitutionally, termination of pregnancy is not legal in this country unless it meets the conditions laid down by the Supreme Court in the X Case. The Supreme Court decided in this case that abortion is permissible in Ireland under the Constitution if it is established as a matter of probability that there is a real and substantial risk to the life, as distinct from the health, of the mother, which can only be avoided by the termination of her pregnancy. The Court accepted that the threat of suicide constituted a real and substantial risk to the life of the mother. Evidence of an increasing acceptance of abortion in at least some circumstances has emerged in social surveys of attitudes. We will examine this evidence in the next chapter.

The final, **fifth question** asks respondents for their attitudes toward emergency contraception (the morning-after pill). The introduction of the Progestin-only pill has led a large number of countries to make EC available over the counter in pharmacies. This trend has been resisted in Ireland where attitudes toward contraception, and particularly EC, are complex.

4.3.1   Attitudes to sex before marriage

IN the ISSHR survey, individuals were asked to indicate whether they believed that 'a man and a woman having sex before marriage' is always, mostly, sometimes or never wrong.

Figure 4.15: Attitudes to sex before marriage: by gender

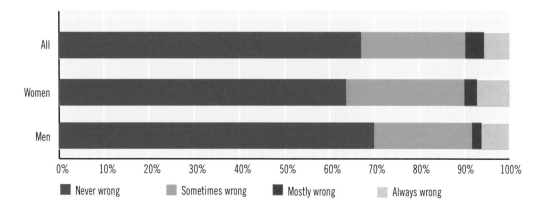

Figure 4.15 shows that most participants (67%) considered premarital sex to be 'never wrong', 24% 'sometimes wrong', 3% 'mostly wrong' and 6% 'always wrong'.

Figure 4.16 compares this overall finding to those in previous surveys in 1975 and 1994. It gives the proportions endorsing the view that sex before marriage is always wrong.

Figure 4.16: Proportion endorsing the belief that 'sex before marriage is always wrong' – social attitude surveys 1975 to 2006

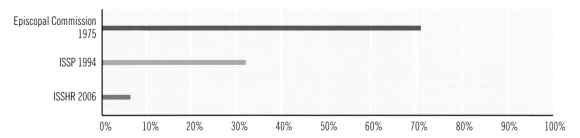

Sources: Fahey 1999:62 and ISSHR 2006

The figure shows a substantial liberalisation in Irish attitudes toward pre-marital sex in the last three decades:

- In the Episcopal Commission Survey in 1973/4, 71% of Catholic respondents (and thus the majority of Irish people) thought sex before marriage was always wrong.[j]
- In the ISSP survey of 1994, the total fell to 32%.
- In the ISSHR survey of 2004/5, the total dropped to just 6.4%.

Research has shown that attitudes toward premarital sex vary considerably across the population, particularly between age groups. *Figure 4.17* gives by age group the proportion of men and women agreeing that premarital sex is never wrong.

Figure 4.17: Attitudes to sex before marriage: by gender and age group

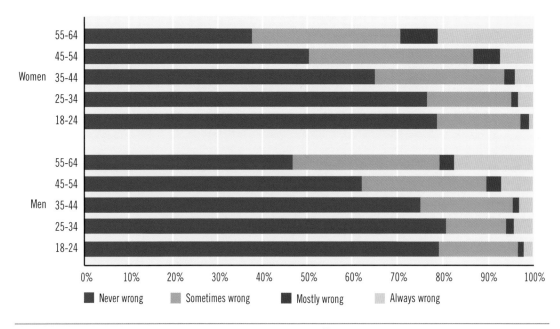

---

j   Episcopal Commission for Research (1975), reported in Inglis (1998).[28]

The figure shows that men are more accepting of sex before marriage than women – a finding replicated in a number of countries[30][31] – and that there are significant differences by age group. Interestingly, the difference between men and women falls with each successive age group.

Further analyses showed distinct differences in attitudes between those who are married and those who are cohabiting, in steady relationships or in casual relationships, even within age groups. For example, 63% of married men and 55% of married women agree that sex before marriage is never wrong, but the figure rises to 86% of men and 78% of women who are cohabiting. Analyses also showed that more religious individuals are less likely to see sex before marriage as acceptable. For more detail on the analyses in this section, see Appendix *Table 2.5*.

4.3.2   Attitudes to 'one-night stands'

ATTTUDES to casual sex were measured by asking participants to indicate whether they believed 'a person having one-night stands' is always, mostly, sometimes or never wrong. *Figure 4.18* shows that 40% considered one-night stands to be always wrong, 14% 'mostly wrong', 30% 'sometimes wrong' and 16% 'never wrong'. Women over 60 are more likely to indicate that one-night stands are 'always wrong': 50% of women endorse this view compared to 31% of men.

Figure 4.18: Attitudes to 'one-night stands': by gender

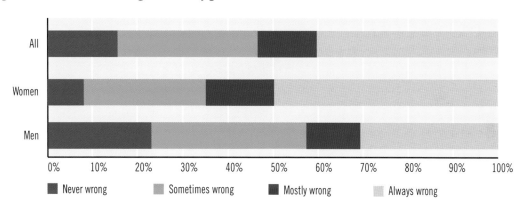

Figure 4.19 shows that, among both men and women, older age is associated with a less accepting stance on this issue. As we move from the youngest age group to the oldest, increasing proportions report that one-night stands are 'always wrong'. For example, 15% of men under 25 endorsed this view, compared to 56% of men aged 55-64, a four-fold increase. Similarly, 29% of women under 25 agreed, compared to 84% of women aged 55-64.

Figure 4.19: Attitudes to 'one-night stands': by gender and age group

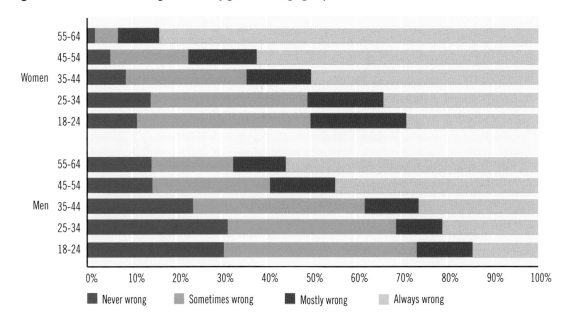

Figure 4.20 shows that those with higher levels of education are also less likely to see 'one-night stands' as 'always wrong' and more likely to see it as 'never', or only 'sometimes wrong'. This relationship holds for women even within age groups. Among men, analysis showed that the differences across education groups reflect the higher proportion of young people among those with higher levels of education (young people are more likely to be liberal on this issue).

Figure 4.20: Attitudes to 'one-night stands': by gender and highest education

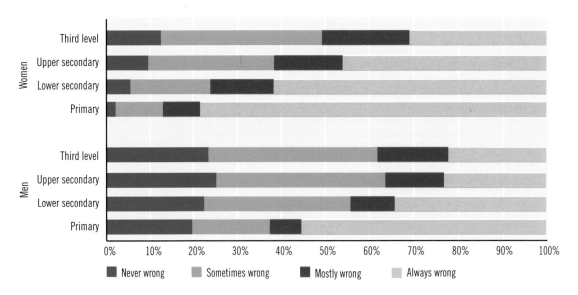

The proportion agreeing that 'one-night stands' are 'always wrong' is highest among those who are married, and lowest among those who are currently single, in casual relationships or cohabiting. Men and women who reported higher levels of religiosity were also more likely to see 'one-night stands' as acceptable.

For further detail on the analyses in this section, see Appendix *Table 2.6*.

4.3.3   Attitudes to homosexual sex

ATTITUDES toward homosexuality in Ireland have significantly softened in recent decades. Homosexuality has been increasingly accepted as a legitimate expression of human sexuality. A similar softening of attitudes has been found in a number of countries in recent decades, including by studies conducted in Australia, Britain and America.

Kelley (2001)[32] compared Australian attitudes measured in 1984 to those from 1999/2000. Most of the population (64%) held that homosexuality is 'always wrong' in 1984. In 2000, fewer people (48%) agreed that homosexuality is 'always wrong'. The percentage of respondents reporting that homosexuality is 'not wrong at all' almost doubled, from 16% in 1984 to 28% in 2000. Findings from ASHR further supported a decline in negative attitudes towards homosexuality; only about one-quarter of respondents agreed that male or female homosexual activity is 'always wrong'.[33]

The first of these Australian studies was held in 1984. The emergence of the AIDS epidemic in the 1980s may have affected attitudes, leading to an increase in anti-gay sentiments as homosexual activity was initially identified as the primary mode of transmission of HIV.[30]

The UK NATSAL studies in 1990 and 2000 also demonstrated a substantial increase in public tolerance of male homosexuality (Copas *et al* 2002).

Research has consistently shown gender differences in attitudes towards homosexuality. A meta-analysis of 112 studies suggested that women hold more positive attitudes toward homosexuality than men.[34] Furthermore, heterosexual individuals tend to express more negative attitudes towards homosexual activity among members of their gender. Again, this negativity is more pronounced among men.[35][36]

Attitudes towards homosexuality appear to be less tolerant in older age groups.[32] Results from the ASHR survey in Australia showed that attitudes to homosexuality were strongly related to age, but the relationship was u-shaped: men over 50 and under 19 were most likely to report conservative attitudes. Similarly, older women reported less acceptance of both male and female homosexual activity.[31]

Figure 4.21: Attitudes to homosexual sex: by gender

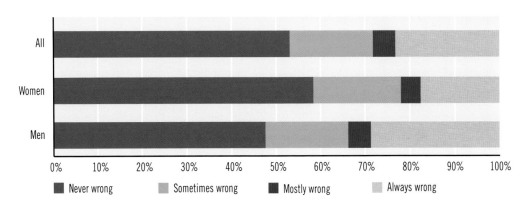

Other factors found to influence attitudes to homosexuality include education and religious beliefs. People with higher education are more likely to accept homosexuality[32] whereas those with stronger religious beliefs are less tolerant.[32][36]

ISSHR respondents were asked:

• "Could you tell me whether you believe that sex between two people of the same sex is always, mostly, sometimes or never wrong?"

Figure 4.21 displays the attitudes of the Irish population aged 18 to 64 on sex between two men or two women. Most (53%) see this as 'never wrong', 19% as 'sometimes wrong', 5% as 'mostly wrong' and less than a quarter (23%) as 'always wrong'.

The figure also shows, as is found across a number of countries, that women are far more likely than men to have more liberal attitudes to homosexuality: 47% of men see sex between two people of the same gender as 'never wrong' compared to 59% of women, a very significant difference.

Figure 4.22: Proportion reporting that homosexuality is 'always wrong'/'never justified' – surveys 1981 to 2006: by age group

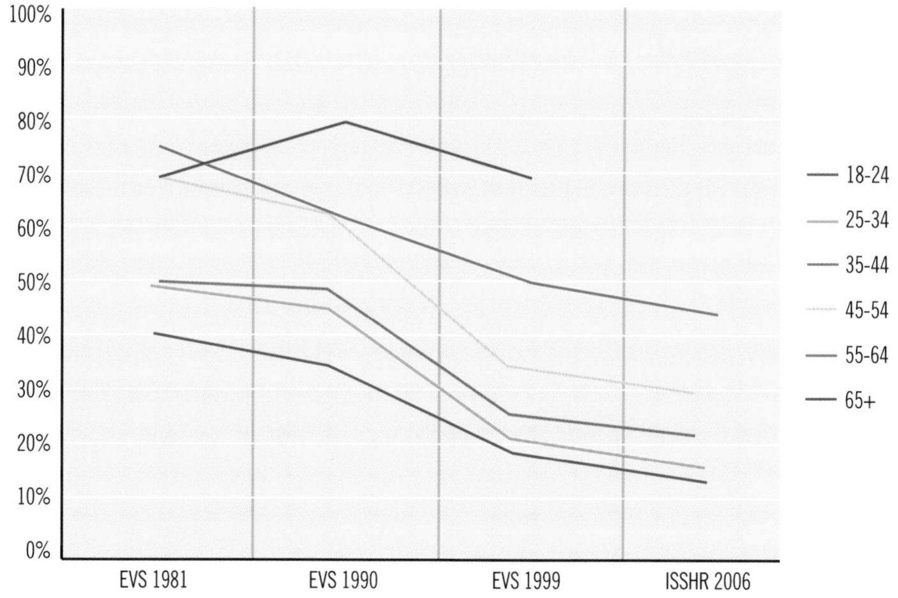

Source: Fahey et al 2005[26] & ISSHR survey 2006

It is useful to see how Irish attitudes to homosexuality have changed. *Figure 4.22* shows attitudes to homosexuality, from successive European Values Surveys (EVS) between 1981 and 1999, together with results from ISSHR 2005. The question used in the ISSHR survey was slightly different from that used in the EVS; it asked respondents whether homosexuality was 'never', 'sometimes', 'mostly' or 'always' wrong' rather than whether it was 'justified' (on a 10-point scale). Here we compare the proportion stating that homosexuality is 'always wrong' in ISSHR to the proportion choosing the first two points on the EVS scale.

Figure 4.22 shows dramatic falls in the proportion of the Irish population who see homosexual relationships as 'never justified'/'always wrong' between the early 1980s and 2005. The fall in the 1990s is particularly steep. Although attitudes have become more liberal across all age groups, with the exception of those over 65, the fall is greatest for younger age groups. For example:

- The proportion of under-25s who hold that same-sex relationships are 'never justified' decreased by 66% between 1981 and 2005.

- The proportion of those aged 55 to 64 with the same attitudes has decreased by just 40% over the same period.

This suggests that liberalisation has been most pronounced among younger Irish people.

Figure 4.23: Attitudes to homosexual sex: by gender and age group

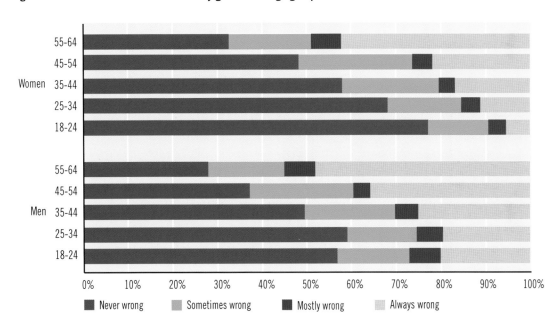

Figure 4.23 further disaggregates responses to this question by age group. It shows that, compared to older age groups, younger individuals among both men and women are more likely to see homosexual sex as 'never wrong'. For example:

- 57% of men and 77% of women aged 18 to 24 see homosexual relationships as 'never wrong'.
- 28% of men and 33% of women aged 55 to 64 see homosexual relationships as 'never wrong'.

Figure 4.24: Atttitudes to homosexual sex: by gender and highest education

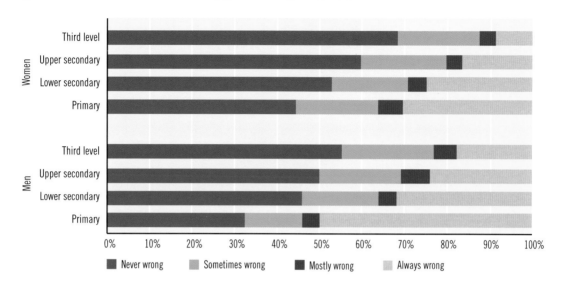

Analyses also showed significant differences in attitudes to homosexual sex across educational groups. *Figure 4.24* shows that 55% of men and 69% of women with third-level qualifications believe that homosexual sex is 'never wrong', but this figure falls to 33% of men and 45% of women with primary education alone.

Lastly, analyses (not shown) also show that level of religiosity is a very important predictor of attitudes: people with no or few religious beliefs are more likely to see homosexual sex as 'never wrong'.

For more detail on the analyses in this section, see Appendix *Table 2.7*.

4.3.4   Attitudes to abortion

ATTITUDES to abortion internationally have been studied in a number of KAB surveys. The ASHR survey in Australia found that fewer than one in five of Australians believed that abortion is 'always wrong', a similar proportion to that found in the NATSAL survey in Britain in 1990 (18%).[31][37] Research from both Australia and Britain indicate that there are only small differences in attitudes to abortion between men and women.

Evidence from Australia and Britain also suggests that attitudes to abortion are more conservative among younger people. The ASHR survey in Australia found that men and women aged between 16 and 19 were significantly more likely than older men and women to believe that abortion is 'always wrong' (Rissel *et al*, 2003).[31]

As regards religion, people who consider it important are more likely to oppose abortion.[36] Moreover, Wellings *et al* (1994)[37] found that British respondents whose religious affiliation was Roman Catholic were more likely to oppose abortion than those of another or of no affiliation.

Attitudes to abortion in the Irish population were measured in the ISSHR survey using the question: "Could you tell me whether you believe that abortion is always wrong, mostly wrong, sometimes wrong or never wrong?"

Figure 4.25: Attitudes to abortion: by gender

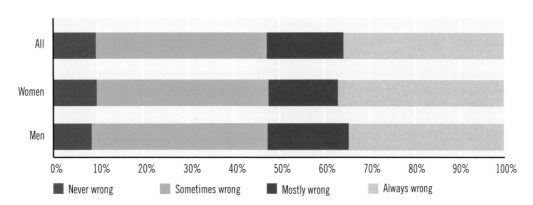

Figure 4.25 shows that, overall,

* 9% of individuals believe that abortion is 'never wrong'
* 38% that it is 'sometimes wrong'
* 17% that it is 'mostly wrong'
* 36% that it is 'always wrong'

These results indicate that a minority of individuals believe that abortion is wrong in all circumstances while 64% believe it is acceptable in at least some circumstances.

There are only small differences between the genders. These differences are not significant, except among those aged 35 to 44 and 55 to 64 where women are significantly more likely to see abortion as 'always wrong'. Fahey et al (2005)[26] have shown, using European Values Survey data from 1999, that attitudes in the Republic of Ireland to abortion are the most conservative in Western Europe after Northern Ireland and Malta.

Figure 4.26: Proportion reporting that abortion is 'always wrong'/'never justified' – surveys 1981 to 2006: by age group

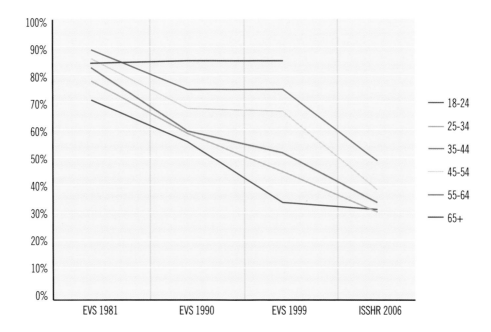

The contentiousness of abortion in the Irish context is, arguably, related to the level of change in Irish attitudes on this subject over the last three decades. The growth of attitudes more accepting of abortion has led to increased calls from groups resistant to change for increased safeguards against the introduction of abortion.

Figure 4.26 gives some measure of the extent of change. It shows attitudes to abortion among Irish people, divided by age group, from 1981 to the ISSHR survey 2006. It also draws on data from the European Values Survey (EVS).

Figure 4.27: Attitudes to abortion: by gender and age group

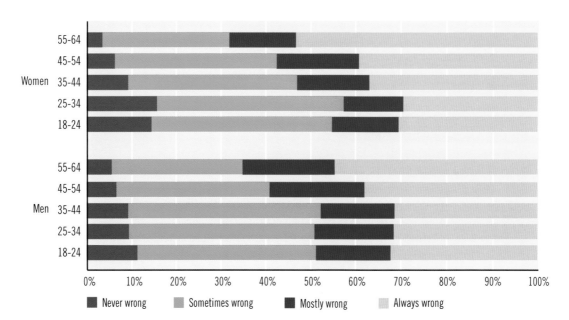

The questions used in the ISSHR survey and in the EVS are slightly different, but highly comparable if dichotomised so as to represent non-acceptance or complete acceptance.

Figure 4.26 shows that attitudes toward abortion have undergone immense change since the early 1980s. Proportions stating that abortion is 'always wrong'/'never justified' fell from between 70% and 90% in 1981 to between 30% and 50% in 2005. If we exclude those aged over 54 in 2005, the proportion runs between 30% and 39% (instead of 50%). The extent of change is greatest among younger cohorts, although between 1999 and 2005 there was a pronounced slow-down in the pace of change among those aged less than 25.

Figure 4.27 gives more detailed age-group breakdowns for the ISSHR survey. It shows that younger individuals are less likely to see abortion as 'always wrong' compared to older respondents. For example:

• 32% of men and 31% of women aged 18 to 24 see abortion as 'always wrong'
• 45% of men and 54% of women aged 55 to 64 see abortion as 'always wrong'

Figure 4.28 shows that education is a very important predictor of attitudes. More educated respondents are less likely to state that abortion is 'always wrong', even within age groups.

Figure 4.28: Attitudes to abortion: by gender and highest edcuation

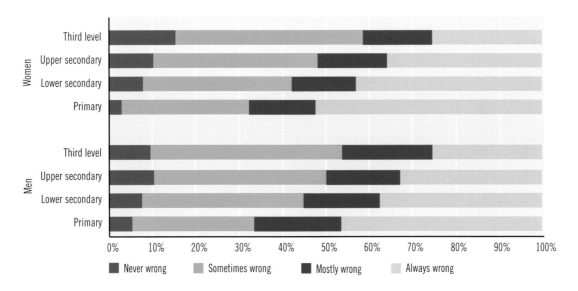

Lastly, as we would expect, level of religiosity is strongly related to attitudes to abortion. The more religious are far more likely to respond that abortion is always wrong.

For more details on the analyses in this section, see Appendix *Table 2.8.*

4.3.5   Attitudes to emergency contraception

THE ISSHR survey asked respondents whether the 'morning-after pill' (emergency contraception or EC) is 'always wrong', 'sometimes wrong', 'mostly wrong' or 'never wrong'.

Figure 4.29 shows that 50% responded that EC is 'never wrong', 33% that it is 'sometimes wrong', 7% that it is 'mostly wrong' and 9% that it is 'always wrong'. The differences between men and women are small, but there is a statistically significant difference in the proportion of women who respond that EC is 'never wrong'; women are less likely to do so than men.

Figure 4.29: Attitudes to emergency contraception: by gender

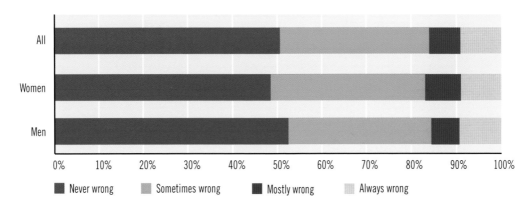

Figure 4.30 shows that younger individuals are more likely to report that use of EC is 'never wrong' and less likely to state that it is 'always wrong'. This difference is statistically significant only among women.

Figure 4.30: Attitudes to emergency contraception: by gender and age group

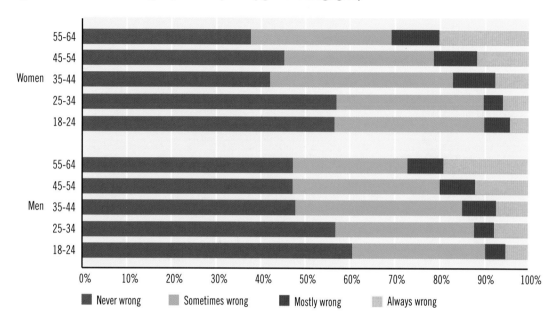

Unlike on other issues, analyses on the question of EC show no differences across educational groups. There are pronounced patterns across individuals with more or fewer religious beliefs. *Figure 4.31* shows that 4% of men and 3% of women who state that they are not religious at all report that EC is 'always wrong', compared to 23% of men and 21% of women who describe themselves as 'very much' religious.

For more detail on the analyses in this section, see Appendix *Table 2.9.*

Figure 4.31: Attitudes to emergency contraception: by gender and religiosity

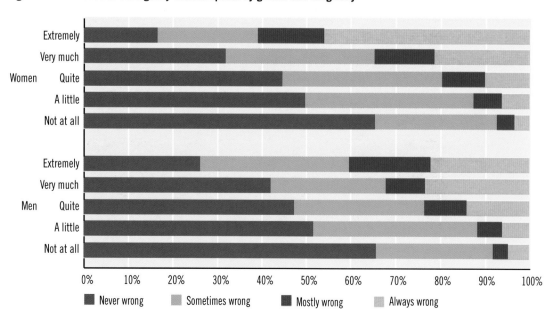

4.4 Beliefs about contraception

SUMMARY

THIS section examines the pattern of beliefs in Ireland concerning the contraceptive pill, condoms and emergency contraception (EC).

The cost of the contraceptive pill is not an issue for most women, but is for a substantial minority, particularly those with lower incomes as proxied by their educational level.

Concerns about the side-effects of the pill were more common among women, but concerns were highest among the two oldest age groups who are less likely to use the pill. However, over half of all women in the youngest age group and two-thirds of those aged 35 to 44 had concerns on this issue. This could have implications for the use of the pill.

Concerns about weight gain on the pill were less common, but women with lower levels of education tended to see this as a concern.

The cost of condoms was a concern for lower-income groups (as measured by age group and level of education).

Most men and women thought that EC should be available.

- 32% of women said the cost of the contraceptive pill would discourage them from using it.

- A significantly lower proportion of women with third-level qualifications felt that cost would discourage them using the pill.

- 63% of women said medical side-effects would discourage them from using the pill. The proportion was significantly lower among younger women.

- Only 12% of women said weight gain as a result of using the pill would discourage them from using it. This proportion was significantly higher among women with lower levels of education.

- 15% of all respondents said the cost of condoms would discourage their use. The proportion was significantly higher among younger respondents and those with lower levels of education.

- Over 90% of respondents felt that the emergency contraceptive pill should be available in Ireland; 52% of men and 42% of women thought it should be available 'over the counter'.

- People in a professional occupation and the unmarried were more likely to support over-the-counter sales of EC.

4.4.1 Beliefs about the contraceptive pill

STUDIES have shown that a significant proportion of women believe that the contraceptive pill is associated with a number of negative outcomes and that this has at least some, though often unspecified, impact on the take-up of the pill and risk of conception (in the absence of other means of contraception). Potential medical side-effects such as mood swings and weight gain have been shown to be important concerns among women.[38] [39] [40] [41] [42]

The ISSHR questionnaire asked respondents to indicate on a five-point scale from 'strongly agree' to 'strongly disagree' (via neither) whether they agreed or disagreed with the following statements:

- "The cost of the contraceptive pill would discourage you from taking it."
- "Possible medical side-effects of the contraceptive pill would discourage you from taking it."
- "Possible weight gain on the contraceptive pill would discourage you from taking it."

The aim of the questions is to get a measure of the overall disposition of women (only women were asked the questions) toward the acceptability of the contraceptive pill on three different counts.

The questions do not attempt to grasp the complex of choices and reasons that shape each woman's judgement about whether to use the pill or not. In this sense, these questions are more like attitude questions in that they attempt to elicit the woman's 'gut feeling' rather than ask her to justify her choice to use the pill or not, in present or past circumstances. This point is particularly important for women in the oldest age group, for many of whom the question of contraception is superfluous because of the menopause. Some women may answer the question in the context of their own life and circumstances. The proportion that choose the non-applicable option may increase in older age groups, but many others may answer the question as intended, as a hypothetical question about their stance on the issue, if they were to need contraception.

Figure 4.32 shows the proportions agreeing/disagreeing with the first of these statements: "The cost of the contraceptive pill would discourage you from taking it".

Figure 4.32: Degree to which the cost of the contraceptive pill would discourage use: for women

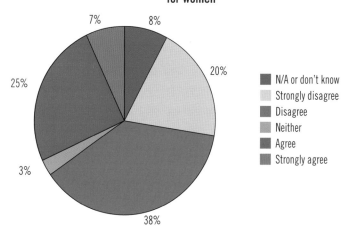

Most women, 58%, either disagree or strongly disagree; slightly less than a third, 32%, agree.

Although a clear majority of women disagree with the statement, concerns about the cost of the pill are higher for women living on lower incomes. The ISSHR survey could not include a measure of household income because of space constraints, but it is well established that highest educational qualification and income are strongly related. Thus education may be used as a proxy for economic situation.

Figure 4.33 gives answers to the question on cost across different levels of education. As level of education increases, the probability of the woman agreeing with the statement decreases while the proportion disagreeing increases. This indicates that affordability is an issue for many lower-income women in the case of the contraceptive pill. The issue of its cost is complicated by its free availability to women with a medical card. The medical card is available to people on low income; however, the income threshold has fallen in real terms in recent years, thus decreasing the proportion in receipt of a card.

Figure 4.33: Degree to which the cost of the contraceptive pill would discourage use: for women, by highest education

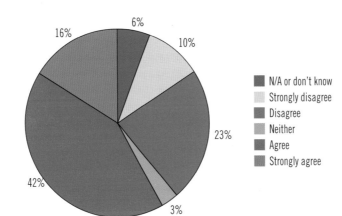

Legend: N/A or don't know | Strongly disagree | Disagree | Neither | Agree | Strongly agree

Figure 4.34 shows the results for the statement: "Possible medical side-effects of the contraceptive pill would discourage you from taking it".

Figure 4.34: Degree to which possible medical side-effects of the contraceptive pill would discourage use: for women

The figure shows that most women (58.1%) agree or strongly agree that possible side-effects would discourage them from using the contraceptive pill. This highlights a substantial level of concern about the health implications of taking the pill and that decisions about whether to use it may be influenced by this issue.

Figure 4.35: Degree to which possible medical side-effects of the contraceptive pill would discourage use: for women by age group

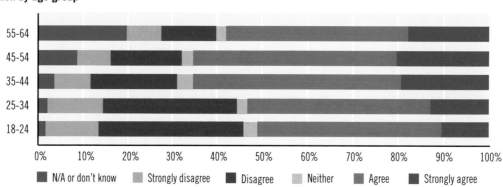

The ICCP survey[9] found that older women are more likely to agree with this statement. *Figure 4.35* shows that this pattern also emerges from the ISSHR data. For example, whereas 33% of women aged 18 to 24 disagree with the statement, the proportion is 20% among women aged 55 to 64. Rundle *et al* (2004)[9] suggested that the relationship may be due to the exposure of older women to the first generation of contraceptive pills where the risk of side-effects was higher. These women may also be aware of the objectively greater risk faced by older women who use the pill.

The final question asked female respondents to agree/disagree with the statement: "Possible weight gain on the contraceptive pill would discourage you from taking it".

Figure 4.36: Degree to which possible weight gain on the contraceptive pill would discourage use: for women

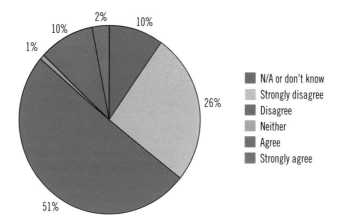

Figure 4.36 shows that the overwhelming majority of women (77%) disagree. Only 12% agree or strongly agree. Unlike with the previous statement, there are no differentials across age groups in the extent of agreement, but analyses show that women with lower levels of education are more likely to agree, as *Figure 4.37* shows.

Figure 4.37: Degree to which possible weight gain on the contraceptive pill would discourage use: for women by highest education

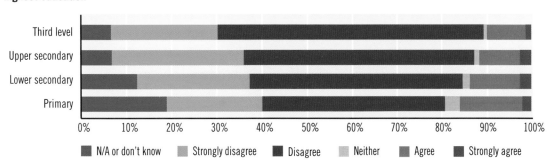

Whereas 83% of women with third-level education disagree or strongly disagree, the proportion is 61% among women with primary education only. Although this relative difference between groups is significant, most women with primary education alone disagree with the statement.

For more detail on the analyses in this section, see Appendix *Table 2.10.*

4.4.2   Beliefs about the cost of condoms

THE important role of barrier methods and the use of condoms in particular in protecting against sexually transmitted infections have prompted considerable research on the reasons for not using them. The perceived impact of condoms on sexual pleasure has often been identified as the primary reason why condoms are not used.[38][43][44] This was confirmed in the Irish context by Rundle *et al* (2004)[9] who found that 43% of men and 27% of women agreed that condoms reduce sexual pleasure.

Figure 4.38: Degree to which the cost of condoms would discourage use: by gender

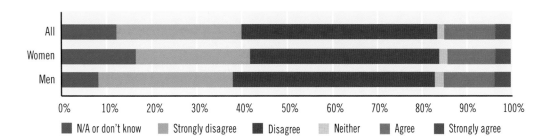

Some research has played down the role of costs in limiting use[46] but younger and poorer respondents may be more likely to find cost an issue.

Figure 4.38 gives the proportions of men and women agreeing or strongly agreeing that the cost of condoms would discourage their use, broken down by age group and sex.

It shows that, overall, 15% agreed that the cost of condoms would discourage their personal use. There was no significant difference between men and women (15% of men and 14% of women). However, as found earlier in relation to the contraceptive pill, groups with lower incomes and less resources may be more likely to agree with the statement.

Figure 4.39: Degree to which the cost of condoms would discourage use: by gender and age group

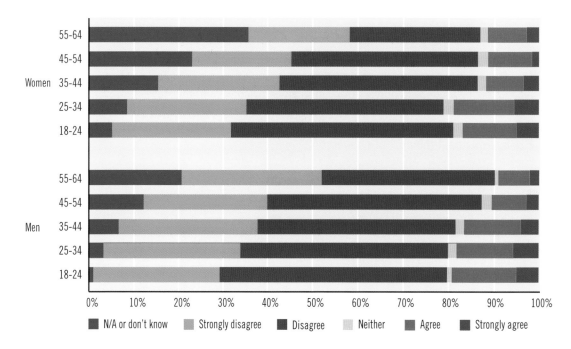

Younger individuals are both more likely to be out of the labour force and, if not, to be on a lower income. Thus they are more likely to have concerns about the cost of condoms. *Figure 4.39*, which disaggregates responses by age, confirms a relationship between agreement with the statement and being younger:

- 19% of men and 17% of women aged 18 to 24 agree with the statement
- 9% of men and 11% of women aged 55 to 64 agree

The overall proportion agreeing with the statement is low, even among younger individuals, but the latter tend more to see cost as in issue.

One complication is the increasing proportion among older age groups who reported that this issue did not apply to them or who responded 'don't know'. This might reflect the fact that older individuals are less likely to need contraception (particularly if they or their partner are post-menopausal), may be using another method, or are in less need of barrier protection because they are in a long-term monogamous relationship. However, if individuals who select N/A or 'don't know' are removed from the analysis, the proportion of those remaining who agree with the statement is larger among younger than among older respondents.

The promotion of condom use, particularly among younger people who are more likely to have new partners on a more frequent basis, is a serious issue in sexual health promotion. It is worrying that the cost of condoms may discourage their use.

As in the analysis of the cost of the contraceptive pill, it is possible to use education as a proxy for income level. *Figure 4.40* disaggregates answers on this issue by highest level of education.

Figure 4.40: Degree to which the cost of condoms would discourage use: by gender and highest education

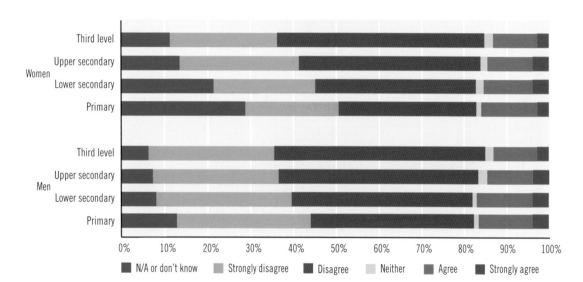

The figure shows that both men and women with higher levels of education are more likely to disagree with the statement that the cost of condoms would discourage their use. As before, the increase in the proportion selecting N/A is a problem, particularly among women, but as before it is clear that the rate of disagreement falls steeply as educational level falls.

For more details on the analyses in this section, see Appendix *Table 2.11*.

4.4.3 Beliefs about emergency contraception

THE development of the progestin-only emergency contraceptive pill (EC) in the 1990s led over 25 countries to allow this form of contraception to be made available 'over the counter'.[47] In Ireland, however, EC has remained a prescription-only medicine. There is little data on whether or not the population supports this stance.

Research shows that, in general, over-the-counter availability of EC leads to greater availability and use,[47] but there is concern that increasing the availability of EC can increase the level of sexual risk-taking, particularly among young women. It is argued that they would be more likely to use the pill instead of barrier methods and thus be at greater risk of STIs. This concern was addressed directly in research by Raine *et al* (2005).[48] They used a 'random control trial' format to assess the impact of (a) over-the-counter access in a pharmacy, without a prescription, (b) advance provision of EC and (c) usual care which required a visit to a clinic to obtain EC. They sampled 2,117 women aged 15 to 24.

The authors assessed the effects of increased access on repeated use of emergency contraceptive, pregnancy rates, acquisition of new STIs, contraception use and sexual behaviour. After six months, women in the advance access group were more likely than those in the clinic access group to report EC use more than once. However, of those in the advance access group, only 7% used it twice and 4% used it three or more times. Those in the pharmacy group were not more likely than women in the clinic access group to use it more than twice. Furthermore, easier access to EC did not compromise regular contraceptive use or lead to risky sexual behaviour. There were no differences by study group in frequency of unprotected sex. Those in the advance access were twice as likely to use EC as those in the clinic access group. However, there was no significant difference by study group in rates of pregnancy. Similarly, there were no differences across study groups in positive STI tests.

Figure 4.41: Beliefs about whether emergency contraception should be available in Ireland and how: by gender

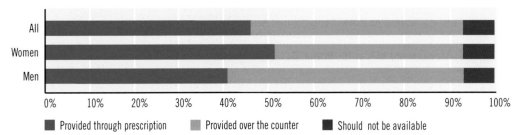

*Figure 4.*21 gives the proportions of men and women in the ISSHR survey supporting the availability of emergency contraception and the manner in which they think it should be available in Ireland. It shows that the overwhelming majority of men and women (93%) believe that EC should be available in Ireland. There is less agreement as to whether EC should be available over the counter or through a pharmacy. A slim majority of men (52%) believe that EC should be provided over the counter, compared to 42% of women.

Earlier analyses in this chapter have shown that younger people tend to be more liberal in their attitudes, particularly on the issue of EC. This suggests that young people would be more likely to favour over-the-counter availability.

Figure 4.42: Beliefs about whether emergency contraception should be available in Ireland and how: by gender and age group

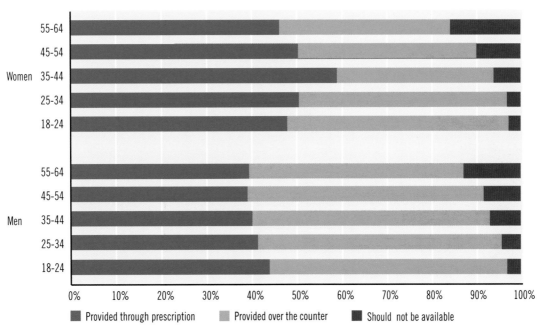

Figure 4.42 shows that young people are less likely than older individuals to state that EC should not be available in Ireland. However, patterns concerning over-the-counter availability are more complex and take different forms for men and women. Both young men and women are more likely to state that EC should be available over the counter. Tests show that the difference between age groups is not significant statistically.

Finally, there are very significant differences by level of religiosity: people with higher levels of religiosity are far less likely to advocate over-the-counter availability, as *Figure 4.43* shows.

Figure 4.43: Beliefs about whether emergency contraception should be available in Ireland and how: by gender and religiosity

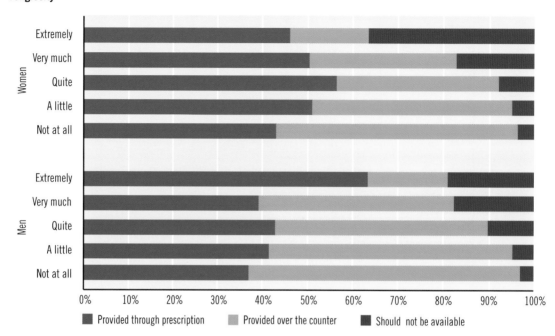

For more detail on the analyses in this section, see Appendix *Tables 2.12* and *2.13*.

4.5 Summary

THIS chapter has examined the pattern of sexual knowledge, attitudes and beliefs in the Irish population. The analyses of the level of sexual knowledge among respondents found both positive and negative patterns.

On the issue of a woman's most fertile period, analyses showed a trend among women across all age groups of weakening knowledge across time. This is a worrying trend. The group with the lowest level of accurate knowledge about a woman's fertility is young men and women: 75% of men and 56% of women aged 18 to 24 could not correctly name the most fertile part of a woman's cycle. This knowledge deficit also seems to be marked among those with lower educational attainment and/or of lower socio-economic position. It could have serious consequences in terms of the level of crisis pregnancy.

In other areas of knowledge, such as the time limit for using emergency contraception, and Chlamydia and HIV/AIDS, young people appeared to have higher levels of knowledge than older people. However, even among young people, 73% of men and 36% of women under 25 did not know the correct time limit for use of EC.

Knowledge of Chlamydia and HIV/AIDS was better, although those with lower levels of education and/or of poor socio-economic position showed a disturbingly high level of inaccurate knowledge about HIV/AIDS: just 53% of men and 45% of women under 35 with primary education alone correctly answered three basic questions about HIV/AIDS. This is a worrying development given the resources put into HIV awareness in Ireland (and the UK). The prominence of social class and educational differences in determining levels of knowledge also underlines the importance of socio-economic inequalities in shaping outcomes.

Chapters 10 and 11 examine the extent of use of contraception and condoms across the population and the distribution of adverse outcomes such as infection with STIs and the experience of crisis pregnancy. The findings from this chapter suggest that the motivation to use contraception and protection could be significantly lower for those of lower education/manual class because of their less accurate knowledge of fertility, contraception and STIs/HIV.

The reasons for this differential in knowledge are complex and unclear at present. As shown in the last chapter, higher levels of education and social class are associated with an increased likelihood of receiving sex education. However, analyses in ISSHR Sub-Report 3: 'Contemporary Sexual Knowledge, Attitudes and Behaviours in Ireland' show that levels of sexual health knowledge are not strongly related to having received formal sex education.

The above does not imply, however, that sex education has no value. Research has confirmed across a number of countries that sex education is crucial for increasing use of protection during sex and even for delaying sexual initiation. These results may indicate that the greater ability of those with higher levels of education to absorb sex-education messages is a more important predictor. That is, given the same level of sex education, those with more education generally will be more likely to absorb this information and put it into practice.[49] If so, this makes effective intervention more problematic. We return to the implications for policy in the final chapter of this report.

The analysis of attitudes toward sex before marriage showed a dramatic liberalisation of attitudes since the 1970s. Only a small minority now see pre-marital sex as 'always wrong'. The young, better educated and less religious tend to be least likely to say that pre-marital sex is wrong. The same strong pattern of attitudes repeats itself on the issue of casual sex or 'one-night stands': younger, better educated and less religious respondents have fewer reservations. This pattern is present across all of the attitude issues, including those on homosexuality and abortion. It indicates a division in world view between the generations in Ireland and considerable differences between those at different socio-economic levels.

Analysis of change in attitudes toward homosexuality and abortion showed that the division between age groups has grown substantially over the last two and a half decades. Attitudes among under-25s may, however, have reached a plateau, as only a small change occurred between 1999 and 2005.

Analysis of comparative data on sexual attitudes shows that the Irish population still holds comparatively conservative attitudes in a West European context. This is as true of young people as of older. The rate of change in attitudes suggests, though, that Irish attitudes are likely to converge with those in the UK in the medium term. This increase in Irish liberalism has been aided by the gradual decrease in the proportion of the population with manual jobs and the increase in that with higher education, both of which are associated with more liberal attitudes.

ISSHR Sub-Report 3: 'Contemporary Sexual Knowledge, Attitudes and Behaviours in Ireland' shows, however, that the relationship between sexual attitudes and behaviours is complex and that increasing liberalism does not directly translate into more risky behaviours or unsafe practices.

The final section of the chapter examined the pattern of sexual beliefs about the contraceptive pill, condoms and emergency contraception (EC). A total of 32% of women reported that the cost of the contraceptive pill would discourage their use of it. Cost is clearly likely to be more of an issue for low-income groups. Using level of education as a proxy for income, analysis showed that women with lower levels of education were more likely to see cost as an issue.

A far higher proportion of women, 59%, believe that the side-effects of the pill would discourage them from using it. As previous studies have indicated, this belief seems to be stronger among older women who perhaps remember the higher risks associated with the first generation of contraceptive pills or realise the higher risks faced by older women using the pill.

Around 12% of women believe that the weight gain associated with the contraceptive pill would discourage them from using it. This view was evenly distributed across age groups, but was significantly related to level of education. Women with lower levels of education were significantly more concerned about weight gain.

Cost was also perceived as an important issue in the use of condoms: 15% of respondents reported that cost would discourage them from using condoms. This proportion was higher among younger respondents and those from a lower socio-economic position. As with the cost of the contraceptive pill, this finding is worrying since it suggests that cost may be a substantial disincentive to use condoms to low-income groups such as the young and less educated.

A large majority of Irish people supported the availability of emergency contraception in Ireland; only 7% of men and women opposed this. Support was far more divided on whether EC should be available without prescription. A small majority of men advocated this option (52%), but only 42% of women.

4.6   Reference list

1   Russell B. *Marriage and Morals*. London: Allen and Unwin, 1929.

2   Wicker AW. 'Attitudes versus actions: the relationship of overt and behavioural responses to attitude objects'. *Journal of Social Issues* 1969; 25: 41-78.

3   Ajzen I, Fishbein M. *Understanding Attitudes and Predicting Social Behavior*. New Jersey: Prentice Hall, 1980.

4   King LA. 'Who is Regulating What and Why? Motivational Context of Self-Regulation'. *Psychological Inquiry* 1996; 7:57-60.

5   Sheeran P, Abraham CH, Orbell S. 'Psychosocial correlates of heterosexual condom use: a meta-analysis'. *Psychological Bulletin* 1999; 125(1):90-132.

6   Grulich AE, de Visser RO, Smith AMA, Rissel CE, Richters J. 'Sex in Australia: Sexually transmissable infection and blood-borne virus history in a representative sample of adults'. *Australian and New Zealand Journal of Public Health* 2003; 27(2):234-241.

7   IFPA. IFPA submission to the Crisis Pregnancy Agency. 2002.

8   Richardson V. *Young Mothers: A Study of Young Single Mothers in Two Communities*. Dublin: University College Dublin, 2000.

9   Rundle K, Leigh C, McGee H, Layte R. *Irish Contraception and Crisis Pregnancy (ICCP) Study. A Survey of the General Population*. Crisis Pregnancy Agency report no. 7, 2004.

10   Wiley M, Merriman B. *Women and Health Care in Ireland*. Dublin: Oak Tree Press, 1996.

11   Dawe F, Rainford L. *Contraception and sexual health 2003. A report on research using the ONS Omnibus Survey produced by the Office for National Statistics on behalf of the Department of Health, London*. London: Office for National Statistics, 2003.

12   Kellock DJ, Piercy H, Rosgstad KE. 'Knowledge of Chlamydia trachomatis infection in genitor-urinary medicine clinic attenders'. *Sex Transm Inf* 1999; 75(36):40.

13   Devonshire P, Hillman R, Capewell S, Clark BJ. 'Knowledge of Chlamydia trachomatis genital infection and its consequences in people attending a genitourinary medicine clinic. *Sex Transm Inf* 1999; 75(409):411.

14   De Visser RO, Smith AM. 'Characteristics of the Situation Are More Important Than Characteristics of the Individual'. *Psychology, Health and Medicine* 1999; 4:265-279.

15   Wulfert E, Wan CK. 'Condom Use: A Self-Efficacy Model'. *Health Psychology* 1993; 12:346-353.

16   Rosenthal D, Smith A, De Visser RO. 'Young people's condom use: an event-specific analysis'. *Venereology* 1997; 10(2):101-5.

17   Marquet A, Zantedeschi E, Huynen P. 'Knowledge of HIV/AIDS Modes of Transmission and Means of Protection in Different European Countries'. *Annali di igiene: medicina preventiva e di comunità* 1997; 9(4):265-274.

18   De Vincenzi I. 'A Longitudinal Study of Human Immunodeficiency Virus Transmission by Heterosexual Partners'. European Study Group on Heterosexual Transmission of HIV. *New England Journal of Medicine* 1994; 331(6):341-346.

19   Pudney J, Oneta M, Mayer K, Seage G. 'Pre-Ejaculatory Fluid as Potential Vector for Sexual Transmission of HIV-1'. *Lancet* 1992; 340(8833):1470-1471.

20   Brien TM, Thombs DL, Mahoney CA, Wallnau L. 'Dimensions of self-efficacy among three distinct groups of condom users'. *Journal of American College Health* 1994; 46:167-174.

21   Thompson SC, Anderson K, Freedman D, Swan J. 'Illusions of safety in a risky world. A study of college students' condom use'. *Journal of Applied Social Psychology* 1996; 26:189-210.

22   Whelan CT. *Values and Social Change in Ireland*. Dublin: Gill and Macmillan, 1994.

23   Cairns E. 'Is Northern Ireland a Conservative Society?' In: Stringer P, Robinson G, editors. *Social Attitudes in Northern Ireland*. Belfast: Backstaff, 1991.

24   Inglehart R. *Modernization and Postmodernization: Cultural, Economic, and Political Change in 43 Societies*. Princeton: Princeton University Press, 1997.

25   Greeley A. *Religion in Europe at the End of the Second Millennium*. London: Transaction Publishers, 2004.

26   Fahey T, Hayes BC, Sinnott R. *Conflict and Consensus: A Study of Values and Attitudes in the Republic of Ireland and Northern Ireland*. Dublin: Institute of Public Administration, 2005.

27   Fahey T. 'Religion and Sexual Culture in Ireland'. In: Eder FX, Hall L, Hekma G, editors. *Sexual Cultures in Europe, National Histories, pp53-70*. Manchester: Manchester University Press, 1999.

28   Inglis T. *Lessons in Irish Sexuality*. Dublin: University College Dublin Press, 1998.

29   Coleman D. 'Demography and Migration in Ireland, North and South'. In: Heath AF, Breen R, Whelan CT, editors. *Ireland North and South: Perspectives from Social Science, pp69-116*. Oxford: Oxford University Press, 1999.

30   Johnson A, Wadsworth J, Wellings K, Field J. *Sexual Attitudes and Lifestyles*. Oxford: Basil Blackwell, 1994.

31   Rissel CE, Richters J, Grulich AE, de Visser RO, Smith A. 'Sex in Australia: attitudes towards sex in a representative sample of adults'. *Australian and New Zealand Journal of Public Health* 2003; 27(2):118-123.

32   Kelley H. 'Attitudes Towards Homosexuality in 29 Nations'. *Australian Social Monitor* 2001; 4(1):15-22.

33   Grulich AE, De Visser R, Smith AM, Rissel CE, Richters J. 'Sex in Australia: homosexual experience and recent homosexual encounters'. *Australian and New Zealand Journal of Public Health* 2003; 27(2):155-163.

34 Kite ME, Whitley BE. 'Sex differences in attitudes toward homosexual persons, behaviors, and civil rights: A meta-analysis'. *Personality and Social Psychology Bulletin* 1996; 22(4):336-353.

35 Herek GM. 'Gender gaps in public opinion about lesbians and gay men'. *Public Opinion Quarterly* 2002; 66:40-66.

36 Stevens SR, Caron SL, Pratt P. 'Decade in review: the importance of religion in shaping the sexual attitudes of college students in the 1990s'. *Journal of College and Character* 2003; 2:1-12.

37 Wellings K, Field J, Whitaker L. 'Sexual Attitudes'. In: Johnson A, Wadsworth J., Field J, editors. Sexual Attitudes and Lifetsyles London: Blackwell Scientific Publications, 1994.

38 Mahon E, Conlon C, Dillon L. *Women and Crisis Pregnancy*. Dublin: The Stationery Office, 1998.

39 Edwards JE, Oldman A, Smith L, McQuay HJ, Moore RA. 'Women's knowledge of, and attitudes to, contraceptive effectiveness and adverse health effects'. *British Journal of Family Planning* 2000; 26(2):73-80.

40 Kihara MO, Kramer JS, Bain D, Kihara M, Mandel J. 'Knowledge of and Attitudes Toward the Pill: Results of a National Survey in Japan'. *Family Planning Perspectives* 2001; 33(3):123-127.

41 Tountas Y, Dimitrakaki C, Antoniou A, Boulamatsis D, Creatsas G. 'Attitudes and behaviour toward contraception among Greek women during reproductive age: a country-wide survey'. *European Journal of Obstetrics & Gynecology and Reproductive Biology* 2004; 116:190-195.

42 Gilliam ML, Warden M, Goldstein C, Tapia B. 'Concerns about contraceptive side-effects among young Latinas: a focus-group approach'. *Contraception* 2004; 70(4):299-305.

43 Abraham C, Sheeran P, Spears R, Abrams D. 'Health beliefs and promotion of HIV-preventive intentions among teenagers: a Scottish perspective'. *Health Psychology* 1992; 11(6):363-70.

44 Pleck JH, Sonenstein FL, Ku LC. 'Contraceptive attitudes and intention to use condoms in sexually experienced and inexperienced adolescent males'. *Journal of Family Issues* 1990; 11(3):294-312.

45 Rundle K, Leigh C, McGee H, Layte R. *Irish Contraception and Crisis Pregnancy (ICCP) Study: A Survey of the General Population*. Dublin, Crisis Pregnancy Agency, 2004.

46 Sutton S, McVey D, Glanz A. 'A Comparative Test of the Theory of Reasoned Action and the Theory of Planned Behaviour in the Prediction of Condom Use Intentions in a National Sample of Young English People'. *Health Psychology* 1999; 18:72-81.

47 Gainer E, Blum J, Toverud EL, Portugal N, Tyden T, Nesheim BI *et al*

48 'Bringing EC over the counter: experiences of non-prescription users in France, Norway, Sweden and Portugal'. *Contraception* 2003; 68(2):117-124.

49 Raine TR, Harper CC, Rocca CH, Fischer R, Padian N, Klausner JD *et al*. 'Direct Access to Emergency Contraception Through Pharmacies and Effect on Unintended Pregnancy And STIs'. *JAMA* 2005; 293(5):54-62.

50 Layte R, Whelan CT. 'Explaining Social Class Differentials in Smoking: The Role of Education'. 12. Dublin, ESRI. Working Papers on *Health Services, Health Inequalities and Health and Social Gain*, 2005.

Chapter 5:

Sexual Attraction, Sexual Identity and Sexual Experience

5.1 Introduction

THIS chapter examines the extent of same-sex and opposite-sex attraction found in the ISSHR survey. It relates self-reported sexual attraction to sexual identity and sexual experience. It seeks to understand the level of same-sex attraction and behaviour in the Irish population and whether this varies between groups, such as by age and sex.

Chapter four showed evidence that Irish attitudes toward sex between two people of the same gender have become more liberal over time. Yet, even by 2005, almost a quarter of people still regarded consensual homosexual sex as 'always wrong' (see chapter four). Even among the youngest age group where attitudes were most liberal, around 13% still thought such behaviour 'always wrong'. Such statistics underline the fact that sexual orientation, identity and expression do not occur in a neutral environment where sexual diversity (in the sense of having sexual relationships with both men and women) is a simple matter of individual choice. Quite the opposite; homosexuality is still widely stigmatised and homosexual identity can come at great personal cost to individuals.

Given this, the extent of same-sex attraction and sexual experience and of homosexual identity in the population, and the extent to which these change over time, is of great interest to sociologists, anthropologists and public-health, health-promotion and health-education specialists. Knowledge of the extent of sexual diversity is also important for epidemiologists attempting to understand the spread of HIV. Even by the mid-1980s, it was clear that most AIDS cases were among homosexual men[1] and that certain practices, most notably anal sex, were much more likely than others to lead to infection. At that time, however, there were no representative statistics on the proportion of men who had sex with other men, or the extent of anal sex and use of barrier protection. This was the primary reason for the development of national KAB surveys in a number of countries in the late 1980s and early 1990s.

Many people tend to think of sexual orientation in an essentialist manner whereby sexuality is the expression of a fundamental biological drive and individuals are either heterosexual or homosexual. Others have argued that the historical and cultural variability of the level of same-sex relations and the manner in which the categories of heterosexual and homosexual are thought of means that, if there is an inherent biological 'drive' toward the same gender, it finds expression through a thick layer of socially constructed practices and beliefs.

We do not intend to rehearse the arguments for these positions here, but research does show that same-sex and opposite-sex sexual expression are better represented as a continuum rather than as a dichotomy of heterosexual and homosexual.[2][3][4][5] Research from the UK, US and Australia all show that the proportion of people who have some level of sexual attraction to the same gender is substantially larger than the proportion who will ever have same-sex genital contact. Research also shows that most individuals who have had a same-sex sexual partner also have had opposite-sex partners. This suggests that attraction to both genders is more common than same-sex attraction.

The ISSHR survey followed similar national KAB surveys in developing an instrument to measure the nature of sexual diversity and then quantify the level of same-sex and opposite-sex attraction and the manner in which this relates to sexual experience with men and women.

The next, **second section** briefly outlines how sexual attraction, identity and experience are measured in the ISSHR survey. The **third section** examines data on the pattern of sexual identity, attraction and experience in Ireland. It also includes analysis of a variant of the 'Kinsey scale' of same-sex and opposite-sex attraction, as well as detailed information on the distribution of same-sex experiences.

In the **fourth section**, we examine the manner in which the spectrum of sexual diversity varies across age groups and, in particular, how the age of first homosexual experience has changed across time. In the **fifth section**, we analyse the extent to which sexual attraction is fulfilled in sexual behaviour.

In the **sixth section**, we examine the socio-demographic predictors of same-sex experience, including through multi-variate analyses. The **seventh section** looks at the exclusivity of sexual orientation over the course of life. In the final, **eighth section** we summarise the findings of the chapter and draw conclusions.

5.2   Measuring sexual attraction, identity and experience

THE estimates of sexual diversity given in this chapter strongly depend on the measures used in the ISSHR questionnaire. The survey questions sought to develop an understanding of three basic dimensions of the individual: sexual identity, orientation of sexual attraction, and same-sex or opposite-sex orientation of sexual relationships.

The ISSHR survey was designed to provide specific, clear and reliable information on a discrete number of important dimensions that can be used to understand the relationship between sexual knowledge, attitudes and behaviour.

The first question in the survey sought to gain an understanding of a person's sexual identity. Respondents were asked:

- "Thinking about yourself, would you define yourself as: heterosexual or straight; homosexual (gay or lesbian); bisexual; not sure; something else?"

This was the only place in the survey where the words homosexual and bisexual were used, as for the most part we sought to learn about sexual behaviours which entailed some risk of disease transmission rather than sexual orientation per se. We did not want to restrict questions on same-sex behaviours to those with a homosexual or bisexual identity. We also sought to measure the spectrum of behaviours and thus avoided using terms such as homosexual that might induce respondents to structure their experiences.

The next question on sexual attraction is a variant of the Kinsey scale, so called because it was first used by Alfred Kinsey in his research. The scale aims to measure the extent of same-sex and opposite-sex attraction by asking individuals to place themselves on a graduated scale which runs from total opposite-sex attraction to total same-sex attraction. The version used in the ISSHR survey is derived from the British NATSAL survey. It asked respondents:

- You have felt sexually attracted:
  only to (male/females), never to (males/females) .... ☐₁
  more often to (male/females), and at least once to a (male/female) .... ☐₂
  about equally often to (male/females) and to (male/females) .... ☐₃
  more often to (male/females), and at least once to a (male/female) .... ☐₄
  only to (male/females), (never to male/female)   .... ☐₅
- You have never felt sexually attracted to anyone at all .... ☐₆
- Refused .... ☐₇

Respondents were asked to stop the interviewer when a statement that best described them was read out.

Sexual behaviour was measured using a number of items. The main aim was to use a rigorous definition of behaviours, often supported with anatomical definitions, rather than generic terms such as 'sex' or 'intercourse'. However, this tight behavioural approach was loosened at the beginning of section G of the questionnaire (see chapter two) so that we could establish the extent of any same-sex contact. Here a single item was used which asked:

- "Have you had any kind of sexual experience or contact with (men/women), even if this was a long time ago or did not involve contact with the genital area?"

A more specific question about genital contact followed:

- "Have you had any sexual contact with a (man/woman) involving the genital area? That is, oral (or anal) sex or any other contact involving the genital area?"

This question was used along with an item asking for the number of same-sex sexual partners over lifetime to measure whether a person had ever had same-sex genital sexual contact.

To establish whether a person had experienced more recent genital sexual contact with someone of the same gender, questions on the number of sexual partners (involving vaginal, oral or anal sex) of the same gender over the last five years and last year were combined with an item asking:

- "When was the last occasion you had any other form of sex with a (man/woman) that involved GENITAL CONTACT but NOT also oral (or anal) sex? Genital contact not involving intercourse is forms of contact with the genital area NOT leading to oral or anal intercourse, but intending to achieve orgasm, for example, stimulating by hand."

Together, these behavioural questions allowed us to quantify the extent of same-sex contact over different periods. These questions do not cover the entire range of same-sex-oriented behaviours. They do not cover simultaneous masturbation by individuals without contact even though this might be regarded by some individuals as a form of sex.

5.3 Sexual identity, attraction and experience

SUMMARY

THE overwhelming majority of individuals defined themselves as heterosexual. Most reported only opposite-sex attraction, but the proportion reporting some level of same-sex attraction was more than double the proportion identifying as other than heterosexual.

Similarly low proportions of men and women have had same-sex sexual experience.

- 2.7% of men and 1.2% of women self-identified as homosexual or bisexual.
- 5.3% of men and 5.8% of women reported some same-sex attraction.
- 7.1% of men and 4.7% of women reported a homosexual experience some time in their life so far.
- 4.4% of men and 1.4% of women reported a genital same-sex experience in their life so far.
- 3% of men and 1.1% of women reported a genital same-sex experience in the last five years.

WE have suggested that sexual expression may be characterised more as a spectrum than a dichotomy and that individual identity, attraction and experience may be combined in complex patterns. The relationship between sexual attraction and experience is important. Though the level of stigma associated with homosexuality has decreased in recent decades, it is still pronounced in Irish society. This means that all estimates of same-sex attraction, experience and identity based upon self-reports should be seen as under-estimates.

However, if sexual attraction can be seen as an indicator of an inclination toward same-sex relationships, we would expect that, given the level of stigma still associated with homosexual behaviour, the level of same-sex experience reported would be lower than the proportion reporting same-sex attraction. By the same logic, we would expect that the prevalence of current homosexual partnerships would be far lower than the proportion that have ever had genital contact with the same gender or homosexual intercourse (ie, anal or oral sex).

Table 5.1 shows the proportions of men and women identifying as heterosexual, homosexual, bisexual or 'something else'/'not sure'. The overwhelming majority define themselves as heterosexual. Women are marginally but statistically significantly more likely to do so than men.

- Only 1.6% of men and 0.4% of women define themselves as homosexual.
- Around 1% of both men and women define themselves as bisexual.

The small proportion defining themselves as anything other than heterosexual means we should be careful in interpreting these statistics. The small numbers involved (1% of the sample defining themselves as homosexual would total just 57 individuals) mean that the standard errors and associated confidence intervals are large. We have no comparable figures for the NATSAL surveys in Britain, but figures from the Australian ASHR survey[6] and US NHSLS[5] are very similar. The figures suggest that very few Irish people could be said to be 'homosexual', but, as already argued, sexual identity is not necessarily aligned with either sexual attraction or sexual experience.

Table 5.1: Sexual identification: by gender

	Men (%)	Women (%)
Heterosexual	96.5	98.6
Homosexual (gay or lesbian)	1.6	0.4
Bisexual	1.1	0.8
Not sure; undecided	0.4	0.1
Something else/other	0.2	0.2
Refused	0.2	0.0
Total	100	100
Base	3,188	4,252

Table 5.2 supports this point. It gives reported sexual attraction for men and women. Although most reported that they were attracted only to the opposite gender, the proportion reporting some same-sex sexual attraction was larger than that identifying as homosexual or bisexual:

- Almost 6% of men and women reported some level of same-sex attraction at some point in their life (men 5.3%).

Unlike in *Table 5.1* where women were less likely to identify as either homosexual or bisexual, here women were marginally more likely to report some same-sex attraction.

Table 5.2: Sexual attraction: by gender

	Men (%)	Women (%)
Only heterosexual	94.3	94.0
Mostly heterosexual	3.6	5.0
Both heterosexual and homosexual	0.2	0.5
Mostly homosexual	0.8	0.2
Only homosexual	0.8	0.1
Never felt sexually attracted	0.1	0.2
Refused	0.3	0.1
Total	100	100
Base	3,182	4,241

The proportion of both men and women who reported mostly homosexual or only homosexual attraction is very small: just 2% of men and less than 1% of women. These patterns of attraction are similar to those found in comparable studies elsewhere. In Britain, for instance, the 1990 NATSAL survey[4] found 6% of men and 5% of women had some level of same-sex attraction. The Australian survey[6] found significantly higher figures: 7% of men and 12.8% of women reported sexual attraction to the same gender at some point in their life.

Research in other countries has shown that there is no necessary reason why sexual identity should follow professed sexual attraction or reported sexual experience. The ISSHR data also show this:

- Among people with some same-sex attraction, over 91% still defined themselves as heterosexual, 8% as bisexual and less than 1% as homosexual.

However, as the degree of same-sex attraction increases and opposite-sex attraction decreases, the likelihood of defining oneself as other than heterosexual increases:

- Among those who reported equal attraction to the same and opposite gender, 74% defined themselves as bisexual and 16% as homosexual.
- Among those with mostly same-sex attraction, the proportion identifying as homosexual increased to 88%.

The extent of same-sex experience found depends largely on the measure used. This can be seen clearly in *Figure 5.1* which gives the proportion reporting specific same-sex experiences and level of same-sex attraction. It shows that 6% of women report some same-sex attraction, but the proportion with same-sex sexual experience, however defined, is lower. The relationship in terms of extent and recency of experience is graduated. The same is true among men, except that the proportion with at least one same-sex sexual experience is higher than that reporting same-sex attraction (7% v 5%). The ISSHR questionnaire did not specify what this 'experience' was, but simply asked respondents if they had experienced any kind of sexual experience with a member of the same gender, even if this did not involve genital contact.

The fact that more men than women report some same-sex sexual experience than report ever having any homosexual attraction may suggest that such experiences occurred during childhood and were part of childhood experimentation. Some evidence for this is the fact that over 50% of men's same-sex experiences occurred before the person was aged 17 and 40% of these men never had a genital same-sex experience. We return shortly to the issue of the stability of same-sex orientation.

Figure 5.1: Proportion with homosexual experience & attraction: by gender

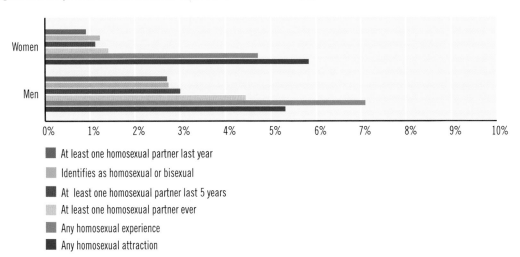

At least one homosexual partner last year

Identifies as homosexual or bisexual

At least one homosexual partner last 5 years

At least one homosexual partner ever

Any homosexual experience

Any homosexual attraction

The proportions of men and women with a same-sex partner (and thus homosexual genital contact with someone of the same gender) are lower than those reporting any homosexual experience:

• 4% of men and over 1% of women reported 'ever' having genital contact with someone of the same gender.

If we confine the population to those having same-sex genital contact in the last five years, the proportion falls still further, to around 3% of men and just 1% of women. Around 3% of men and 1% of women reported genital homosexual contact in the last year. It is largely those respondents who reported a same-sex partner 'in the last five years' who identified as homosexual or bisexual.

Compared to the 1990 NATSAL survey in Britain (figures for the 2000 NATSAL survey are not available), the Irish figures reveal a slightly higher proportion of Irish men and women who have had at least one sexual experience with someone of the same gender (7% of men and nearly 5% of women, compared to NATSAL's 6% of men and 3% of women). Rates of genital contact, however, are essentially the same:

• Over 4% of Irish men reported ever having a homosexual partner (genital contact) compared to 5% of British men, and 1% of Irish women compared to 2% of British women.

The Irish figures should be treated with caution, given the small numbers of respondents. The NATSAL samples were 13,765 in 1990 and 11,161 in 2000, which allows greater precision in estimates, particularly for low-prevalence behaviours.

5.4 Sexual identity, attraction and experience by age group

SUMMARY

THIS section examines in more detail the pattern of same-sex sexual experiences by age group.

Younger respondents are more likely to report homosexual and bisexual identity as well as some level of same-sex attraction. Among women, the youngest age group are far more likely than all other age groups to report some same-sex non-genital experience, but a far lower proportion have ever had same-sex genital experience.

The age of first same-sex genital experience falls steeply across female age groups.

Among men, patterns of same-sex sexual contact by age are complex. Men between 45 and 54 are most likely to have had some same-sex experience and a genital same-sex experience, but men aged 25 to 44 are more likely to have had a same-sex experience in the recent past. This suggests that, among men aged 45 to 54, early same-sex contact was not carried forward into adulthood.

■ Younger Irish women are far more likely than older women or men to report some same-sex attraction and experience.

■ Among women, the probability of ever having had genital contact with a same-sex partner or with one in the recent past is highest for women aged 25-34.

■ Men aged between 35 and 54 have the highest probability of ever having had genital contact with a same-sex partner.

■ The median age for first genital same-sex experience is 16 among men and 23 among women.

■ Men aged between 45 and 54 are not only most likely to have had a same-sex experience, but also to have had this earlier than all other age groups (median of 14).

■ Women under 35 experience same-sex relationships far earlier than was the case with older age groups.

TABLE 5.3 shows the same information as *Figure 5.1*, but disaggregated for different age groups. This shows some distinct differences in patterns of identity, attraction and experience across age groups, but the patterns are not uniform across the different measures.

Younger age groups are more likely to identify themselves as homosexual or bisexual, except that the peak among men occurs among those aged 25 to 34. As shown in chapter three, younger age groups tend to have more liberal attitudes to sexual issues. This may be reflected in them feeling more secure in adopting a homosexual identity. Although the absolute number of individuals covered in this table may be small, it appears that the youngest age group of women are six times more likely than women in other age groups to define themselves as homosexual or bisexual. Interestingly, most women aged 18 to 24 who do not identify as heterosexual define themselves as bisexual.

The age pattern is also reflected in the proportions reporting 'any homosexual attraction'. Younger men and women, and particularly those in the youngest age group, are far more likely to report some attraction to the same gender. Again, the pattern is most pronounced among young women: under-25s are almost nine times more likely to report same-sex attraction than women in the oldest age group (age 55+).

The measures of homosexual experience show a pattern that, compared to the patterns of identity and attraction, is not quite as simple for women and very dissimilar for men. The youngest age group of women are almost 10 times more likely than the oldest age group, and twice as likely as the next oldest age group, to have had some same-sex sexual experience.

The measures of genital same-sex experience or homosexual intercourse show that, although there is an age gradient, women between 25 and 34 have the highest prevalence. Whereas young women were far more likely than older women to report some same-sex attraction and a homosexual/bisexual identity, there is less difference across age groups in same-sex genital experience.

Interestingly, *Table 5.3* also shows that the median age[k] of first genital same-sex partner has decreased significantly across age groups. Whereas women aged over 34 had their first same-sex experience in their 30s, 50% or more of women between 25 and 34 had the experience at or before 22. The median age drops to 18 for women in the youngest age group.

Among men the pattern is more complex for all categories of sexual experience. Those aged between 35 and 54 have the highest prevalence of any same-sex sexual experience or same-sex genital contact. For any same-sex sexual experience, men aged between 45 and 54 have the highest prevalence, at almost 10%, followed by those aged 35 to 44, at 8%.

Table 5.3: Proportion of respondents with specific homosexual experiences: by gender and age group (%)

Men	18-24	25-34	35-44	45-54	55-64	**Total**	Base
Identifies as homosexual or bisexual	2.7	3.6	2.9	2.0	1.8	**2.7**	3,188
Any homosexual attraction	7.3	6.4	5.6	3.9	2.4	**5.3**	3,182
Any homosexual experience	5.2	6.3	7.9	9.8	6.3	**7.1**	3,169
Median age of first genital homosexual partner	**16**	**18**	**19**	**14**	**18**	**16**	**3,188**
At least one homosexual partner ever	2.5	3.8	5.6	6.8	3.3	**4.4**	3,188
At least one homosexual partner in last 5 years	2.4	3.5	4.3	3.0	1.4	**3.0**	3,188
At least one homosexual partner in last year	1.9	3.3	3.8	2.4	1.4	**2.7**	3,188
Base range	754-759*	699-701*	640-647*	570-574*	506-507*		
Women	18-24	25-34	35-44	45-54	55-64	**Total**	Base
Identifies as homosexual or bisexual	2.6	0.7	1.2	0.7	0.4	**1.2**	4,252
Any homosexual attraction	11.6	7.3	4.5	2.7	1.3	**5.8**	4,241
Any homosexual experience	10.7	4.9	3.7	2.1	0.9	**4.7**	4,231
Median age of first genital homosexual partner	**18**	**22**	**30**	**32**	**–**	**23**	
At least one homosexual partner ever	1.4	2.0	1.7	1.1	0.2	1.4	4,253
At least one homosexual partner in last 5 years	1.4	1.6	1.5	0.8	0.0	**1.1**	4,253
At least one homosexual partner in last year	0.8	1.1	1.3	0.7	0.0	**0.9**	4,253
Base range	908*	964-966*	1007-1114*	751-755*	601-610*		

*The base range reflects differential non-response across different questions.

---

k   The median age here is the age at which 50% or more of individuals who report a same-sex genital experience had this experience.

The same pattern holds for having genital contact with someone of the same gender (7% and 6%), although the pattern weakens as we move from ever having a same-sex partner to at least one in the last five years or in the last year. Here those aged 35 to 44 tend to have the highest rates. (Again, we should exercise caution here as the number of respondents involved is small and confidence intervals will be wide and overlapping.)

For women, the age of first same-sex partner is falling. For men, the trend is similar in recent years. However, the median age for men aged 45-54 falls to 14. Men aged 35 to 44 have the oldest median, 19. (We return later to this issue.)

As well as asking whether respondents had had same-sex sexual partners, the ISSHR questionnaire asked at what age this first occurred, for both all same-sex experiences and those involving genital contact. This allows us to examine whether certain age groups are more likely than others to have had homosexual experiences earlier.

Figures 5.2 and *5.3* show the proportion, by current age group, of men and women who reported a same-sex genital experience at any age. The earlier the line rises and the steeper the curve, the earlier the experience and the greater the proportion of each age group with a same-sex genital experience. If a line for one age group rises earlier and is steeper than the lines for other age groups, the members of that age group experienced same-sex relationships earlier. This is the case even if the line finishes lower in the graph, showing that a lower proportion overall had such an experience.

Figure 5.2: Proportion of men with genital same-sex experience by a given age: by current age group

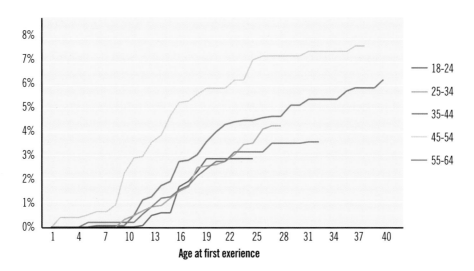

A minority of men report same-sex genital contact. The scale on the left side reflects this.

Figure 5.3: Proportion of women with genital same-sex experience by a given age: by current age group

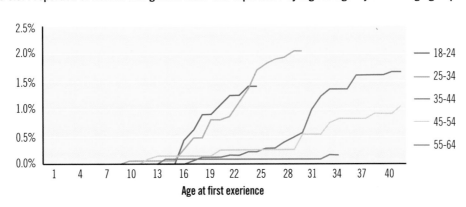

A minority of women report same-sex genital contact. The scale on the left side reflects this.

If we compare *Figures 5.2* and *5.3*, what is initially striking is the different shapes of the curves as between men and women. The male curves rise steeply from the early teenage years and begin to flatten in the mid-20s. The curve for women varies greatly by age group. For women aged 35 or more, the curves rise gently from the early 20s and do not flatten out until the mid-30s. For women under 35, the curves climb steeply from mid-adolescence and do not flatten out until the late 20s. The line for the youngest age group climbs most steeply. The graphs suggest very different features for men and women, and different features within genders according to age group.

Men aged 45 to 54 were not only more likely to have had genital homosexual experiences than either younger or older age groups, they were also more likely to have these earlier. These men would have been aged between 10 and 20 in 1970. This was not only the beginning of a period of intense change in attitudes and behaviour in Ireland, but was shortly after the change in the legal status of homosexual acts in Britain, in 1967. This generation may thus have been in the forefront of sexual change in Ireland, but there are other possible explanations. A second explanation is that this age group may have been more likely to experience abusive homosexual experiences.

Whereas around half of men who reported a genital homosexual experience dated this to before age 17, this was true of over 70% of men in the 45-54 age group. The median age of first homosexual experience for men aged 45-54 was 14, compared to 19 among those aged 35-44. The ISSHR survey did not request information on first homosexual partner; it is thus not possible to verify, but experience of abuse may explain the young age at which this age group had their first same-sex experience, compared to other groups.

Among women, the pattern of homosexual experience is quite different from that among men. The median age of first experience is 23, compared to 16 among men. For women over 34, the pattern is one of later experience and far more variability. For under-35s, there is a steep increase in the proportion having same-sex genital experience between 18 and 20. This rise occurs slightly later than among men but indicates a very pronounced change in behaviour among young women.

5.5 The relationship between sexual identity, attraction and experience

SUMMARY

PEOPLE who report same-sex attraction are far more likely to also report same-sex sexual experience. As the level of same-sex attraction increases, so does the level of same-sex genital experience. Of people who report some level of same-sex attraction, though, a minority have experienced a same-sex genital partnership.

■ Orientation of sexual attraction is strongly related to orientation of sexual experience.

■ 2% of men and 0.2% of women who report opposite-sex attraction alone report ever having had a same-sex partner.

■ 25% of men and 12% of women who are 'mostly attracted' to the opposite gender have had a same-sex partner.

■ 47% of men and 24% of women who have some degree of same-sex attraction report having had a same-sex genital sexual experience.

Table 5.4: Relationship between sexual attraction and life-time genital sexual experience: by gender (%)

				Sexual attraction				
Men	**All opposite**	**Mostly opposite**	**Equally**	**Mostly same**	**All same**	**None**	**Refused**	**All**
Just heterosexual experiences	93.6	69.5	0.0	7.1	0.0	0.0	59.6	91.0
Heterosexual & homosexual experiences	2.1	24.9	38.6	53.8	13.3	0.0	0.0	3.4
Just homosexual experiences	0.0	0.0	22.7	39.1	79.6	0.0	0.0	1.0
No sexual experiences	4.3	5.7	38.8	0.0	7.2	100.0	40.4	4.6
N	2,982	126	8	23	29	3	6	3,177
Women	**All opposite**	**Mostly opposite**	**Equally**	**Mostly same**	**All same**	**None**	**Refused**	**All**
Just heterosexual experiences	94.8	85.3	33.4	0.0	0.0	36.2	70.8	93.6
Heterosexual & homosexual experiences	0.2	11.5	66.7	87.6	0.0	0.0	0.0	1.3
Just homosexual experiences	0.0	0.0	0.0	12.4	76.3	0.0	0.0	0.1
No sexual experiences	5.0	3.2	0.0	0.0	23.7	63.8	29.2	5.0
N	3,965	226	19	5	3	6	4	4,228

THE ISSHR data show that the proportions of people reporting sexual attraction to the same gender are not radically different from those reporting same-sex experience of different kinds (see last two sections). This suggests that there are not large proportions of the population that would like to experience same-sex partnerships but feel they can not, for some reason. But to what extent have those who profess an attraction to the same gender experienced same-sex relationships?

Table 5.4 shows the distribution of same-sex and opposite-sex relationships for people with different levels of attraction to the same gender. Sexual experience is defined here as any same-sex genital contact, rather than anal or oral sex with someone of the same gender.

The table shows a great deal of consistency between the orientation of sexual attraction that people report and their sexual experience. For example:

- Only 2% of men and 0.2% of women who reported opposite-sex attraction alone also reported some same-sex genital experience; this is true of 25% of men and 12% of women who reported 'mostly opposite' attraction.

As we move from left to right in *Table 5.4* (ie, as attraction becomes increasingly focused on the same gender), the proportion with homosexual and bisexual experience increases. Given the small number of respondents available for analysis in some of these cells, we do not interpret the results for those who declined to indicate orientation of attraction.

If all people who express some level of same-sex attraction are included, we find that 53% of men and 76% of women have never translated this attraction into experience.

5.6 Socio-demographic variation in prevalence of homosexual experience

SUMMARY

ANALYSIS of the ISSHR data shows that the likelihood of having a same-sex genital relationship is related to socio-demographic characteristics as well as age.

Married men and women are significantly less likely to report a same-sex relationship over all periods. Those who are cohabiting tend to have the highest probability of same-sex experience over all periods.

- Unmarried men and women are most likely to have had a same-sex relationship 'ever' and 'in the recent past'.

- Geographical location seems to be a factor, but only for men. Men in large cities including Dublin are over twice as likely to report same-sex genital experience. Women with same-sex experience tend to live in 'smaller' geographic locations.

THE prevalence of homosexual experience is strongly patterned by age and gender (see previous sections), but other factors may be implicated. Research in Britain (by Johnson *et al*)[4] has shown that people in higher non-manual positions are more likely to report same-sex experiences, although this class difference was not evident for recent homosexual experience in Britain. However, since tolerance and acceptance of homosexuality also increase with social status (see chapter four), higher social-status groups may be more likely to report homosexual experience.

Johnson *et al* also show that where a person lives is an important factor: people living in London and the south-east of Britain were far more likely to report both ever having a homosexual partner and having one 'in the last five years'. Again, reporting bias may be an issue here. However, analysis of past geographical movements among this British sample also showed that those with homosexual experience were more likely to move to the capital, perhaps because of its greater anonymity and its population of people with same-sex experience. Johnson *et al* also showed that having attended a same-sex school and/or having attended a boarding school were strong predictors of both ever having a same sex partner and having a homosexual partner 'in the last five years'.

Attraction to the same gender may affect the probability of an individual becoming involved in a long-term opposite-sex relationship and getting married, with the probability of marriage decreasing as the extent of same-sex attraction increases. Of course, the motivation to get married is complex and some individuals with a dominant same-sex attraction may marry, for many reasons, but on average same-sex attraction should lead to a lower probability of marriage. On the other hand, analyses may find a higher probability of cohabitation for individuals with same-sex experience, since they may be cohabiting with someone of the same gender.

Figure 5.4: Proportion of men with a genital same-sex experience over different periods: by relationship status

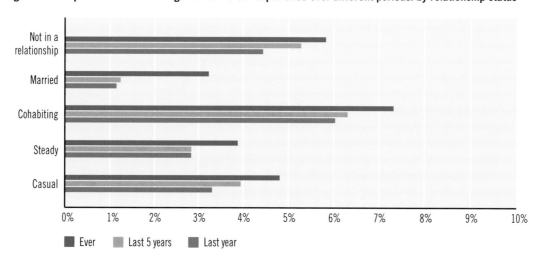

Figure 5.4 gives the proportions, by current relationship status, of men experiencing same-sex relationships over different periods. It offers some support to the hypothesis concerning marriage and same-sex attraction. It shows that married men have the lowest probability of same-sex relationships over all periods, though the differential is highest over the two most recent periods. *Figure 5.4* also supports the idea that cohabiting people are most likely to have had same-sex experience.

Figure 5.5: Proportion of women with a genital same-sex experience over different periods: by relationship status

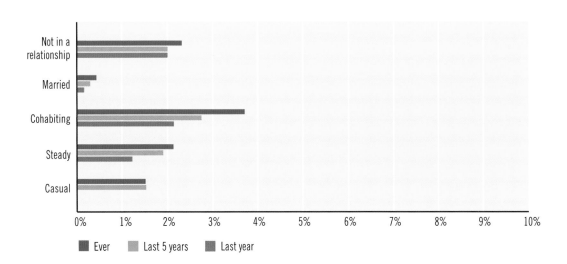

Figure 5.5 gives the proportions, by relationship status, of women reporting a same-sex genital experience over different periods. It gives support to the hypothesis that, as with men, women who desire same-sex relationships will be less likely to enter into marriage. It shows that married women are significantly less likely to have had a same-sex genital relationship over all periods.

Figure 5.5 also shows higher levels of same-sex contact among women who are currently cohabiting. This suggests that these women may be living with someone of the same gender.

Figure 5.6: Proportion of men with a genital same-sex experience over different periods: by current location

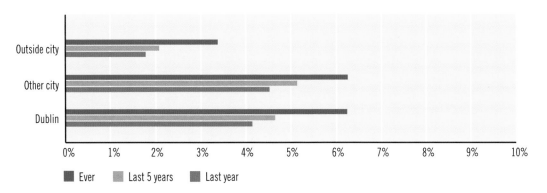

As discussed above, the British NATSAL survey 1990[4] found a strong relationship between current location and likelihood of a same-sex experience; people resident in London had almost twice the likelihood of same-sex experience. Similar patterns were found in the ISSHR survey, although the impact of living in a city was not confined to Dublin.

Figure 5.6 shows that the probability of same-sex genital experience 'in the past five years' or 'in the last year' is over twice as high in Dublin and other Irish cities as it is elsewhere, although only for men. Analyses suggest that homosexual relationships among women are more evenly spread across Ireland. The pattern among men suggests that those who would like to have same-sex relationships tend to move to areas with a large population.

5.7 Exclusivity of sexual preference over lifetime

SUMMARY

THE survey respondents infrequently reported same-sex experience. Most of those with same-sex experience also reported opposite-sex experience. This could imply that individuals' sexual preferences are stable within distinct periods, but analyses confining results to recent periods show that most people with same-sex relationships also have had opposite-sex relationships. This suggests that the widely held belief that individuals are either heterosexual or homosexual is wrong and that most people having same-sex relationships are bisexual in orientation.

- Most men and women currently having same-sex relationships identified themselves as bisexual.

- Only 35% of men with a same-sex experience 'in the last year' have had sex with men alone.

WHILE results show that homosexual experience is comparatively infrequent in the Irish population, it varies strongly between different age groups and between men and women. To what extent is same-sex experience exclusive over the course of life?

Table 5.5: Sex of partners over time intervals: by gender

	Ever %	Last 5 years %	Last year %
Men			
Exclusively female	91.0	94.8	90.1
Men and women	3.4	1.8	1.3
Exclusively male	1.0	0.4	0.7
No partners	4.6	3.0	8.0
Base	3,181	2,990	2,984
Women			
Exclusively male	93.6	93.0	87.3
Men and women	1.3	0.9	0.4
Exclusively female	0.1	0.2	0.4
No partners	5.0	5.9	11.9
Base	4,233	3,979	3,971

Table 5.5 shows that, of men and women who have ever had a homosexual experience including genital contact, a minority have experienced same-sex partners only. The proportion with only same-sex experience is larger among men. The proportion having same-sex experience alone increases as the time period is shortened. However, even if we examine experiences 'in the last year', only 35% of men (0.7/(1.3+0.7)) with same-sex experience have had male partners alone. This finding

underlines the point that no simple distinction can be made between the heterosexual and homosexual populations.

If we increase the period over which we include partnerships and move from only genital contact to any homosexual experience, we find a larger proportion of both men and women have had some homosexual contact. Moreover, of those who have had a same sex-experience, most have had experiences with both men and women, even if we only survey the most recent year.

5.8 Summary

MANY people tend to think that individuals are either heterosexual or homosexual. However, research shows that same-sex and opposite-sex attraction are better represented as a continuum. Analysis of the ISSHR data in this chapter has confirmed this by showing that the rate of same-sex attraction for men is over twice that of homosexual or bisexual identification. In other words:

• twice as many men report some level of same-sex attraction as identify themselves as homosexual or bisexual.

Among women the ratio is even larger:

• over five times as many women report some level of same-sex attraction as identify themselves as bisexual or lesbian.

Similarly, a smaller proportion of the population identify themselves as homosexual or bisexual than report a same-sex genital experience, although the rates are closer among women than men. Among men, just over 4% of the population have had a same-sex genital experience, compared to 3% identifying as homosexual or bisexual. Among women, the proportions are closer; 1% of women have ever had a same-sex sexual experience and 1% identify themselves as homosexual or bisexual.

These figures are, however, the aggregate picture. The ISSHR data show that the prevalence of same-sex attraction and experience vary widely across a number of dimensions, particularly in terms of current age. Among men, same-sex attraction is more common among younger men: the rate among under-25s is three times that among men between 55 and 64. This might suggest that the preference of men is changing, but it is more likely that younger men feel more able than older men to express their desire for same-sex relationships and are more comfortable in admitting to same-sex attraction. Younger men are more liberal than older men in their attitudes to homosexuality (see chapter four); this is likely to affect responses to surveys such as ISSHR.

Among women the pattern is even starker: 12% of women under 25 report some same-sex attraction compared to 3% of women aged between 45 and 54 and just 1% of those aged between 55 and 64. This suggests dramatic changes in attitudes to homosexuality among women over time.

The pattern of same-sex experience among women largely replicates that found for sexual attraction. Young women are much more likely to report some form of same-sex experience, but the pattern of same-sex genital contact is flatter across age groups, suggesting a far smaller degree of change. One reason for this may be that same-sex genital contact among women tends to occur much later than among men. Peak rates do not emerge until the mid to late 20s, although this pattern seems to be changing for younger women. This may be the reason why the highest proportions with a same-sex genital partner among women are found among women between 25 and 34. That indicates a slow development toward more same-sex relationships among women, but this has yet to emerge fully as the youngest age group has yet to experience such relationships.

Among men the picture is much more complex. Although young men are more likely to report same-sex attraction, the highest proportion of non-genital same-sex experiences is found among those aged between 45 and 54. Around half of these same-sex experiences occurred before the individual was 17, and this rises to over 70% among those aged 45 to 54. This may represent adolescent or child sex play, but the ISSHR data do not include the age of the partner for this experience so it is not possible to be definitive about the contact.

Men aged between 45 and 54 are also the most likely to report ever having a same-sex partner, including genital contact. The rates for the age groups immediately above and below are lower but similar. The lowest rates of same-sex genital contact, as with any same-sex contact, are among the youngest age group. It is hard to be definitive about the nature of this contact.

More evidence that sexual orientation is a spectrum rather than a dichotomy comes from the finding that the vast majority of people who have had same-sex (genital) partners have also had opposite-sex partners. Among men, only a fifth of those who have ever had a same-sex partner have had sexual experience only with other men. Among women, the small numbers of respondents make it difficult to draw conclusions, but most of those with same-sex contact have had both female and male partners over their lifetime to date.

Analysis of the other factors related to same-sex experience show that a person's relationship status is an important predictor. Married men and women are significantly less likely than all other groups to have had a same-sex partner over all periods, whereas those who are cohabiting are far more likely.

A second predictor is living in a large city (including Dublin), but only for men. This is likely to result from the movement of men with a same-sex orientation to large cities and the capital, rather than from a higher rate of homosexual preference among city-dwellers.

5.9   Reference list

1   Institute of Medicine. *Confronting AIDS: Directions for Public Health, Health Care and Research.* Washington DC: National Academy Press, 1986.

2   Kinsey AC, Pomeroy WB, Martin CE. *Sexual Behaviour in the Human Male.* Philadelphia: Saunders, 1948.

3   Kinsey AC, Pomeroy WB, Martin CE, Gebhard PH. *Sexual Behaviour in the Human Female.* Philadelphia: Saunders, 1953.

4   Johnson A, Wadsworth J, Wellings K, Field J. *Sexual Attitudes and Lifestyles.* Oxford: Basil Blackwell, 1994.

5   Laumann EO, Gagnon JH, Michael TM, Michaels S. *The Social Organisation of Sexuality: Sexual Practices in the United States.* Chicago: University of Chicago Press, 1994.

6   Grulich AE, De Visser R, Smith AM, Rissel CE, Richters J. 'Sex in Australia: homosexual experience and recent homosexual encounters'. *Australian and New Zealand Journal of Public Health* 2003; 27(2):155-163.

Chapter 6:

First Heterosexual Intercourse

6.1 Introduction

FIRST sexual intercourse is a highly significant event in most societies. Even though sex is no longer so intimately tied to marriage, it retains this importance. Most people can remember the first time they had penetrative sex. This testifies to its continuing significance as well as making it possible for researchers to investigate the factors associated with first intercourse.

The timing of a person's first sexual intercourse is a key variable influencing the probability of a negative outcome: younger age at first coitus is associated with an increased risk of unintended pregnancy. This is mostly due to lower use of contraception at younger ages.[1][2][3] Early parenthood has itself been associated with lower educational and occupational attainment and an increased risk of poverty.[4]

Given the influence that first sexual intercourse can exert on an individual's future life, it is important to understand the timing, circumstances and nature of this event in the lives of Irish people. This information will be particularly useful for policy-makers in the areas of sexual health and education, and especially for those designing education and prevention strategies for young people.

In the next, **second section**, we examine the striking decline in age of first intercourse in Ireland and other developed countries. In the **third section**, we look at the factors that influence the experience of first sex before age 17. In the **fourth section**, we analyse the extent of use of contraception at first intercourse and the factors associated with this.

In the **fifth section**, we look at the reasons that respondents in the ISSHR survey gave for not using contraception. In the **sixth section**, we examine the main reasons given for having first intercourse, the extent of planning and willingness between partners, and whether the decision to experience intercourse led to regret in later years. In the final, **seventh section**, we summarise our findings and draw conclusions.

6.2 The age of first vaginal intercourse

SUMMARY

THE average age of first vaginal intercourse has steadily declined for both men and women over the last half century. Most people now in their 20s had their first experience of vaginal sex before they were 18. This is true of a small minority among those aged over 50.

- The median age of first vaginal intercourse is 18 for men and 19 for women.

- The median age of first vaginal intercourse for men aged 60 to 64 is 22; for women it is 23.

- For men and women under 25, the median age of first intercourse is 17.

THIS section examines the pattern of decrease in age of first vaginal intercourse across age cohorts in the Irish population. Estimating the age across a population is complicated by the fact that some respondents will not yet have had sex; there is thus no age of first sex that can be used in the calculation. The proportion who have had sex increases with age, so a simple average or median will be particularly biased for younger age groups. To allow for this we use the Kaplan Meier estimator, which takes into account the fact that some respondents may not yet have had sex, to estimate the mean and median age of first vaginal intercourse.

Figure 6.1 gives the median age of first vaginal intercourse by the current age of the individual. This is listed again in *Table 6.1* alongside figures for the mean age as well as the proportion who have had vaginal sex in each age group. These statistics shed light on different aspects of the age of first sex.

The *mean age of first sex* represents most people's notion of the 'average' age, but this can be unduly influenced by extreme values (for instance, when a small number of individuals have sex very early). The *median*, however, is not influenced by these values, as it is the age at which 50% or more of the age group has had vaginal sex. *Table 6.1* shows that the median and mean ages of first sex are actually reasonably close in most age groups, but a gap appears in older age groups due to the larger number of individuals with very high ages at first intercourse.

Figure 6.1 gives the median age. It shows a clear pattern of decreasing age at first vaginal intercourse across age groups for both men and women:

- Whereas 50% of men currently aged 60 to 64 had their first vaginal sex when 22 or younger, 50% of men under 25 in 2004/5 had done so by the age of 17, a decrease of five years.

As we move from those born between 1940 and 1944, there is a steadily decreasing average and median age of first sex for both men and women.

Figure 6.1 also shows that, in each age group except the youngest and that of those aged 30-34, on average men have their first experience of vaginal sex before women.

Figure 6.1: Median age of first vaginal sex: by gender and age group

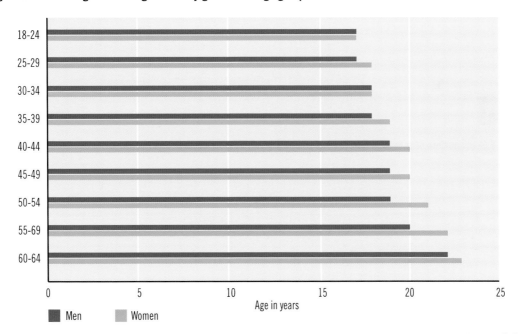

People born between 1960 and 1964 (aged 40-44 in 2004/5) were likely to have had vaginal sex a full three years earlier than the oldest age group. The age falls another year for those born after 1970, and another again for those born after 1980.

The median for men aged between 18 and 24 in Ireland is the same as that for men between 20 and 24 in the British sample gathered as part of the NATSAL 2000 survey. However, Irish men over 29 and women over 24 are more likely than their British counterparts to have had sex at a slightly older age. This suggests that age of first sex for Irish people has been converging with that of the British population over the last two decades and has largely done so now.

Table 6.1: Median and mean age of first vaginal intercourse: by gender and five-year age group

	Men				Women			
	% Had vaginal sex	Median	Mean	N	% Had vaginal sex	Median	Mean	N
18-24	84.3	17	16.9	759	81.8	17	17.4	908
25-29	95.0	17	17.7	454	94.7	18	18.1	587
30-34	95.4	18	18.2	247	97.9	18	18.9	357
35-39	97.2	18	18.8	300	97.8	19	19.8	573
40-44	98.3	19	19.6	347	97.7	20	20.6	441
45-49	94.6	19	19.6	309	97.9	20	20.7	389
50-54	95.1	19	20.2	265	98.5	21	21.7	366
55-59	95.3	20	21.5	302	94.7	22	22.1	368
60-64	90.0	22	23.0	205	95.6	23	23.1	242

Concerning the proportion that have had vaginal sex in each age group, that among men reaches its peak in age group 40-44 whereas that among women does so among those aged 50 to 54. Interestingly, the proportion decreases among those in older age groups, a pattern that reflects the high rate of non-marriage among Irish people in previous decades. In most other countries of Western Europe, a similar table would show increasing proportions by age of people who have had sex (see chapter seven).

Mean and median ages of first sex do not show the full picture of how age of first sex has changed over recent decades. These are much more easily grasped using *survivor curves* (as first seen in chapter five). Here, these show the proportion of each age group who have had sex by a given age.

Figure 6.2: Proportion of men who had vaginal sex by a given age: by current age group

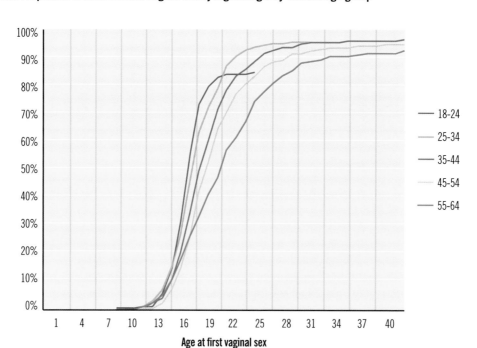

The steeper the survivor curve and the higher the line reaches, the earlier sex occurred and the greater the proportion of the age cohort who have experienced it. *Figure 6.2* shows (as suspected from *Table 6.1*) that the line for the youngest age group of men (this time using 10-year age groups) rises most steeply, while the lines for each older age group take a steadily shallower path. There is a particularly large difference in patterns between the oldest age group of men and all others. It is also notable that:

• whereas only 33% of the oldest age group had had sex by the age of 20, this was true of 86% of men aged under 25 (at the time of the ISSHR survey).

This difference can be seen in *Figure 6.1* in the large proportion of the curve which occurs after age 20 for the oldest age group.

Figure 6.3 shows that the pattern for women is very similar to that found for men. The lines for older age cohorts (using 10-year age groups) rise less steeply and, in the case of the oldest group, plateau at a lower age than for younger cohorts (indicating that a lower proportion had actually had sex – see chapter seven).

Figure 6.3: Proportion of women who had vaginal sex by a given age: by current age group

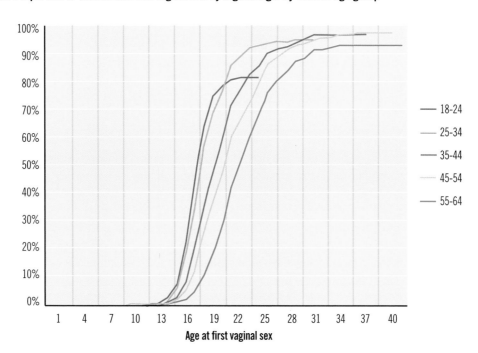

6.3   First vaginal intercourse before age 17

SUMMARY

THE steady decline in age of first vaginal sex during recent decades means that the proportion reporting vaginal sex before age 17 is significantly higher among younger individuals than among older people.

Early vaginal sex is associated with lower levels of educational achievement and being in the manual working class, although the latter only for men.

Age of menarche (onset of menstruation) has been falling among women across generations. This may contribute to the earlier experience of vaginal sex among young women.

■ 21% of men and 12% of women first experienced vaginal intercourse before they were 17.

■ The proportion experiencing first vaginal sex before 17 has increased across age cohorts, from 11% of men and 2% of women currently aged 60 to 64 to 31% of men and 22% of women aged 18 to 24.

■ People with lower levels of education are more likely to experience vaginal sex before 17. The differential is larger for men than women: 29% of men with lower secondary education report vaginal sex before 17, compared to 16% of men with third-level education. The proportions for women are 14% and 9%.

■ Manual and particularly unskilled-manual social class is associated with earlier vaginal sex.

■ 18% of women who experienced their first period before age 13 reported vaginal sex before 17, compared to 9% of women whose periods began after age 13.

THE decreasing age of first intercourse among both men and women in Ireland raises the issue of whether a substantial and increasing proportion of young people may be having sexual intercourse below the legal age of consent. (For a description of the law on the age of consent in the Republic of Ireland, see section 1.5.)

Figure 6.4 gives the proportions of Irish men and women who have had vaginal sex before age 17. It shows that men are more likely than women to report this: 21% compared to 12%. The prevailing pattern tends to be that men have relationships with younger women; thus it is likely that most men who have had sex below the age of 17 did so with a female partner under 17 (see ISSHR Sub-Report 1: 'Learning About Sex and First Sexual Experiences').

Figure 6.4: Proportions having sex before age 17: by gender

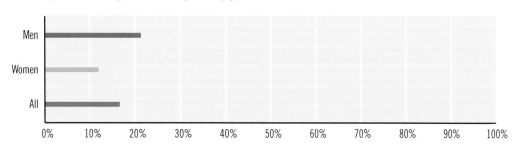

The difference by gender is an average across age groups. *Figure 6.5* shows a clear increase in the proportions having vaginal sex before 17 in younger age groups, for both men and women. The probability of men under 25 having first vaginal intercourse under age 17 is three times that of men aged over 54 and significantly higher even than for men aged 25 to 34. The rate among men has almost tripled between those born before 1950 and those born after 1980. The rate for the latter group is 50% higher than that for men born before 1970.

The rate of change has been even greater among women. Rates of sex before 17 are extremely low in women born before 1950 (2.2%), but 22% of women born after 1980 have had vaginal sex before age 17.

Figure 6.5: Proportion having sex before age 17: by gender and age group

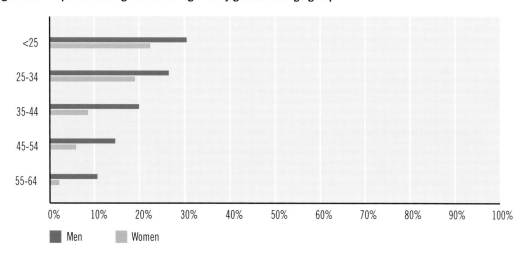

Lower levels of education are significantly associated with a greater probability of vaginal sex under age 17, as can be seen in *Figure 6.6*. However, the rate is higher for both men and women with a lower secondary (Intermediate Certificate) qualification than it is for those with primary education alone. This pattern is due to the fact that those with primary education alone are likely to be older; as we have seen, older respondents are less likely to have had vaginal sex at a young age because of the sexual and moral climate of the time.

This difference in behaviours across educational groups seems paradoxical given the more conservative attitudes (noted in chapter four) among less educated groups, but it is a well-established finding across a number of surveys of sexual behaviour, particularly the NATSAL surveys carried out in Britain.[36]

Earlier vaginal sexual initiation is associated with a higher risk of negative outcomes such as early child-bearing and STIs. It has also been associated with more risky behaviours in later life.[2]

Figure 6.6: Proportion having vaginal sex before age 17: by gender and highest education

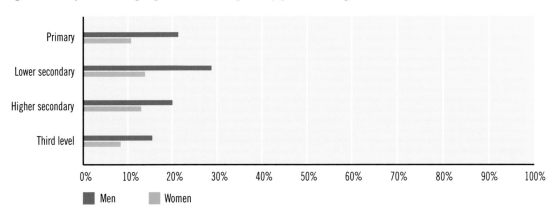

The proportion of people who have experienced vaginal sexual intercourse before age 17 is almost 100% higher among men with lower secondary qualifications than among men with a third-level qualification.

The socio-economic gradient in under-age vaginal sex is also prominent in analysis by social class among men. Rates among non-manual groups are lower than those among manual groups (see Appendix *Table 4.1*). The class differential is not so clear among women. Statistical tests show no significant differences by social class for women.

Age at menarche has been shown in other countries to be strongly associated with age of first vaginal sex[16] as it is associated with level of physical development which itself interacts with the development of interest and desire for sexual intercourse.

Table 6.2: Age of menarche: by 10-year age group

	<25	25-34	35-44	45-54	55-64	N
10 or less	2.1	2.7	3.3	2.8	1.4	94
11 or 12	40.4	35.6	33.3	29.1	27.7	1,438
13 or 14	44.2	46.8	47.7	48.7	47.2	2,012
15+	13.3	15.0	15.8	19.4	23.7	693
Total	100	100	100	100	100	4,237
Mean	12.9	13.0	13.0	13.2	13.5	

In Western countries, age at menarche has been steadily falling across the generations. The ISSHR data show that women in Ireland are no exception.

Table 6.2 shows that age at menarche has fallen steadily across generations of women in Ireland, from a mean of 13.5 among women aged over 55 in 2004/5 to a mean of 12.9 among those aged under 25 (born after 1980). Whereas less than a third of women in the oldest age group had their first period before age 13, this is true of over two-fifths of women aged under 25.

Appendix *Table 4.1* shows that age of menarche is strongly associated with age of first vaginal intercourse: women who had first menarche before 13 are more than twice as likely to have early vaginal sex as women whose first period was at age 13 or higher.

The ISSHR Sub-Report 1: 'Learning About Sex and First Sexual Experiences' shows that current level of religiosity is also strongly related to age of first sex. People with weaker religious beliefs are far more likely to have first vaginal sex before 17. This pattern has been found in research in other countries,[7][8] although these studies examined religious practice (ie, attendance) rather than level of belief.

ISSHR Sub-Report 1 also shows that certain contextual factors are associated with vaginal sex before age 17. First, early vaginal sexual initiation is more likely to occur with a 'casual' partner (no prior personal relationship). Secondly, vaginal sex before 17 is associated with less stability in the relationship; the relationship is significantly less likely to continue into the future if sex occurs before 17.

6.4   Use of contraception at first intercourse

SUMMARY

THIS section examines the factors associated with use and non-use of contraception at first vaginal sex.

A higher proportion of women than men report using contraception at first intercourse.

Use of contraception at first intercourse has increased across time: younger respondents are more likely to report use than older respondents.

The proportion using contraception at first intercourse has increased from around 40% among those currently aged 55 to 64 to over 90% among those aged 18 to 24. This increase in use is largely due to the greater availability of contraception in recent decades, but may also be associated with a rising average level of sexual knowledge among younger Irish people through time.

Higher levels of use are associated with higher level of education and being in a non-manual social class.

Younger age at first sex (under 17) is associated with a lower likelihood of using contraception, among both men and women.

Analyses suggest that having received sex education on contraception and being able to talk to parents about sexual matters increase the probability of using contraception at first intercourse.

- 67% of men and 74% of women report using contraception at first intercourse.

- Use of contraception at first intercourse has risen steadily across age cohorts: from 39% of men and 40% of women currently aged 55 to 64, to 88% of men and 94% of women aged 18 to 24.

- 79% of men and 86% of women with third-level education report using contraception at first intercourse, compared to 43% and 42% of men and women with primary education alone.

- 69% of men whose first vaginal intercourse occurred after age 17 report using contraception, compared to 58% of those who had sex before 17.

THE ISSHR survey included a range of questions about first experience of vaginal intercourse, including about use of contraception. Contraception in this instance includes withdrawal and use of emergency contraception (this was explained to respondents).

A small number of participants (37) reported that their first experience of intercourse was of anal sex. This group were excluded from all analyses relating to contraceptive use since they may differ from those reporting that their first intercourse was vaginal, particularly in their contraceptive decisions.

The analyses here also distinguish those who risked an unintended pregnancy at first sexual intercourse from those who were intending to conceive. Individuals who reported wanting to conceive, being post-menopausal or being infertile at the time of first sex are thus excluded from the analyses.

6.4.1   Current age

BOTH researchers and policy-makers are interested in the factors leading to conception among women under 20. For that reason, a great deal of research has examined the factors associated with use of contraception at first sexual intercourse.

One of the primary findings is that use of contraception has become more frequent across generations: younger cohorts are much more likely to take precautions. This pattern has been seen in national surveys worldwide,[9][10][1] including by the British NATSAL study, which reported increasing contraceptive use at first intercourse among younger age groups.[11] This pattern of increasing contraceptive use was also identified in the Australian ASHR study: contraceptive use rose steadily from 17% of men and 35% of women who experienced first intercourse in the 1950s to 90% of men and 95% of women first having intercourse in the 2000s.[12] Svare *et al* (2002)[10] also reported an increase in contraceptive use with later year of first intercourse among Danish women aged 20-29.

6.4.2   Highest education level attained

RESEARCH has established that lower levels of educational attainment and aspiration are associated with lower likelihood of having used contraception at first intercourse[13] and during intercourse generally.[14]

The relationship between educational level and age and using a contraceptive at first intercourse is complex. Recent research has found that many teenagers have a positive or ambivalent attitude towards pregnancy[15][16][17][18] and that considerable numbers of pregnant teenagers report having intended or wanted to become pregnant.[17][19] Among pregnant teenagers who had not used contraception at the time of conception, those who had dropped out of school were more likely to have an ambivalent or positive attitude towards pregnancy.[17] Additionally, many studies have found that teenage mothers are more likely to have low educational attainment or aspirations.[14][11][20][21][4][22][23][24][25]

This relationship was previously assumed to indicate that teenage pregnancy itself reduced educational and career opportunities; however, recent interpretations conclude that teenagers with low educational attainment often view pregnancy more positively, since it offers them a social identity as a parent where the possibility of other social roles may be limited. This is further supported by research reporting that young people who felt most strongly about avoiding pregnancy and had other life ambitions (eg, educational or career aspirations, or travel) used contraception.[26][27]

6.4.3 Relationship status

RELATIONSHIP status may influence sexual behaviour and contraceptive use in a number of ways. Some research indicates that people in a casual relationship, or not in a relationship with their first sexual partner, are less likely than those in a steady relationship to use contraception at first intercourse.[28] [29] A US study of women's retrospective reports of first intercourse, Manning *et al* (2000),[29] found that 52% of those whose first intercourse was with someone they had just met had not used contraception, compared to 24-25% of those whose first intercourse occurred within a steady relationship.

Alternatively, the effect of relationship status on contraceptive use during first intercourse has been investigated in terms of the partner's ability to communicate about contraception. Research has found that young people were more likely to use contraception at first sexual intercourse if partners had discussed contraception prior to first intercourse,[30] [31] if their relationship lasted longer than one month, and if intercourse was planned.[30] They were also more likely to use contraception throughout their first sexual relationship if they had discussed contraception prior to first sex, or if they had delayed first sex with a partner for a longer time after the start of the relationship.[32]

Stone and Ingham 2002[31] found that male students aged 16-18 were more likely to have used contraception at first sexual intercourse if they had discussed contraception prior to sex, if they gave an intimate reason for having sex on that occasion, and if their parents portrayed sexuality positively. Contraceptive use at first intercourse among women aged 16-18 was predicted by: age at first intercourse, having discussed contraception prior to sex, being comfortable interacting with males of their age, and having planned sex. Factors that increased the likelihood among men of having discussed contraception were: lower levels of social deprivation, longer relationship length, and greater openness of parents in talking about sex. For women, factors were: giving a greater number of intimate reasons for having sex and greater parental warmth and availability.

6.4.4 Age at first intercourse

EARLIER age at first intercourse has also been associated in a number of studies[14] [31] [28] [10] with lower likelihood of using contraception at first intercourse. Other studies have related non-use of contraception at first intercourse to continuing risk behaviours and negative outcomes. In their study of Danish women aged 20-29, Svare *et al* 2002[10] noted that not using contraception at first intercourse was significantly related to increased likelihood of: never using condoms, subsequent experience of abortion, and having over 20 sexual partners. Conversely, condom use at first intercourse by adolescents has been related to increased likelihood of subsequent condom use.[33]

6.4.5 Parent-child communication

RESEARCH has linked parent-child communication about sex with increased contraceptive use by adolescents and young people.[34] [31] [35] Other research has found that mother-daughter communication about sex increases the likelihood of contraceptive use in adolescents and reduces the likelihood of teenage pregnancy.[55] Similarly, Wellings (1999)[36] found that women who found it easier to communicate about sex with their parents were less likely to be teenage mothers. Other studies have suggested that it is also important to consider what has actually been communicated[35] and that parent's attitudes and values may be important determinants of adolescent sexual behaviour.[37]

A few studies have looked at parent-child communication in relation to contraceptive use at first sexual intercourse. Wellings *et al* (2001)[11] found that young men were more likely to report having used contraception at first intercourse if they had discussed sexual matters with parents. Stone and Ingham (2002)[31] found that students aged 16-18 were more likely to have used contraception at first sexual intercourse if they had discussed contraception prior to sex, and that male students were more likely to do so if their parents portrayed sexuality positively. Furthermore, the likelihood of having discussed contraception prior to sex was greater among boys reporting greater openness of parents in talking about sex. Girls who reported greater warmth and availability of parents were more likely to have discussed contraception prior to first intercourse. The authors suggest that family communication and openness in discussing sexual matters is an important influence on young people's contraceptive behaviour at first intercourse.

6.4.6   Results from the ISSHR survey

Figure 6.7 shows that 70% of individuals who had experienced vaginal sex reported using contraception at first vaginal intercourse; women were more likely to report use than men (74% v 67%).

Figure 6.8 shows that contraceptive use at first vaginal intercourse has increased steadily across age cohorts, from 39% of men and 40% of women currently aged 55-64 to 88% of men and 94% of women aged 18-24. These significant patterns suggest a pronounced change in behaviour across time, although much of this may be due to contraception having become increasingly available in the Republic of Ireland in recent decades. The proportion of young people receiving sex education over this period has also steadily increased (see chapter three). The increase in use of contraception may be due to a combination of both improved availability of contraceptives and increased sexual knowledge and preparedness among young people.

Figure 6.7: Proportion using contraception at first vaginal intercourse: by gender

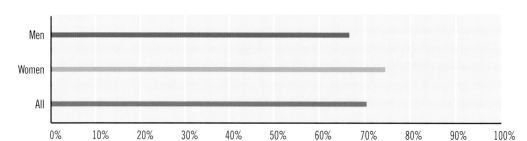

Figure 6.8: Proportion using contraception at first vaginal intercourse: by gender and age group

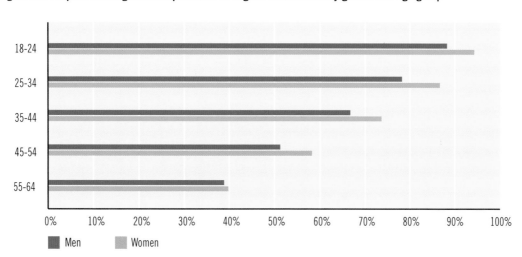

Figure 6.9 shows that contraceptive use at first intercourse is positively associated with highest educational qualification for both men and women:

- Only 43% of men and 42% of women with primary education alone reported using contraception at first intercourse, but this is true of 79% of men and 86% of women with a third-level qualification.

Analyses have shown that people with higher levels of education were more likely to have also received sex education, to have received it both at home and in school, and to have parents that they found it easier to talk to about sex (see chapter four).

Figure 6.9: Proportion using contraception at first vaginal intercourse: by gender and highest education

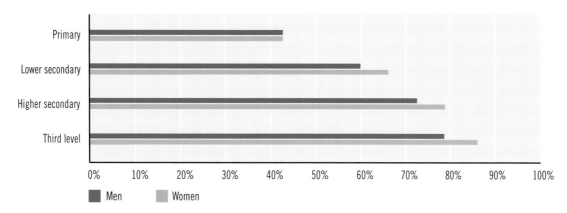

These factors may have influenced their decision-making and preparedness concerning use of contraception at first vaginal intercourse. (We discuss in more depth shortly the influence of sex education and communication with parents.)

Figure 6.10 shows that the gradient in use of contraception that was found across levels of education is also seen across social-class groups, although only among men. Higher professional men are significantly more likely than semi-skilled or unskilled men to have used protection at first vaginal sex. There is a clear increase in use of contraception in the classes, between higher professional and unskilled manual.

The impact of education and social class underlines the importance of socio-economic factors in shaping risky sexual behaviours. Analyses earlier in this chapter showed that individuals with lower levels of education and/or of lower social class were far more likely to experience early sexual initiation. This risk is confounded here with a lower overall probability of using protection at first intercourse.

The lack of impact of social class among women may reflect the fact that the measure of social class used reflects that of the household if the person has no present or past occupation. This will be far more common among women, who are more likely to be out of the labour force, than among men, and may decrease the impact of social class among women.

Figure 6.10: Proportion using contraception at first vaginal intercourse: by gender and social class

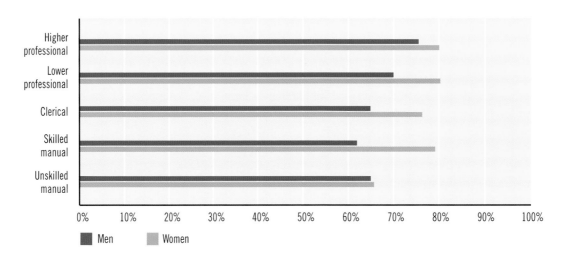

Age at first intercourse has been shown by previous research to be an important factor influencing use of contraception. Earlier sex is associated with lower likelihood of using contraception. This pattern was also found in analyses of the ISSHR data. *Figure 6.11* shows that, across all age groups, men and women who had vaginal sex before age 17 were less likely to have used contraception.

Figure 6.11: Proportion using contraception at first vaginal intercourse by age group and whether sex occurred before the age of 17

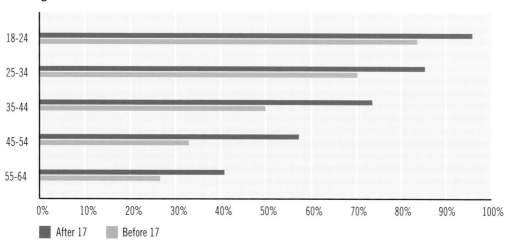

For example, among individuals aged 55 to 64, 26% of those whose first vaginal sex was before age 17 used contraception, compared to 41% whose first experience came after their 17th birthday. Similarly, among those currently aged 18 to 24, 83% of those whose first experience was before 17 used contraception, compared to 95% of those having vaginal sex for the first time at a later age. The impact of age of first sex is important for both men and women, except among women aged 55-64 (among them, there is no clear difference in use of contraception at first intercourse before or after 17).

The other ISSHR reports provide important insights into the complex processes around use of contraception at first intercourse. ISSHR Sub-Report 1: 'Learning About Sex and First Sexual Experiences' shows, for example, that certain contextual factors are important. A person who was not already in a relationship with their first partner, before sex occurred for the first time, is significantly less likely to have used contraception. Non-use is also associated with sex occurring 'on the spur of the moment' or when either or both of the partners have been drinking alcohol or taking drugs. (For more evidence on these issues, see next section).

Sub-Report 1 also sheds light on the relationship between sex education and use of contraception at first intercourse. Cross-nationally, research shows that sex-education programmes can increase rates of contraceptive usage. This is also found in the ISSHR data: men who received sex education on contraception are almost 60% more likely and women 70% more likely to use contraception at first intercourse.

Sub-Report 1 shows that communication with parents, too, is a crucial factor. Men who said it was easy to communicate with their father about sex were significantly more likely to have used contraception, whereas easy communication with their mother had no association with behaviour. For women, the relationship was reversed. Women who reported that it was easy to communicate with their mother were significantly more likely to use contraception at first intercourse, but easy communication with their father had no association.

For more detail on the analyses in this section, see Appendix *Table 4.2*.

6.5   Reasons for not using contraception

SUMMARY

THIS section examines the reasons people gave for not using contraception at first intercourse.

The most cited reason is that contraception was not available at the time. This is unsurprising, since controls on the distribution of contraception were not withdrawn until the early 1990s. Younger age groups are significantly less likely to cite this as a reason for non-use.

Both men and women cite a lack of planning for sex on the first occasion as the next most frequent reason, followed by a lack of understanding of the risks.

Women with lower levels of education are more likely than other women to cite a lack of understanding of the risks as a reason for non-use.

- Of all participants who had not used contraception at first intercourse (but were not trying to become pregnant/infertile), 31% of men and 24% of women reported that this was because none was available.

- The proportion reporting non-availability as a reason fell from 42% of men aged 45-64 to 10% of men under 30. Among women the proportion dropped from 33% to 8%.

- Around 60% of men and women under 30 cite lack of planning, forethought or understanding of risks as the main reasons why contraception was not used at first vaginal intercourse.

- Alcohol or drug use was cited as a reason by around 3% of respondents overall – but by around 12% of respondents under 30.

THE previous section showed that a number of factors influenced the use of contraception at first intercourse, including educational attainment, age of first intercourse, relationship status and level of communication with parents. These 'objective' factors explain a good deal of the variation in use of contraception, but the ISSHR survey also asked respondents why they did not use contraception so that we could understand their subjective interpretations.

Since many respondents will be recalling events from years or decades earlier, such reports should be handled with care, but it is instructive to examine the reasons given. All responses to this question (including those not covered by the questionnaire) were recorded so that a full account could be attained. As before, individuals who reported that they did not use contraception because they were trying to become pregnant or were infertile have been excluded from the analysis.

There has been considerable research on why individuals do not use contraception and specifically on why they do not do so at first intercourse. A qualitative study of pregnant Irish teenagers[38] found that spontaneity of sex was one of the main reasons given for low levels of contraceptive use. In the same vein, a recent nationally representative study of contraceptive use among the adult Irish population[39] found that the most common reasons for non-use (though not at first intercourse) were that sex was unplanned and that alcohol or drugs had been used.

These reasons for non-use were particularly common among those aged 18-25; among them, 58% of non-users of contraception over the previous year reported that non-use was due to sex having been unplanned, while 33% cited use of alcohol or drugs.

Since these reasons are so prevalent among this age group in particular, it is necessary to determine whether these issues also play a part in non-use of contraception at first intercourse among the Irish population.

6.5.1   Attitudes towards contraception

ATTITUDES to contraception have also been investigated as major determinants of contraceptive use. Research has shown that a negative attitude to condoms among adolescents, particularly among young men who believe that they reduce sexual pleasure, can lead to less use of condoms.[40 41 42] Other studies have identified a moral/judgemental perspective as a factor; for example, some have found that a small number of adolescents believe that contraception is morally wrong,[40] and that carrying or using contraception gives a message that a person is promiscuous or looking for sex, particularly in the case of women carrying condoms.[40 43 44]

6.5.2   Accessing contraceptive services

EASE of access to contraception is likely to be very important in determining contraceptive behaviour, particularly in retrospective reports from older Irish people who began having sex during a period when contraception was not generally available. However, even for those who have recently had sex for the first time, access can be a problem.

Irish research into levels of access to and experiences of contraceptive services is limited. Current information for service planning is based mainly on small studies and international research. The Irish Family Planning Association[45] has suggested that young Irish people may be reluctant to use their family doctor for contraceptive services due to embarrassment. A number of studies have highlighted issues seen by adolescents as preventing them from availing of contraceptive services. For example, Dempsey et al (2000)[38] noted that pregnant Irish teenagers listed as barriers to obtaining or using contraception: cost of contraception, relationship with GP, locality and fear of being seen buying contraception, tendency to procrastinate, feeling embarrassed and denial of the possibility of their fertility.

Concerning barriers to consultation with a GP regarding contraception, many adolescents have reported concerns about confidentiality and the possibility that their parents could be informed of their discussions with the doctor.[38 46 43 47] Confidentiality and anonymity in accessing services and in behaviour generally may be of particular concern to people living in rural areas where anonymity is unlikely. The report 'Young people's self-identified health needs' suggests that a rural environment can restrict adolescent behaviour and experimentation.[48] Simply being seen visiting a GP (perhaps more likely in rural areas) may lead to teenagers having to explain the visit to family members.[46] Similarly, Mason (2003)[49] reported that young people were worried about seeing friends or neighbours in waiting rooms, or when buying condoms in chemists, in small towns.

It has also been suggested that GPs may further block access by refusing to provide contraception because of their moral attitude to sex outside marriage or because of a client's age. Some Irish women, particularly adolescents, have reported avoiding GP visits because they feared disapproval.[43]

Additionally, 21% of GPs in a small-scale Irish study[49] reported personal objections to at least one contraceptive method: the methods most commonly objected to were emergency contraception, IUCDs and Mirenas.

Mason (2003)[49] also reported that, while 64% of GPs contacted would provide general advice and prescribe to under-16s, 18% would prescribe only if a parent was present and 16% would give advice but not prescribe to under-16s.

Jacobson et al (2000)[50] investigated English 15-and-16-year-olds' health-related concerns and whether they had consulted a health professional about them. Nearly a quarter (23%) of the girls and 6% of boys were concerned about issues relating to pregnancy. While 25% had seen a GP and 30% had visited a clinic in relation to their pregnancy concerns, 34% had not spoken to anyone about them. The authors suggest that teenagers concerned about their health need greater encouragement to use health services.

Cost may also be a relevant factor. In the Republic of Ireland, only holders of medical cards can attend a GP and receive free contraception on prescription. The costs of visiting a doctor and of contraception itself can further limit access to contraception, particularly for young people on low incomes.[45] [43]

A Belgian qualitative study found that the costs of visiting a GP and of contraceptives were among the biggest obstacles to contraceptive access among 17-year-old girls.[51] In Ireland, the Irish Family Planning Association (2002)[45] recommended that young people should have free access to sexual and reproductive health services, in order to increase uptake of contraceptive services and to provide choice of services.

Hosie (2002),[52] in a review of sexual health policies throughout Europe, suggested a number of important issues relating to availability of sexual health services for young people. These include: convenient geographic locations with suitable opening times, services away from parental view, confidentiality, informal and user-friendly staff, an approachable demeanour and respectful attitude among professionals, using terms familiar to young people, and recognition of the needs of young men.

6.5.3 Results from the ISSHR survey

FIGURE 6.12 gives the proportions in the ISSHR survey, by age group, of men citing particular reasons for not using contraception at first vaginal intercourse. Three broader age groups are used in this section because the questions asked were answered by a subset of individuals and this smaller number cannot be disaggregated finely without introducing statistical problems. Individuals who said they had not used contraception because they were trying to conceive, or who were post-menopausal or infertile, were excluded from the analysis.

Figure 6.12: Men's reasons for not using contraception at first intercourse: by age group

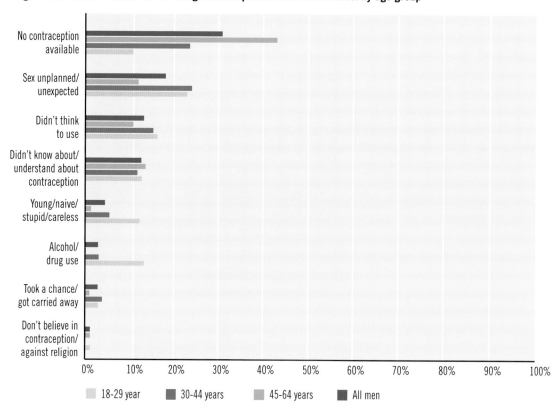

Fewer age groups are used here than in the report generally, because fewer individuals were available for analysis.

Figure 6.12 shows that, among all men, the most frequently stated reason for not using contraception at first intercourse is that no contraception was available, either because it was 'illegal' in the Republic of Ireland at the time or for some other reason. A far larger proportion of those aged over 44 cite this reason compared to other age groups. However, a significant 10% of under-30s would have been having sex for the first time in the 1980s when contraception became more widely available. This may indicate that other restrictions on availability (but not cost, embarrassment or fear, which were also given as reasons) may have played a role; these include non-compliant GPs and local unavailability.

After non-availability, the most frequently cited reason is that sex was unplanned/unexpected. This was suggested by over 17% of men (23% of men under 44). A total of 12% said they 'didn't think to use' contraception, while 12% cited a plain lack of knowledge (at the time) about the need for contraception.

These figures suggest that around 40% of men did not use contraception due to a lack of planning and forethought or lack of understanding. The figure rises to over 60% of men under 30 if we add in the group stating that they were 'young, naïve, stupid or careless'.

Interestingly, alcohol or drug use was mentioned by a small 3% of men overall, but almost 13% of those aged under 30. This suggests that alcohol and drug use is increasing in importance as an issue that promotion of safe first vaginal sex needs to tackle.

Figure 6.13: Women's reasons for not using contraception at first intercourse: by age group

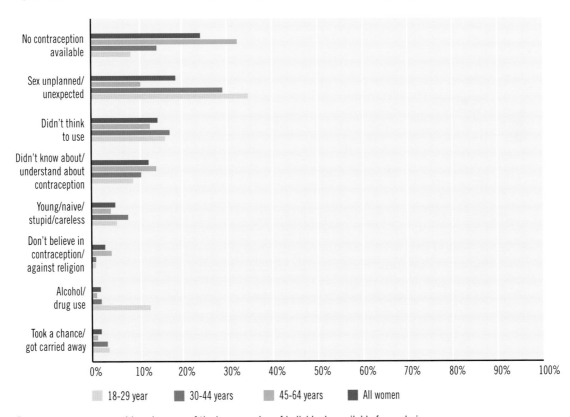

Fewer age groups are used here because of the lower number of individuals available for analysis.

Figure 6.13 shows a similar general pattern among women. The same four reasons dominate, although there are some differences in the distribution of reasons across age groups.

Overall, slightly more women than men said they had not used contraception because of a lack of planning, but this was volunteered by a striking 35% of under-30s and 29% of those under 44. Aside from this, the patterns across women are the same as for men, including the significant role of alcohol and drugs for the youngest age group.

Figure 6.14: Men's reasons for not using contraception at first intercourse: by highest education

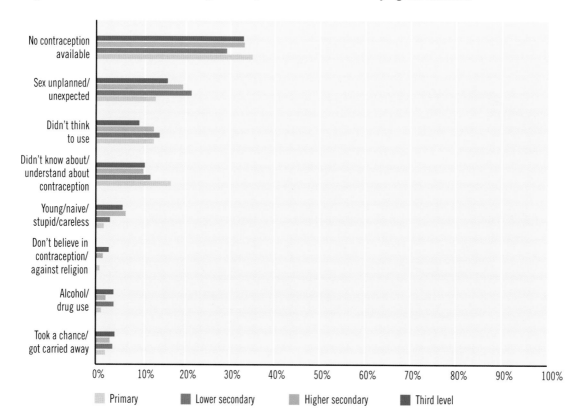

Figure 6.14 shows that the differences across educational groups among men who cited unavailability as an issue in non-use are relatively small. Men with lower secondary qualifications are somewhat less likely to offer this reason, but the difference between groups is not significant statistically. This could be because the restrictions on contraception were national and applied to all groups relatively equally.

Figure 6.15 gives some differences across educational groups for women, although few are statistically significant. One exception is the difference between women with lower secondary education or less and other women:

- 18% of women with primary education alone who did not use contraception cite not knowing about it or the risks of not using it.
- Only 6% of those with third-level qualifications who did not use contraception cite not knowing about contraception or the risks of not using it.

Another exception is that women with lower levels of education are more likely than women with third-level qualifications to state that alcohol or drugs had a role in non-use.

Figure 6.15: Women's reasons for not using contraception at first intercourse: by highest education

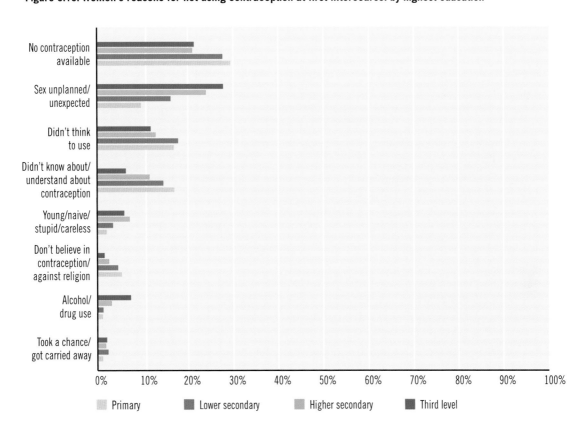

6.6 Planning, willingness and regret

SUMMARY

THIS section shows that most men (64%) and almost half of women (48%) who have had vaginal sex state that neither they nor their partner planned the first occasion.

There is some evidence of greater planning among the oldest group of women, but no overall trend across age groups. This suggests little change in patterns across time.

Most people report that they willingly had sex on the first occasion, although women are more likely than men to report that their partner was more willing than they were.

The level of willingness among women is significantly related to their age at first event; younger age is associated with lower levels of equal willingness.

Most men cite being curious as the main reason for sex occurring at the time it did, followed by it being 'about the right time'. Women are more likely to report first that it was 'about the right time'. The second most common reason given by women is that sex was a natural follow-on in the relationship.

Younger individuals are more likely to cite curiosity and peer behaviour as chief reasons. Older respondents are more likely to say they were in love, that it was a natural follow-on, or that they were carried away by their feelings.

Most men and women say sex occurred at around the right time, but women are more likely to express regret, as are younger respondents. Younger age at first sex is associated with a higher probability of later regret.

- 92% of men and 86% of women report that they and their partner were equally willing at first intercourse. The unwilling partner is more likely to be female.

- Women who first had vaginal sex at a young age are far more likely to report that they were less willing than their partners.

- Older age groups are more likely to cite 'love' and 'being carried away by feelings' as reasons for first intercourse. Younger respondents are more likely to cite being 'curious', that 'most people the same age seemed to be doing it' or a desire to lose virginity.

- Men under 35 are 50% more likely than men over 54 to say they 'should have waited longer' before first having sex. Women under 25 are 2.4 times more likely than women over 54 to express regret.

THE previous sections provide indirect evidence that lack of planning at first vaginal intercourse often affects use of contraception.

The ISSHR survey included questions on the extent of planning and on why sex occurred at the time it did. These questions were taken from the NATSAL survey (1990) which in turn took them from the Schofield survey (1965).[53]

As with the questions on why contraception may not have been used, these questions assume that respondents have good recall of past events and that they are not reconstructing their state of mind in the light of their current beliefs, attitudes and emotions. This caveat may be particularly important in the case of questions on the extent to which the respondent entered into sex willingly.

We also examine whether or not respondents later regretted having first intercourse at the time they did.

6.6.1   Planning

FIGURE 6.16 shows, by sex and age group, the extent of planning for first vaginal intercourse. Around two-thirds of men across all age groups said neither they nor their partner planned their first vaginal experience, or that it happened on the spur of the moment.

Figure 6.16: Level of planning: by gender and age group

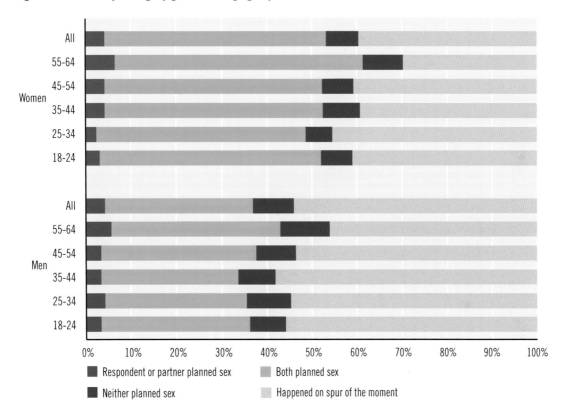

Around 50% of women report lack of planning, although there is evidence of significantly greater planning among women in the oldest age group.

These findings support the picture presented in the last section of low levels of planning, but also suggest that the age trend we detected there may overestimate the extent of planning in older age groups.

6.6.2 Willingness

FIGURE 6.17 shows that the vast majority of respondents felt that both partners were equally willing at their first vaginal sex:

• around 92% of men and 86% of women agree that both partners were equally willing.

There seems to be no age trend across any of the categories of willingness for either men or women. Among respondents who report that both were not equally willing, it was more often the male partner who was more anxious to have sex:

• around 13% of women said their partner was more willing, but only 4% of men.

Figure 6.17: Level of willingness: by gender and age group

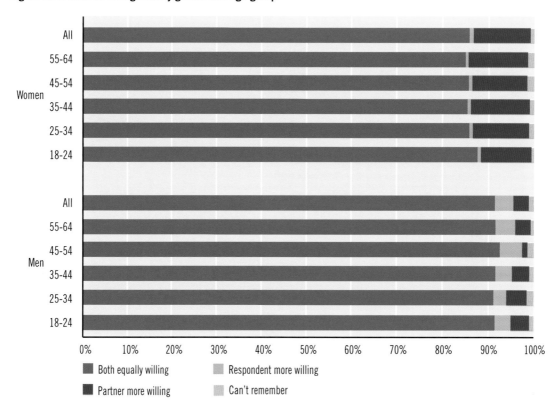

Further analyses in ISSHR Sub-Report 1 show that a woman's age at first intercourse is strongly related to the partners being equally willing. The proportion reporting equal willingness rises from:

• 62.8% among women who had sex before age 15
• to 85% among women who had sex aged 15 or 16
• to 89.1% among those who had sex aged 17 to 20
• to 90% among those who had sex after age 20
  (for the population aged less than 30)

This result is consistent with international findings that lower age at first intercourse is associated with a lower likelihood of equal willingness.[11 54]

6.6.3   Contextual factors

THE ISSHR survey listed eight statements about why first vaginal intercourse occurred at the time it did. Respondents were asked which statement(s) applied. These statements are listed in *Figure 6.18*.
       Figure 6.18 shows that:
*   Men cited being 'curious' about sex most frequently (92%), followed by feeling that it was 'the right time' (86%) and sex being 'a natural follow-on in the relationship' (85%).
*   Women cited 'the right time' most frequently (92%), followed by 'a natural follow-on in the relationship' (90%).

Figure 6.18: Agreement with contextual statements relating to first vaginal intercourse: by gender

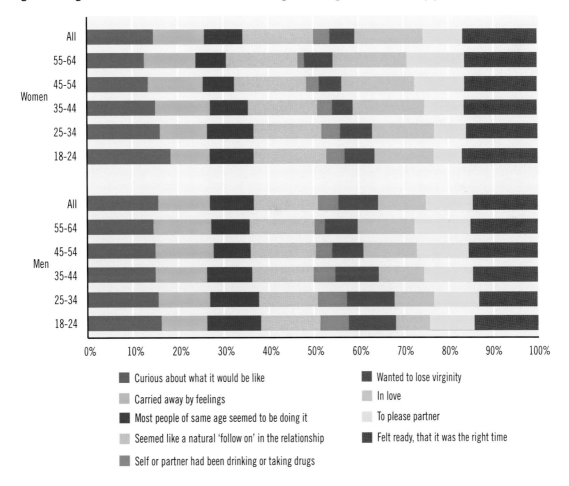

A similar pattern emerged in the 1990 NATSAL survey.[2] Men were most likely to state that being 'curious' was the prime factor followed by 'a natural follow-on'. Among women in the British survey, 'being in love' was the most cited reason, followed by 'a natural follow-on'.

In the ISSHR survey, older men and women were significantly less likely than younger people to cite 'curiosity', or say they had sex because 'most people the same age seemed to be doing it' or they wanted to lose their virginity. They were more likely to cite being 'carried away by feelings', 'a natural follow-on' or being 'in love'. In essence, older age groups were far more likely to cite classically 'romantic' notions about why they first had sex. Younger people were more likely to give more pragmatic reasons.

Figure 6.18 shows a very significant age trend in the proportions reporting use of alcohol or drugs at first sex: men under 35 are almost three times more likely to report this than men over 55; women under 35 are almost four times more likely to do so than the oldest age group. (Note the similar age trend in the previous section concerning non-use of contraception.)

Significantly, however, younger age groups are significantly less likely to report having sex 'to please partner', a trend that is particularly pronounced among women. Whereas 80% of women in the oldest age group cited 'to please partner', this was true of around a third of women under 25. The age trend between these two age groups is steep. This suggests an increasing confidence among younger women in their ability to assert themselves and their wishes at the time of first vaginal sex.

6.6.4   Regret

FIGURE 6.19 shows that the first experience of vaginal sex of most men (80%) and women (78%) occurred at 'about the right time'. However, women are more likely to say they 'should have waited longer' (19% of women v 14% of men) and less likely to say they 'should not have waited so long' (3% of women v 6% of men).

Figure 6.19: Level of regret: by gender and age group

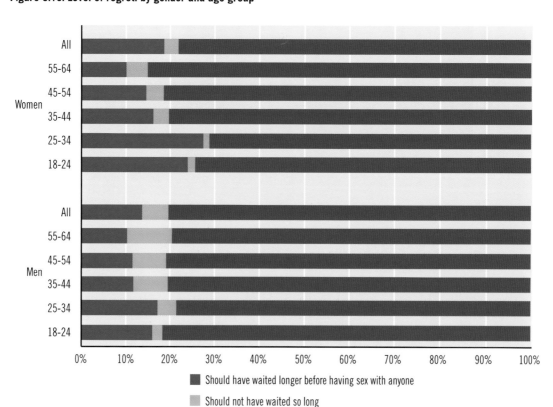

These are averages across age groups, however. There is a clear age trend among both men and women. Younger age groups are significantly more likely to say they 'should have waited longer'. Men under 35 are over 50% more likely to report this than men over 55. The difference is even more pronounced among young women: under-25s are 2.4 times more likely and those between 25 and 34 are 2.8 times more likely than women over 55 to say they 'should have waited longer'. Interestingly, both older men and older women are more likely to say they 'should not have waited so long'.

In an analysis of the population under 30, ISSHR Sub-Report 1 shows that men and women who had sex before 17 were considerably more likely to say they 'should have waited longer':

- Among men who had sex before 15, the proportion expressing regret at the timing is 47%, compared to just 11% of men who had sex after age 19.
- Among women the difference is even more pronounced: 78% of women who had sex before age 15 expressed regret, compared to 17% among women who had sex after age 19.

6.7   Summary

FIRST sexual intercourse remains a significant event, both for individuals and for researchers trying to understand the factors associated with first coitus and its implications for later experiences, health and well-being. In this chapter we have examined the patterning of first sex among Irish people, use of contraception at first sex and the degree of planning, willingness and regret.

As found in other countries, the ISSHR data reveal a steady decline in age for first vaginal sex:

- The median age of first vaginal sex for people born between 1940 and 1944 is 22 for men and 23 for women.
- For those born between 1955 and 1960, the age drops to 19 for men and 20 for women.
- For the youngest age group (born in the early 1980s), the age falls to 17 for both men and women.

The decreasing age of first sex means that increasing numbers of Irish people are having sex before the age of 17. Our results show that whereas just 2.2% of women aged over 54 report having sex before 17, this is true of 19% of those aged between 25 and 34 and 22% of those under 25.

Various factors are associated with early experience of vaginal sex. These include highest educational qualification; men and women with few qualifications are much more likely to begin having sex before 17:

- Men with less than higher secondary-level qualifications have over three times the probability of having had sex before 17, compared to men with third-level qualifications.
- For women this relationship is even stronger: women with primary education alone are over seven times as likely as those with third-level qualifications to have had sex before age 17.

A second factor is social class. Respondents in manual occupations are much more likely than those in non-manual occupations to have had vaginal sex before 17.

These differences by education and social class underline the importance of socio-economic factors in both risky behaviours and poor outcomes. Research suggests that earlier age of intercourse is strongly associated with lowered 'competence' at first intercourse, as evidenced by less willingness and planning and less use of contraception and protection. This results in a higher risk of poor outcomes such as early child-bearing and higher rates of STIs, which can have a long-lasting effect on health. There is also substantial evidence that lower age of first sex is associated with risky behaviours in later life.

Much policy research and development is aimed at increasing levels of contraceptive use at first vaginal intercourse. Although the ISSHR research shows that age of first intercourse is decreasing, it is clear that rates of use of contraception at first intercourse are increasing, suggesting better preparation for sex among younger Irish people:

• People under 25 are 11 times more likely to use contraception at first intercourse than were individuals aged over 54.

To a certain extent such comparisons are misleading, since contraception was not widely available until the recent period. The comparison of contraceptive use across age groups is also complicated by the fact that people who had sex for the first time before 1970 often did so after getting married and in the hope of having children. However, if we compare only age groups who would have had general access to condoms, we see significant increases in the use of protection in younger age groups. This welcome development should help to improve outcomes for younger respondents. However, around 10% of the youngest cohort report not using protection.

The pattern of socio-economic difference in rates of contraceptive use at first intercourse is also important. Although young people with fewer qualifications are more likely to first have sex before age 17, they are also less likely to use contraception. Being under 17 at first intercourse also has an independent association with the probability of using contraception. The fact that respondents who had sex at a younger age are more likely to be unprepared and less able to negotiate safer sex practices contributes to the lower use of protection, no matter what the level of education and social class.

Research in other countries has identified the role of sex education in increasing the use of contraception at first coitus. The results of the ISSHR project tend to support these findings. First, receiving sex education on contraception is positively associated with the use of contraception, among both men and women; it leads to around a 60% increase in use. Secondly, communication with parents about sex also seems to have a positive influence, and in an interesting way. Among young men, 'easy' communication with their father, but not with their mother, is associated with greater use of contraception at first sex. For young women, communication with their mother is important.

Respondents gave a variety of reasons for not using contraception at first intercourse. For older respondents, unavailability of contraception was the primary issue, followed by naivety about the need for contraception. For younger respondents, not being prepared for sex or sex being unplanned had a more important role. More worryingly, the youngest age group was also most likely to report that alcohol or drug use was a reason why precautions were not used.

Further evidence of many young people's lack of preparedness for first intercourse was gleaned from questions on the extent of planning. Older people reported more planning than did younger respondents. As well, the level of planning decreases with decreasing age of first intercourse.

The ISSHR survey also gathered data on other factors that influenced the timing of first sex. Responses revealed some interesting age patterns. Older age groups were far more likely to cite classically 'romantic' factors, such as 'it seemed like a natural follow-on' or being 'in love'. Younger people were much more likely to indicate they were simply curious to know what sex was like, or say that 'most people of same age seemed to be doing it' or that they wanted to lose their virginity.

Finally, the chapter examined the issue of regret after first intercourse and the patterns of regret across socio-demographic characteristics. The results found that, for the overwhelming majority of Irish people, first vaginal intercourse occurred at 'about the right time'. However, women were more likely to say they should have waited longer, as were younger age groups. Men under 35 were

50% more likely to report regret than men over 55. Among women the age differential is even larger: those under 25 were 2.4 times more likely than those aged over 54 to express regret.

6.8   Reference list

1   Wellings K, Nanchahal K, Macdowall W, McManus S, Erens B, Mercer C *et al.* 'Sexual behaviour in Britain: Early heterosexual experience'. *Lancet* 2001; 358:1843-1850.

2   Johnson A, Wadsworth J., Wellings K, Field J. *Sexual Attitudes and Lifestyles.* Oxford: Basil Blackwell, 1994.

3   Hayes CD. *Risking the Future: Adolescent Sexuality, Pregnancy and Child Bearing.* Washington DC: National Academy Press, 1987.

4   Wellings K, Wadsworth J, Johnson A, Field J, Macdowall W. 'Teenage Fertility and Life Chances'. *Reviews of Reproduction* 1999; 4(3):184-190.

5   Ryan F. ''Queering' the Criminal Law: Some Thoughts on the Aftermath of Homosexual Decriminalisation'. *Irish Criminal Law Journal* 1997; 7(1):38-45.

6   Bingham CR, Miller BC, Adams GR. 'Correlates of Age at First Sexual Intercourse in a National Sample of Young Women'. *Journal of Adolescent Research* 1990; 5(1):18-33.

7   Hardy SA, Raffaelli M. 'Adolescent religiosity and sexuality: an investigation of reciprocal influences'. *J Adolesc* 2003; 26(6):731-9.

8   Bozon M, Kontula O. 'Sexual Initiation and Gender in Europe. A Cross-Cultural Analysis of Trends in the 20th Century'. In: Hubert M, Sandfort T, editors. *Sexual Behaviour and HIV/ AIDS in Europe. A Comparison of National Surveys.* London: UCL Press, 1998.

9   Boyle FM, Dunne MP, Purdie DM, Najman JM, Cook MD. 'Early patterns of sexual activity: age cohort differences in Australia'. *International Journal of STD & AIDS* 2003; 14(11):745-52.

10   Svare EI, Kjaer SK, Thomsen BL, Bock JE. 'Determinants for non-use of contraception at first intercourse; a study of 10841 young Danish women from the general population'. *Contraception* 2002; 66(5):345-50.

11   Wellings K, Nanchahal K, Macdowall W, McManus S, Erens B, Mercer CH *et al.* 'Sexual behaviour in Britain: early heterosexual experience'. *Lancet* 2001; 358(9296):1843-50.

12   Rissel CE, Richters J, Grulich AE, de Visser RO, Smith AM. 'Sex in Australia: first experiences of vaginal intercourse and oral sex among a representative sample of adults'. *Australian and New Zealand Journal of Public Health* 2003; 27(2):131-7.

13   Singh S, Darroch JE, Frost JJ. 'Socioeconomic disadvantage and adolescent women's sexual and reproductive behavior: the case of five developed countries'. *Fam Plann Perspect* 2001; 33(6):251-8.

14   Kirby D. 'Antecedents of adolescent initiation of sex, contraceptive use, and pregnancy'. *Am J Health Behav* 2002; 26(6):473-85.

15   Jaccard J, Dodge T, Dittus P. 'Do adolescents want to avoid pregnancy? Attitudes toward pregnancy as predictors of pregnancy'. *J Adolesc Health* 2003; 33(2):79-83.

16   Condon JT, Donovan J, Corkindale CJ. 'Australian Adolescents' Attitudes and Beliefs Concerning Pregnancy, Childbirth and Parenthood'. *Journal of Adolescence* 2001; 24(6):729-742.

17   Stevens-Simon C, Kelly L, Singer D. 'Absence of negative attitudes toward childbearing among

pregnant teenagers. A risk factor for a rapid repeat pregnancy?' *Arch Pediatr Adolesc Med* 1996; 150(10):1037-43.

18   Zabin LS, Astone NM, Emerson MR. 'Do adolescents want babies? The relationship between attitudes and behavior'. *J Res Adolesc* 1993; 3(1):67-86.

19   Forrest JD, Singh S. 'The Sexual and Reproductive Behaviour of American Women 1982-1988'. *Family Planning Perspectives* 1990; 22(5):206-214.

20   Richardson V. *Young Mothers: A Study of Young Single Mothers in Two Communities.* Dublin: University College Dublin, 2000.

21   Frost JJ, Oslak S. *Teenagers' pregnancy intentions and decisions: A study of young women in California choosing to give birth.* New York: The Alan Guttmacher Institute, 1999.

22   Manlove J. 'The influence of high school dropout and school disengagement on the risk of school-age pregnancy'. *Journal of Research on Adolescence* 1998; 8(2):187-220.

23   Kiernan KE. 'Becoming a Young Parent: A Longitudinal Study of Associated Factors'. *British Journal of Sociology* 1997; 48(3):406-428.

24   Babb P. 'Teenage conceptions and fertility in England and Wales, 1971-1991'. *Population Trends* 1993; 74:12-7.

25   Adler NE. 'Contraception and Unwanted Pregnancy'. *Behavioral Medicine Update* 1984; 5(4):28-34.

26   Free C, Lee RM, Ogdan J. 'Young women's accounts of factors influencing their use and non-use of emergency contraception: an in-depth interview study'. *British Medical Journal* 2002; 325(7377):1393.

27   Kirby D. 'Effective approaches to reducing adolescent unprotected sex, pregnancy, and childbearing'. *J Sex Res* 2002; 39(1):51-7.

28   Schubotz D, Simpson A, Rolston B. *Towards Better Sexual Health: a survey of sexual attitudes and lifestyles of young people in Northern Ireland.* 2002. London, fpa.

29   Manning W, Longmore M, Giordano P. 'The relationship context of contraceptive use at first intercourse'. *Family Planning Perspectives* 2000; 32(3):104-110.

30   Henderson M, Wight D, Raab G, Abraham C, Buston K, Hart.G *et al.* 'Heterosexual Risk Behaviour Among Young Teenagers in Scotland'. Journal of Adolescence 2002; 25:483-494.

31   Stone N, Ingham R. 'Factors affecting British teenagers' contraceptive use at first intercourse: the importance of partner communication'. *Perspect Sex Reprod Health* 2002; 34(4):191-7.

32   Manlove J, Ryan S, Franzetta K. 'Patterns of contraceptive use within teenagers' first sexual relationships'. *Perspect Sex Reprod Health* 2003; 35(6):246-55.

33   Richard R, van der Pligt J, de Vries N. 'The influence of habits, self-efficacy and affective reactions on condom use among adolescents'. [Dutch]: 'De invloed van gewoontes, persoonlijke effectiviteit en gevoelsmatige reacties op condoomgebruik bij jongeren'. Gedrag & Gezondheid: *Tijdschrift voor Psychologie & Gezondheid* 1991; 19(2):65-76.

34   Stanton B, Li X, Pack R, Cottrell L, Harris C, Burns J. 'Longitudinal Influence of Perceptions of Peer and Parental Factors on African American Adolescent Risk Involvement'. *Journal of Urban Health* 2002; 79(4):536-548.

35   Whitaker DJ, Miller KS, May DC, Levin ML. 'Teenage partners' communication about sexual risk and condom use: the importance of parent-teenager discussions'. *Fam Plann Perspect* 1999; 31(3):117-21.

36   Wellings K, Wadsworth J, Johnson A, Field J, Macdowall W. 'Teenage fertility and life chances'.

Reviews in Reproduction 1999; 4(3):184-90.

37 Miller BC, Benson B, Galbraith KA. 'Family relationships and adolescent pregnancy risk: A research synthesis'. *Developmental Review* 2001; 21(1):1-38.

38 Dempsey M, Heslin J, Bradley C. *The Experience of Teenage Pregnancy*. Waterford: South-Eastern Health Board, 2000.

39 Rundle K, Leigh C, McGee H, Layte R. *Irish Contraception and Crisis Pregnancy (ICCP) Study. A Survey of the General Population*. Crisis Pregnancy Agency Report no. 7. 2004.

40 Pesa JA, Turner LW, Mathews J. 'Sex differences in barriers to contraceptive use among adolescents'. *J Pediatr* 2001; 139(5):689-93.

41 Pleck JH, Sonenstein FL, Ku L. 'Changes in adolescent males' use of and attitudes toward condoms, 1988-1991'. *Family Planning Perspectives* 1993; 25(3):106-10.

42 Pleck JH, Sonenstein FL, Ku LC. 'Contraceptive attitudes and intention to use condoms in sexually experienced and inexperienced adolescent males'. *Journal of Family Issues* 1990; 11(3):294-312.

43 Mahon E, Conlon C, Dillon L. *Women and Crisis Pregnancy*. Dublin: The Stationery Office, 1998.

44 Abraham C, Sheeran P, Spears R, Abrams D. 'Health beliefs and promotion of HIV-preventive intentions among teenagers: a Scottish perspective'. *Health Psychology* 1992; 11(6):363-70.

45 IFPA. IFPA submission to the Crisis Pregnancy Agency. 2002.

46 Walker ZA, Townsend J. 'The role of general practice in promoting teenage health: a review of the literature'. *Fam Pract* 1999; 16(2):164-72.

47 Donovan C, Mellanby AR, Jacobson LD, Taylor B, Tripp JH. 'Teenagers' views on the general practice consultation and provision of contraception'. The Adolescent Working Group. *Br J Gen Pract* 1997; 47(424):715-8.

48 Shucksmith J, Spratt J. *Young People's Self-Identified Health Needs: A Literature Review*. Health Education Board for Scotland, 2002.

49 Mason C. *A Needs Assessment for Contraceptive Services in the North-Western Health Board*. Faculty of Public Health Medicine, Royal College of Physicians of Ireland, 2003.

50 Jacobson LD, Mellanby AR, Donovan C, Taylor B, Tripp JH. Teenagers' views on general practice consultations and other medical advice. The Adolescent Working Group, RCGP. Fam Pract 2000; 17(2):156-8.

51 Peremans L, Hermann I, Avonts D, Van Royen P, Denekens J. 'Contraceptive knowledge and expectations by adolescents: an explanation by focus groups'. *Patient Education & Counseling* 2000; 40(2):133-41.

52 Hosie A. *Sexual health policy analysis in selected European countries*. Edinburgh: Health Education Board for Scotland, 2002.

53 Schofield M. *The Sexual Behaviour of Young People*. London: Longman, 1965.

54 Dickson N, Paul C, Herbison P, Silva P. 'First sexual intercourse: age, coercion, and later regrets reported by a birth cohort'. *BMJ* 1998; 316(7124):29-33.

55 Pick S and Palos PA. 'Impact of the family on the sex lives of adolescents'. *Adolescence* 1995; 30(119): 667-675.

Chapter 7:

Heterosexual Partnerships: Number of Partners
and Male Experience of Commercial Sex

7.1 Introduction

THE pattern and distribution of heterosexual partnerships is of key importance for a number of reasons. For example, knowing the number of partnerships over a given period and whether they are monogamous or concurrent is important for understanding the nature of social relations, how these are related to societal attitudes and morals, and the extent to which these have changed over generations. Knowledge of the frequency of partner change, the extent of concurrent relationships and the impact on these of socio-demographic characteristics is also critical for understanding the dynamics of STI transmission.

This chapter examines:

- the number of sexual partners that Irish people have had over three periods (lifetime, last five years and in last year)
- the extent of concurrency in relationships
- the extent of and nature of commercial sex use by Irish men

The central aim of the chapter is to understand the nature of heterosexual partnership in Ireland and the implications that this has for the risk profile of the population in terms of STI infection. By relating these patterns to a number of socio-demographic and economic characteristics, the chapter will be able to describe those groups who are most at risk of both contracting and propagating STIs.

Surveys of sexual behaviour in other countries have shown a great deal of variability in number of partners. Although most report one or a few partners, a substantial minority report a large number.[1][2][3][4][5] Analyses show that this variability can be explained by a number of key variables, but most importantly the person's age and marital status.

Young people are less likely to have started having sex (and thus have no partners yet) but, if they have begun having sex, are also most likely to have a high number of partners over recent periods. Young people tend to experience relationships with a number of partners before establishing a stronger, monogamous relationship for a substantial period.

This transition in relationship status also explains the importance of marital status for number of partners; married people are least likely to have more than one partner in recent periods, followed by those who are cohabiting and those in steady relationships.

Other factors have also been shown to influence the likelihood of a high number of partners in a recent period, including social class (non-manual groups tend to have higher numbers of partners) and age of sexual debut.

These examples show that the variability in number of partners has a distinct social structure that is as yet poorly understood in the Irish context.

However, the pattern of partnerships not only varies across the population, but also across time as social, economic, demographic and cultural change occurs. Research in a number of countries shows dramatic changes in sexual behaviour and partnership formation during the last three decades. These changes were driven by economic growth, increased mobility, technical change and profound legal and cultural shifts.

Ireland has not been immune to such changes. It is likely that behaviours here may also have altered substantially in recent decades. Yet, just as industrialisation and economic growth occurred in Ireland later than in other Western countries, cultural and legal change was also delayed. Ireland may still lag behind other countries in terms of sexual behaviour. On the other hand, as the dizzying pace of economic growth has seen Ireland pass the living standards of other nations, the country may have moved far from its conservative sexual culture and associated behaviours of the relatively recent past.

The next, **second section** discusses the average number of partners experienced by Irish men and women over lifetime, last five years and past year. It shows substantial differences in the numbers reported by men and women; in the **third section**, we discuss this difference in more detail. The **fourth section** examines in detail the patterns of partner numbers according to age groups.

The **fifth section** examines the socio-demographic factors associated with a high number of partners. The **sixth section** looks at patterns of monogamy and concurrency. The **seventh section** examines use of commercial sex by Irish men. The last, **eighth section** summarises the results and discusses their implications.

7.2 Number of partners over different time intervals

SUMMARY

THE overwhelming majority of Irish men and women have had vaginal, oral or anal sex. 29% of men and over half of women have had a single sexual partner in their life so far. A quarter of men and 6% of women report 10 or more partners.

The average number of sexual partners is influenced substantially by a small number of men and women who report a large number of partners.

The shorter the period over which the number of partners is recalled, the higher the proportion that have had a single partner.

International comparisons show that Irish people tend to have fewer partners on average than people in other countries, but this varies substantially by age: young Irish people have as many partners as their peers in other countries (see section 7.4).

■ 94% of both Irish men and women have had a sexual partner.

■ 29% of men and 51% of women have had a single sexual partner in their life to date.

■ The proportion with a single partner increases as the period covered decreases:

58% of men and 68% of women have had a single partner in the last five years, while 70% and 75% have had a single partner in the last year.

■ Less than 1% of men and women report 10 or more partners in the last year.

■ 7% of men and 1% of women report 10 or more partners in the last five years.

THIS section examines the number of partners with whom respondents have had sex over different periods. Sex is defined as vaginal, oral or anal sex.

Results from other national surveys of sexual behaviour show that analysis of the number of sexual partnerships is complex. This is because a relatively small number of individuals who report a large number of partners influence the data. Standard distributional measures such as mean number of partners are an unreliable guide to the average number of partners because a few cases with a high number of partners draw this average upward. Other measures such as the median are used, therefore, and number of partners is grouped into categories that can be compared more readily.

In the British National Sexual Lifestyle Survey (NATSAL) of 1990,[3] Johnson *et al* (1994) show that around a quarter of men and almost half of women reported one or no partners over their lifetime so far. Among men, another quarter reported 10 or more partners over lifetime, and the top

1% of men reported 30% of all partners in the whole sample of men. Among women the proportion with a high number of partners was lower, at just 7%, but their impact was still large as they contributed 15% of all partners to the sample of women.

More recent figures for Britain, from the 2000 NATSAL survey,[4] show that the overall distribution of partners among both men and women had increased substantially across all age groups and both genders.

The Australian ASHR study reported higher numbers of partners on average among Australians than were found among the British population.[4][5] A total of 44% of Australian men reported 10 or more partners, compared to 35% of British men (even though the British study was confined to people under 45 and younger cohorts tend to have more partners on average). Among women, the pattern was reversed: fewer Australian women reported three or more partners (59% v 66% for men), but roughly equal proportions reported 10 or more partners.

Figure 7.1 gives, by gender, the numbers of partners reported by respondents to the ISSHR study over lifetime so far, in the last five years and in the last year. Men and women differ substantially in the reported number of partners.

Figure 7.1: Number of heterosexual partners over different time periods: by gender

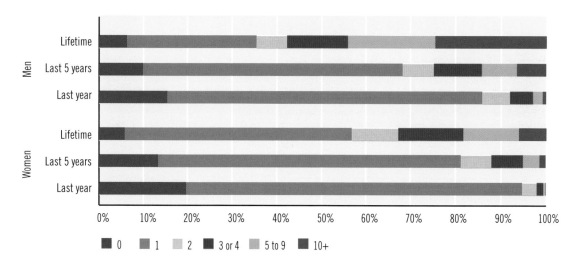

Figure 7.2: Mean and median heterosexual partners over different time periods: by gender

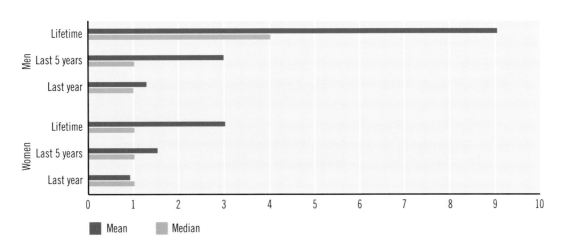

Over lifetime, 6% of men and women reported never having had a sexual partner, while 25% of men and 6% of women reported 10+ partners. The largest single grouping is those reporting a single partner over lifetime so far: around 29% of men and 51% of women.

The Irish sample shows the same pattern of reported partners as found in other national studies of sexual behaviour:[1 3 5 6 7] most people report a small number of partners while a small minority report a large number of partners.

Figure 7.2 shows clearly that, among both men and women, the *mean* number of partners (the total number of partners across all individuals divided by the number of individuals) is substantially higher than the *median* (the number of partners of the person at the 50th percentile of the cumulative distribution) for lifetime number of partners and number over the last five years. For example, among men, the mean number of partners over lifetime is more than nine, compared to a mean of four. This difference stems from the small proportion of men and women who report a large number of partners:

- Over lifetime, 1% of men report more than 70 partners (a maximum of 600 partners) and 1% of women more than 18 (maximum 167).

It is likely that people reporting a large number of partners over lifetime are estimating rather than giving an exact total, as there is a clear preference for multiples of five and 10. The accuracy of their reports may grow worse the longer the recall period, particularly among older people who may be casting back over four decades or more.

Over shorter recall periods, the distributional pattern in the data becomes significantly less skewed and the mean number of partners for the sample comes closer to the median:

- 58% of men and 68% of women report a single partner over the last five years, and just 7% of men and 1% of women report 10+.
- 70% of men and 75% of women report a single partner in the last year, and 1% of men and 0.1% of women report 10+.

Overall, it is clear that most of the Irish population aged between 18 and 65 will have had a single partner over 'the last five years' and 29% of men and 51% of women a single partner over their lifetimes so far.

Figure 7.3: Number of heterosexual partners in lifetime: by gender and country

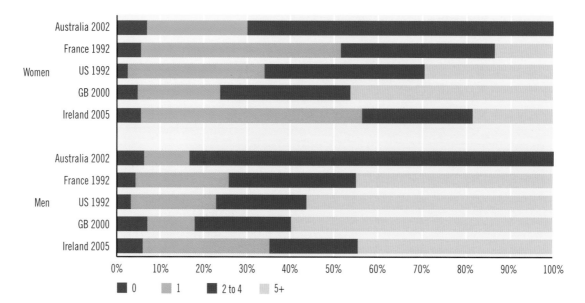

Note: Australian proportion for 2 to 4 represents proportion 2+ partners.

Figure 7.3 compares the findings for Ireland to those from other countries. It shows that, over lifetime, both Irish men and women are more likely to have had a single partner and less likely to have two or more partners than men and women in the UK, US, France and Australia.

Figure 7.4, comparing number of heterosexual partners 'in the last year', reveals a more complex pattern. Compared with men and women in the UK, France and Australia, Irish people are more likely to report no partners over the period, but as likely to report two or more partners (though significantly less likely than men and women in the US).

The marked differences in distributions over lifetime but similarity in those over the last year reflect the substantial change that has occurred in Ireland across age cohorts. Older Irish people are much less likely than their peers in other countries (for which there is data) to have more than one partner. Among younger age groups, the proportions for number of partners 'in the last year' or 'last five years' are as high as, if not higher than in other countries. This means that lifetime numbers of partners in younger Irish age groups are around the same level as in other counties.

Figure 7.4: Number of heterosexual partners in last year: by gender and country

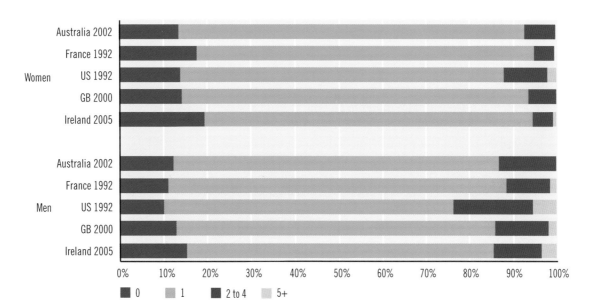

The level of partners among younger Irish people points to a change in behaviour that may be related to the change in sexual attitudes (analysed in chapter four). This development has implications for the spread of sexually transmitted infections (STIs) in Irish society, since an increase in average numbers of partners is associated with an increase in STI incidence if there is no concomitant increase in the use of protection.

A small number of individuals report high numbers of sexual partners:

• 1% of men account for 31% of the total number of sexual partners 'in the last year' over the whole sample of men and 1% of women account for 32% of the total number among women.

This highlights the existence of a core group who have a very active sex life. This group may be very important for maintaining or increasing the level of STIs in the population, depending on how much they use protection. Understanding the characteristics of this core group is essential for understanding the dynamics of STI transmission.

For more detail on the analyses in this section, see Appendix *Tables 5.1* to *5.4*.

7.3   Difference in number of heterosexual partners between men and women

FIGURES 7.1 to *7.4* show that, irrespective of the time period, men report a higher number of sexual partners than women. This is reflected in both the mean and median. This finding is consistent with results from other surveys in countries such as Britain, France, the US and Australia[2][3][4][5][8] which have all reported that men of all ages report higher numbers of sexual partners than women.

A *priori*, the expectation is that, in a closed population, the number of heterosexual partners in a given period should be equal between men and women. The finding that this is generally not so has been explained in a number of ways:

- First, respondents may have partners outside the sampled population. This is increasingly true as international travel grows.
- Secondly, female partners who are under-represented in the sample, such as women who work in prostitution, may account for some of the discrepancy. (More analysis on this subject is presented later in this chapter.)
- Thirdly, men may be having sex with women outside the age range covered in the study (in the ISSHR survey, this is 18-64).
- Fourthly, men and women may differ in what they consider as a sexual partner. Although the ISSHR questionnaire asked respondents to count all heterosexual partners with whom they had vaginal, oral or anal sex, men may count all encounters and women discount some, possibly because they were brief, inconsequential or regretted.
- Fifthly, the pattern of age mixing (men tending to have relationships with younger women) combined with recall error may lead to some inconsistency, particularly for statistics on lifetime number of partners.
- Sixthly, men may exaggerate the number of their sexual partners and women may under-report, or there may be some combination of the two tendencies.

Irish society, like many others, tends to look positively at men with a high number of partners and negatively at such women. This double standard remains even though attitudes toward female sexuality and sex outside marriage have become substantially more liberal in recent decades. In sex-behaviour surveys, however, as long as the recall bias is similar across different groups within the same gender, the essential patterns necessary for analysis are preserved.

Research on the inconsistency between the reports of men and women tends to support the hypothesis that recall bias is the prime factor, followed by the age mixing of partners and the impact of use by men of women who work in prostitution.[9]

7.4 Current age of individual and number of heterosexual partners

SUMMARY

THIS section shows that younger Irish people have more sexual partners on average than older people, both over lifetime and in recent periods. This is partly because of a pronounced pattern of non-marriage and celibacy among the oldest age group, but also reflects a substantial change in behaviour, with sex before marriage becoming the norm rather than the exception.

International comparisons suggest that the behaviour of younger Irish people has now converged with that of younger people in Britain and Australia.

■ Younger men and women report substantially higher numbers of sexual partners than older respondents:

- 46% of men aged 55 to 64 have only ever had a single partner compared to 23% of men aged 18 to 24.

- 76% of women aged 55 to 64 have had a single partner compared to 35% of women aged 18 to 24.

■ A small absolute number of young people have high numbers of partners. Only 2.5% of men and 0.4% of women aged 18 to 24 reported 10 or more partners 'in the last year'.

THE overall distribution of partners noted in the last section is heavily influenced by the pronounced difference in patterns across age groups, as *Figure 7.5* shows. For example:

- Although 29% of men overall have had a single partner over lifetime, this proportion increases across age cohorts: 46% of men aged 55-64 reported a single partner compared to 23% of those aged 18 to 24.

Figure 7.5: Number of heterosexual partners for men in lifetime: by age

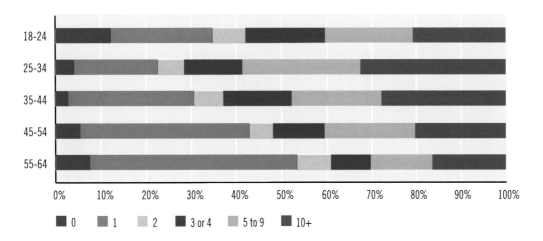

This cohort difference is even more marked among women. *Figure 7.6* shows that:

- 76% of women in the oldest age group reported a single partner compared to 35% among those aged 18 to 24.

These patterns are slightly complicated by the higher proportions among people in the youngest age group who have not yet had a sexual partner; this proportion is highest among those aged 18 to 24, at 12% of men and 15% of women.

A higher number who have not had sex is to be expected among the youngest age group, but it is interesting to note that, after reaching a low of 3% among both men and women aged 35 to 44, the proportion who have never had sex increases thereafter to 7% among men and 6% among women. Whereas UK results show that the proportion who have never had sex decreases by age, in Ireland the increasing proportion reflects the historical pattern of non-marriage and celibacy which was slow to change until recent decades.

Figure 7.6: Number of heterosexual partners for women in lifetime: by age

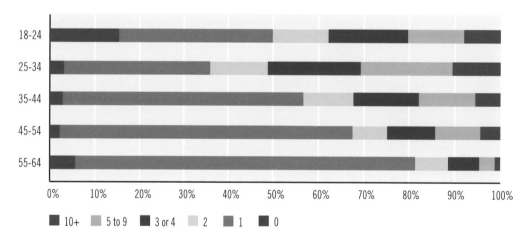

While virginity is higher among older Irish age groups than among their British peers, the proportion in the youngest Irish age group who have not yet had sex is lower than that found in a recent British sample.[7]

These results suggest a pronounced cohort change in behaviour in the Irish population over time. This can also be seen in the change in the mean and median number of partners over lifetime, shown in Appendix *Table 5.1*. Here, the youngest age group have the lowest average number of partners (as they have had a shorter period over which to acquire partners), but for men the mean and median partners peak in the 35-44 age group and among women in the 25-34 group. The same pattern can be seen for the proportion with 10 or more partners. This suggests a strong generational shift among people born after the mid-1960s (and who thus reached sexual maturity from around 1980 onwards). They are much more likely to report a higher number of partners.

Even among younger age groups, however, around a third reported a single sexual partner over lifetime so far.

Figure 7.1 showed that over 70% of men and 75% of women reported only a single sexual partner 'in the last year'. The proportion for those aged 18 to 24 is around 46% of men and 62% of women. We would expect that younger people would be more likely to report a higher number of partners in the recent period, as they will be starting out on their sexual careers and might have a number of relationships before finding a more long-term match (as we see in older age groups).

Cross-national comparisons show that the proportion of Irish people aged 18 to 24 having five or more partners 'in the last year' is three times higher than that in the 1990 National Sexual Lifestyle Survey (NATSAL) in Britain. (The same figures for the 2000 NATSAL survey are not available.) Figures for number of partners 'in the last five years' show young Irish men to be marginally more likely (36.8% ISSHR v 33.6% NATSAL) and young Irish women significantly less likely (17% ISSHR v 25.2% NATSAL) to report 5+ partners over the last five years. This could indicate that patterns of behaviour among younger Irish people are currently very similar to those among their British peers, although there are pronounced differences between the genders.

For more detail on the variation in number of partners over different periods, see Appendix *Table 5.1* to *5.3*.

7.5 The influence of other factors on number of sexual partners

SUMMARY

THIS section examines the determinants of having multiple partnerships 'in the last year' (multiple is defined as two or more partners).

Having two or more partners is associated with being in a higher social class and having higher levels of education, even among younger age groups where multiple partnerships are more common.

Age of first intercourse is a strong predictor of having two or more partners.

Men and women under 25 are far more likely than all other age groups to report more than one partner in the last year:

- 37% of men and 16% of women under 25 report two or more partners, compared to 9% of men and 2% of women aged 35 to 44.

- People in casual relations (46% of men, 29% of women) or not in a relationship (30% of men, 12% of women) are most likely to report two or more partners in the last year.

- Respondents who had vaginal sex before the age of 17 are almost three times more likely, than those who had sex after 17, to report a higher number of partners in the last year.

AGE and gender have a significant influence on the number of sexual partners reported (see last section). In this section we examine other factors and their impact on the probability of multiple partnership over the most recent period (ie, in the last year).

Defining *multiple partnership* as two or more partners (in the last year) may appear to set a low threshold, but this definition is well established in the research literature.[3][4]

Figure 7.7: Proportion having two or more partners in the last year: by gender

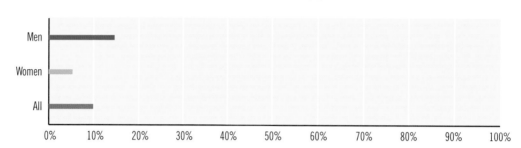

Figure 7.7 shows the proportions of men (14%) and women (6%) with two or more sexual partners in the last year. It underlines the earlier finding that few individuals have a high number of partners, particularly over a period as short as a year.

Relationship status is associated with number of sexual partners 'in the last year'. Although changes in attitudes mean that sex in Ireland is now far more likely to occur outside of marriage than previously, there is still likely to be an expectation among most couples of monogamy within marriage or informal unions. Among those who are not married or living together, the commitment to sexual exclusivity will usually be weaker, but the expectation is likely to grow as the duration and depth of the relationship increases.

Figure 7.8 shows married men and women are significantly less likely than all other groups to report two or more partners in the last year:

- People not currently in a relationship or in a casual relationship are most likely to report two or more partners.
- Married people are least likely to report two or more partners (2% of men and <1% of women), followed by those who are cohabiting (5% of men and 2% of women).

Figure 7.8: Proportion having two or more partners in the last year: by gender and current relationship status

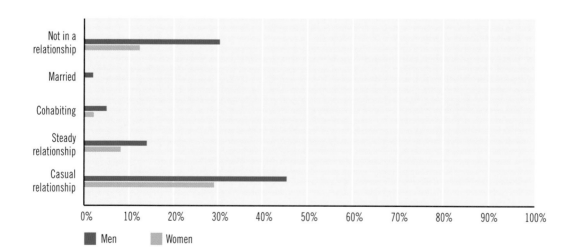

Figure 7.9: Proportion having two or more partners in the last year: by gender and social class

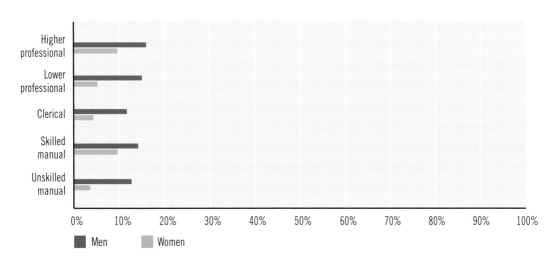

Research has also shown a substantial relationship between social class and aspects of sexual behaviour including age of sexual debut[10][11] and number of partners.[3][12] Evidence for the latter is mixed; some studies[12] find larger numbers of partners among manual social classes, whereas others[3] find higher numbers of partners among married people in the professional and managerial classes.

Figure 7.9 shows that, among the higher professional and managerial classes, higher proportions of both men and women reported two or more partners, compared to all other classes. We would expect a similar relationship with education, given the close relationship between social class and education (see section 2.12.3). Analyses (not shown) show that education is related to number of sexual partners.

Previous research has found that early sexual debut is related to a higher number of sexual partners in later life. For example, Johnson *et al* (1994)[3] found that those who reported sex before the legal age of 16 were more likely to have a higher number of partners later.

Figure 7.10: Proportion having two or more partners in the last year: by gender and age of first vaginal sex

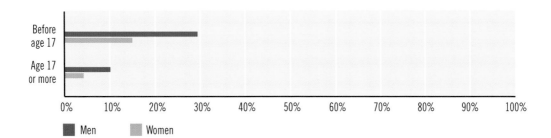

Figure 7.10 shows a similar relationship in the ISSHR data. People whose sexual debut was before 17 are significantly more likely than those who had first intercourse after 17 to report two or more partners in the last year.

ISSHR Sub-Report 3: 'Contemporary Sexual Knowledge, Attitudes and Behaviours in Ireland' includes more in-depth analyses of the relationship between other characteristics and multiple partnerships 'in the last year'. These show an association with use of alcohol: currently drinking more than the recommended number of alcohol units per week was significantly related to having a higher number of partners in the last year. This was true of both men and women, even controlling for age and marital status.

Drinking high levels of alcohol may increase the risks associated with multiple partnerships in so far as it affects protective practices. Indeed, analyses in Sub-Report 3 show that consumption of alcohol above guideline thresholds is associated with not using condoms on the last occasion of sex. (We return to this issue in chapter 10.)

Sub-Report 3 also shows that men who have 'ever' paid for sex are more likely to report multiple partnerships 'in the last year', whether we include paid partners or not. Use of commercial sex is an important risk factor for STIs at the individual level, but this result is also important as multiple partnerships increase the risk that infections will be spread among the population more quickly.

7.6   Monogamy and concurrency in relationships

SUMMARY

ONLY a small proportion of men and women reported two or more partners in the last year, but among men there is a relationship between number of partners and concurrency (more than one relationship occurring at the same time).

The pattern of increasing concurrency with higher number of partners is particularly strong if both homosexual and heterosexual relationships are counted.

■ Men with a higher number of partners were more likely to report concurrent relationships.

■ 61% of men with 10 or more sexual partners in the last year reported concurrent relationships.

CERTAIN groups are more likely to have a higher number of partners (see previous sections). However, counting the number of partners a person has over a given period does not give a full picture of the overall pattern of relationships.

First, the social implication of a higher number of partners depends upon whether the relationships were experienced sequentially, with no overlap, or whether two or more of the relationships were held concurrently. For example, serial monogamy (one relationship is experienced after another has ended) implies that the person is focused on one individual. On the other hand, concurrent relationships (an individual has a new relationship during the course of another) imply that the person, and possibly their partner, accepts that relationships need not be exclusive.

Secondly, the pattern of relationships has epidemiological implications. For example, if a person has three partners sequentially over a year and the last of these has an STI (and assuming, for simplicity, that infection is certain if they have sex and protection is not used), the first two partners will not be infected. However, if the individual has concurrent relationships with all four partners, all four will become infected.

This section examines the extent of concurrency in the ISSHR data, using a question asked of any individual who had reported two or more partners in the last year. As noted, this is a small group of around 14% of men and just 6% of women (a total of 669 unweighted individuals). We are particularly interested in the extent to which those with a higher number of partners have concurrent relationships.

Figure 7.11: Proportion of individuals with 2 or more partners in the last year also having concurrent relationships: by gender and number of sexual partners

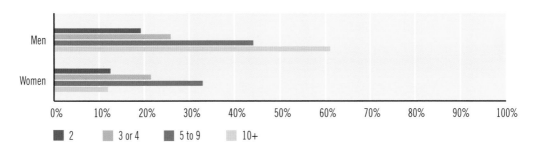

Figure 7.11 shows, by gender, the pattern of concurrency by number of partners in the last year. It provides evidence that there is indeed a relationship between number of partners and degree of concurrency (although the numbers involved are relatively small): people with a higher number of partners are more likely to have had a concurrent relationship with two or more of these partners.

This pattern is clearer among men than women. Although the proportion of women experiencing concurrent relationships initially increases with the number of partners, women with 10 or more partners in the last year have a lower probability of concurrency. The relationship becomes even more pronounced among men if both heterosexual and homosexual partnerships are counted (see Appendix *Table 5.6*).

The results suggest that probability of concurrency is strongly linked to overall number of partners, particularly among men.

These findings have two implications:

- First, the higher the number of partners that a person has, the more likely that he or she will have multiple partners concurrently, thus increasing the risk of infection with STIs.
- Secondly, the relationship between number of partners and concurrency increases if homosexual partnerships are included.

7.7 Men's use of commercial sex

SUMMARY

A SMALL but significant proportion of Irish men have paid a woman for sex at some time. A smaller proportion have done so recently.

The oldest age group of men are most likely to have paid a woman for sex at some time. Men aged 25 to 34 are most likely to have paid for sex 'over the last five years'. Men aged 18 to 24 are the second most likely group to have paid for sex over the same period.

The results suggest that there may be an increasing trend toward payment for sex among younger age groups.

■ 6.4% of men reported having paid for sex; 3.3% reported doing so in the last five years.

■ Age-cohort patterns suggest an upward trend in men paying for sex.

■ Single men and those with higher professional occupations are most likely to have paid for sex both 'ever' and in the last five years.

■ Men who have had a same-sex partner are 80% more likely than other men to have paid a woman for sex.

■ Men with a higher number of unpaid female sexual partners are more likely to have paid for sex.

■ 44% of men who have paid for sex did so with one paid partner, 50% with between two and nine partners and 6% with 10 or more.

■ 83% of men who have paid for sex reported that they had always used a condom, 7% used them inconsistently and 11% never used them.

PAYMENT for sex is a particularly difficult area to research. It has received comparatively little attention both in Ireland (where there is no representative research) or abroad. However, as well as being an interesting subject that aids understanding of sexual expression and the mismatch between reported partners as between men and women, the extent and nature of commercial sex could also be an important factor in the spread of sexually transmitted infections (STIs).

Prostitution was the subject of a great deal of popular writing in the 19th century but was not the subject of systematic enquiry until the KAB surveys of the 1980s and 1990s. There has been some recent research on levels of HIV among women who work in prostitution in Britain,[13] but overall there is little understanding of the role of prostitution in propagating STIs in the population.

Johnson *et al* (1994),[3] using the 1990 NATSAL survey for Britain, showed that 6.8% of men had 'ever' paid a woman for sex and just 1.8% had done so 'in the last five years'. Admitted female use of prostitutes was found to be so low as to be almost non-existent. This study also found a fivefold increase in the probability of ever paying for sex among men aged over 45, compared to under-25s, but the opposite trend was true for commercial sex 'in the last five years'.

It was not possible to fully ascertain whether the difference between experience over lifetime and 'in the last five years' was due to a cohort change in behaviour, or simply because younger groups had not had time to reach the same level. However, the distribution did indicate a decline in the prevalence of commercial sex among men, perhaps because of the greater availability to men in recent decades of non-paid and, more importantly, non-married partners.

In Australia, the ASHR survey (2003) found a higher prevalence of 'ever' having paid for sex (16%), although the age gradient was not as pronounced.

The sensitivity of questions around commercial sex may mean that these figures underestimate the true proportion that have paid for sex. It is possible that, in a more open sexual culture, men are more likely to admit paying for sex. If so, the more conservative sexual culture of Ireland would tend to depress the true proportion for Ireland.

Figure 7.12: Proportion of men paying for sex with a woman over different time periods

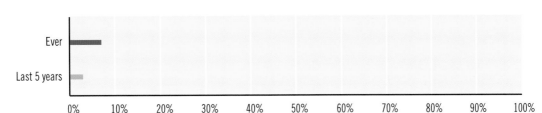

Questions on use of commercial sex and 'most recent occasion' were asked in the ISSHR study. *Figure 7.12* shows the overall proportion of men paying for sex 'ever' and 'in the last five years'. Questions on payment for sex were also asked of women, but just one case was reported, making analysis impossible. Questions were also asked about payment for sex with same-sex partners; once again, incidence was so low that analysis was not possible.

Figure 7.12 shows that 6% of Irish men between 18 and 64 have 'ever' paid for sex with a woman, a rate identical to that found in the 1990 NATSAL survey (lifetime prevalence figures for the 2000 NATSAL survey have not yet been published) and significantly less than that found in Australia (16%). (A rate for the 'last five years' was not available from the ASHR literature.)

The Irish 'last five years' rate of 3% is higher than the 2% found in the 1990 NATSAL survey, but lower than the 4% found in the 2000 NATSAL survey. However, the latter includes only men up to age 44, so the comparison is not simple.

Figure 7.13 shows that the oldest Irish age group, as in Britain, are the most likely to have paid for sex and all older age groups are significantly more likely to report paid sex than the youngest age group. However, the second highest 'ever' proportion is for those aged 25-34. This may suggest that among younger groups there is increasing use of paid sex. This is supported to an extent by the high rate of 'last five years' among the 25-34 age group (although 6% here represents just 40 individuals).

Figure 7.13: Proportions of men who have paid a woman for sex over different time periods: by age

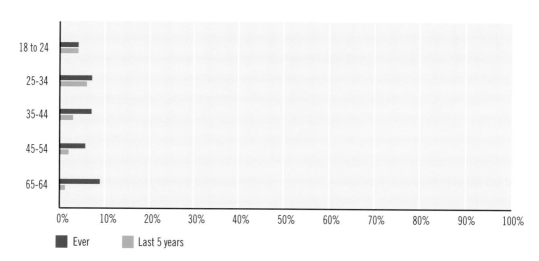

Figure 7.14 gives the pattern by social class. It shows that men in higher professional and managerial occupations are most likely to have 'ever' paid for sex and also to have done so 'in the last five years', although the differences between groups over lifetime are small.

Figure 7.14: Proportion of men paying a woman for sex over different time periods: by social class

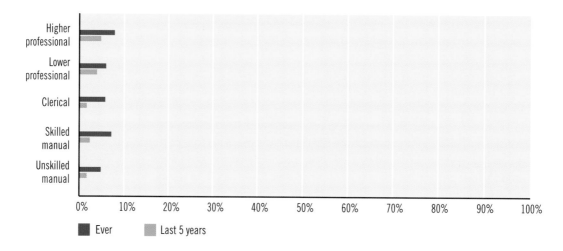

Rates of paying for sex are also high among the skilled manual group, but this group's 'last five years' rate is not relatively high.

The pattern of higher levels of payment for sex among professional and managerial groups was also found in the NATSAL surveys in Britain. It may reflect the fact that such men have higher incomes and may be more able to afford the expense.

Analyses of the ISSHR data also show that other characteristics are important predictors of having paid for sex (see Appendix *Table 5.7*).

Dividing respondents by relationship status shows that single men (not in a relationship) are most likely to have paid for sex, followed by those in a casual relationship or cohabiting. This order remains when we look at payment for sex 'in the last five years'. Married or cohabiting men are significantly less likely to have paid for sex in their lifetime compared to those who are currently single. Similarly, married men and those in a steady relationship are significantly less likely to have paid for sex 'in the last five years'.

Johnson *et al* (1994)[3] found in their British sample a significant positive relationship between ever having a homosexual partner and payment for sex. The ISSHR results show a very strong relationship: men who have ever had a genital same-sex experience are five times more likely to have paid for sex (with a woman) both 'ever' and 'in the last five years'.

Lastly, analyses showed a relationship between the number of unpaid heterosexual partners over lifetime and paying a woman for sex, although the main difference is between men reporting fewer than 10 partners and men reporting 10 or more. Of the former, less than 6% have ever paid a woman for sex; of the latter, 14%. The difference between groups is not so marked for payment for sex 'in the last five years', but the difference is still statistically significant.

Studies in the UK[13] show that payment for sex is an important risk factor for STIs and HIV, although this risk depends a great deal on the profile of women who are providing sexual services. Where sex workers are also heroin users, the risk of HIV and STI infection is high and use of protection less consistent. The high rate of paid sex among men with a larger number of sexual partners is worrying since it would facilitate the spread of infection in the wider population.

Of men who have paid a women for sex, 44% reported that they had paid one partner (we do not know how many times), 50% reported between two and nine partners, and 6% reported 10 or more. These figures are quite close to those found in the 1990 NATSAL survey,[3] although the proportion with one partner is slightly higher (44% ISSHR v 39% NATSAL). The proportion with 10 or more partners is almost identical (50% ISSHR v 51% NATSAL).

As with the proportion of men who have ever paid a women for sex, these figures indicate that the pattern of commercial sex in Ireland is similar to that in Britain, albeit Britain of the early 1990s. Since then, rates of commercial sex among men in Britain have increased: men aged 25-34 are most likely to have paid a woman for sex 'in the last five years'. Thus the pattern of development in Ireland may be similar to that in Britain. We may see an increase in commercial sex in the next decade in Ireland.

As with the level of concurrent sex, the level of STI infection in the population associated with commercial sex is related to:

- the use of protection by women who work in prostitution and by their clients
- the extent to which those using commercial sex have a high number of partners (including paid partners)

Figure 7.15: Proportion of men who have ever paid for sex with a woman: by number of heterosexual and homosexual partners in lifetime

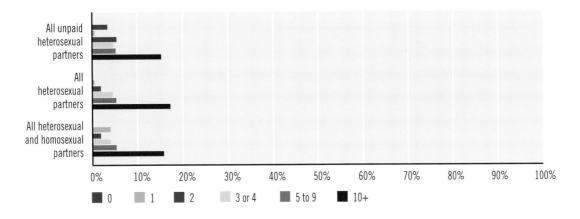

Figure 7.15 shows more detail on the relationship between number of sexual partners and payment for sex. Three sets of figures are provided:

- numbers of unpaid heterosexual partners
- total number of heterosexual partners including those who were paid
- total number of heterosexual and homosexual partners

The results show that, irrespective of whether we count unpaid heterosexual partners, all heterosexual partners, or heterosexual and homosexual partners, men with a higher number of partners are most likely also to have paid for sex with a woman.

The proportion of men who have paid a woman for sex is highest among those who report 10 or more partners; this proportion increases if we also count paid partners. Doing this also produces a more graduated relationship between number of partners 'ever' and the probability of 'ever' having paid for sex. The relationship is also pronounced if we include homosexual partners.

These results show an accumulation of risk factors among a core group of individuals who are more likely:

- to have a higher number of partners
- to have concurrent sex with these partners
- to have had homosexual partners
- to have paid for sex

This does not mean that the 'sets' of men with these different risk behaviours directly overlap. A higher number of partners over lifetime, for instance, does not mean that the individual also has concurrent, homosexual and paid sex, simply that the probability of this being true increases. *Figure 7.15* shows, for example, that only 15% of men with 10 or more unpaid partners had also paid a woman for sex – and those with 10 or more partners made up only 19% of the male sample.

Lastly, *Table 7.1* shows condom use among men who have ever paid a woman for sex.

Table 7.1: Use of condoms when paying for sex, among men who have ever paid a woman for sex

	%	N
Used on every occasion	82.9	150
Used on most occasions	2.4	5
Used on roughly half of occasions	2.0	3
Used on some occasions	2.2	6
Never used condoms	10.5	18

Table 7.1 shows that, while 83% of men who have paid for sex report that they always used a condom, a sizeable 7% report using them inconsistently and almost 11% never using them. Since the absolute number of individuals used for analysis here is small, results should be interpreted cautiously. For example, using a confidence interval based on 95% probability, the proportion never using a condom could vary between 6% and 17%.

For more details on the analyses in this section, see Appendix *Table 5.8*.

7.8 Summary

UNDERSTANDING the pattern and distribution of partnerships in a society is vitally important for a number of reasons, but it is essential for specifying the pattern of STI risk. This chapter has drawn on the extensive data in the ISSHR survey to examine the number of partners that Irish people reported for three periods: ever, the last five years and over the last year.

Studies in a number of countries have shown that the distribution of number of partners is complex; most people report relatively few partners over lifetime and most only one partner 'in the last five years' or 'in the last year'. However, a minority report a high number of partners. This factor tends to make problematic standard measures such as the mean since a small number of very high values inflates the average.

Analysis of the patterns for Ireland also show this pattern: around a third to a half of the population report a single partner over lifetime thus far, but one in four men and one in 16 women report 10 or more partners. Compared to the UK, US, France and Australia, Irish people are more likely to report a single partner over lifetime so far and less likely to report two or more partners.

However, analysis of partnership patterns over more recent periods ('last five years' and 'in the last year') and by age group shows that young Irish people have converged with their peers in other countries in terms of numbers of partners. As in other countries, the trend of larger numbers of young Irish people with a high number of partners points to the emergence of an important sub-population for the spread of STIs.

This change in behaviour is particularly stark when compared to that of older Irish generations who were more likely than their peers in other countries to have a single partner and to remain celibate throughout their lives. This leads to a pattern in the Republic of Ireland that is very rare internationally, whereby the proportion of people ever having had a sexual partner increases with age initially and then decreases among the oldest age groups.

Analysis of the factors aside from age that are associated with number of partners shows that both men and women in a casual relationship are most likely to report two or more partners 'in the last year'. Similarly, both men and women with more education or in a higher social class are more likely to report two or more partners.

Importantly, people who began having heterosexual sex before 17 are significantly more likely to have two or more partners 'in the last year'. A higher number of sexual partners increases the risk of transmitting STIs. The spread of STIs increases if multiple partnerships are held concurrently. Men with a higher number of partners 'in the last year' were far more likely also to have had concurrent relationships.

The final section of the chapter examined the pattern of commercial sex among Irish men. The extent of payment for sex and characteristics of those who pay for sex has never been studied in Ireland before using a representative national study. The results, therefore, are important for understanding both the social patterning of sex and the pattern of risk of STIs in the Irish population.

Almost 7% of Irish men reported having paid for sex. Just over 3% reported having done so 'in the last five years'. Men over 54 are most likely to have paid for sex, but there is evidence that payment for sex has become more common in younger cohorts; the highest 'in the last five years' proportion is among men aged 25-34, while the proportion among men aged 18-24 is greater than that of men aged over 35.

Analysis of other predictors of paying for sex shows that single men, men in casual relationships or those cohabiting were most likely to report paying for sex 'in the last five years', as were men with professional and managerial occupations.

One important finding was that men who also reported same-sex genital contact were 80%

more likely to have recently paid for sex.

Men with a higher number of heterosexual partners were also more likely to report paying for sex, even if we exclude those partners for whom payment was made.

The results suggest, as with concurrent sex, that multiple risk factors for transmitting STIs tend to coalesce around the same, relatively small group of individuals.

7.9   Reference list

1   Laumann EO, Gagnon JH, Michael TM, Micheals S. *The Social Organisation of Sexuality: Sexual Practices in the United States*. Chicago: University of Chicago Press, 1994.

2   ACSF Investigators. 'AIDS and Sexual Behavior in France'. *Nature* 1992; 360:407-409.

3   Johnson A, Wadsworth J., Wellings K, Field J. *Sexual Attitudes and Lifestyles*. Oxford: Basil Blackwell, 1994.

4   Johnson A, Mercer C, Erens B, Copas A. 'Sexual Behaivour in Britain: Partnerships, Practices and HIV Risk Behaviours'. *Lancet* 2001; 358:1835-1842.

5   De Visser R, Smith AM, Rissel CE, Richters J. 'Sex in Australia: Heterosexual Experience and Recent Heterosexual Encounters Among a Representative Sample of Adults'. *Australian and New Zealand Journal of Public Health* 2003; 27(2):146-154.

6   Spira A. *Sexual Behaviour and AIDS*. Aldershot: Averbury, 1994.

7   Wellings K, Nanchahal K, Macdowall W, McManus S, Erens B, Mercer CH *et al.* 'Sexual behaviour in Britain: early heterosexual experience'. *Lancet* 2001; 358(9296):1843-50.

8   Laumann EO, Gagnon JH, Michael RT. 'A Political History of the National Sex Survey of Adults'. *Family Planning Perspectives* 1994; 26(1):34-38.

9   Wadsworth J, Johnson A, Wellings K, Field J. 'What's a Mean? - An Examination of the Inconsistency Between Men and Women in Reporting Sexual Partnerships'. *Journal of the Royal Statistical Society* 1996; 159(Part 1):111-123.

10   Rundle K, Leigh C, McGee H, Layte R. *Irish Contraception and Crisis Pregnancy [ICCP] Study: A Survey of the General Population*. 2004. Dublin, Crisis Pregnancy Agency.

11   Dunnell K. *Family Formation*. 1979. London, HMSO.

12   Gorer G. *Sex and Marriage in England Today*. London: Nelson, 1971.

13   Ward H, Day S, Mezzone J. 'Prostitution and Risk of HIV: Female Prostitutes in London'. *British Medical Journal* 1993; 307(356):358.

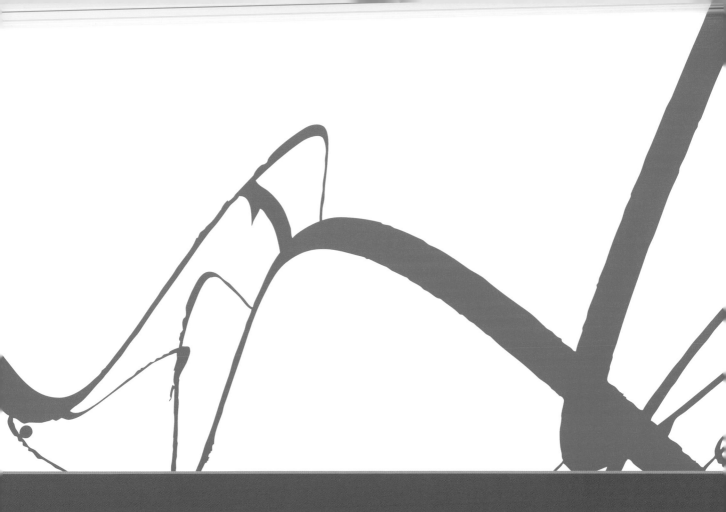

Chapter 8:

Heterosexual Practices and Frequency of Sex

8.1   Introduction

OF all areas of human sexuality, sexual practices have received the least amount of systematic attention. Studies of numbers of partners and age of first sex are not common, but have at least been carried out. Studies of the behaviours that sexual partners share are conspicuous by their absence.

As in most areas of sex research, the work of Alfred Kinsey and colleagues[1][2] stands out as the first attempt to study sexual practices systematically, albeit using rather flawed methods. Only with the advent of HIV and AIDS did researchers begin to take seriously the need for detailed information on specific practices, on how these are related to the characteristics of the individual, and on the context of the behaviour.[7]

Heterosexual practices encompass a wide variety of behaviours including penile-vaginal intercourse, oral sex (oral-penile and oral-vaginal contact), anal sex (penile-anal intercourse) and manual genital stimulation. These are just some of the biological combinations, but sexual practices can encompass a huge variety of forms. The prevalence and acceptance of these practices has varied hugely throughout history[3] and their popularity has been influenced by a host of both cultural and technological factors.

Our prime interest in this report is the risk of infection from HIV/STIs and the risk of unintended conception. These risks are significantly influenced by the sexual behaviours practised and the frequency of these behaviours (as well as by number of partners and risk-reduction strategies). In this chapter, we focus only on behaviours that have implications for the spread of sexually transmissible disease or hold a risk of pregnancy. This means that we focus on vaginal and anal intercourse and oral sex rather than on mutual masturbation which is associated with less risk. However, since sexual practices are extremely important sociological indicators, we also look at the broader set of genital sexual behaviours when we examine the frequency of sex.

In the next, **second section**, we describe how sexual practices were investigated in the ISSHR study. In the **third section**, we examine the relative frequency of vaginal, anal and oral sex. In the **fourth section**, we look at how 'ever' experiencing and 'recently' experiencing these behaviours varies across age cohorts and other important socio-demographic categories.

In the **fifth section**, we use reports of the frequency of sexual events to get a better sense of their relative density. In the **sixth section**, we examine the extent to which individuals see as optimal their current frequency of sex and how this level compares to what they perceive as the average frequency of the Irish population. This section also examines the extent of physical pleasure and emotional satisfaction derived from sex.

8.2   Investigating sexual practices

THE ISSHR survey included questions that attempt to measure the repertoire of sexual practices among the Irish population. These were of two types. The **first set of questions** explored the frequency of a range of practices by asking respondents when they had last experienced them (if ever). Eight possible responses were available:

In the last 7 days .... ☐₁
Not in the last 7 days but within the last 4 weeks .... ☐₂
Not in the last 4 weeks but within the last 3 months .... ☐₃
Not in the last 3 months but within the last 6 months .... ☐₄
Not in the last 6 months but within the last year .... ☐₅
Not in the last year but within the last 5 years .... ☐₆
More than 5 years ago .... ☐₇
Never .... ☐₈

This question was asked about the last time the respondent had experienced vaginal sex, gave oral sex, received oral sex, gave anal sex and received anal sex. Each of these behaviours was accompanied by an anatomical definition making clear what the behaviour entailed. Due to limited interview time, the survey did not ask about non-penetrative genital contact unless the respondent did not report any of the other behaviours. In such a case, the following question was used:

> 'When, if ever, was the last occasion you had GENITAL CONTACT with a (man/woman) NOT involving intercourse? GENITAL CONTACT NOT INVOLVING INTERCOURSE are forms of contact with the genital area NOT leading to vaginal, oral, or anal sex, but intended to achieve orgasm, for example, stimulating by hand.'

Preparatory research for the NATSAL survey[4] showed that respondents were often unclear as to what non-penetrative genital contact included. The rather cumbersome question/definition given above was found to be the most effective way of gaining information.[I]

Non-penetrative practices play an important role in the repertoire of sexual behaviours. They are often used as a substitute for penetrative sex by those in the early stages of a sexual relationship or as part of 'casual sex', particularly among homosexual men[5] or people wanting to avoid pregnancy or risk of STIs.[4] The decision to ask about non-penetrative behaviours only in cases where no other contact was reported was made on the basis that, given limited interview time, we had to concentrate on practices that carried a significant risk of either STI transmission or conception.

The **second set of questions** on practices was asked in a section on the most recent sexual event. Here respondents were asked whether their most recent genital sexual event included vaginal sex, anal sex and oral sex. As with the first set of questions, this section identified non-penetrative sexual practices only in cases of the absence of all other practices. If no other practices were reported it was clear that the event included a non-penetrative practice.

The term 'oral sex' covers two anatomically distinct practices: oral contact with female genitals and oral contact with the penis. A number of terms could be used to refer to these practices, but in this chapter we use 'cunnilingus' for the former and 'fellatio' for the latter.

[I] The ISSHR project was fortunate to be able to draw on the development work already carried out for other KAB surveys such as NATSAL.

8.3   The repertoire and frequency of different practices

SUMMARY

VAGINAL intercourse is the most widely experienced sexual practice among both men and women, followed by oral sex. A minority of individuals (and more men than women) report having experienced heterosexual anal sex.

Around half of all individuals reported vaginal sex 'in the last week' and around two-thirds 'in the last month'.

- 94% of men and women have experienced vaginal sex.

- 76% of men and 61% of women have experienced oral sex.

- 11% of men and 8% of women have experienced anal sex.

- Around half of Irish men and women report vaginal sex 'in the last week' and 68% 'in the last month'.

- 39% of men and 29% of women report oral sex 'in the last month'.

- Oral sex appears to be largely reciprocal: a large majority of men and women who report any oral sex report both fellatio and cunnilingus. Less than 10% of people only give or only receive oral sex.

REPRESENTATIVE data on sexual practices are almost entirely confined to those gathered as part of national KAB surveys. The British NATSAL survey[4] showed that vaginal sex predominated in heterosexual partnerships, with over 92% of men and women having experienced vaginal sex. Although oral sex in the form of cunnilingus and fellatio was common, with over 70% of respondents having some experience of either or both, both recent and lifetime experience of oral sex was strongly related to age. There was considerable evidence that oral sex had become more common in recent decades, suggesting an increase in its popularity over time in Britain.

The 1990 NATSAL survey found much lower recent and lifetime experience of anal sex: just 14% of men and 13% of women reported ever experiencing anal sex. There was no indication that its popularity had increased in recent decades. The NATSAL survey did find, however, as with oral sex, that anal sex was more likely to have been recently experienced by younger age groups.

NATSAL found that the frequency of different practices was also shaped by a person's relationship status: non-married individuals had a wider repertoire of practices, including manual stimulation and oral and anal sex.

Figure 8.1 shows the cumulative proportion of men reporting different sexual practices from 'in the last seven days' up to 'ever' in their life. The curves in the figure slope upward from left to right, showing that as the period grows more recent a smaller proportion of men have experienced each of the behaviours. The height of the curves shows the overall proportions who have experienced each behaviour at each period.

Figure 8.1: Last occasion of different sexual practices among men

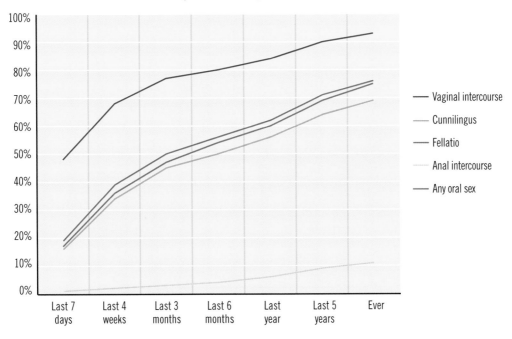

'Any oral sex' refers to either cunnilingus or fellatio.

Figure 8.1 shows that vaginal intercourse is the most widely experienced behaviour, both 'ever' and within all periods: 93% of men have experienced vaginal sex, 69% cunnilingus and 75% fellatio. A far smaller proportion, 11%, have experienced anal sex.

A total of 48% of men report vaginal sex 'in the last week' and over two-thirds 'in the last month'. These proportions are marginally lower than those found in the NATSAL survey (56% 'in the last seven days' and 73% 'in the last month').

Interestingly, of those men who report ever having vaginal sex, around 10% report not having done so 'in the last year'. Although most men have experienced oral sex, only a fifth have done so 'in the last week' and two-fifths 'in the last month'. A smaller proportion of men reported cunnilingus than reported fellatio. The NATSAL survey found the opposite for the British sample.

Figure 8.2: Last occasion of different sexual practices among women

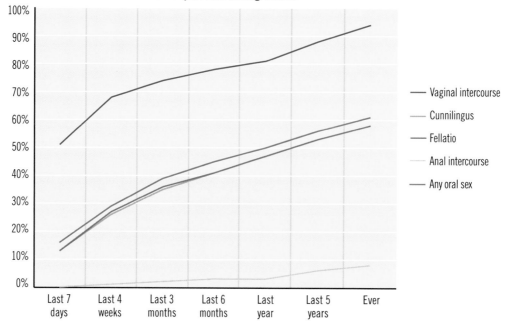

Figure 8.2 shows that the proportion of women who have experienced vaginal sex is roughly equal to the proportion of men and very close to the proportions reported in the NATSAL survey. The Irish proportions experiencing both oral (61% ISSHR v 69.2% in the UK) and anal sex (8.1% ISSHR v 12.9% in the UK) are substantially lower. The fact that these proportions are also lower than among Irish men may indicate some under-reporting by Irish women. (Some evidence for this is available below, where the experience of oral sex by age group is examined.) As among men, a substantial minority of women (11%) who have experienced vaginal sex have not done so 'in the last year'.

Oral sex is common experience among Irish men and women. Most have experienced it at some point, though rather more men report doing so than women and more men report fellatio than cunnilingus.

Table 8.1 shows a strong association between both types of oral sex among those having oral sex 'in the last year'. Of the 62% of men who experienced oral sex 'in the last year', the vast majority (83%) experienced both cunnilingus and fellatio (the data do not indicate whether this was during the same sexual event). The same pattern emerges among women (81% have experience of both 'in the last year'), suggesting that oral sex is reciprocal for most Irish men and women who practise it.

For more detail on the analyses in this section, see Appendix *Tables 6.1* and *6.2*.

Table 8.1: Experience of oral sex in the last year*

	Men (%)	Women (%)
Cunnilingus only	7.6	12.9
Fellatio only	9.4	6.5
Both	83.0	80.7
Total	100	100
N	2,020	2,184

* By those reporting oral sex 'in the last year'.

8.4   Determinants of the repertoire of sexual practices

SUMMARY

AN individual's sexual repertoire both in the past and in the more recent period is associated with a number of factors. The oldest age group in Ireland are more likely than their peers in other countries to never have married and to have remained celibate (see chapter seven). This is reflected in lower rates of having experienced vaginal sex among this group. This leads to an inverted u-shaped pattern: young people and the oldest age group are least likely to have experienced vaginal sex.

The recent experience of vaginal sex is also strongly related to relationship status: married people are most likely to have experienced it 'in the last year', followed by those who are cohabiting or in a steady relationship.

Age is also important for the experience of oral and anal sex. There is good evidence that both oral and anal sex have become more common through time. Older individuals are less likely to report oral sex and much less likely to report it in the most recent period. Among younger individuals, oral sex is now an established part of the sexual repertoire and an integral aspect of most sexual episodes.

Relationship status is also important for the recent experience of oral sex: people in less formal relationships are more likely to have experienced it.

■ The proportions that have experienced vaginal sex increase with age but decline in the oldest age groups.

■ Age is the major determinant of ever experiencing oral sex: 87% of men and 77% of women aged 25 to 34 have had oral sex compared to 48% and 24% of men and women aged 55 to 64.

■ Anal sex is increasing in prevalence: just 6% of men and 4% of women aged 55 to 64 have experienced it, compared to 18% of men and 13% of women aged 25 to 34.

■ Individuals with higher levels of education are more likely to have recently experienced vaginal and oral sex.

A PERSON'S repertoire of sexual practices, as noted in the introduction, may be influenced by many factors. These include stage of life, sexual attitudes and beliefs, education and relationship status, as well as the dynamics between partners (such as how well they know each other).

In this section we examine the impact of the most important of these, the age of the person. In the following section, we look at the wider determinants, including age.

Previous research has found that age is strongly related to both a person's number of partners and sexual repertoire.[4][6][7] Age can be related to sexual practices in a number of ways.

First, current age is strongly related to sexual attitudes: more recent cohorts are far more likely to be more liberal and accepting of a wider range of sexual practices (see chapter four). This is likely to lead to a greater acceptance of practices outside of vaginal sex and a greater prevalence of these practices.

Secondly, older age groups may experience a fall in the availability of partners for sexual contact, a particularly acute problem for older women as differential mortality for men leads to increasing proportions of women in each age group over 45.[8]

Thirdly, a decreasing appetite for sex emerges among older age groups.[9]

Fourthly, a factor affecting the level of experience of all types of sex among older cohorts in Ireland is the high level of non-marriage and celibacy (still more common among Irish men and women than among their British counterparts until the 1960s; see chapter one). Whereas rates of experience of vaginal sex tend to increase with age in most countries, in Ireland they rise and then fall again for older age groups.

Figures 8.3 and *8.4* show the proportions, by gender and age group, of people who have experienced vaginal, oral and anal sex 'in the last year' and 'ever'.

Looking first at the proportions by age group for 'ever' experiencing vaginal sex, we can see the pattern just noted: increasing proportions up to age 44 (among men) and 54 (among women) and then a slight decline for the older age groups. The proportions having vaginal sex 'in the last year' follow the same pattern, but are five to 10 points lower in general, although even among the oldest age group (55 to 64) over three-quarters of men and two-thirds of women report vaginal sex 'in the last year'.

Figure 8.3: Prevalence of different sexual practices among men in the last year and ever: by age

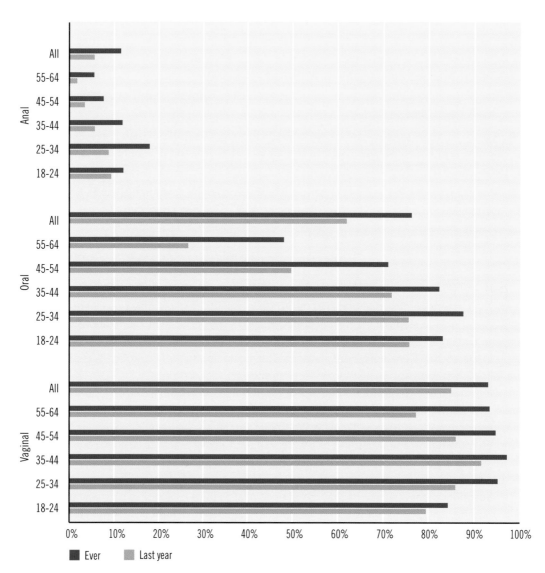

For oral sex, we see a very different pattern: a decreasing prevalence with age among men and women for having oral sex both 'ever' and 'in the last year'.

Figure 8.4: Prevalence of different sexual practices among women in the last year and ever: by age

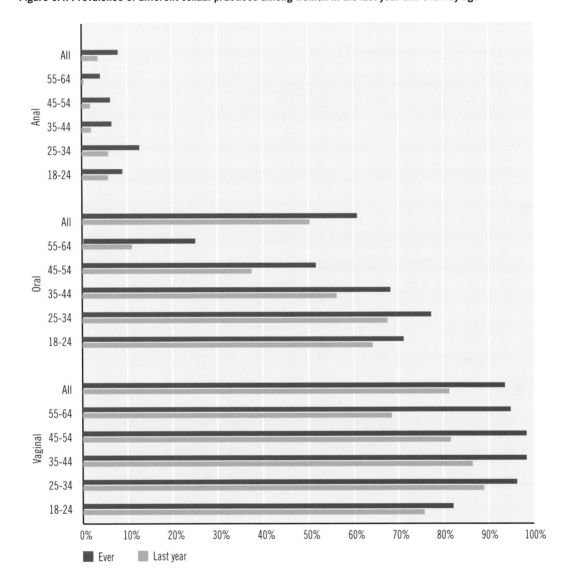

Over 80% of men aged 18 to 24 have experienced oral sex but less than half of men aged over 54. There is a particularly big fall (of over 23%) between those aged less than 55 and those aged 55 to 64.

The age pattern for those who have ever had oral sex is even more pronounced among women: over 77% of those aged 25 to 34 report it compared to just 24% of those aged over 54.

These results suggest a pronounced generational change in the acceptance and practice of oral sex. People born after 1950 and particularly those born after 1960 are much more likely to see oral sex as a standard part of their sexual 'script' and repertoire of practices. The growth in the prevalence of oral sex may have much to do with increasingly liberal sexual attitudes. Improved personal hygiene in recent decades, with greater availability of bathrooms and frequency of baths and showers, may also be a factor.

Figure 8.5: Sexual practices at most recent event: by gender and age group

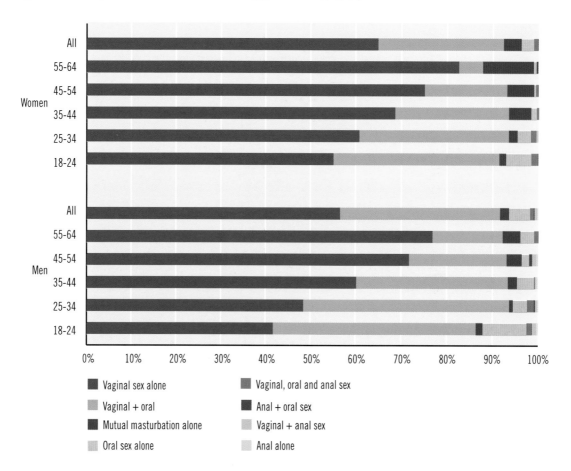

Figures 8.3 and *8.4* also show that the practice of heterosexual anal sex has increased in prevalence across the age cohorts. It has more than tripled between men aged over 54 (6%) and those between 25 and 34 (over 18%). Almost 12% of the youngest cohort have already experienced anal sex (and the proportion having done so 'in the last year' is higher than that among those aged 25 to 34). It is likely that the final proportion among this group will equal or exceed that of those aged 25 to 34. Among women the proportions are slightly lower but the overall pattern is the same: increasing prevalence among younger age groups.

Overall, however, anal sex is practised currently by a far smaller proportion of people than have 'ever' experienced it. Rates for 'in the last year' are typically 30% to 77% lower than the proportions that have 'ever' experienced anal sex, while the ratio of recently to 'ever' having anal sex increases across age groups. This implies that, of those who have ever experienced anal sex in older age groups, around half or less currently have anal sex.

The preceding tables show which practices were most recently experienced, but not the manner in which these practices were combined. For example, did vaginal and oral events occur in the same sexual episode, or did they occur in different episodes? Did anal sex replace vaginal sex in a subsequent episode or were both practised in the same episode?

To examine the manner in which practices were combined, we use the ISSHR questions on most recent genital sexual event. These questions asked respondents to reflect on their most recent event even if this was some time ago and irrespective of the status and sex of the partner. Questions were then asked about the nature of the sex, the characteristics of the partner and the context. Analysing only heterosexual events, *Figure 8.5* shows the combination of vaginal, oral and anal sex and the prevalence of mutual masturbation alone.

The results show that, for both men and women, vaginal sex alone tends to be the dominant practice, except among men aged 18 to 24 where the proportion having vaginal *and* oral sex is the largest group.

As age increases, the proportion having vaginal sex alone also increases. It was suggested earlier that mutual masturbation and oral sex may be practised instead of vaginal sex by those wishing to avoid the risk of pregnancy and STIs. To a certain extent this is supported in *Figure 8.5*: the largest proportion having oral sex alone is among the youngest age group of both men and women. On the other hand, mutual masturbation tends to be highest among the oldest age group.

For more detail on the analyses in this section, see Appendix *Tables 6.5* and *6.6*.

8.4.1   Other determinants of sexual practices

THE last section showed that age is strongly related to the probability of different sexual practices. In this section, we briefly examine the findings of research in other countries on the factors that influence the pattern of vaginal, oral and anal sex before examining several factors that were found to be important in the Irish data.

A number of studies have found relationship status to be an important factor. First and foremost, it is likely to be related to the probability of vaginal sex through the availability of sexual partners: married or cohabiting people have more access to sexual partners. For example, vaginal sex has been found to be far more common in settled relationships and marriage in particular, since issues around contraception and protection tend to have been dealt with in longer and more formal unions.

Relationship status can also influence sexual practices more indirectly, through sexual attitudes. For example, those who cohabit are more likely to be younger and more liberal sexually. Cohabitation has become a more general practice in recent years among Irish couples but is not as common as in the Scandinavian countries or even the UK.[10] However; its increasing prevalence does indicate more liberal attitudes.

Lastly, relationship status can influence sexual practices through the extent of familiarity between partners. In young relationships where partners are still becoming familiar, sexual practices may be confined to non-penetrative. As familiarity and trust grow, other practices may be suggested and the partners may experiment more.[9]

Education has been shown to influence sexual behaviours by a number of studies, including recent Irish research.[11] Higher levels of education are associated with greater levels of knowledge and judgement in the use of abstract information. This means that people with higher levels of education are more likely to avoid higher-risk behaviours.[12] This may affect practices such as anal sex. Johnson *et al* (1994)[4] found a weak relationship between social class and the probability of anal sex (individuals in the manual class were more likely to practise anal sex). Since education is strongly related to class, this finding may suggest a relationship to education also. On the other hand, higher education is also associated with more liberal attitudes (see chapter four), so it is not clear *a priori* how education affects practices.

Lastly, it is likely that people with a higher number of partners may also be more likely to have more varied sexual practices. This has been found in research in Britain[4] where higher levels of oral and anal sex were found among those with higher numbers of partners.

Analyses of the factors influencing whether the individual had experienced vaginal sex 'in the last year' confirmed the importance of age. *Figure 8.6* shows that both men and women in the middle age group (35 to 44) are most likely to have experienced vaginal sex 'in the last year'. This is because this group are more likely both to have a stable relationship and to still have a desire for sex.

Figure 8.6: Proportion having vaginal sex in the last year: by gender and age group

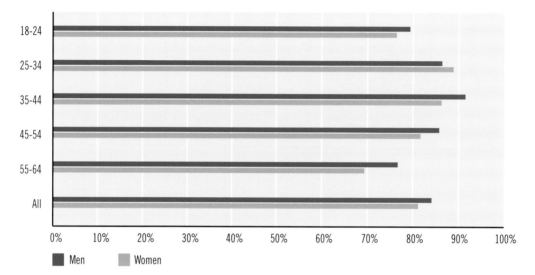

Figure 8.7 shows the proportion of respondents having vaginal sex 'in the last year' but disaggregated according to relationship. As expected, the more 'stable' the relationship (from no relationship to married via steady, cohabiting and casual), the more likely it is that both men and women report vaginal sex. Married men and women are significantly more likely to have had vaginal sex 'in the last year' than all other groups, followed by those who are cohabiting or in a steady relationship.

Analyses did not find that level of education or social class influenced the probability that the person had experienced vaginal sex 'in the last year', but did show, as we might expect, that individuals with two or more genital sexual partners 'in the last year' were more likely to report vaginal intercourse than individuals who reported either no partner or a single partner 'in the last year'.

Figure 8.7: Proportion having vaginal sex in last year: by gender and relationship

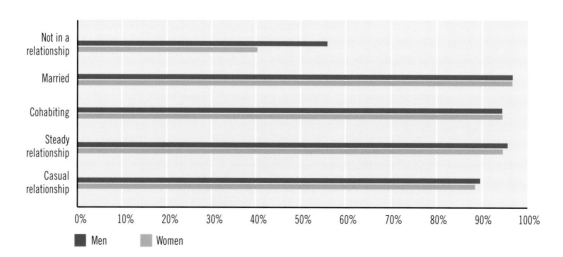

Figure 8.8 again shows the importance of age: younger men and women are significantly more likely than older to have experienced oral sex 'in the last year'. Men in the youngest age group are over twice as likely as those in the oldest to have had oral sex 'in the last year'.

Figure 8.8: Proportion having oral sex in last year: by gender and age group

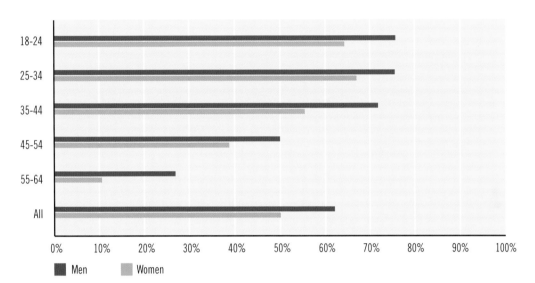

Among young women the difference is even larger: women aged 18 to 24 are almost six times more likely than the oldest group to have had oral sex in the recent period.

The clear and steep age gradient reveals a pronounced cohort change in the practice of oral sex: younger age groups see it as an integral part of their 'sexual script'.

Relationship status has a different influence on oral sex to that found for vaginal intercourse. *Figure 8.9* shows that cohabitees and people in steady relationships are more likely to have experienced oral sex than those who are married. These patterns recur even within age groups. That suggests that older individuals who are not married have more varied practices, perhaps because of more liberal sexual attitudes.

Figure 8.9: Proportion having oral sex in last year: by gender and relationship

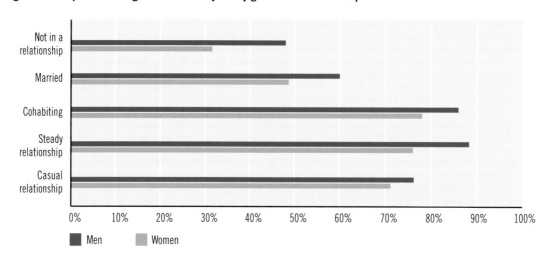

Figure 8.10 shows that both men and women in the highest educational grouping are significantly more likely to report oral sex 'in the last year' than all other groups.

Figure 8.10: Proportion having oral sex in last year: by gender and highest education

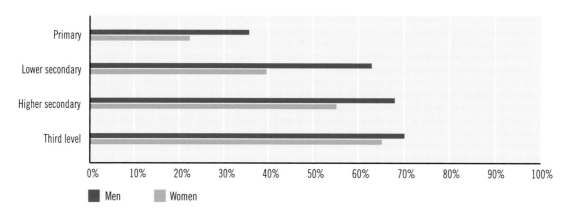

These patterns suggest that sexual attitudes play a significant role in shaping experience of oral sex; more educated people are more likely to see cunnilingus and fellatio as a standard part of their sexual repertoire.

Analyses (not shown here) also found that men and women in the higher professional class are significantly more likely to practise oral sex compared to men in the unskilled manual class, even within age groups.

Having experienced two or more sexual partners 'in the last year' is also associated with a higher probability of experiencing oral sex in the same period.

Lastly, *Figure 8.11* shows that, as with vaginal and oral sex, age is significantly related to the probability of experiencing anal sex 'in the last year'. Men and women under 35 are significantly more likely than those aged 35 or more to practise anal sex. This suggests a pronounced behavioural change among those born after 1970. Men aged 18 to 24 are almost six times more likely to currently practise anal sex than men aged 55 to 64. The difference among young women is even larger –

young women are 10 times more likely – but this is largely due to the very small proportion of the oldest cohort who report anal sex. These results suggest that anal sex is becoming a more accepted part of the heterosexual sexual repertoire among under-35s.

Figure 8.11: Proportion having anal sex in last year: by gender and age group

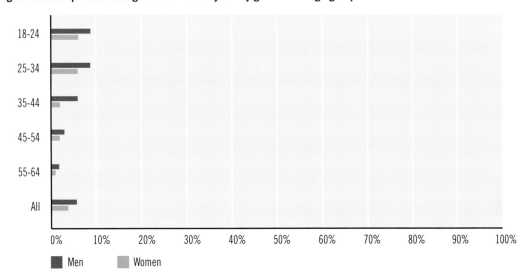

Analyses show that, apart from age, few other socio-demographic factors are strongly related to the experience of anal sex, except for a significantly higher rate among both men and women with two or more partners 'in the last year'. Among women, this group was four times more likely than women with a single partner to report anal sex in the most recent period.

For more detail on the analyses in this section, see Appendix *Tables 6.7* to *6.9.*

8.5 Frequency of sex

SUMMARY

MOST adults aged 18 to 64 have sex less than once a week and a quarter less than once a month.

The age of individuals is crucial factor: frequency is lower among the oldest and youngest groups.

Age interacts with relationship status. For example, among the youngest age group, those in a sexual relationship have the highest frequency of sex.

Women with higher levels of education have a higher frequency of sex.

- 58% of men and 57% of women aged 18 to 64 have sex less than once a week.

- 14% of men and 17% of women have sex less than twice a year.

- 50% of married people have sex less than weekly.

- Age and relationship status are the primary determinants of frequency of sex.

THIS chapter has examined the frequency with which individuals experience different sexual practices. It is also important to gain an understanding of the overall density of sexual events; that is, how many times do individuals have sex (of different kinds) over a given period?

Since the risk of infection from STIs is a function of type and number of partners, type of behaviour, risk-reduction practices and frequency of sex, knowing the density of sexual events is important. Knowing this pattern is also important for those outside epidemiology such as social scientists and psychologists who wish to understand the role that sex plays in maintaining relationships and how this varies across the population.

Attention is often focused on the biological 'drive' for sex, but not only does an individual's desire for sex vary enormously[13] over time, the frequency of sex is influenced by a large number of other factors. These include: the length and stability of a relationship (if a person has a current partner), the ages of the partners, and their health, since poor health may limit sexual functioning.

Comparisons of the frequency of sex across countries are problematic as the measures used vary widely. In general, US and UK research[4][9] has found roughly similar frequencies of sex among men and women. European and Australian[14] research has found higher levels of reported sex among men.[15] In all research, however, increasing age is associated with a lower frequency of sex, and marriage and cohabitation are associated with a higher frequency, although frequency tends to decrease as the length of the marriage increases.

In Australian[14] and French[15] research, the level of physical and emotional satisfaction from sex is also positively associated with increased frequency.

Individuals with more than one regular partner, or a series of short relationships over a compressed period, may report higher frequency of sexual events, since young relationships are usually associated with a greater frequency of sex (Johnson *et al* 1994).

The overwhelming majority of Irish respondents reported only one sexual partner over the last year or five years (see chapter seven). Frequency of sex is also determined to a considerable extent by a sexual partner, by their characteristics, circumstances and desires. The ISSHR survey could not collect information on sexual partners, aside from that reported for last sexual event. Most of our analyses concentrate on the respondent and their characteristics. It is not possible to analyse to any great depth the relationship between respondent and partner.

British research[4] has shown a weak relationship between frequency of sex and social class: frequency is higher among higher social-class groups. This could suggest that frequency of sex is also positively related to education (since class and education are strongly related). As with number of partners, class may be related to frequency of sex through the availability of partners rather than through more sexual events with any one partner.

This section examines the frequency of *all* rather than of *specific* genital sexual events (examined in the previous sections). All genital sexual events encompasses a broad range of practices, from vaginal and anal penetrative sex to oral sex and mutual masturbation plus other genital contact not necessarily leading to orgasm.

The frequency of this broadly defined sex was assessed in the ISSHR survey by asking respondents who reported sex 'in the last four weeks': "How often in total have you had sex in the last 4 weeks?" Respondents were given eight response categories, from '1 to 3 (less than once a week)' to '25 or more (at least once a day)'. There were also categories for 'don't know' and refusal. This variable has been combined with that employed in the previous section to create a combined variable which measures the total self-defined number of sexual events.

Figure 8.12 gives the proportions for the different frequency categories for men and women who reported at least one genital sexual event in their life so far. It shows no difference between men and women overall; the frequency of reported sex is the same. Age appears to be a very significant factor, but its effect is somewhat u-shaped. Frequency of sex rises for both men and women as age increases, with a peak among those aged 35 to 44, before decreasing again among older groups.

Figure 8.12: Total frequency of genital sexual events: by gender and age group

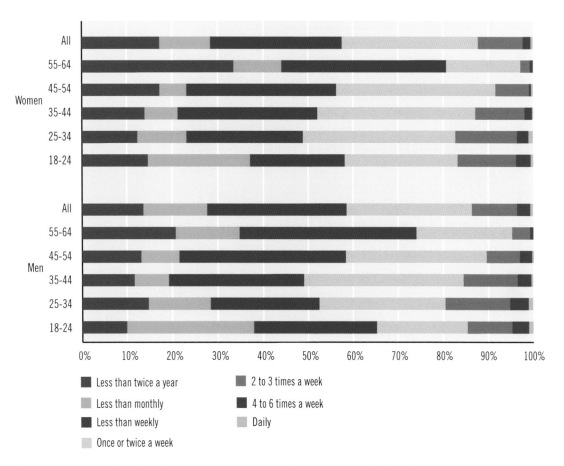

Legend:
- Less than twice a year
- Less than monthly
- Less than weekly
- Once or twice a week
- 2 to 3 times a week
- 4 to 6 times a week
- Daily

This pattern seems largely due to a combination of the greater availability of partners to people in the middle age groups (who are more likely to be married or cohabiting) and a decreasing appetite or ability to have sex (combined with falling partner numbers – see chapter seven) among the older age groups.

Interestingly however, the youngest age group are more likely to inhabit the two extremes of the distribution. This group has both the largest proportion reporting sex less than monthly (twice that even of the oldest age group) and one of the highest proportions reporting sex daily. This suggests that, when in sexual relationships, people aged 18 to 24 are more likely to have very high frequencies of sex.

Some evidence of the impact of availability of partners can be found in the results by relationship status (see Appendix *Table 6.10* and *6.11*). These show that married people or those living together have significantly higher frequencies of sex than those in casual relationships or who are not in a relationship. However, the relatively high frequencies for categories other than those who are married and the strong impact of not having a current relationship show that non-marriage is no longer a bar to sexual experience; instead, the availability of partners is the crucial factor.

Appendix *Tables 6.10* and *6.11* also show the distribution of frequencies of sex by educational group. There is some suggestion of a greater frequency of sex among people with an upper-secondary qualification or higher. Women with higher levels of education have a significantly higher frequency of sex, although the highest frequency is among women with higher-secondary qualifications.

For social class, on the other hand, no obvious relationship is apparent, particularly among women. Johnson *et al* (1994)[4] found similar results for their British sample – a very weak association between class and frequency of sex 'in the last four weeks'.

It is interesting to note that, among the Irish population aged 18 to 64 who have ever had sex, most have sex less than once a week (58% of men and 57% of women) and over a quarter have sex less than once a month (28%). One in six women and one in seven men reported sex less than twice a year. Even among married people, half have sex less than weekly and one in eight less than once a month. It is not possible to compare with other studies as these statistics are usually presented as frequency of sex 'in the last four weeks' (which would encompass about three-quarters of our sample), but these findings do not present a picture of a population where the majority are having daily or even weekly sex.

8.6   Preferred frequency of sex, physical pleasure and emotional satisfaction

SUMMARY

OVERALL, significantly more women than men report that their frequency of sex is 'about right'. More men than women report that they would like to have sex more frequently.

Among women, greater frequency is associated with greater agreement that the frequency is 'about right'.

Among men, the pattern is more complex. Men who report the lowest and highest frequencies of sex say they would like a higher frequency, whereas men with a medium level of frequency are more likely to say the frequency is 'about right'.

Men are more likely than women to report that sex with their current or last partner is 'extremely' pleasurable. A higher proportion of women report that sex is 'moderately' or only 'slightly' pleasurable.

Patterns of emotional satisfaction are almost identical for men and women. Levels of emotional satisfaction and sexual pleasure rise after age 24, are highest in men and women aged 25 to 44, and decrease among older age groups.

- 57% of men and 70% of women believe that their current frequency of sex is 'about right' for them.

- The highest proportion of those who would like less frequent sex is among those currently experiencing the least frequency.

- 79% of people report that sex is 'extremely' or 'very' pleasurable.

- 40% of men find sex 'extremely' pleasurable compared to 33% of women.

- 78% report that sex is 'extremely' or 'very' emotionally satisfying.

THE last section showed that frequency of sex varies enormously across the population and is influenced by a number of factors. However, this gives us no insight into whether people consider the frequency of sex to be close to ideal or into the pleasure and fulfilment that people derive from their sex lives.

The ISSHR survey contained questions on all these issues. One question asked about the frequency of sex by asking respondents whether they would like greater frequency, about the same or less frequent sex than they were currently experiencing. Two other questions examined the issue of physical pleasure and emotional satisfaction that individuals derived from the sexual partner they last had sex with.

Figure 8.13 (overleaf) gives the results for the question on whether sex is frequent enough. It shows that 57% of men and 70% of women (who have had sex at least once in their life) perceive their level of frequency to be 'about right'. More men than women said they would like a higher frequency of sex (42% of men compared to 25% of women). This proportion is smallest among both men and women where sexual frequency is 'less than monthly'. It reaches a peak for men at 'twice or three times a week' and for women at 'once a day', although the latter proportion is based upon the responses of just 20 women.

The pattern of men wanting more sex is complex. It is highest among men having the lowest frequency, falls among men having sex once to three times a week, but increases again among men having sex more frequently than that. Around a third of men reporting sex four to six times a week still feel that they would like a greater frequency.

Among women the pattern is simpler. The proportion wanting more sex decreases as frequency increases.

For both men and women, the proportion wanting less sex is highest for those who currently have the lowest frequency. This suggests that a low frequency of sex is not a problem for some individuals in this group, although most would like increased frequency.

For more detail on the analysis of preferences for frequency of sex, see Appendix *Tables 6.12* and *6.13*.

Figure 8.14 gives the results for the question that asks respondents whether their sexual relationship with their current or last partner is or was physically pleasurable or not. Men were significantly more likely than women to report 'extremely pleasurable' sex with their current or most recent partner (40% of men compared to 33% of women). Women were more likely than men to report 'moderately pleasurable'.

The difference in the proportions of men and women reporting sex as 'extremely pleasurable' does not necessarily indicate a significant difference between the genders in their experience of sex. Women may experience the same levels of pleasure as men during sex, but be less likely to report this as 'extremely pleasurable'. However, the greater proportion of women than men reporting sex as only moderately pleasurable suggests that more women than men find sex with their current or last partner lacking in some respects.

Figure 8.13: Frequency and desired frequency of sex: by gender

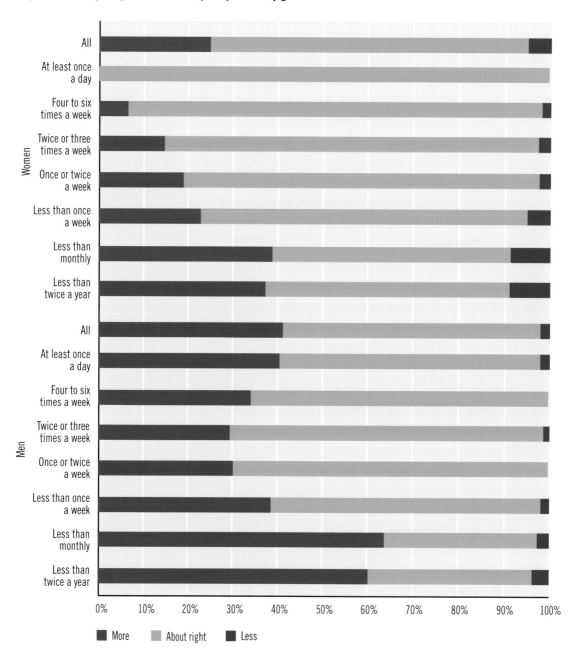

Figure 8.14: Extent of physical pleasure with current or last partner: by gender

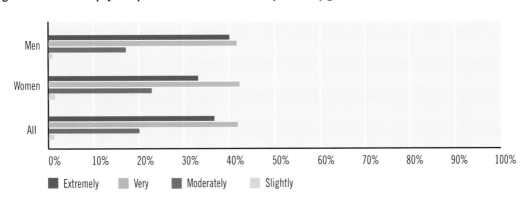

Analyses found that the degree of physical pleasure derived from sex varied strongly by age group, as shown in *Figure 8.15*.

Figure 8.15: Extent of physical pleasure with current or last partner: by gender and age group

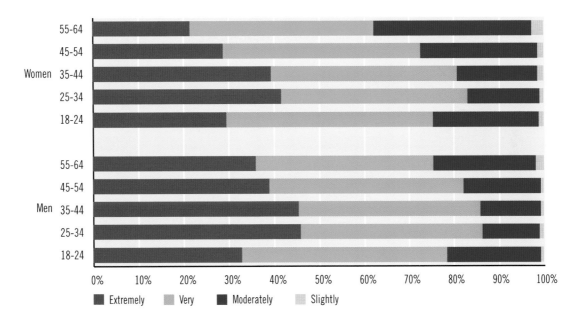

Reported pleasure from sex is highest among both men and women aged 25 to 34 and lowest among the oldest age group of women where the proportion reporting sex as 'moderately' or 'slightly' pleasurable is 38%.

Overall, the level of pleasure increases with age before decreasing again after age 44.

Analyses also found (not shown here) that level of sexual pleasure also varied significantly by relationship status. Satisfaction was lowest for sex between partners who had just met and highest for those in a steady relationship or who were engaged; it fell back again among married people. This pattern is one reason why sexual pleasure varied by age group in the manner shown above; people in a steady relationship or who are engaged are likely to be younger, and married people older.

Overall, these patterns suggest that sexual pleasure increases as partners' experience of one another increases, but that this factor then diminishes with age and duration of relationship.

Figure 8.16 gives the overall reported levels of emotional satisfaction that men and women derived from sex with their current or most recent partner. It shows almost identical results for men and women: around a third report being 'extremely' emotionally satisfied with their current or last partner.

Figure 8.16: Extent of emotional satisfaction with current or last partner: by gender

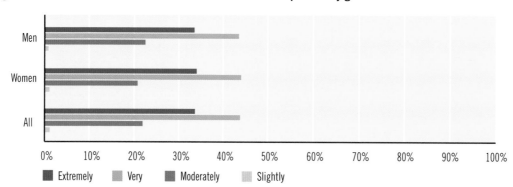
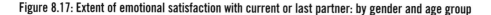

Figure 8.17: Extent of emotional satisfaction with current or last partner: by gender and age group

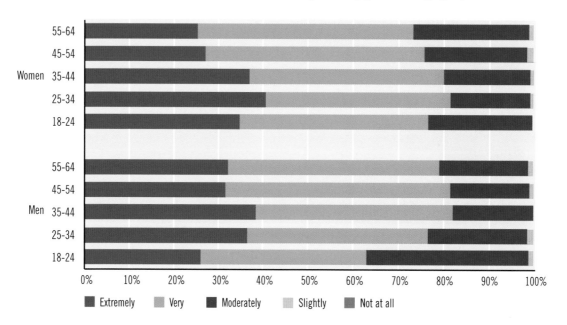

Figure 8.17, however, shows that responses vary significantly by age group. As with physical pleasure, the extent of emotional satisfaction increases with age. It peaks among women between 25 and 34 and among men aged 35 to 44, then falls thereafter.

8.7 Summary

THE study of human sexual practices has until comparatively recently been confined to a biological perspective. This perspective was only partially widened by the work of Alfred Kinsey and his associates in the first half of the 20th century. Since the 1980s, a number of national studies of sexual behaviour allow us to look more closely at sexual practices and how they are related to the wider set of social and demographic determinants.

This chapter used data from the ISSHR study (the first Irish study of sexual knowledge, attitudes and behaviours) to give an overview of the pattern of sexual practices in heterosexual partnerships.

The results show that vaginal sex is by far the most commonly experienced sexual practice: 94% of men and women have experienced vaginal sex at some point in their life so far. Around 70% of both men and women report vaginal sexual intercourse 'in the last month'. Oral sex is less common than vaginal sex: around three-quarters of men and just under two-thirds of women report experiencing oral sex. Anal sex appears to be practised by a relatively small minority: 11% of men and 8% of women.

An examination of the factors associated with the experience of different practices shows that age is the main determinant. Older respondents are less likely to report experience of each of the practices in the recent period. However, as in studies elsewhere, the popularity of oral sex appears to have increased over time; younger individuals are far more likely than older respondents to have experienced it. There is also some evidence of an increase in the experience of anal sex through time, although the relatively small numbers involved make it difficult to be certain of this.

For younger respondents, the 'average' sexual event is now likely to include oral sex; among older respondents, vaginal sex only is still the dominant pattern.

Oral sex has become more important in heterosexual sexual relationships, and is almost always reciprocal; over 80% of men and women who had oral sex at their most recent event report experiencing both fellatio and cunnilingus together.

An analysis of the wider determinants of practices shows that vaginal sex tends to become the dominant practice in more stable and formalised relationships. There is some evidence that mutual masturbation and oral sex alone are often practised as an alternative to vaginal intercourse among people in more casual or younger relationships where contraception and protection are an issue.

There is some evidence that, even within age groups, level of education is a significant predictor of oral sex; more educated groups are much more likely to include oral sex within their repertoire. This pattern is particularly strong among women and could be related to sexual attitudes among these groups, since less educated and more manual working-class groups tend to have more conservative attitudes.

As with other practices, age and relationship status was a significant predictor of anal sex. Having a higher number of partners 'in the last year' was also a strong predictor. This could be because this group are more liberal in attitude and have a wider sexual repertoire as well as a higher number of partners than average. It is notable that this group combines higher levels than average of anal sex and number of partners, two important risk factors for risk of infection with an STI and the HIV virus.

8.8 Reference list

1   Kinsey AC, Pomeroy WB, Martin CE. *Sexual Behaviour in the Human Male*. Philadelphia: Saunders, 1948.

2   Kinsey AC, Pomeroy WB, Martin CE, Gebhard PH. *Sexual Behaviour in the Human Female*. Philadelphia: Saunders, 1953.

3   Weeks J. *Sex, Politics and Society: The Regulation of Sexuality Since 1800*. London: Longman, 1981.

4   Johnson A, Wadsworth J, Wellings K, Field J. *Sexual Attitudes and Lifestyles*. Oxford: Basil Blackwell, 1994.

5   Grulich AE, De Visser RO, Smith AM, Rissel CE, Richters J. 'Sex in Australia: homosexual experience and recent homosexual encounters'. *Australian and New Zealand Journal of Public Health* 2003; 27(2):155-163.

6   Johnson A, Mercer C, Erens B, Copas A. 'Sexual Behaviour in Britain: Partnerships, Practices and HIV Risk Behaviours'. *Lancet* 2001; 358:1835-1842.

7   Laumann EO, Gagnon JH, Michael RT. 'A Political History of the National Sex Survey of Adults'. *Family Planning Perspectives* 1994; 26(1):34-38.

8   Layte R, Fahey T, Whelan C. 'Income, Deprivation and Well-Being among Older Irish People'. ESRI Books and Monographs [No. 151]. Dublin: National Council on Ageing and Older People, 2000.

9   Laumann EO, Gagnon JH, Michael TM, Michaels S. *The Social Organisation of Sexuality: Sexual Practices in the United States*. Chicago: University of Chicago Press, 1994.

10 Coleman D. 'Demography and Migration in Ireland, North and South'. In: Heath AF, Breen R, Whelan CT, editors. *Ireland North and South: Perspectives from Social Science*, pp69-116. Oxford: Oxford University Press, 1999.

11 Rundle K, Leigh C, McGee H, Layte R. *Irish Contraception and Crisis Pregnancy (ICCP) Study: A Survey of the General Population*. 2004. Dublin, Crisis Pregnancy Agency.

12 Mondon CWS, van Lenthe F, de Graaf ND, Kraaykamp G. 'Partner's and own education: does who you live with matter for self-assessed health, smoking and excessive alcohol consumption?' *Social Science and Medicine* 2003; 57:1901-1912.

13 Masters WH, Johnson VE. *Human Sexual Response*. Boston: Little, Brown, 1966.

14 Richters J, Grulich AE, de Visser RO, Smith M, Rissel CE. 'Sex in Australia: sexual and emotional satisfaction in regular relationships and preferred frequency of sex among a representative sample of adults'. *Australian and New Zealand Journal of Public Health* 2003; 27(2):171-179.

15 Sandfort T, Bos H, Haavio-Mannila E, Sundet J. 'Sexual Practices and Their Social Profiles'. In: Hubert M, Bajos N, Sandfort T, editors. *Sexual Behaviour and HIV/AIDS in Europe*. London: UCL Press, 1998.

Chapter 9:

Homosexual Partnerships and Practices

9.1 Introduction

SEXUAL practices are an important determinant of the risk that an individual faces of infection from STIs and HIV. This is particularly true among homosexual men. The role of anal sex in the transmission of HIV was highlighted early on in studies of the spread of HIV in North America and the UK.[1] Research has shown that anal sex is a core element of homosexual sex among men in other countries.[1,2] It is thus important to establish the frequency of this behaviour among men who have sex with men in Ireland. Since oral sex is also accompanied by risks of transmission, it, too, is an issue examined in this chapter.

Our aims are not all epidemiological, however. The pattern of homosexual partnerships and practices is important for understanding the pattern of homosexual relationships. The homosexual and heterosexual populations are firmly enmeshed (as chapter five shows). Only a small minority of men and women report genital contact with the same gender only. The overwhelming majority of people who have had same-sex partnerships have also had sexual relationships with the opposite gender. This is true even if we confine analysis to the most recent period. In this sense, exclusive 'homosexuality' is rare and bisexuality far more common.

However, only 4% of the male population and around 1% of the female population have ever had a same-sex genital experience (see chapter five). This means that the numbers of respondents available for analysis are very small in absolute terms: 4% of men (weighted) means 145 individuals (unweighted) over a sample of 3,188 men, and 1% of women (weighted) means 56 individuals over a sample of 4,253 (unweighted). This severely limits the analyses that can be performed; the samples cannot be disaggregated without cells becoming perilously small and statistical inference breaking down. Because of this, this chapter is relatively short, but it still provides important insights into same-sex partnerships and practices.

In the next, **second section**, we examine how the ISSHR survey measures same-sex partnerships and practices and the implications this has for the results. In the **third section**, we analyse the pattern of sexual partnerships, in particular the number of same-sex partnerships experienced over different periods. The **fourth section** examines the frequency of oral and anal sex in same-sex relationships, while the **fifth section** looks at the extent of reciprocity in these practices. The **sixth section** summarises the main findings and reaches conclusions as to their implications.

9.2 Measuring same-sex partnerships and practices

THE ISSHR survey instrument was designed to collect detailed information on various dimensions of sexual relationships, but the limited time available to interview respondents meant that choices had to be made about the focus of the study and thus the content of the questionnaire. As described in the introduction to this report, one of the primary objectives of the project was to generate a better understanding of the factors that contribute to infection with an STI and to unplanned pregnancy. The questionnaire thus concentrated on collecting information that was directly relevant to this. As noted in the last chapter, this focus had implications for the measurement of sexual practices; only questions on behaviours that carry a risk of conception or STI infection were included. Only if respondents reported genital sexual contact in their life but no penetrative practice in the last year were they questioned on non-penetrative practices.

The same approach was adopted for same-sex sexual relations. For men, only questions on same-sex oral and anal intercourse were included in the section on frequency of different sexual practices. For women, only oral sexual practices were included. As before, only if the respondent did not report any of these practices 'in the last year' were they then questioned on mutual masturbation. Thus no form of vaginal or anal sex would be counted for women, even though this might be an integral part of practices through the use of sex toys.

This approach also had implications for the measurement of number of sexual partners. Because vaginal sexual intercourse dominates in heterosexual partnerships, restricting the definition of 'sexual partner' to encounters including vaginal, oral or anal sex does not produce a pronounced bias in the results. However, among respondents experiencing same-sex relationships, non-penetrative events may form a far larger part. These partnerships would not be counted, which may mean that the figure for number of same-sex partners over different periods is far lower than would have been the case if a wider definition had been used. This issue is especially important when findings from the ISSHR survey are compared with those produced by the Sigma Research and Gay Health Network study of men.[3] Carroll *et al* did not include a breakdown of the behaviours which define a 'sexual partner'; respondents were simply asked "how many men have you had sex with?"

9.3 Numbers of same-sex sexual partners over different periods

SUMMARY

THIS section examines the number of partners over different periods experienced by men and women who reported at least one same-sex partner over lifetime so far.

Men who have had same-sex contact tend to have as many (male) partners as men who have only had sex with women. However, around a third report 10 or more partners, a larger proportion than that found among men with opposite-sex experience alone.

The absolute number of women who report same-sex contact is small. Analyses, thus, are difficult, but results suggest that such women tend to have had a smaller number of partners than women with heterosexual experience alone.

■ Most men who have sex with men (MSM) have a similar number of partners to the general male population.

■ However, 32% of MSM have had 10 or more partners in their life so far, compared to 21% of the general male population.

■ Women with homosexual experience tend to have fewer partners than the general female population aged 18 to 64.

THIS section examines the number of same-sex sexual partners that men and women who report same-sex genital contact have had over different periods. Sex is defined as anal or oral sex; partnerships that did not include these practices are not counted.

Representative KAB surveys in a number of countries tend to show that men who report same-sex genital experience have a greater number of sexual partners than men who report heterosexual experience alone.[4][5][6] The findings are not as clear for women; some suggest that women with same-sex experience have a lower number of partners overall.[7]

The Australian ASHR study reported that, over three time periods, men had a higher number of same-sex partners than women. However, a similar proportion of men and women (around 3%) reported two or more same-sex partners over lifetime. (A greater proportion of men than women reported 10 or more same-sex partners over lifetime (1.8% v 0.2%), but these small proportions have wide confidence intervals around them and the difference is not statistically significant.) Men and women who identified themselves as homosexual or bisexual had significantly more same-sex partners than heterosexual individuals; men identifying themselves as homosexual had the highest number of same-sex partners, followed by bisexual men. Both groups of men reported more same-sex partners than homosexual or bisexual[m] women.[2]

Figure 9.1 gives the numbers of partners reported by male and female respondents who reported ever having a same-sex partner (with whom they had anal or oral sex). It shows that just over 40% of such men have had a single partner in their lifetime and just under another fifth have had two to four partners. These proportions are very similar to those found for heterosexual partnerships among Irish men overall (40% had a single partner and 21% two to four).[n] However, whereas 25% of Irish men overall reported 10 or more (heterosexual) partners, 32% of men with same-sex experience reported 10 or more. This suggests a degree of polarisation among men with homosexual experience; that is, most have patterns of partnership similar to those having heterosexual relationships, but a minority have a higher number of partners.

Figure 9.1: Distribution of number of same-sex partners over three time periods by gender – for those having same-sex genital contact

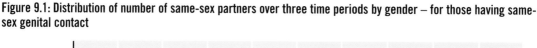
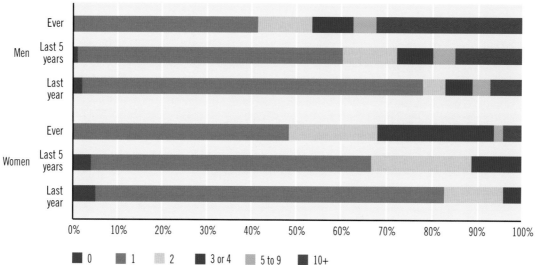

Around 10% of men with same-sex experience reported 30 or more partners over lifetime so far, and 5% over 100. However, this is 10% and 5% of the 4.5% who had had a same-sex partner, so the absolute number of individuals is low.

These proportions are made slightly problematic by missing data on number of sexual partners. Of respondents reporting same-sex genital contact over lifetime, 41 cases, among men, were missing a response for the number of sexual partners and, among women, 13 cases. These are small numbers, but large relative to the numbers reporting same-sex contact. Analysis suggests, however, that these respondents are unlikely to have had large numbers of partners as almost all reported same-sex experience 'more than five years ago'. If we assume that all had a single same-sex partner, this would imply that the proportion of men with a single partner over lifetime so far (as shown in *Figure 9.1*) would increase substantially, from 41% to 57%. Among women, the proportion would increase from 47% to 58%.

When we look at the patterns of partnership 'in the last five years', the proportions display the same pattern: three-fifths reported a single partner, a fifth two to four and 15% 10 or more. These figures are close to those for heterosexual partnerships over the same period except that, once again, the prevalence of men with 10 or more partners is twice as large among those with homosexual experience.

The same pattern is repeated for partners 'in the last year', except the proportion with one partner increases (from the 'in the last five years' figure) to almost four-fifths, while that with 10 or more decreases to around 7%, compared to 3% for heterosexual partnerships.

The Sigma Research and Gay Health Network by Carroll *et al* (2002) (from here forward referred to as the Sigma survey)[3] have carried out several studies among men who have sex with men in Ireland and have published figures on numbers of partners. These show substantially higher numbers of partners over the 'last year' than the ISSHR results. Although the categories used are not strictly comparable, Carroll *et al* (2002: 23)[8] show that around a quarter of their sample had between five and 10 partners 'in the last year' and another quarter 11 or more. This compares to 4% with five to nine in the ISSHR sample and a further 7% with 10 or more. This raises the question of how this difference arose:

- Part of the difference may be due to the more open definition of 'sex' used in the Sigma survey (only oral and anal sex were counted in ISSHR).
- Another possible reason for the difference may be the small ISSHR sample and associated confidence intervals. Only 84 men had a male partner 'in the last year'; this means that the proportion having more than nine partners could be anywhere between 3% and 18%. Although the non-random sampling of the Sigma survey means that normal standard errors are not applicable, if we assume normality, the 95% confidence interval on a sample of 1,056 individuals is 4.1%, giving a lower and upper range of 19.7% and 27.9%. This means that the confidence intervals don't overlap; if, however, we take both at their extremes they are relatively close (this is making some heroic assumptions).
- A third explanation may be the sampling strategy used in the Sigma survey. To obtain a large enough sample, the questionnaire was distributed at the Gay Pride parade and in pubs and clubs. Those attending these events and venues were likely to be younger than the general population. There is, indeed, a difference in average age between the two surveys; a median of 29 in the Sigma sample compared to 43 in the ISSHR sample. The younger profile and higher level of social participation of the Sigma sample may have led to a greater prevalence of higher numbers of partners.

If the above is true, the ISSHR data suggest, in contrast to the Sigma survey, that a majority of men who currently have same-sex partners have partner frequencies close to those of men who have sex only with women.°

The numbers of same-sex partnerships among Irish men are very different to those found in the Australian ASHR study[2] where the distribution was significantly skewed upward: 95% of homosexual men reported three or more partners over lifetime (as did 83% of bisexual men), compared to just 46% of Irish men with genital homosexual experience. The proportion having 10 or more partners over lifetime is also very different: in the Australian study, 77% of homosexual men and 58% of bisexual men reported 10 or more partners, compared to 32% of Irish men with same-sex genital experience.

The patterns found among women are different from those among men. Less than 4% of women reported 10 or more partners over lifetime and around half reported a single partner. These patterns are similar to those found for women's heterosexual partnerships, except that a far higher proportion of women with homosexual experience reported between two and four partners and smaller proportions five or more. Men with homosexual experience were more likely to report a larger number of partners than men without same-sex experience, but the opposite is true for women.

Patterns 'over the last five years' and 'last year' show a similar pattern. Few women with same-sex partnerships reported a single partner but, as well, fewer reported five or more, compared to women with heterosexual partnerships.

It should be understood, however, that the ISSHR sample has very few men and women with homosexual experience; this leads to large standard errors and confidence intervals. For example, although the proportion of women with one partner over lifetime is given as 49% in *Figure 9.1*, the wide confidence interval means the actual proportion could be anywhere from 32% to 66%. Similarly, for those with 10 or more partners, the proportion could be as low as 1% and as high as 16%.

Although it is difficult to make comparisons given the small number of individuals in the ISSHR data, results from the ASHR survey show that Irish women with same-sex experience tend to have fewer partners than Australian women identifying as homosexual or bisexual: 86% of the former and 53% of the latter report three or more partners over lifetime compared to 31% of Irish women with same-sex genital experience.

In the proportions with 10 or more partners, the differences are even more pronounced: 20% of homosexual Australian women reported this number of partners compared to just 4% of Irish women. However, 60% of Australian women with some same-sex experience identified themselves as bisexual and just 7% of this group reported 10 or more partners – which is closer to the Irish pattern.

° It should be emphasised that targeted research such as the Sigma survey is essential for identifying patterns of behaviour, knowledge and attitudes among population sub-groups, such as gay men, who may not be interviewed in sufficient numbers by a national population survey such as the ISSHR study.

9.4 Frequency of oral and anal sex

SUMMARY

AMONG both men and women who have experienced a same-sex partnership, only a minority reported practising oral and anal sex.

The majority of men (70%) who have had same-sex genital contact have never either given or received anal sex and less than 10% have had anal sex 'in the last month'.

- A minority of men (33%) who have had homosexual contact reported homosexual oral sex 'in the last year'.

- 17% of men who have had homosexual contact had homosexual anal sex 'in the last year'.

- 27% of men who have had homosexual contact reported never having homosexual oral sex.

- 68% of men who have had homosexual contact reported never having homosexual anal sex.

- 20% of women who have had homosexual contact reported never having homosexual oral sex.

THE ISSHR survey included a number of questions that sought to measure the frequency of different practices (as noted in chapter eight). In section G of the questionnaire, these were tailored to the task of measuring the frequency of oral and anal sex among men and women who reported any same-sex genital contact over lifetime so far.

One important question which needs to be addressed is the prevalence of giving and receiving oral and anal sex.[p] This has particular importance in epidemiological models. Questions were asked, therefore, on these four behaviours.

Where individuals did not report oral or anal sex 'in the last year', they were asked when they had last experienced mutual masturbation (the question used is identical to that described in chapter eight).

Results from a French survey[9] show that the most common practice in male same-sex encounters is manual stimulation of the partner; over 70% of respondents reported this at their last same-sex experience. Just 36% reported insertive anal intercourse and 28% receptive anal intercourse. These results were closely replicated in the Australian ASHR study. It found that the majority of 'most recent' male same-sex encounters included manual stimulation (89% received, 90% gave), while 38% reported insertive anal intercourse and 30% receptive anal intercourse. Receiving and giving oral sex was reported by around 75% of men. Of women, over 90% reported manual stimulation at 'most recent' same-sex encounter; around two-thirds reported both giving and receiving oral sex.

For the ISSHR study, *Figure 9.2* gives the proportions of men, who have had a same-sex genital partner, experiencing different frequencies of the four behaviours. It shows that:

---

[p] Giving oral sex is defined as putting the mouth on a partner's genitalia and receiving oral sex as vice versa. Giving anal sex is defined as inserting the penis in a partner's rectum, and receiving anal sex as vice versa. The terms 'insertive anal intercourse' and 'receptive anal intercourse', respectively, are also used.

- Around a fifth of men (with same-sex genital experience) have both received and given oral sex 'in the last month', a further fifth have both received and given oral sex 'in the last five years' and between a fifth and a quarter have 'ever' given and received oral sex.

Figure 9.2: Last occasion of different sexual practices among men who report same-sex genital experience in their lifetime

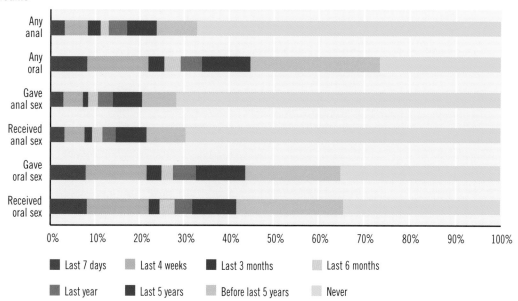

This suggests that among men who have had genital same-sex contact, only around 40% are currently practising or have recently practised oral sex. Perhaps more surprisingly, around a third have not experienced oral sex at all with someone of the same gender.

Figure 9.3: Last occasion of different sexual practices among women who report same-sex genital experience in their lifetime

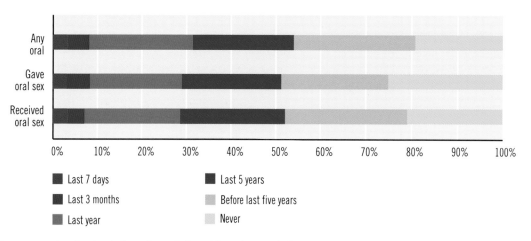

The proportion for both 'last 4 weeks' and 'last 6 months' were zero percent.

The pattern of frequency of anal sex is even more polarised:

- Around 70% of men (who have had genital contact with other men) reported that they had never either given or received anal sex, and just a fifth reported anal sex 'in the last five years'. Only around 7% reported either giving or receiving anal sex in the last month.

Care should be taken in interpreting these results as numbers of individuals are low, but they suggest that the population frequency of homosexual anal sex is very low:

- Only 0.5% to 1% of the male population have homosexual anal sex 'at least once a month' (using a 95% confidence interval).

Figure 9.3 gives the proportions of women (who have ever had a same-sex genital partner) having different frequencies of oral sex. The numbers of women available for this analysis are very low, so it is impossible to derive any clear conclusions. However, the numbers suggest that a very small proportion of women practise homosexual oral sex regularly ('more than once a month'). Around a quarter have experienced oral sex 'in the last year' and another quarter oral sex 'in the last five years'.

9.5 The reciprocity of oral and anal sex

> **SUMMARY**
> THE ISSHR data suggest that, as found with oral sex in opposite-sex relationships, oral and anal sex in same-sex relationships is largely reciprocal, although the small number of individuals in the sample makes definitive statements difficult.
> - Oral sex tends to be reciprocal among homosexual partners, although the level of reciprocity is lower among women.
> - Reciprocity of anal sex (both giving and receiving) among men who have sex with men is lower than for oral sex.

ORAL sex is essentially a reciprocal practice in heterosexual relationships (as shown in chapter eight). Men and women who had received oral sex were just as likely to give oral sex, at the 'most recent' sexual event. The ISSHR survey did not have a large enough sample of same-sex sexual practices at the 'most recent' event (section H of the questionnaire) to be able to draw any conclusions about practices in homosexual partnerships. However, analyses can approximate a measure of the degree of reciprocity in oral and anal sex by examining whether individuals experienced both giving and receiving (or neither) in same-sex events that occurred 'in the last year'. This is not ideal as receptive and (for men) insertive oral and anal sex may have occurred on different occasions and with different partners, but we can still gain an approximate of practices.

Those who reported oral sex 'in the last year' are a very small group in our data, but the findings in *Table 9.1* are fairly conclusive in showing high levels of reciprocity.

Table 9.1: Experience of homosexual oral sex 'in the last year'*

	Men (%)	Women (%)
Received only	2.5	8.7
Gave only	4.8	7.4
Both	92.8	83.8
Total	100%	100%
N	50	13

* For those reporting oral sex 'in last year'

Among men who reported oral sex 'in the last year', over 90% both gave and received oral sex. Among women the figure was lower, but the vast majority (84%) experienced both. This figure, however, is based on 13 individuals and is thus highly unreliable. These findings do suggest, though, that oral sex is a reciprocal homosexual activity, with partners both receiving and giving on most occasions that it occurs.

The pattern for anal sex among men, shown in *Figure 9.4,* is slightly different.

Figure 9.4: Experience of homosexual anal sex in the last year for men who have had homosexual sex in the last year

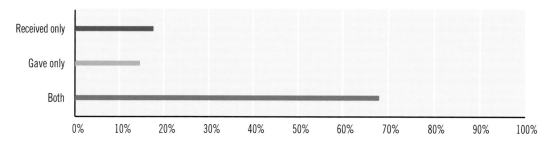

Although the absolute numbers of men involved here are low, reducing reliability, the results suggest that men may prefer either giving or receiving anal sex since the proportion doing both is substantially lower than that both giving and receiving oral sex. For example, 18% of men (who experienced anal sex in the last year) received only and 14% gave only, while 68% did both, compared to 93% for oral sex. This suggests a pattern of behaviours among some men who have sex with men that has both sociological and epidemiological implications.

9.6 Summary

THIS chapter, using the data available on men and women who have experienced a genital same-sex relationship, has examined the pattern of homosexual partnership and practices.

Our analyses show that the pattern of partnerships among such men is quite different to that found in male heterosexual relationships, but the picture is to a significant extent bipolar. On the one hand, the proportions of men with same-sex contact having four or fewer partners are similar to those found among all men having heterosexual partnerships, but a far larger proportion have had 10 or more partners than men with heterosexual partners:

• Most men who have sex with men have partnership patterns (in terms of numbers) similar to those found for heterosexual partnerships, but a larger minority have a very high number of partners – 10% have 30 or more over lifetime and 5% over 100.

Among women, homosexual contact is associated with a lower number of partners than is found for heterosexual partnerships among women. The proportion of women with more than four sexual partnerships over lifetime is low at around 6%, although the small numbers of individuals involved makes clear analyses problematic.

Analysis of practices shows that, among those who have experienced a same-sex genital event, only a minority are currently practising:

• Of men, only 22% have had oral sex in the last month and just 8% anal sex.
• Of women, the proportion reporting recent oral sex is even lower, at 3%.

This suggests that not only is homosexual contact relatively uncommon in Ireland but, even among those who have had homosexual contact, the majority would not currently be having same-sex oral or anal sex. This means that the overall population prevalence of these practices is extremely low. For more detail on the analyses in this chapter, see Appendix seven.

9.7 Reference list

1) Johnson A, Wadsworth J., Wellings K, Field J. *Sexual Attitudes and Lifestyles.* Oxford: Basil Blackwell, 1994.

2 Grulich AE, De Visser R, Smith AM, Rissel CE, Richters J. 'Sex in Australia: Homosexual Experience and Recent Homosexual Encounters'. *Australian and New Zealand Journal of Public Health* 2003; 27(2):155-163.

3 Carroll D, Foley B, Hickson F, O'Connor J, Quinlan M, Sheehan B *et al.*' Vital Statistics Ireland: Findings from the All-Ireland Gay Men's Sex Survey', 2000. 2002. Dublin, Gay Health Network.

4 Bound J, Johnson G. 'Changes in the Structure of Wages During the 1980s: An Evaluation of Alternative Explanations'. American Economic Review 1992; 82:371-392.

5 Cochran SD, Mays VM. 'Lifetime Prevalence of Suicide Symptoms and Affective Disorders Among Men Reporting Same-Sex Sexual Partners: Results From NHANES III'. *American Journal of Public Health* 2000; 90:573-578.

6   ACSF Investigators. 'Analysis of Sexual Behaviour in France (ACSF). A Comparison Between Two Modes of Investigation: Telephone Survey and Face-to-Face Survey'. *AIDS* 1992; 6:315-323.

7   Leridon H, van Zessen G, Hubert M. 'Europeans and Their Sexual Partners'. In: Hubert M, Bajos N, Sandfort T, editors. *Sexual Behaviour and HIV/AIDS in Europe*. London: UCL Press, 1998.

8   Carroll D, Foley B, Hickson F, O'Connor J, Quinlan M, Sheehan B *et al*. Vital Statistics Ireland. 'Findings from the All-Ireland Gay Men's Sex Survey', 2000. 1-5-2002.

9   Messiah A, Nouret-Fourme E. 'Socio-Demographic Characteristics and Sexual Behaviour of Bisexual Men in France'. *American Journal of Public Health* 1995; 85:1543-1546.

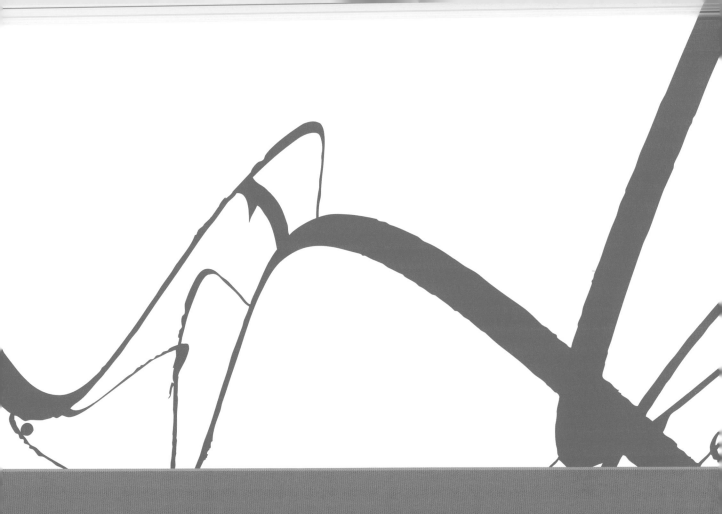

Chapter 10:

Risk-Reduction Practices

10.1 Introduction

FOR most adults, sex is a fundamental part of the human experience and contributes greatly to personal well-being. It is important to make this point as much of the research literature on sex tends to concentrate on its pathological side in terms of crisis pregnancy, STIs and the risk of HIV. Yet most Irish people have not and will not experience these outcomes. On the other hand, a minority have and will, and, particularly in terms of STIs and HIV, this proportion seems to be increasing, as the first chapter of this report documents.

Some possible reasons for this increase – in the context of changing patterns of sexual behaviour among younger age groups – have been outlined in previous chapters. These behaviours, however, will not increase the prevalence of STIs and crisis pregnancy if they are accompanied by sufficient risk-reduction methods (use of contraception and protection in the form of condoms and other barrier methods). This chapter investigates the extent of use of contraception and protection, using data from the ISSHR study.

The next, **second section** briefly outlines the methodological approach used to measure contraception and use of protection. The **third section** analyses the pattern of contraceptive use at 'most recent' vaginal intercourse, and the **fourth section** the distribution of types used.

The **fifth section** examines the reasons that respondents gave for not using contraception at last vaginal intercourse.

The pattern of condom use is looked at in two ways: first, the **sixth section** examines the consistency of condom use 'in the last year' and how this varies according to a range of socio-economic characteristics. The **seventh section** examines how condom use varies at 'most recent occasion' of vaginal or anal sex.

The **eighth section** analyses the reasons that respondents gave for not using protection. The **ninth section** summarises the findings of the chapter.

10.2 Measuring contraception and protection use

STUDIES of contraceptive behaviour use two methods for measuring contraceptive use:

* consistency of use 'in the last year' (for people who have experienced sex in the last year)
* use of contraception at 'most recent event'

The ISSHR survey was carried out in the year following the Irish Survey of Contraception and Crisis Pregnancy[1] which used both these approaches. ISSHR thus concentrated on the second measure: use at 'most recent event'. This approach has the benefit of focusing on a specific event rather than asking respondents to recall a number of past events over the space of the last year; it thus tends to decrease the problems involved with recall. Nonetheless, it does make the assumption that the last event represents a good cross-section of all intercourse events for each individual over a longer period.

Clearly it would be preferable to have information on each case of intercourse and whether contraception was used, but this is not practical. Instead it is assumed that, for most of the sample, the last intercourse event is representative and that there is no systematic bias associated with the period of the survey. The ISSHR survey did adopt a measure based on recall 'over the last year' to measure consistency of use of protection. This measure was integrated into sections F and G of the questionnaire which examined the number of partners and the practices that respondents had experienced.

In analyses of use of contraception, only respondents at risk of conception are included. The analyses do not include individuals who were either pregnant or trying to become pregnant or who had had a hysterectomy. However, respondents who had been sterilised are included as this is a form of contraception. This means that, as well as older men, older women remain in the analysis even though they may be menopausal and unlikely to conceive and thus may not use contraception. This inclusion is intentional. Previous research in Ireland (Rundle *et al* 2004) has found that a sizeable number of women in their 40s report not using contraception because they are menopausal. The instance of menopause in women of this age group is very small; thus many women over 40 may assume that they have low levels of fertility and may not use contraception even though their risk of conception may be quite considerable. All women, aside from the groups listed above, are therefore included in the analyses.

10.3 Use of contraception at most recent sexual intercourse

SUMMARY

THIS section examines the use of contraception on the 'most recent' occasion of vaginal sexual intercourse.

Results show that most individuals reported using contraception if not intending to conceive, although rates of use vary significantly across groups. Younger, unmarried people are most likely to use contraception; among older men and women who are married, but not post-menopausal, there is a significant pattern of non-use.

Almost a fifth of women aged 35 to 44 did not use contraception on 'most recent' occasion, even though they were at risk of conceiving. They may, therefore, risk crisis pregnancy.

Irrespective of age, women with higher levels of education were more likely, and women with lower levels less likely, to use contraception on the 'most recent' occasion.

Early first sexual intercourse is associated with less use of contraception later in life.

- 74% of men and 69% of women who wished to avoid pregnancy used contraception on their 'most recent' occasion of vaginal sex.

- Use of contraception varies widely by age: 93% of men and 94% of women aged 18 to 24 (not intending to conceive) used contraception at last event compared to 81% of men and 82% of women aged 35 to 44.

- Men and women in less formalised relationships are more likely to use contraception.

- Knowledge and attitudes around contraception are not associated with use, but experience of vaginal sex before 17 and use of contraception on the first occasion are.

WE begin by examining the pattern among ISSHR respondents of contraceptive use at 'most recent' sexual intercourse. This approach, as noted above, limits the extent of recall required from respondents, although for some the recall period will be longer than for others. For respondents not in a sexual relationship but who were in the past (such as widowed, divorced or separated people), the last sexual event may have been some time previously and the recall period could be substantial.

However, for the overwhelming majority of respondents recall should not be a problem, as the following figures show. Around 93% of the ISSHR sample reported having had vaginal sexual intercourse; of this 93%, around three-quarters reported vaginal intercourse 'in the last month'. A further 18% of men and 14% of women reported vaginal intercourse 'in the last year', but this leaves just 9% of men and 13% of women who had not had sex 'in the last year'.

The authors of the 1990 NATSAL report estimated that around 10% of British respondents who were at risk of pregnancy did not use any method of contraception or take precautions.[2] The recent Irish survey of contraception and crisis pregnancy, the ICCP survey,[3] found approximately the same proportion for Ireland for use of contraception at last intercourse, although rates varied considerably across groups.

Relationship status was a particularly important factor; people in long-term relationships were more likely to use contraception than those who had just met their partner, or knew them but were having intercourse for the first time. Age was also a significant predictor; younger respondents were more likely to use contraception. So, too, were people with higher levels of education.

Figure 10.1: Proportion using contraception at most recent sexual intercourse: by gender

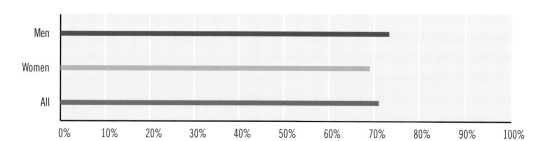

Figure 10.1 gives the proportions of people who reported using some form of contraception – including the rhythm method or withdrawal – on 'most recent' occasion of vaginal sexual intercourse. Respondents who were pregnant or trying to become pregnant, or who could not conceive because of hysterectomy or infertility are *not* included; individuals who reported that they were menopausal or post-menopausal *are* included (reasons explained in section 10.2).

Figure 10.1 shows that, overall, 71% of individuals reported using contraception on 'most recent' occasion, but that men were significantly more likely than women to report doing so. This is a common pattern found in surveys of contraceptive behaviour.

The overall proportion of men and women using contraception in Figure 10.1 is slightly less than that found in the ICCP survey (Rundle *et al* 2004), which found that around 90% of the entire sample had used contraception at 'most recent' event. However, the ICCP survey was restricted to people under 45. If the ISSHR sample is restricted to people under 45, the proportion using contraception rises to 89% of women and 90% of men, figures almost identical to those in the ICCP survey.

Figure 10.2: Proportion using contraception at most recent sexual intercourse: by gender and age

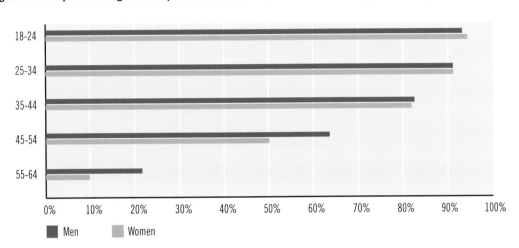

Figure 10.2 shows that use of contraception by both men and women varies widely by age. Younger respondents are more likely to use contraception. Section five examines the reasons for non-use, but Rundle *et al* (2004)[3] showed that the major reason for lower use of contraception among older age groups is a belief that they have a lower level of fertility. In fact, as noted earlier, their risk of conception may be considerable.

It is worrying that around 19% of women between 35 and 44 are not using contraception even when they do not intend to become pregnant.

Figure 10.3: Proportion using contraception at most recent sexual intercourse: by gender and highest education

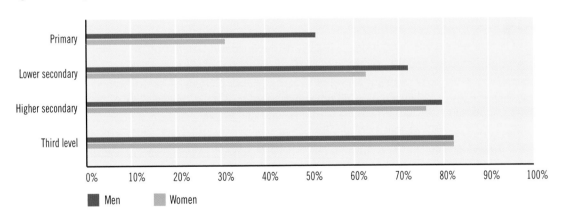

Figure 10.3 shows that people with higher levels of education are more likely to have used contraception on 'most recent' occasion of intercourse. The relationship between age and education (older people are less likely to have educational qualifications – see section 2.12.1) is the main reason for the pronounced pattern by age in *Table 10.1*. Once the influence of age is removed, analyses show no significant difference across educational groups among men, but women with primary education alone are significantly less likely to use contraception, even within age groups.

Figure 10.4: Proportion using contraception at most recent sexual intercourse: by gender and relationship status

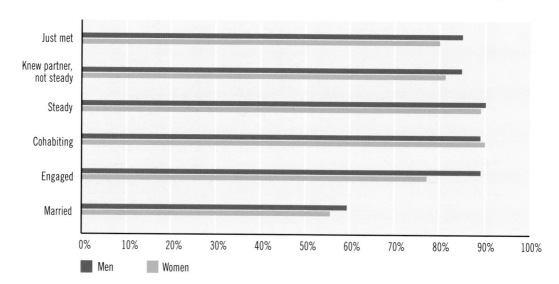

Men   Women

Finally, *Figure 10.4* shows that, compared to married people, all other groups are more likely to use contraception on 'most recent' occasion. People in a steady relationship or cohabiting are most likely to use contraception. Married individuals are more likely to be older and some post-menopausal, which explains the non-use to an extent (see section five). However, analyses show that, even among younger age groups, married people are less likely to use contraception even though they do not want to conceive. This may suggest higher levels of risk-taking among this group, perhaps because they perceive that becoming pregnant would not be a 'crisis' (see next chapter).

The analyses above have shown the patterns using a fairly limited number of predictors. Other factors, most notably a person's sexual knowledge and attitudes, may also have a bearing on use of contraception. However, more in-depth analyses in ISSHR Sub-Report 3: 'Contemporary Sexual Knowledge, Attitudes and Behaviours in Ireland' show that use of contraception on 'most recent' occasion is not related to a person's level of knowledge about fertility or contraception. They also show that attitudes to contraception do not significantly predict use. However, they do show that a significant predictor of current practices is past behaviours, in particular age at first intercourse and whether contraception was used at first intercourse.

Research in Britain[4] and Australia[5] has shown that having sex at a young age is a risk factor for negative outcomes such as contracting an STI and having a termination later in life. These findings appear to be replicated in the ISSHR data. They show that both younger age at first intercourse and non-use of contraception at first intercourse are significantly associated with lower contraceptive use later in life, even where the person did not wish to conceive.

For more detail on the analyses in this section, see Appendix *Table 8.1*.

10.4 Type of contraception used

SUMMARY

THE most common forms of contraception used by people who reported use at 'most recent' event are condoms and the contraceptive pill.

Patterns of usage are similar across men and women, but the type of contraceptive used varies significantly across age groups; younger people are more likely to use condoms. The proportion using the pill increases with age until the age of 35 at which point it decreases among both men and women. In older age groups, the coil/IUD/Mirena and particularly sterilisation become much more common.

The type of contraception used is also strongly related to relationship status. Condoms are the dominant form used among people just beginning a relationship. As the duration and seriousness of the relationship increase, so does the proportion using the pill.

Among married people, sterilisation is almost as common as use of the pill.

■ Condoms are the most frequently reported method of contraception: 57% of men and 52% of women report using condoms on the most recent occasion of vaginal sex.

■ Around 30% of partners used the contraceptive pill on the most recent occasion.

■ Younger respondents are more likely to use condoms; 82% of men and 74% of women aged 18 to 24 used a condom on the most recent occasion.

■ The contraceptive pill is used more often by younger respondents when they are in relatively settled relationships.

RESEARCH has shown that method of contraception varies systematically across the population. There is also substantial evidence that patterns of contraceptive use have changed substantially over time in Ireland as the legal and social position of contraception has changed. See section 1.5 for details of legal developments concerning the sale of contraceptives.

Given these legal changes, it is difficult to directly compare patterns of contraceptive use in Ireland over time. There have been a number of surveys:

- The Wilson-Davies survey of married women in 1974 found that 'natural' methods (following a woman's cycle) were the most commonly used, followed by oral contraception (16%) and withdrawal (10%).
- O'Neill (1985) reported that, of 198 postpartum women, 39% were using an oral contraceptive, 30% rhythm methods, 19% condoms and 27% no method.
- By the mid-1990s, Wiley and Merriman (1996) found that 22% used condoms, 22% used oral contraceptives and 14% the rhythm method.
- In the most recent study prior to the ISSHR, the ICCP survey (Rundle *et al* 2004) found that 11% used no method 'in the last year', 55% used condoms, 38% the contraceptive pill, 6% withdrawal, 6% the rhythm method, 7% sterilisation and 5% the coil/IUD/Mirena.

Figure 10.5: Contraception and precautions (as a proportion of those reporting contraceptive use) on most recent occasion of sexual intercourse: by gender

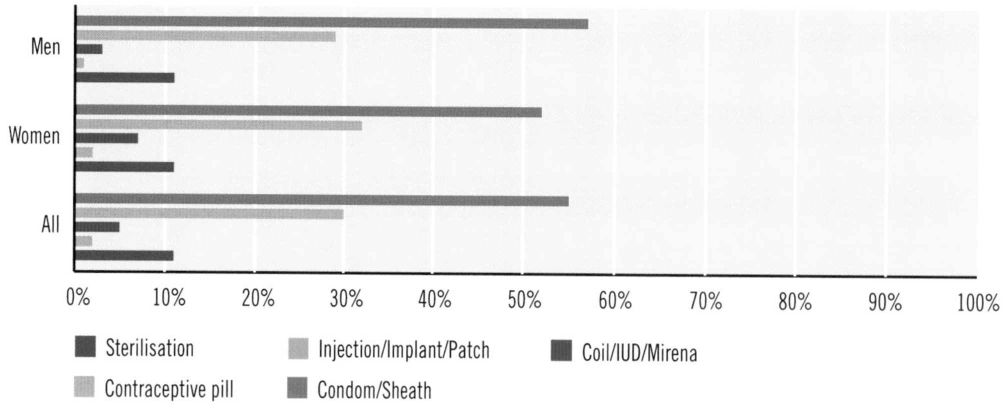

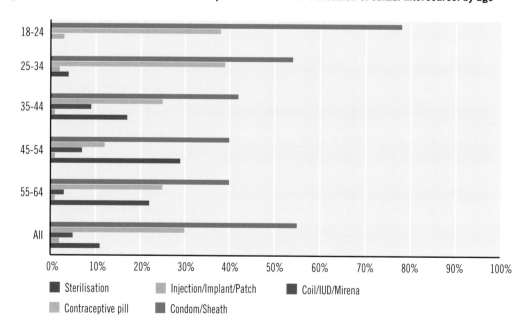

Figure 10.5 gives the proportions of men and women in the ISSHR survey who reported using contraception at 'most recent' event, using the most common forms of contraception. It shows similar results for men and women. Condoms are the most common method, followed by the contraceptive pill, sterilisation and the coil/IUD/Mirena.

Around 7% of men and 11% of women reported using more than one method. In most of these cases of multiple protection, condom and contraceptive pill were combined; in a small number, condom was combined with coil/IUD/Mirena/implants. For almost all these individuals, the primary stated aim in using contraception was to protect against infection as well as conception. A small number of women provided extra protection by also using a spermicidal gel.

Figure 10.6: Use of common forms of contraception on most recent occasion of sexual intercourse: by age

Overall, 55% of women and men report using a condom on 'most recent' occasion, but this proportion varies considerably by age group. *Figure 10.6* shows that the youngest age group is almost twice as likely as the oldest group to use this method. There is a clear trend of decreasing condom use across the age groups. There is also a clear differentiation in condom use between those aged under 25 and all other age groups

Figure 10.7: Use of common forms of contraception on most recent occasion of sexual intercourse: by relationship type

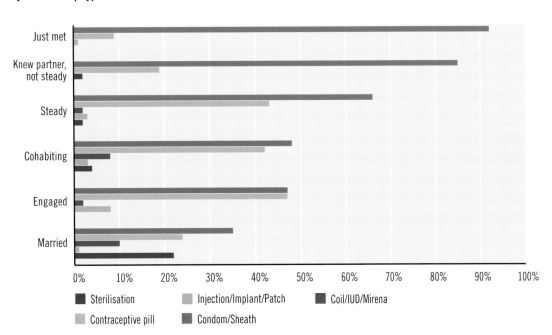

The pattern of use of the contraceptive pill is more complex. Around a third of men and women up to age 34 reported using the pill at most recent event but, after that age, use of it dropped steeply. Among both men and women, use of coil/IUD/Mirena increases with age until age 44 but decreases after that, whereas the proportion relying on sterilisation increases with age until 54. These proportions are almost identical to those found by Rundle *et al* (2004) in the ICCP study and have been found widely in studies in a number of countries.[6]

Figure 10.7 shows the strong association between contraceptive method and relationship status:

- Condoms are the most prevalent choice for people in the early stages of a sexual relationship or in a casual partnership.
- The contraceptive pill, coil, IUD and Mirena become more prevalent as the stability and duration of the relationship increases.
- Among married people, sterilisation becomes more common as partners with children seek a more permanent form of contraception; among this group the proportion who report sterilisation as their method of contraception is almost as large as the proportion using the contraceptive pill.

For more details on the analyses in this section, see Appendix *Table 8.2*.

10.5 Reasons for not using contraception on most recent occasion of vaginal intercourse

SUMMARY

PEOPLE in the ISSHR survey who did not use contraception were asked why not.

The most common reason cited overall was being post-menopausal. While most common among those in the oldest age group, this was cited by a significant proportion of women in younger age groups, even though other evidence suggests that only a small proportion of under-45s are post-menopausal.

Drinking alcohol/taking drugs was quoted as a contributory cause of not using contraception by 20% of respondents under 25 who did not use contraception.

■ 15% of women aged 35 to 44 who have a risk of pregnancy report not using contraception because they believe they are post-menopausal.

■ The most common reasons for non-use among respondents aged 18 to 24 are: drinking alcohol/taking drugs (20%), no contraception available (18%), sex not planned (16%) and not thinking to use contraception (15%).

THE main reasons for not using contraception have only recently been studied in Ireland.[1][7][8][9] Previous research abroad has shown that alcohol plays a major role in non-use and that this is particularly true of first sexual intercourse.[3][10] There is also evidence that simple unpreparedness is a serious issue.[1]

Unplanned or unexpected intercourse is less of an issue among older age groups who are more likely to be in settled relationships, but other issues have emerged for these groups. For example, in the recent ICCP study, Rundle *et al* (2004)[3] found that some women in the 36-45 age group believed they were unlikely to conceive because of the menopause. Yet very few women under 45 are likely to be post-menopausal. This quite common belief among women suggests that more education and information needs to be targeted at older women.

Rundle *et al* (2004) found that, overall, being unprepared was the most common reason given for not using contraception. This reason was far more common among respondents under 26 (58% of non-users) than among older groups and particularly those over 35 (29%). The next most common reason given was drinking alcohol or taking drugs; this was reported by 21% of respondents and, again, was far more prevalent among those aged under 26. Older respondents were much more likely to report not using contraception because they were 'unlikely to conceive'.

Figure 10.8 gives the distribution, by age group, of reasons that respondents gave for not using contraception at 'most recent' event. Included in this figure are non-users who were (or whose partner was) not pregnant or trying to become pregnant, not infertile or who had had a hysterectomy. Although those citing being post-menopausal could be excluded, the pattern of responses was interesting enough to be retained. The responses to the question were entered as open answers and only coded after fieldwork, to a coding frame created from the answers given.

Figure 10.8: Reasons for not using contraception at most recent sexual intercourse

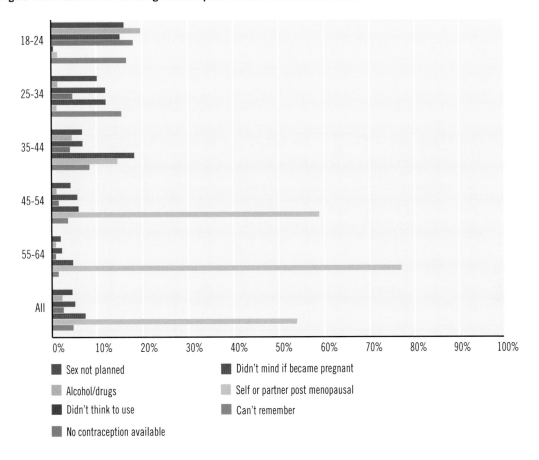

All responses were noted. *Figure 10.8* gives the proportions citing each response; no attempt is made to show the most important reason (respondents could list as many as they felt necessary). The figure shows that, across all age groups, being post-menopausal/unlikely to conceive is the most commonly reported reason, at 54%. As we would expect, this is cited by a large proportion of non-users over 54, but it is also stated by 59% of those between 45 and 54 and 15% of those between 35 and 44. Since only a small proportion of women in their 40s would have entered menopause, a large number of women may be taking quite substantial risks in the false belief that their fertility has declined substantially. Rundle *et al* (2004) also found this pattern, although at a lower level because of the younger age range interviewed.

Figure 10.8 shows 'not minding if became pregnant' as the next most common group overall, followed by 'didn't think to use' contraception and 'sex not planned', but there are substantial differences across age groups. Of those who would welcome pregnancy, it is not surprising that the highest proportion are aged between 25 and 44. However, what is striking is the large proportion of those aged 18 to 24 who suggest that 'drinking alcohol/taking drugs' was a contributory factor (20%), a pattern also seen in Rundle *et al* (2004).[3] This proportion drops to no more than 5% among the other age groups. A further 18% of those aged 18 to 24 report 'no contraception available', 16% that sex was 'not planned' and 15% that they 'didn't think to use'.

The results suggest that, for the 18-24 group at least, unpreparedness and situational factors such as alcohol and drugs are the major reasons for failing to use contraception.

For more detail on the analyses, see Appendix *Table 8.3*.

10.6 Consistency of condom use in the last year

SUMMARY

THE ISSHR survey asked individuals who reported vaginal or anal sex 'in the last year' how consistent their condom use had been over this period.

Only a minority consistently used a condom, but use varied strongly with age group and relationship status. Among younger groups in casual relationships, consistency of use was far higher, but even here substantial minorities used condoms inconsistently.

■ Men are more likely than women to report consistently using condoms 'in the last year'.

■ Younger respondents are more likely to consistently use condoms 'in the last year':

■ 57% of men and 51% of women aged 18 to 24 consistently use a condom compared to 15% of men and 13% of women aged 45 to 54.

■ 47% of men and 45% of women in casual relationships report consistently using a condom 'in the last year', but only 13% of men and 11% of women who are married.

■ Respondents who began having sex before age 17 are more likely to be inconsistent users of condoms 'in the last year'.

USE of contraception varies across the population in a number of different dimensions (as shown in section three). Condoms and other barrier methods such as the female condom have been shown to be the most effective means of preventing the transmission of HIV[11] and STIs[12] during intercourse. From a public health and epidemiological perspective, it is imperative to understand the factors that promote or decrease the use of condoms, particularly in high-risk sexual encounters.

The advent of the HIV virus and the public-health campaigns of the late 1980s and early 1990s did much to increase the use of condoms in certain countries. Research in the US, for instance, showed a significant increase in condom use among men between 1988 and 1995.[13] The NATSAL surveys of 1990 and 2000 found a significant increase in consistent condom use in Britain.[14] However, these studies also highlighted the fact that condoms are often used infrequently or inconsistently.[2] Similarly, French, Dutch and Belgian national studies of sexual practices have revealed inconsistent condom use, reporting that 25-30% of adults had used condoms consistently 'in the last year'.[15] In a recent British study of adults aged 16-69, of those who reported using condoms in the past year, just 56% of men and 64% of women said they always used a condom when they had sex.[16]

Research has found a pronounced age effect, with younger respondents reporting higher levels of condom use.[16 17 6 18 19]

• The Irish Contraception and Crisis Pregnancy (ICCP) national study of contraceptive practices found that people aged 18-25 were more likely (78%) to report condom use in the last year than those aged 26-35 (54%) or 36-45 (36%). As well, condom use at most recent intercourse was more likely among younger respondents (Rundle *et al*, 2004).

• Similarly, the Slán study[20] found that condom use among Irish men decreased with increasing age.

• Dawe & Rainford (2003)[16] found that 96% of men aged 16-19 reported using a condom in the past year compared to 74% of men aged 20-24 or 31% of those aged 40-44.

• The national Australian study also showed a significant relationship between age and condom use: older women reported much lower use over the past year.[6]

Dubois-Arber & Spencer (1998)[15] argue that these patterns may be due to younger generations being the first to adapt their behaviour in light of the HIV epidemic and exposure to health-promotion campaigns. This is supported by the reasons respondents give for recent condom use. For example, in the French study, the reasons that respondents aged 18-19 gave for using condoms during the previous 12 months were: AIDS (75%), contraception (53%) and protection against STIs (76%). In contrast, older respondents (aged 40-49) indicated AIDS (3%) and STIs (43%) as a concern less frequently, and were more likely to report contraception as a reason for using condoms (60%).

The higher use of condoms among young people may also be related to their higher average number of partners and consequent need for barrier protection. Respondents under 30 tend to report greater numbers of partners, particularly for the year preceding the study.[4 21 22] There is, however, a generalised effect of having a higher number of partners; respondents who report more than one partner in the previous year are more likely to report condom use than those who report having only one partner in the year[16] and this condom use is more likely to be consistent.[4]

Whereas a higher number of partners over the last year tends to lead to more consistent use of condoms, increasing duration of a relationship can lead to lower levels of use. Research has found that consistent condom use is higher in casual relationships or among single people as opposed to those in long-term relationships.[23]

Sheeran *et al* (1999)[24] conducted a meta-analysis of 30 studies that examined predictors of condom use. They analysed 11 studies that compared use by people with a steady partner to that by those with a casual partner. They found that the mean percentage of respondents who always used a condom with a steady partner was 17% compared to 30% among those with a casual partner. Similarly, findings from the ICCP study revealed that condom use at most recent sexual encounter was five times more likely among those in casual relationships compared to those living together/engaged/married.

Buysse (1998)[25] has argued that typical features of stable relationships, such as closeness, intimacy and exclusivity, discourage condom use as it may suggest mistrust and formality. A national US study of American women found that those in the early stage of a relationship (six months or less) were much more likely to use condoms than those in a long-standing relationship.[18] Similarly, the ACSF study conducted in late 1991 in France found that condoms were more likely to be used during the early stages of relationships, while couples tended to use other methods as their relationship became more stable.[26] Also, condom use has been shown to be greater at the start of a relationship, with oral contraceptive use increasing as the relationship develops.[27]

Other factors found to be related to condom use include level of education; people with higher education are more likely to report using condoms. This relationship has been found across a number of countries (Dubois-Arber & Spencer, 1998).[6 28] A meta-analysis of 30 studies by Sheeran *et al* (1999)[24] also found greater education was associated with greater condom use. Consistent with these findings, Rundle *et al* (2004),[3] using Irish survey data, found that those with incomplete second-level education were significantly less likely to report using a condom at most recent sexual encounter than those with complete second-level or third-level education.

Despite the above, the apparent effects of education on condom use must be interpreted cautiously, as education is not a constant for all age groups; for instance, the average level of education of younger generations is higher. This factor may confound the relationship between education and condom use.[15]

Gender also seems to be a factor in level of condom use. Men have a higher level of condom use across a number of studies, including the Irish Contraception and Crisis Pregnancy Survey.[3 15 24] However, these findings also must be interpreted with caution as the social acceptability or desirability of condom use may partly account for the difference. Dubois-Arber & Spencer (1998) argued that women may under-report condom use for a number of reasons; as it is the man who wears the condom, women may not see themselves as using one or may be embarrassed to report use. Bajos *et al* (1997)[29] postulated that women may feel that reporting use of a condom devalues their relationship, particularly in the case of casual relationships which do not fit society's image of female sexuality. However, gender differences have been found to be smaller in certain countries, including the Netherlands, West Germany and Switzerland, where lifetime use is high. Similarly, lifetime use is relatively high in the UK where gender differences are marginal.[15] Small gender difference may reflect a more open society where use of condoms is widely accepted by both men and women.

Situational or contextual factors may also play an important role in condom use. In the Irish context, Rundle *et al* (2004)[3] found that almost a third of people not using condoms at most recent sexual intercourse cited simply being unprepared; a further 15% said they had been drinking alcohol or taking drugs. We will explore these factors further, using data from the ISSHR project.

Figure 10.9: Profile of condom use in the last year: by gender

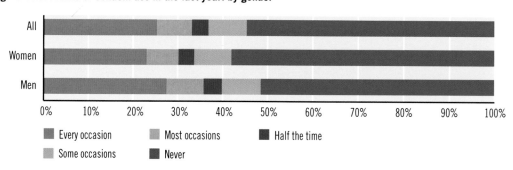

Figure 10.9 shows the proportions of people who had vaginal or anal sex in the last year who reported consistently using a condom in that period.

A total of 25% of both men and women reported always using a condom in the past year, while 8% mostly used a condom. However, 55% of individuals reported never using a condom in the past year. As found across almost all studies, the figure shows a significantly higher level of consistent condom use among men.

Figure 10.10 shows consistency of condom use across age groups by gender. The difference between age groups is extremely pronounced:

- The youngest age group among men are over seven times more likely than the oldest age group to use condoms consistently.
- Young women are over 16 times more likely than the oldest age group to use condoms consistently.

Figure 10.10: Profile of condom use in the last year: by gender and age

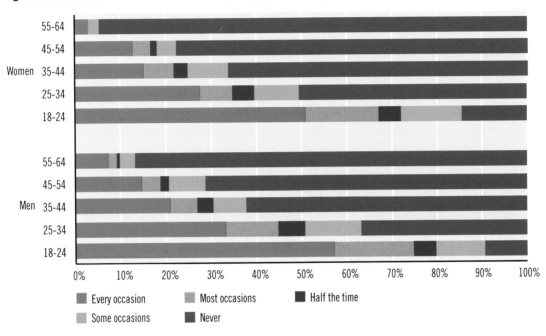

There may be a number of reasons why use of condoms varies so strongly according to age. Condoms tend to be used as a form of contraception early in relationships and younger people are far more likely to be in new relationships (as discussed in section four). As well, people in the oldest age groups may be post-menopausal; this would remove the need for contraception, except as protection from STIs.

Figure 10.11: Profile of condom use in the last year: by gender and relationship status

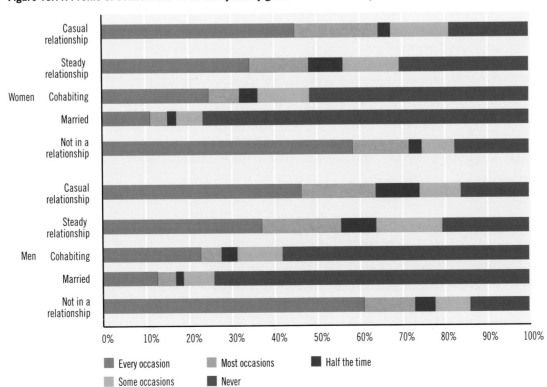

Duration of relationship is also a factor in use of protection against infection. Since older individuals are far more likely to be in established, monogamous relationships, it is unsurprising that a large majority in the older age groups report not using a condom in the past year.

The ISSHR results confirm the importance of relationship status for consistency of condom use. *Figure 10.11* shows that men and women who are not in a relationship (but have had sex in the last year), in a casual relationship or in a steady relationship are far more likely to report consistently using condoms in the last year. The proportion reporting non-use in the last year rises as the stability of the relationship increases from casual relationship to steady, cohabitation and married.

Interestingly, the proportions reporting that they used condoms 'most' or 'some' of the time are highest among those in steady and casual relationships. This may suggest a certain level of risk-taking among these groups.

The results above show the relationship between age, relationship status and use of condoms in the last year. However, these are 'distal' influences in the sense that they summarise many other reasons why behaviours may differ. For example, although age has been found to be a major determinant of condom use, it is unlikely that there is a *direct* relationship between being older and lower condom use. As discussed above, being older is an indicator of other differences such as number of sexual partners, but it can also be an *indirect* indicator of differential attitudes, beliefs and levels of knowledge about the need for protection. To fully understand the factors influencing level of condom use (examined in the sections to come), it is necessary to look at the role of sexual knowledge, attitudes and behaviour.

The ISSHR Sub-Report 3: 'Contemporary Sexual Knowledge, Attitudes and Behaviours in Ireland' examines in more depth the data on consistency of condom use 'in the last year' and, in particular, the role of sexual knowledge and attitudes. It shows that knowledge of fertility, Chlamydia and HIV/AIDS seems to play no significant role in shaping the consistency of condom use 'in the last year'. A similarly negative result was found for a person's perceived risk of HIV infection, number of partners in the last year, and alcohol consumption. However, Sub-Report 3 did find, as already seen with use of contraception in general, that having had intercourse before the age of 17 is a significant predictor of lower consistency in use of condoms in later life.

Sub-Report 3 also shows that people who reported that the cost of condoms discouraged their use of them were less likely to use condoms consistently. This suggests that the cost of condoms may be a serious disincentive to their consistent use and perhaps even to their use at all. If so, this has implications for the transmission of STIs and HIV.

For more detail on the analyses in this section, see Appendix *Table 8.4*.

10.7 Condom use on last occasion of sexual intercourse

SUMMARY

PATTERNS of condom use on the last occasion of vaginal or anal sex largely replicate the patterns found for consistency of use in the last year.

Once again, men are more likely to report condom use, as are young people and those whose relationship to their partner was casual. Higher levels of education are also associated with higher condom usage, even across age and relationship-status groups.

People who first had vaginal sex before age 17 were significantly less likely to use a condom on the last occasion of sex, as were those reporting high levels of alcohol consumption.

- Men (37%) are more likely than women (31%) to report using condoms on the last occasion of vaginal sex.

- Younger respondents are more likely to report use on the last occasion: 76% of men and 68% of women aged 18 to 24 compared to 22% of men and 17% of women aged 45 to 54.

- Lower levels of education among both men and women are associated with a lower likelihood of using condoms.

- The less time partners have known each other and the less formalised the relationship, the more likely they are to use condoms: 78% of men and 71% of women who had just met their partner before the time of intercourse used a condom compared to 17% of married men and 16% of married women.

THE patterns of condom use on the last occasion of vaginal or anal sex are similar to those found for consistency of use in the last year.

Figure 10.12 gives the proportions by gender of people who reported using a condom on their last occasion of sexual intercourse.

Figure 10.12: Proportion using a condom at most recent sexual intercourse: by gender

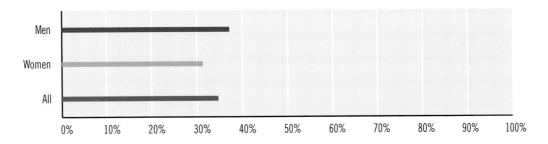

This confirms the findings of the last section; men are significantly more likely than women to report using a condom on the last occasion of sexual intercourse.

Figure 10.13 shows that age is once again a significant predictor of condom use. Younger people were far more likely than older respondents to report using a condom at last event:

- 76% of men and 68% of women aged 18 to 24 reported using a condom at last event compared to 22% of men and 17% of women aged 45 to 54.

The reasons for such a differential (discussed above) apply here also; younger respondents are more likely to be in relationships of a shorter duration where trust in the other partner is less well developed. Analysis by relationship status (not shown here) confirms this.

Figure 10.13: Proportion using a condom at most recent sexual intercourse: by gender and age

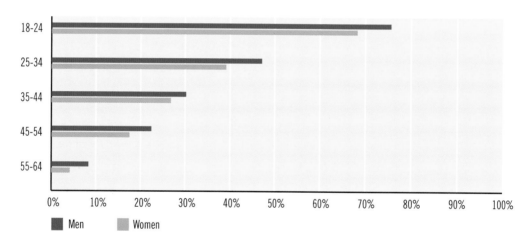

Figure 10.14 shows distinct differences by educational qualifications. Men and women with higher levels of education are significantly more likely to report using a condom on last occasion. For example, women with third-level qualifications are almost four times more likely to do so than women with primary education alone. These patterns apply even across the age groups.

Fixture 10.14: Proportion using a condom at most recent sexual intercourse: by gender and highest education

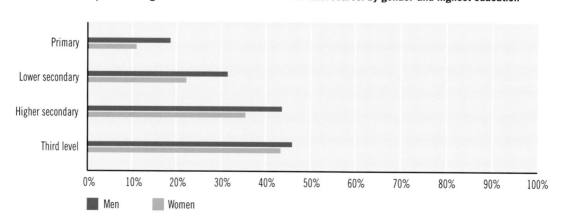

As with condom use 'in the last year', ISSHR Sub-Report 3: 'Contemporary Sexual Knowledge, Attitudes and Behaviour in Ireland' also examines the role of attitudes and knowledge in the use of condoms at most recent event. It looks at the influence of knowledge of fertility, STIs and HIV/AIDS as well as that of perceived risk of contracting HIV/AIDS, and finds no significant relationship. However, it does find a significant relationship between the age of a person at first sexual intercourse and current use of condoms. Both men and women who reported first sexual intercourse before age 17 were significantly less likely to report using a condom on their last occasion of sex. This confirms the important relationship between early sexual experience and a number of risk behaviours.

Sub-Report 3 also shows that condom use on last occasion is related to alcohol consumption. Among men, those who reported consuming six or more standard drinks when they drink alcohol (defined as 'binge' drinking) were significantly less likely to have used a condom on last occasion of sex. This is a troubling relationship as men and women with high levels of alcohol consumption are also more likely to have higher numbers of sexual partners (as already discussed).

For more details on the analyses in this section, see Appendix *Table 8.5*.

10.8 Reasons for not using condoms on last occasion of intercourse

SUMMARY

THE majority of individuals who did not use a condom on the last occasion of sexual intercourse report that this was because they trusted their partner not to have an STI/HIV. This proportion is lower among younger age groups and those in casual relationships but, even among those who had just met their partner, a substantial minority said trust in their partner was the main reason why they did not use a condom.

- 69% of respondents not using a condom on last occasion cite as a reason their trust in their partner.

- The proportion trusting their partner varies by age and nature of relationship.

- 27% of respondents who knew their partners but had not previously been in a sexual relationship with them reported not using condoms because they trusted that they would not have an STI.

- 14% of respondents who had only just met their partner before having sex for the first time reported not using a condom because they trusted that their partner would not have an STI.

THIS section examines the reasons offered by respondents for not using contraception on the last occasion of vaginal or anal intercourse.

Table 10.1 gives the proportions reporting particular reasons for not using a condom.

Table 10.1: Reasons for not using a condom at most recent sexual intercourse (%)

	<25	25-34	35-44	45-54	55-64	All
Sex not planned/unexpected	3.2	0.3	0.3	0.1	0.1	0.5
Drinking alcohol/taking drugs	4.0	0.1	1.0	0.2	0.0	0.7
Couldn't be bothered	0.8	0.2	0.1	0.1	0.1	0.2
Didn't think to use	3.8	1.3	1.5	1.0	1.4	1.5
Took a chance/got carried away	0.0	0.3	0.2	0.1	0.2	0.2
Young/naïve/stupid/careless	0.3	0.3	0.0	0.1	0.2	0.1
No condoms available	5.5	0.5	0.1	0.1	0.0	0.6
Doesn't like/allergic to condoms	2.6	1.4	0.6	0.3	0.4	0.8
Doesn't believe in condoms/against religion	0.0	0.1	0.1	0.0	0.0	0.1
Didn't know about protection or didn't understand the risk	0.0	0.0	0.2	0.0	0.1	0.1
Didn't think was at risk from STIs	6.6	11.0	9.2	10.2	6.3	9.0
Trusted partner not to have STI	54.2	68.3	70.0	69.9	72.9	69.0
Tested/checked for STI	3.6	1.0	0.2	0.3	0.0	0.6
Can't remember	14.0	13.2	13.4	14.3	14.0	13.8
N	370	899	1,125	1,003	935	4,332

The results show that, across all age groups, the most commonly given reason (69%) is trust that one's partner would not have an STI. However, the proportion giving this reason varies considerably across age groups: from 73% among those aged 55 or more to around 54% among those in the youngest age group. Younger respondents are less likely to be in settled relationships and more likely to be having sex with someone they met comparatively recently. The findings thus reflect respondents' different levels of information about and trust of their partners.

Figure 10.15 shows that the proportion citing trust in their partner as the reason for non-use is higher among people who are married, cohabiting or engaged. However, this response was also given by 27% of those who knew their partner but were not in a relationship with them, and also by 14% of those who had recently met their partner. This suggests that a substantial minority of people trust that their sexual partners will not have an STI on the basis of little evidence.

Figure 10.15: Proportion reporting that the reason no condom was used on the last occasion of intercourse was because they trusted their partner: by relationship status

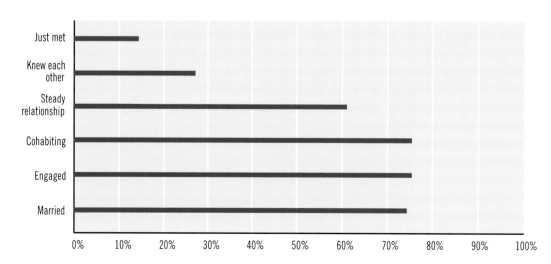

If the 'can't remember' category is discounted, the next most prevalent reason reported is that the person did not think that they were at risk of an STI. Since this answer is substantively similar to the 'trusted partner' reason, it is not surprising that the distribution across age groups is similar.

10.9 Summary

FOR most people, sex is a source of pleasure and well-being and the way to give birth to children, both of which enrich their lives and those of other people. However, conception at the wrong point in a person's life can be experienced as a crisis and affect both their own life chances and those of the child. In this context, a primary aim of this chapter is to examine why some individuals and groups do not use contraception when they would, at face value at least, want to avoid conception.

This chapter has also investigated the use of contraception as protection against STI infection, and the factors that promote or decrease the use of condoms, particularly in high-risk sexual encounters.

The third section of the chapter showed, as did the recent ICCP survey (Rundle *et al* 2004), that around 10% of people aged under 45 did not use contraception at their most recent sexual intercourse even though they or their partner did not want to conceive. Encouragingly, analysis showed that young people were more likely to use contraception than older age groups.

However, lower levels of education and, in particular, having no qualifications led to a lower propensity to use contraception, a finding which supports a great deal of research both in Ireland and abroad. Such findings underline the relationship between unintended pregnancy and poor life chances, and the processes that consolidate this pattern. They are yet further evidence in this report of the extent to which socio-economic inequalities structure health behaviours and outcomes.

Findings from the ISSHR data show that a person's level of knowledge about contraception and their attitudes toward it do not predict their contraceptive behaviour. On the other hand, their past behaviour does: respondents who had sex at an early age (before 17) or who did not use contraception on this first occasion were much more likely to not use contraception at 'most recent' event.

Analysis of the forms of contraception used showed that condoms and the contraceptive pill were the most frequently used methods, but that the distribution of methods was significantly related both to the individual's age and marital status. People in less formalised relationships, who are more likely to be younger, are more likely to use condoms, but as the relationship is stabilised and formalised other methods begin to dominate, the pill becoming particularly common. Other methods such as the coil/IUD and Mirena and more permanent methods such as contraceptive implants and sterilisation also become more common.

People who did not use contraception at last vaginal intercourse gave a range of reasons for this. A large proportion did not mind conceiving but, if this group is discounted, a large proportion 'didn't think' to use contraception, reported that sex was not planned and so they were not prepared or had been drinking/taking drugs, which impaired their judgement. These responses were particularly common among under-25s; alcohol and drug use were the most common.

Although young people are more likely to use contraception when having sex, this is not true of a significant minority. These findings, which replicate those found in the ICCP survey, underline the serious issue facing Irish society of getting young people under 25 to protect themselves during sex from both unintended pregnancy and infection from STIs.

Analysis of the consistency of use of condoms 'in the last year' showed again that young people were more likely to use protection during sex – particularly in casual relationships or less formalised partnerships, which is encouraging.

It was important to find out whether use of condoms was also related to a person's level of knowledge about the risks of having unprotected sex. Results showed no significant relationships between professed knowledge and behaviours.

The relationship between knowledge, attitudes and behaviour can be very complex (as discussed in chapter four). It may be that more work should be carried out on the relationship between these factors in the Irish context, using data from the ISSHR survey. However, analyses did show that consistency of use of condoms, as with use of contraception, is related to the person's age of first sexual intercourse. Those who had intercourse before 17 are less likely to use condoms later on and also less likely to be consistent users.

The analysis of condom use on the last occasion of sex confirmed many of the results found in the analysis of consistency. Young people and people in less formalised relationships were more likely to have used condoms on the last occasion. This event-specific analysis also highlighted more strongly that men and women with lower levels of education are less likely to use condoms. We have seen this pattern of higher-risk behaviours and lower-protective behaviours throughout this report. It underlines the importance of socio-economic processes in shaping behaviour and outcomes.

Explaining such patterns is harder than describing them, however. ISSHR Sub-Report 3: 'Contemporary Sexual Knowledge, Attitudes and Behaviours in Ireland' shows that levels of knowledge about STIs and HIV are very weakly related to use of condoms on the last occasion of sex. It is, thus, unlikely that, among people with higher levels of education, knowledge or an ability to absorb and use knowledge is the main reason for the difference across educational levels.

Other explanations should be sought. There is some anecdotal evidence that disadvantaged men have attitudes that militate against using condoms, whatever the risk, although this has not been examined thoroughly using nationally representative data. Research has also suggested that poor health behaviours are strongly related to higher levels of socio-economic deprivation and the fatalism that these generate. More research would be needed to examine this question in the Irish context but, if it is a correct explanation, a far broader and more integrated policy response than is currently in place would be required. (Chapter 12 returns to this issue.)

The final section of the chapter examined the reasons that people gave for not using condoms on the last occasion of sex. The primary reason given was trust that one's partner would not be infected with an STI. Levels of trust increased with the duration and formalisation of the relationship, but around a quarter of people having unprotected sex with someone with whom they did not have a steady relationship trusted their partner not to have an STI. Around 14% of those having unprotected sex with a casual partner also reported that they did not use a condom because they trusted their partner.

10.10 Reference list

1   Rundle K, Leigh C, McGee H, Layte R. *Irish Contraception and Crisis Pregnancy (ICCP) Study: A Survey of the General Population*. Dublin, Crisis Pregnancy Agency, 2004.

2   Johnson A, Wadsworth J, Wellings K, Field J. *Sexual Attitudes and Lifestyles*. Oxford: Basil Blackwell, 1994.

3   Rundle K, Leigh C, McGee H, Layte R. Irish Contraception and Crisis Pregnancy (ICCP) Study. A survey of the general population. Crisis Pregnancy Agency Report no. 7. 2004.

4   Wellings K, Nanchahal K, Macdowall W, McManus S, Erens B, Mercer CH et al. 'Sexual behaviour in Britain: early heterosexual experience'. *Lancet* 2001; 358(9296):1843-50.

5   Smith AM, Rissel CE, Richters J, Grulich AE, de Visser RO. 'Sex in Australia: reproductive experiences and reproductive health among a representative sample of women'. *Australian and New Zealand Journal of Public Health* 2003; 27(2):204-209.

6   Richters J, Grulich AE, de Visser RO, Smith AM, Rissel CE. 'Sex in Australia: contraceptive practices among a representative sample of women'. *Australian and New Zealand Journal of Public Health* 2003; 27(2):210-6.

7   Mahon E, Conlon C, Dillon L. *Women and Crisis Pregnancy*. Dublin: The Stationery Office, 1998.

8   MacHale E, Newell J. 'Sexual behaviour and sex education in Irish school-going teenagers'. *International Journal of STD & AIDS* 1997; 8(3):196-200.

9   Hyde A. 'Unmarried Pregnant Women's Accounts of their Contraceptive Practices: A Qualitative Analysis'. *Irish Journal of Sociology* 1996; 6:179-211.

10 Strunin L, Hingson R. 'Alcohol, drugs, and adolescent sexual behavior'. *International Journal of the Addictions* 1992; 27(2):129-46.

11 De Vincenzi I. 'A longitudinal study of human immunodeficiency virus transmission by heterosexual partners'. European Study Group on Heterosexual Transmission of HIV. *New England Journal of Medicine* 1994; 331(6):341-346.

12 Bryan AD, Aiken LS, West SG. 'Young women's condom use: the influence of acceptance of sexuality, control over the sexual encounter and perceived susceptibility to common STDs'. *Health Psychology* 1997; 16:468-479.

13 Murphy JJ, Boggess S. 'Increased condom use among teenage males, 1988-1995: the role of attitudes. *Family Planning Perspectives* 1998; 30(6):276-280.

14 Johnson A, Mercer C, Erens B, Copas A. 'Sexual Behaviour in Britain: Partnerships, Practices and HIV Risk Behaviours'. *Lancet* 2001; 358:1835-1842.

15 Dubois-Arber F, Spencer B. 'Condom Use'. In: Hubert M, Bajos N, Sandfort T, editors. *Sexual Behaviour and HIV/AIDS in Europe*. London: UCL Press, 1998.

16 Dawe F, Rainford L. *Contraception and sexual health 2003. A report on research using the ONS Omnibus Survey produced by the Office for National Statistics on behalf of the Department of Health, London*. London: Office for National Statistics, 2003.

17 Michael RT, Wadsworth J, Feinleib J, Johnson AM, Laumann EO, Wellings K. 'Private sexual behaviour, public opinion and public health policy related to sexually transmitted disease: a US-British comparison'. *American Journal of Public Health* 1998; 88(5):749-754.

18 Bankole A, Darroch J, Singh S. 'Determinants of trends in condom use in the United States, 1988-1995'. *Family Planning Perspectives* 1999; 31(6):264-271.

19 Tountas Y, Dimitrakaki C, Antoniou A, Boulamatsis D, Creatsas G. 'Attitudes and behaviour toward contraception among Greek women during reproductive age: a country-wide survey'. *European Journal of Obstetrics & Gynecology and Reproductive Biology* 2004; 116:190-195.

20 Shiely F, Kelleher C, Galvin M. 'Sexual Health and the Irish Adult Population: Findings from Slán. Report 11'. Dublin: Crisis Pregnancy Agency, 2004.

21 De Visser R, Smith AM, Rissel CE, Richters J. 'Sex in Australia: heterosexual experience and recent heterosexual encounters among a representative sample of adults'. *Australian and New Zealand Journal of Public Health* 2003; 27(2):146-154.

22 Leridon H, van Zessen G, Hubert M. 'Europeans and their Sexual Partners'. In: Hubert M, Bajos N, Sandfort T, editors. *Sexual Behaviour and HIV/AIDS in Europe*. London: UCL Press, 1998.

23   Martin K, Wu Z. 'Contraceptive Use in Canada: 1984-1995'. *Family Planning Perspectives* 2000; 32(2):65-73.

24   Sheeran P, Abraham C, Orbell S. 'Psychosocial correlates of heterosexual condom use: a meta-analysis'. *Psychological Bulletin* 1999; 125(1):90-132.

25   Buysse A. 'Safer sexual decision-making in stable and casual relationships: a prototype approach'. *Psychology & Health* 1998; 13(1):55-66.

26   Spira A, Bajos N. *Sexual Behaviour and AIDS*. Aldershot: Avebury, 1994.

27   Ku L, Sonenstein FL, Pleck JH. 'The dynamics of young men's condom use during and across relationships'. *Family Planning Perspectives* 1994; 26(6):246-51.

28   Castilla J, Barrio G, de la Fuente L, Belza MJ. 'Sexual Behaviour and Condom Use in the General Population of Spain'. *AIDS Care* 1998; 10(6):667-676.

29   Bajos N, Ducot B, Spencer JM, Spira A. 'Sexual Risk-Taking, Socio-Sexual Biographies and Sexual Interaction: elements of the French National Survey on Sexual Behaviour'. *Social Science and Medicine* 1997; 44(1):25-40.

Chapter 11:

Experience of Crisis Pregnancy, Abortion and Sexually Transmitted Infections

11.1 Introduction

SEX and sexual intercourse are an important component of individual well-being and a major dimension of the relationship between partners. Yet sex is also associated with the risk of transmission of infections and viruses which can seriously damage health.

Common sexually transmissible infections (STIs) such as Chlamydia, herpes simplex and human papilloma virus can have long-term consequences for individuals. Untreated Chlamydia, for example, is a major cause in women of pelvic inflammatory disease, ectopic pregnancy and infertility.

In the Irish context, since 1989 there has been a steady increase in STIs notified to the Health Protection Surveillance Centre (HPSC, formerly the National Disease Surveillance Centre):

- The total number of new STI infections notified increased from 2,228 annually in 1989 to nearly 10,500 in 2003. Rates of non-specific urethritis, genital warts and Chlamydia trachomatis rose strongly, particularly after 1994.

Despite the fact that women have gained the ability to control their fertility, failure to use and misuse of contraception, as well as chance, still lead to unintended pregnancies, the largest component of what have been termed 'crisis' pregnancies.[1]

A definition of a crisis pregnancy was laid down in the statutory instrument that founded the Crisis Pregnancy Agency (CPA). It describes a crisis pregnancy as: "a pregnancy which is neither planned nor desired by the woman concerned, and which represents a personal crisis for her".[q] But, since 'crisis pregnancy' encompasses a far broader set of circumstances, CPA has suggested that the definition also include the experience of women for whom a planned or desired pregnancy develops into a crisis over time due to a change in circumstances.[2] Replacing the terms 'unplanned' or 'unintended' with 'crisis' pregnancy would allow us to examine that broader set of issues.

Rundle *et al* (2004)[1] found a wide range of reasons reported by women as to why their pregnancy was a crisis pregnancy. Some suggested that the primary reason for the crisis was changed circumstances. Most suggested that unintended pregnancy at the wrong moment in their life was the most important factor. The ISSHR survey yields further evidence of this:

- 91% of women reported that their crisis pregnancy was such from the beginning; 9% said it subsequently became a crisis.

Because of these findings, this chapter builds on the previous work of the ICCP survey[1] and analyses the influence of factors associated with use and non-use of contraception on the experience of crisis pregnancy; it does not attempt to tease out the other multiple factors that may explain why a pregnancy becomes a crisis pregnancy.

The next, **second section** analyses the pattern of crisis pregnancies in the ISSHR survey. It looks at the prevalence of crisis pregnancy according to a large number of factors, including the person's knowledge of contraception and fertility and their sexual behaviours.

Section three examines the outcomes of the crisis pregnancies reported. **Section four** looks at one of these outcomes, abortion, and in particular the factors that predict a woman having an abortion. As with the section on crisis pregnancy, this section also examines the role of socio-demographic factors.

Section five examines the correlates of experiencing an STI. ISSHR respondents were asked whether they had ever been told by a health professional that they had an STI. Their responses are

---

q Statutory Instrument No. 446, 2001:1.

used to examine the prevalence of reported STIs across a large number of different characteristics. **Section six** looks at the factors that explain the probability of seeking advice on STIs, where this advice was sought and from where individuals would prefer to receive it. Finally, **section seven** draws together the findings of the chapter and their implications.

11.2 Experience of crisis pregnancy

SUMMARY

THE overwhelming majority of crisis pregnancies are defined as such because the pregnancy was unplanned and occurs when circumstances are not suitable.

The ISSHR survey shows that 21% of women who have been pregnant have experienced a 'crisis' pregnancy. This amounts to 13% of *all* women aged 18 to 64.

Pregnancies among young women are more likely to be defined as crisis pregnancies because of their circumstances. The proportion experiencing a crisis pregnancy decreases with age.

The average age at which crisis pregnancies occur has fallen through time. Women aged 18 to 24 are likely to experience a crisis pregnancy at a younger age. This may be related to more widespread early sex among younger age groups in recent decades.

- A fifth (21%) of women who had been pregnant had experienced a crisis pregnancy.

- A larger proportion of young women's pregnancies were experienced as 'crisis' pregnancies: 56% among under-25s, compared to 16% among women aged 35 to 54. However, overall, younger women experienced fewer crisis pregnancies.

- The median age at which women experience crisis pregnancy has fallen significantly across age cohorts. In women under 25 it is 19, compared to 32 among women aged 55 to 64.

- Higher social class is weakly associated with an increased probability of crisis pregnancy.

- Women who had vaginal sex before the age of 17 are almost 70% more likely to experience a crisis pregnancy than women who began to have sex after 17.

THIS section examines the experience of crisis pregnancy among women in the ISSHR survey. Although general rates of use of contraception are high, a sizable minority of Irish men and women do not use contraception, even though they would like to avoid conception (see chapter 10). Almost 10% of men and women under 45 reported not using contraception at last intercourse, thus leaving themselves and their partner open to the risk of unintended conception.

Unplanned pregnancy is the most common reason women report for explaining crisis pregnancy; not using contraception along with contraceptive failure are the main reasons why unplanned pregnancies occur. Unplanned pregnancy makes it impossible for the mother and foetus to benefit from pre-pregnancy measures such as taking folic acid, giving up smoking and reducing alcohol intake, which have been shown to improve infant outcomes.[3]

Defining a crisis pregnancy and thus determining true prevalence is difficult. Even though a pregnancy may be unplanned, it may be 'wanted'; thus it does not always present a crisis (as defined in the introduction to this chapter). We suggested that a pregnancy, even if planned, might be a crisis for a range of reasons, particularly if the circumstances of the person's life change substantially.

Much of the research on 'unplanned' or 'crisis pregnancy' has been concerned with the situation of young people and teenagers. Conception among this group is a concern, but research suggests that crisis pregnancy is just as much of an issue for those aged over 20 and often for those aged over 30. Mahon (1998)[4] found that 30% of pregnant women who described their pregnancy in negative terms were over 30. Subsequent research (Rundle *et al*, 2004)[1] using a nationally representative survey found that conceptions among women under 25 are most likely (42%) to be experienced as a 'crisis' pregnancy, but the rate is still 15% among women between 26 and 35 and 7% among women over 35. Crisis pregnancies are, thus, a substantial issue even among women over 20.

The ICCP study showed that, overall:

• 28% of women who had been pregnant had experienced one or more crisis pregnancies

This proportion varies significantly across age groups: among women under 26, the proportion was 55%, falling to 31% among those aged 26-35, and 21% of those aged 36-45. These figures should be interpreted with caution as they are the proportion of women who *have experienced a pregnancy*. This is itself highly determined by the age of the woman. As the proportion experiencing a pregnancy among a cohort of women increases, the proportion with a 'crisis pregnancy' is likely to fall. As we have seen, 'unplanned' is the most frequently reported reason for a pregnancy to be a crisis, and younger women are less likely to want to be pregnant as they are less likely to be in a long-term relationship and more likely to still be in education or developing their careers.

Almost by definition, thus, pregnancies among young women are more likely to be a 'crisis'. This does not necessarily mean that younger women are more likely to have a crisis pregnancy over *lifetime*. However, the ICCP results show a substantial difference in the experience of crisis pregnancy among women under 36 compared to those over 36. This may suggest that, compared to older generations, women born after 1970 are more likely to have a crisis pregnancy over their lifetime. A good proportion of this cohort of women have yet to complete their fertility; thus it is not possible to know definitively, but the large difference does suggest that the number of crisis pregnancies may have increased among young women.

In the ISSHR survey, questions on pregnancy and crisis pregnancy were asked of women only, as the relatively recent ICCP survey[1] had looked at this issue in depth among both men and women.

Figure 11.1: Proportion of women who have been pregnant who have experienced a crisis pregnancy: by current age

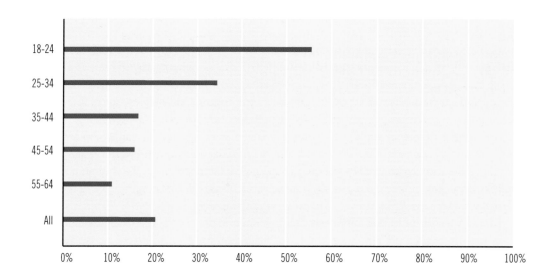

Figure 11.1 shows, by age group, the proportion of women who have experienced one or more crisis pregnancies (note that the crisis pregnancy may have occurred some time previously). It shows that:

- 21% of women in the ISSHR survey who have been pregnant have experienced a crisis pregnancy

This is a slightly lower figure than the 28% found in the ICCP survey. However, the ICCP survey was restricted to those under 46. Adjusting the ISSHR results in the same way reveals an identical figure to that found in the ICCP survey. The proportion of those under age 46 experiencing more than one crisis pregnancy (16%) is very similar to the 13% found in the ICCP survey.

As found in the ICCP survey, there is a strong age gradient in the experience of crisis pregnancy:

- 56% of women under 25 who have had a pregnancy report one or more crisis pregnancies, and 35% of women aged between 25 and 34.
- After age 34, the proportion drops considerably: to 17% among women aged 35-44 and 16% among women aged 45-54.

These figures also replicate the ICCP figures, to within 1%. It should be emphasised that these proportions are of those women who have had a pregnancy – a small proportion of women under 25 but a larger proportion of those in older age groups.

Pregnancies among young women are more likely to be defined as a 'crisis' because of their circumstances (as discussed in the introduction to this chapter). As much fewer young women than older women have been pregnant, their rate of crisis pregnancies will be higher. However, as these women age and their circumstances change, subsequent pregnancies will not be as problematic; thus the overall proportion of crisis pregnancies among this group will fall.

If we include all women whether they have had a pregnancy or not, the proportion who have experienced a crisis pregnancy is just 8% of women under 25 and 21% of those between 25 and 34. (For an analysis of the risk factors for crisis pregnancy across all women, see ISSHR Sub-Report 3: 'Contemporary Sexual Knowledge, Attitudes and Behaviours in Ireland'.)

It is important to know the age at which women experience crisis pregnancy and whether this is changing in younger age groups compared to older: are women having crisis pregnancies now at the same ages as in the past?

An answer to this question may be found using the kind of 'survivor curves' that were used in earlier analyses (see chapters five and seven). Survivor curve is the generic name for a technique that examines the rate of change in a variable over time. By plotting the proportion of women experiencing a crisis pregnancy against the woman's age, we can examine whether the age at which women in younger age groups have crisis pregnancies is lower on average than in older groups, controlling for the fact that most women in all cohorts will never experience a crisis pregnancy. Survivor curves usually plot the proportion of the population who have not yet experienced some outcome, but here we will be plotting what is termed the 'failure rate', or the proportion of women experiencing a crisis pregnancy. If the line representing a particular age cohort rises at an earlier age and more steeply, this would suggest that this group are having crisis pregnancies earlier and at a greater rate than women in other age groups. If so, this suggests that their behaviours are likely to be quite different, with consequences for their experience of crisis pregnancy.[r]

---

[r] The question in the ISSHR survey asked for the year of 'most recent' crisis pregnancy. Since women who had had more than one crisis pregnancy could bias the results, we excluded them from the analysis. Tests showed that including them increased the average age of crisis pregnancy among older age groups.

Figure 11.2: Age at crisis pregnancy for women: by current age group

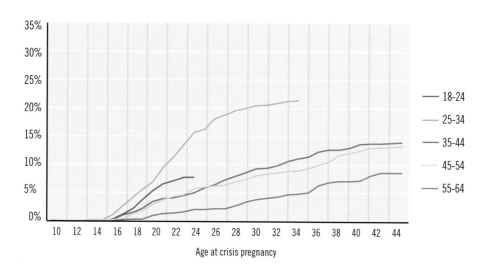

Figure 11.2 shows the 'failure' curves for crisis pregnancy among women of different age groups. The most noticeable pattern is the difference in the track of the two lines for women aged less than 25 and 25-34 compared to women aged 35 or more (and particularly women aged 55-64). The lines for the two youngest age groups rise earlier and much more quickly than those of later cohorts. This suggests that younger women are having crisis pregnancies at a younger age than later cohorts.

Analysis of the age of crisis pregnancy shows this as well. Women under 25 and aged 25-34 have 'median' ages of 19 and 22 at the time of crisis pregnancy, compared to 26 for women aged 35-44, 25 for women aged 45-54 and 32 for women aged 55-64. It is clear, too, that women aged 25-34 are more likely than women over 34 to experience a crisis pregnancy. The youngest cohort seem to be following the same track.

Both these findings show substantially different patterns among women under 35. This could be because younger women are more likely than older ones to have risky behaviours, to have vaginal sex earlier and to have more partners (as seen in chapters six and seven). However, younger women are also more likely to use contraception both at first sex and in the 'recent' period (as chapter 10 showed). This suggests that some of the other risk factors will be moderated. It may be that younger women are more likely than older generations to define a pregnancy as 'crisis'. A much larger proportion of young women now enter higher education and look to establish themselves in a career than has been true of any past cohort.[5] This changing context may colour the view that young women have of their pregnancies.

As already argued, the vast majority of crisis pregnancies are defined as such because they occur at a point in the woman's life when conditions are not appropriate or her future opportunities would be limited. Changing the average conditions of Irish women's lives would be likely to lead to a change in their perception of whether a pregnancy is a crisis or not. It is not easy to test this hypothesis with the present data, though a reanalysis of the ICCP data (which included women's reasons for defining their pregnancy as a crisis) by age may provide some insight.

Figure 11.3: Proportion of women who have been pregnant who have experienced a crisis pregnancy: by current relationship status

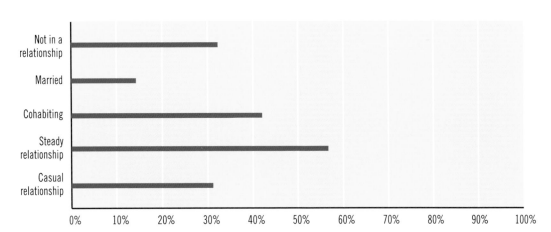

Figure 11.3 gives, by current relationship status, the proportion of those women who have been pregnant who have experienced a crisis pregnancy. It is important to bear in mind that the crisis pregnancy may have occurred a number of years previously and the woman may have had a different relationship status at the time. This may be one reason why, as Figure 11.3 shows, relationship status is related to the probability of a crisis pregnancy in a rather complex way. Women in a steady relationship (but not married or engaged) are most likely to have experienced a crisis pregnancy, followed by those who are not in a relationship. Married women are least likely. *Figure 11.1* showed that young women are most likely to have experienced a crisis pregnancy (as a proportion of all pregnancies). These women are also more likely to be cohabiting or in steady relationships, leading to the pattern that we see in *Figure 11.3*.

Age of first intercourse has been found, in studies in other countries,[6 7] to be associated with a range of negative outcomes. The direct cause of this relationship is not fully known. It is likely that early sexual intercourse is related to socio-economic and attitudinal factors that make risk-taking behaviour more likely both in adolescence and in adulthood and that this leads to higher rates of negative outcomes.

Figure 11.4 shows that, across all age groups except the youngest, having had vaginal sex before 17 leads to an increase in the probability of a crisis pregnancy.

Figure 11.4: Proportion of women who have been pregnant experiencing a crisis pregnancy: by age of first vaginal sex

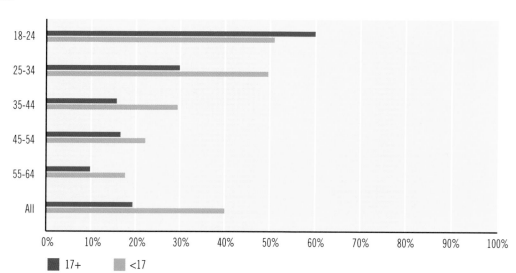

Of women who have been pregnant, the proportion that have experienced a crisis pregnancy is over twice as high among those who began having vaginal sex before the age of 17, compared to those starting later. This suggests a pronounced relationship, although the underlying processes are not clear. It may be, for instance, that the women who are likely to have early sexual intercourse are also those who have unprotected sex later. There may be no necessary casual relationship between early sex and later crisis pregnancy, just an underlying propensity on the part of some women to experience both events. On the other hand, the relationship may be more direct. Women who had sex before the age of 17 are less likely to use protection and are less able to negotiate safe sex (see chapter six). This may contribute to an increased risk of early and unplanned pregnancy among these women.

Age and relationship status are to a certain extent 'distal'[s] characteristics in the sense that they represent the impact of other factors likely to affect behaviours, such as use of contraception, which in turn are likely to influence the probability of a crisis pregnancy. For example, lower levels of contraceptive knowledge may be associated with an increased risk of non-use of contraception, although results described in the last chapter cast doubt on this. The relationship between knowledge and outcomes such as crisis pregnancy is, of course, complex; experience of crisis pregnancy itself may lead to an increase in knowledge as, armed with what they have learnt from their experience, individuals seek to protect themselves in future. Simple causal statements should be avoided, therefore, although gaining an understanding of the relationship would be both interesting and constructive.

ISSHR Sub-Report 3: 'Contemporary Sexual Knowledge, Attitudes and Behaviours in Ireland' examines the relationship of attitudes, knowledge and behaviours with the probability of crisis pregnancy. It shows that a number of factors are related to crisis pregnancy, but that the relationship is complex. Once other factors are controlled for, level of knowledge about fertility is not a significant predictor of crisis pregnancy. Knowledge of emergency contraception is, however – but it is a *higher* level of knowledge about the latter that is associated with a higher probability of crisis pregnancy. This may indicate that women who have had a crisis pregnancy have learnt through experience about emergency contraception.

---

[s] Distal is an anatomical term that means: situated away from the centre of the body or of a point of attachment.

Concerning the impact of sexual attitudes, Sub-Report 3 finds a general relationship between liberal attitudes and a higher risk of crisis pregnancy. It is likely that more liberal attitudes are associated with both more risky sexual behaviours and an earlier age of first sex (which, as we saw in the last chapter, is associated with a lower use of contraception). This is likely to lead to a higher risk of negative outcomes. Sub-Report 3 also finds a positive relationship between negative attitudes to using oral contraceptives (agreeing that side-effects would discourage use) and the risk of crisis pregnancy. This suggests that negative attitudes are related to lower use of contraception both currently and/or in the past and thus an increased risk of crisis pregnancy.

11.3 Outcomes of crisis pregnancy

SUMMARY

ANALYSIS of the outcomes of pregnancy shows that most women in the ISSHR survey became a parent. However, the outcomes of crisis pregnancy have changed profoundly through time.

The ISSHR survey shows that women currently aged 45 or over who had a crisis pregnancy are far more likely than younger women to have become a parent or offered their child for adoption. Although becoming a parent is still the dominant outcome among women in younger age groups, these women are more likely to have experienced abortion than their older peers.

Among women under 35, there are no instances of women having their child adopted. This pattern is reflected in official adoption figures where numbers have fallen dramatically in recent decades.

- 75% of women became a parent after their crisis pregnancy and 15% had an abortion.
- The child was adopted after 1.2% of crisis pregnancies.
- Miscarriage or still birth was experienced in 9% of cases of crisis pregnancy.
- The proportion of younger women who became a parent following crisis pregnancy is lower (73% among women under 25) than among older age groups (82% among women aged 45-54 and 81% among women aged 55-64).
- 20% of women aged 25-34 aborted their crisis pregnancy compared to 7% of women aged 55-64.
- Older age at crisis pregnancy is associated with a greater likelihood of becoming a parent; younger age with a higher probability of abortion.

WOMEN who reported a crisis pregnancy in the ISSHR survey were asked the outcome for this pregnancy. Respondents who said they were *currently* pregnant with a crisis pregnancy were excluded from the analysis.

Figure 11.5 shows, across age groups, the proportions of women who reported becoming a parent, having the baby adopted, having an abortion, experiencing stillbirth or having a miscarriage.

Figure 11.5 Outcomes of crisis pregnancy: by age group

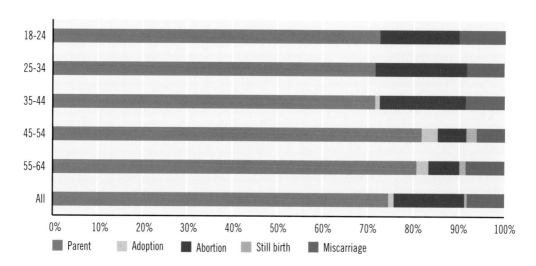

The results show that the proportion of women who became a parent increases with current age, whereas the proportion having an abortion decreases with age.

There is also a clear relationship between current age and having the baby adopted. Among women under 35 who had a crisis pregnancy, the proportion having the baby adopted falls to zero in the two youngest age groups. This reflects the sharp fall in the number of children offered for adoption in recent decades.[8]

Figure 11.5 shows the historical changes which have occurred in the outcomes of crisis pregnancy, but it is also interesting to examine the different outcomes by the age of the woman at the time of the crisis pregnancy.

Figure 11.6: Crisis pregnancy outcomes: by age of crisis pregnancy

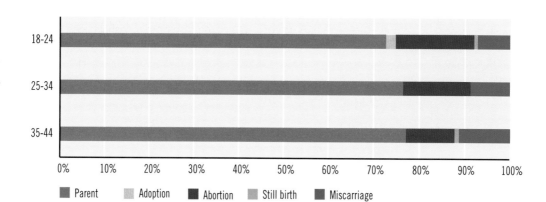

Although the pattern is quite weak, *Figure 11.6* shows that the proportion of women becoming a parent increases as her age at pregnancy increases, whereas the proportion opting for abortion decreases.

11.4 Experience of abortion

SUMMARY

OFFICIAL sources in Britain show an increasing number of women with Irish addresses having abortions in British clinics over recent decades. However they also show that numbers have declined in the last five years. The ISSHR survey asked women whether they had ever had an abortion.

Higher education and non-manual social class are associated with higher levels of abortion, as is having vaginal sex before the age of 17.

■ Between 1980 and 2000, the absolute number of women travelling to Britain for an abortion almost doubled: from 3,320 to 6,381.

■ Overall, 4% of women in the ISSHR survey reported having an abortion. Compared to international figures, this prevalence is low to average.

■ Women in less formalised relationships are more likely to have experienced an abortion.

■ Women who had vaginal sex before 17 are almost three times more likely to experience an abortion than women who had sex for the first time after 17.

THE last section showed a number of outcomes of crisis pregnancy. The prohibition on abortion in Ireland coupled with the availability of abortion across the Irish Sea has meant that a great deal has been written on the subject. However, there is surprisingly little evidence available on the prevalence of abortion among Irish women, apart from figures published by the British government and the recent ICCP survey.[1] This section examines the experience of abortion among Irish women in more detail.

Since abortion is not available either north or south of the Irish border, Irish women have availed of abortion services in Great Britain since the reform of abortion law there in 1967 (as well as much further afield). The UK's National Statistics Office has shown that the number of Irish women seeking an abortion in Britain has risen steadily, from 3,320 in 1980 to 6,673 in 2001 (see *Figure 11.7*).

Figure 11.7: UK Office of National Statistics abortion figures: for women with Irish addresses

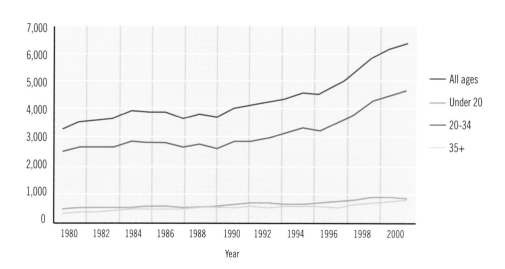

These figures are based on the addresses given by these women to the clinic they attend. They do not include abortions sought elsewhere in the world; thus it is highly likely that these figures underestimate the true number of Irish women seeking abortions.

The ICCP study[1] found that around 2% of all conceptions among Irish women aged between 18 and 45 ended in abortion. This figure is far lower than that found in the US (9.7%) and Australia (9.8%).[7] Information on the abortion rate in Britain was presented slightly differently, but the figure there is also substantially higher.

In the ISSHR survey, abortion was reported on a per woman rather than per conception basis, as in the reports for Britain, Australia and the US. We would expect this to lead to a higher level of abortion than that found in the ICCP survey. This is the case (4% ISSHR compared to 2% ICCP), but the rate is still low internationally.

Henshaw *et al* (1999)[9] have estimated that, in countries where there is no restriction on abortion, the rate on a per woman basis ranges from 0.7% of those aged 15-44 in Belgium and the Netherlands to 8.3% in Vietnam. This suggests that the Irish rate is in the low to mid range.

Figure 11.8: Proportion of women who have been pregnant experiencing an abortion: by age

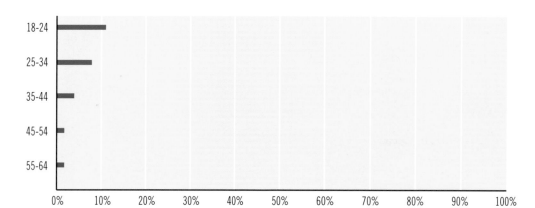

Figure 11.8 shows that, among women who have been pregnant, the proportion that have experienced an abortion varies systematically by age group:

• Whereas only 1.5% of those over 54 have experienced an abortion, the figure rises to 4% among those aged 35-44, 8% among those aged 25-34 and 11% among those aged 18-24.

As in the analysis of crisis-pregnancy figures, it should be born in mind when analysing these figures that the denominator group is important. This here is the proportion of women who have experienced a conception, which is a much smaller proportion among the younger age group.

Figure 11.9: Proportion of women who have been pregnant experiencing an abortion: by highest education

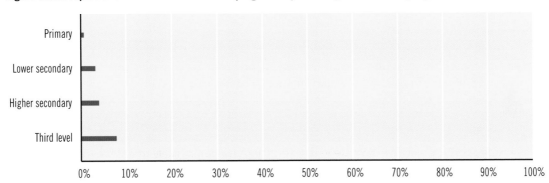

Figure 11.9 shows that higher levels of education are associated with a higher probability of abortion:

• Whereas just over 8% of women with a third-level qualification who have become pregnant have had an abortion, this is true of less than 1% of women with primary education alone or less.

This pattern by education is statistically significant; educational differences are important, even within age groups.

Analyses (not shown) also found that social class is related to the probability of abortion; women in professional and managerial occupations are more likely to have experienced an abortion than women in manual working-class jobs.

Figure 11.10: Proportion of women who have been pregnant experiencing an abortion: by current relationship status

Figure 11.10 shows the probability among women who have been pregnant of experiencing an abortion, according to the woman's current relationship status. As in the analysis of crisis pregnancy, it is important to note that the abortion may have occurred some time ago and that current relationship status may no longer apply.

The figure shows that the probability of an abortion is positively associated with less formalised forms of relationship. Married women have the lowest rate and those in steady or casual relationships the highest. This pattern emerges even if we take account of the impact of age (since younger women are less likely to be married and more likely to be cohabiting or in a steady relationship).

Finally, we come to the role of age of first vaginal intercourse. This chapter and the last have given several examples of the importance of age of first intercourse, for both use of contraception and experience of crisis pregnancy. It is also positively associated with the risk of abortion; women who had sex first before 17 have almost three times the risk of subsequently experiencing an abortion (see Appendix *Table 9.2*).

As in the analysis of crisis pregnancy, it is useful to examine how levels of knowledge and specific behaviours help to explain the distribution of abortions. ISSHR Sub-Report 3 examines in depth the role of these factors. It shows that knowledge of fertility and emergency contraception are positively associated with the experience of abortion; that is, better knowledge is associated with a higher likelihood of abortion. As with the experience of crisis pregnancy, this unexpected relationship may stem from a process of 'reverse causation', where the experience of abortion leads to an increase in knowledge about fertility and contraception. This finding underlines the complexity of the processes at work and the difficulty in assigning causal significance when using cross-sectional data.

Sub-Report 3: 'Contemporary Sexual Knowledge, Attitudes and Behaviours' also shows that sexual attitudes are related to probability of abortion. More liberal attitudes generally are associated with a higher likelihood of abortion, perhaps through an association with higher-risk behaviours. A higher number of partners over lifetime is also associated with a higher risk of abortion.

11.5 Experience of sexually transmitted infections

SUMMARY

THE ISSHR survey shows that around 3% of men and 2% of women reported having been diagnosed with a sexually transmitted infection (STI) in the past.

Younger individuals were more likely to report an STI diagnosis, and those aged 25-34 most likely.

Among women, those with higher levels of education and/or with professional or managerial occupations were most likely to report an STI diagnosis, even within age groups.

Among both men and women, those in casual relationships or not in a relationship were more likely to report being diagnosed, as were those who began having vaginal sex before the age of 17.

Men reporting a same-sex partner 'ever' in their life were significantly more likely to report being diagnosed with an STI. It is not clear whether this is due to higher levels of infection or higher levels of knowledge and health-seeking behaviour among such men.

- 3.4% of men and 1.8% of women had been diagnosed with an STI.
- Experience of STIs was most likely among men and women aged 25-34.
- Higher education and non-manual class among women are associated with a higher risk of experiencing an STI.
- Men and women in casual relationships or not in a relationship were most likely to report an STI.
- Both men and women who had sex before 17 were more likely to report having experienced an STI.

KNOWLEDGE, attitude and behaviour surveys (KABS) offer researchers the chance to examine the relationship between a person's history of STI infection and their sexual knowledge, attitudes and behaviours. Unlike national disease-surveillance systems, such surveys do not attempt to present complete reviews of the prevalence of a disease in a population. Instead they seek to find relative differences in reported prevalence between groups with different characteristics. In this way, KAB surveys complement surveillance figures by providing insights into the processes that underlie overall prevalence.

Various KAB surveys have assessed STI and blood-borne virus history in different ways. The first NATSAL survey in Britain[6] (in 1990) did not ask respondents for their STI history, arguing that it was not possible to define STIs in terms comprehensible to respondents. Instead they assumed that the vast majority of STIs were treated at genito-urinary clinics and asked respondents if they had ever attended such a clinic. This approach may have led to an underestimate of STI prevalence in that survey.

The later, 2000 NATSAL survey asked respondents directly if they had ever been diagnosed with an STI. It found rates of 11% among men and 13% among women, compared to the previous survey's figures of 8% among men and 6% among women. However, the 2000 NATSAL survey also showed that some risk behaviours had also increased between the two surveys, so it is possible that the lower estimate was accurate. The Australian ASHR survey[10] found much higher lifetime rates of STIs, at 20% among men and 17% among women. Such figures place Australia at the upper end of the international spectrum, which tends to range between 10% and 20%.[10]

In most European studies[11] men are more likely to report gonorrhoea than women, whereas women are more likely to report Chlamydia. However, in the 2000 NATSAL survey both genders were most likely to report genital warts, and Chlamydia was more common than gonorrhoea among both men and women.[12]

The Australian ASHR survey found that pubic lice or 'crabs' was the most commonly reported STI among men over lifetime, followed by NSU[t] and genital warts (discounting thrush which is also transmitted non-sexually). Among women, the most commonly reported STIs over lifetime were genital warts and the associated virus (HPV), followed by pubic lice and Chlamydia. Figures were also reported for STIs 'over the last year', which were less prevalent; genital herpes was most prevalent among both men and women, followed by genital warts (HPV).[13]

The ASHR survey[10] also analysed the correlates of ever being diagnosed with an STI. It found that older age, higher education, social class and homosexual identity were all strongly predictive, as were ever having paid for sex and being a sex worker.

Figure 11.11: Proportion diagnosed with a sexually transmitted infection: by gender

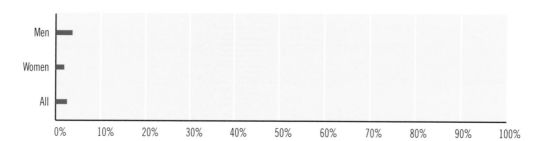

In the ISSHR survey, respondents were asked if they had ever been told by a health professional that they had a sexually transmissible disease or illness.

Figure 11.11 shows that 3% of men and 2% of women reported having been diagnosed with an STI. This rate places Ireland outside and below the usual range of rates reported in KAB surveys. The large differences between the ISSHR figures and those in other national studies could be explained by a number of factors.

- First, the difference may reflect a lower prevalence of STIs in Ireland. To evaluate this, it is necessary to compare risk behaviours, such as rate of partner exchange, across different populations. Although the lifetime rate of partners is lower in Ireland (see chapter seven), the number 'in the last year' is close to that in other countries. The likelihood of contracting an STI is, of course, also determined by risk-reducing strategies such as use of condoms. There is some evidence (see last chapter) that the rate of reported condom use is higher in Ireland than in some other European countries.

---

[t] Non-specific urethritis (NSU) is an inflammation of the urethra. It affects men only. It is called 'non-specific' because a range of infections can cause it. It is usually caused by vaginal, oral or anal sex with a partner who has an STI, but other causes include: other genital or urinary tract infections, damage to the urethra through vigorous sex or masturbation, or, rarely among young men.

- Secondly, STI prevalence may be reported as low in Ireland if uptake of screening differs between Ireland and countries where opportunistic screening (for instance, for Chlamydia) is provided. This issue is discussed in more detail in ISSHR Sub-Report 2: 'Sexual Health Challenges and Related Service Provision'. It shows that in Ireland levels of testing for all STIs and HIV are far lower than in most other European countries and that this is likely to affect the prevalence of STIs found in Irish surveys as well as data from surveillance agencies such as the HPSC. Section 11.6 examines these issues in more detail and profiles the characteristics of people in the ISSHR sample who have sought advice about STIs.

Figure 11.12 shows that both men and women aged 25-34 report the highest lifetime prevalence of STIs, at 5% and 4% respectively; among men, this rate is matched among those aged 35-44.

Figure 11.12: Proportion diagnosed with a sexually transmitted illness: by gender and age

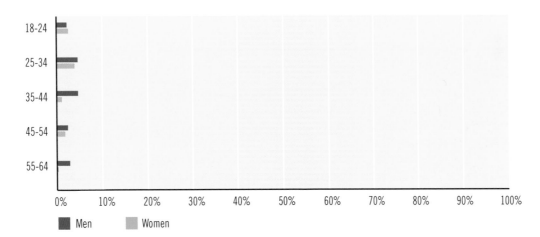

In the international context, this age pattern is unusual. The peak prevalence usually occurs later, since older respondents have had more time to acquire an STI. Older Irish people have unusually low numbers of sexual partners (see chapter seven), which may contribute to the unusually low rates of STIs among them, when compared internationally. However, given the differences in surveillance and detection in Ireland compared to other countries, it is not possible to be definitive.

As well as age group, several other factors are important (see Appendix *Table 9.3*). For example, the prevalence of being diagnosed with an STI is lower among manual working-class groups and people with lower levels of education, although this pattern is statistically significant only among women. This may reflect differences in health-seeking behaviour between groups rather than rates of infection.

Current relationship status is also important. Among both men and women, people in casual relationships report the highest prevalence (7% among men and 6% among women), while married respondents report the lowest. Again, it is difficult to disentangle the level of diagnosis from level of infection, but people who are not in a relationship or in casual relationships are more likely to have had higher numbers of partners over the most recent period (see chapter seven), and this may be associated with a higher level of infection.

A person's age of first vaginal sex is an important determinant of outcomes such as crisis pregnancy and abortion (see previous sections). Analyses show (see Appendix *Table 9.3*) that a similar pattern holds here: people who had vaginal sex before the age of 17 have a significantly higher risk of STIs in later periods.

ISSHR Sub-Report 3: 'Contemporary Sexual Knowledge, Attitudes and Behaviours in Ireland' points to other behavioural factors being associated with STI diagnosis. Analyses there show that, among both men and women, having five or more partners over lifetime to date is associated with a significant increase in STI diagnosis. Similarly, ISSHR Sub-Report 2: 'Sexual Health Challenges and Related Service Provision' shows that 'ever' having a same-sex partner or paying for sex (among men) are associated with a pronounced increase in STI diagnosis.

As with other issues in previous sections, it is useful to examine the correlation of sexual health knowledge and specific behaviours with rates of STIs. These are examined in depth in ISSHR Sub-Report 3. It shows that, among both men and women, knowledge of both HIV/AIDS and Chlamydia is associated with a higher prevalence of STIs over lifetime. However, a person's level of knowledge (as also argued in the last section) can have a complex relationship to outcomes since good knowledge can be acquired through experience, particularly adverse experiences.

11.6 Use of STI services

SUMMARY

USE of sexual health services is an important issue for sexual health. The ISSHR survey included questions on whether an individual had ever sought advice on sexually transmitted infections (STIs) and, if so, where they had sought this advice and from where they would prefer to get it.

Results showed no significant differences between men and women. Younger people were more likely to have sought advice, as were those with higher levels of education, particularly third-level. Relationship status also proved important: unmarried people were significantly more likely to have sought advice on STIs.

Concerning availability of services as a possible factor, people living in a city were significantly more likely than others to have sought advice.

GPs were the most common source of advice on STIs, especially for women (used by 43% v 32% for men).

- In total, 9.4% of men and 8.3% of women had sought advice about STIs.

- Men and women who were cohabiting, in a steady relationship, in a casual relationship or not in a relationship were more likely than married men and women to have sought advice about STIs.

- Men and women who resided in a city were more likely than those living in a town/rural area to have sought advice about STIs.

- Women were more likely than men to have got advice on STIs from family planning/Well Woman clinics (22% v 4%).

- Men were significantly more likely than women to have used an internet site as a source of advice about STIs (14% v 3%).

- Most men and women (60% and 51% respectively) said they would prefer to seek advice from their GP.

ONE of the factors likely to contribute to differences in reported STIs across studies internationally is the fact that the level of STI screening varies from country to country.

Some countries, such as Sweden and more recently the UK, have adopted widespread screening for Chlamydia. Prevalence data show that reported cases of Chlamydia have increased in the UK and the US since the early 1990s. Rates in Finland and Sweden have started to increase in recent years, following a decline in the early 1990s. It is notable that the national sexual-behaviour studies in the US and Finland were done in the early 1990s, so it is possible that reported STI prevalence may have increased since then.

Information on the level of testing across Europe is scant. Swedish figures show that 13% of the population aged 15-39 underwent testing for Chlamydia in 2003 (384,000 tests); 25% of these tests were on men. In Denmark, 275,000 Chlamydia tests were done in 2002 (15% of the population aged 15-39). About 60% of those tests were conducted as part of a screening programme. Although Norway does not have a national screening programme for Chlamydia, screening is nonetheless common. One Norwegian study showed that, by age 25, 85% to 90% of women had undertaken a Chlamydia test. The cumulative incidence of Chlamydia by age 25 was 15% for women born between 1976 and 1979.

In the ISSHR survey overall, 10% of men and 9% of women had 'ever' attended for a sexual health check-up. For those aged 18-49, these figures were 12% for men and 13% for women. The ISSHR figures are not directly comparable with the northern European figures, but it is clear that they fall far behind them. In Sweden and Denmark, for instance, a larger proportion underwent Chlamydia testing in a *single* year than the proportion of ISSHR participants who had 'ever' undergone a test. The British NATSAL figures reported that 14% of men and 12% of women had 'ever' attended a GUM (genito-urinary medicine) clinic. However, half of the women and almost a quarter of the men had an STI diagnosed in a facility other than a GUM clinic, which suggests that a larger proportion of the population had undertaken an STI screen.

In summary, it is clear that levels of testing for STIs are lower in Ireland than in these other European countries. This will contribute, though to an unquantifiable extent, to the differential in reported STI rates between ISSHR and other national surveys (as found in the last section). Combining this information with international comparisons of sexual-risk behaviour (specifically, number of partners and condom use), as outlined in chapters seven and 10, balances the explanation for low rates of reported STIs in the ISSHR survey.

ISSHR participants reported lower numbers of lifetime sexual partners and higher levels of condom use than those in other studies. These factors support the lower STI rate found in the survey. However, they also reported notably lower levels of lifetime testing for STIs. This factor suggests a higher level of undetected STIs among ISSHR participants than among participants in the other European studies. Thus the lower levels of STIs reported in Ireland are likely to be a combination of genuinely lower levels, because of a lower sexual-risk profile, and less awareness of existing STIs because of less testing. A national prevalence study such as the one proposed for Chlamydia would provide valuable evidence of the gap between detected STIs and their real prevalence in Ireland.

This section examines the profile of people in the ISSHR survey who had presented for STI testing.

Figure 11.13 gives the proportion of people who had 'ever' sought advice about sexually transmitted infections. It shows that around 9% of men and 8% of women had sought advice about STIs. The figure also shows some differences across age groups; men and women aged 18-24 were most likely to report seeking advice, particularly when compared to those aged over 44.

Figure 11.13: Proportion who have ever sought advice about STIs: by gender

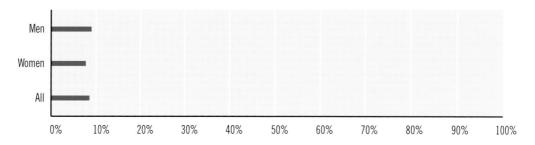

Figure 11.14: Proportion who have ever sought advice about STIs: by gender and age

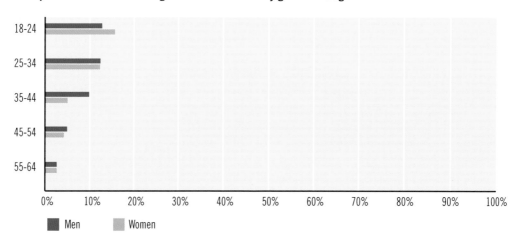

Figure 11.15: Proportion who have ever sought advice about STIs: by gender and highest education

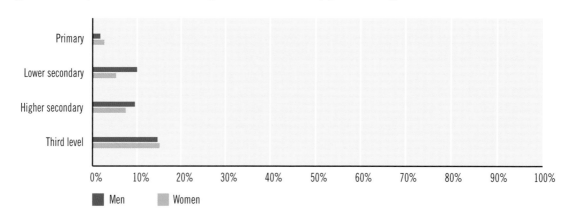

Level of highest education also appears to be a significant predictor of seeking advice. People with higher levels of education, and particularly those with third-level qualifications, are significantly more likely. Among men, for example, 15% of those with third-level qualifications reported seeking advice compared to 2% among those with primary education only.

A person's relationship status is also an important predictor (see Appendix *Table 9.4*). Unmarried people are significantly more likely to have sought advice than married people, even within age groups.

A person's ability to seek advice might be constrained by the fact that there are limited services available to them in their area. Analyses (see Appendix *Table 9.4*) show that geographical location is an important predictor. People living in a city are significantly more likely to have sought advice about STIs than individuals living in rural areas or in towns, even if the influence of factors such as age and relationship status has been removed. This suggests that a person's ability to get the services required strongly depends on availability of services.

Figure 11.16: Source of advice about STIs: by gender and age

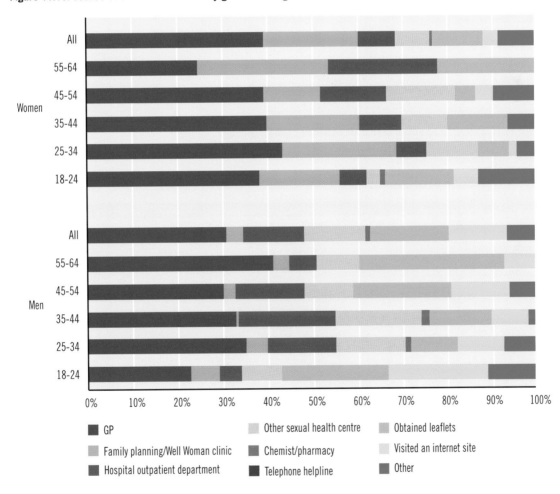

Participants who had sought advice about STIs were asked about their source of advice. *Figure 11.16* shows that GPs were the most common source. More women than men got information from GPs (43% v 32%). Women were also more likely than men to have got advice from family planning/Well Woman clinics (22% v 4%). Leaflets were also a common source of information (used by 18% of men and 13% of women).

There were no gender differences in use of hospital outpatient departments, other sexual health centres, and chemist/pharmacy. Men were significantly more likely than women to have used an internet site as a source of advice (14% v 3%). A number of men and women gave another source of advice; the most common of these were college health services and family or friends.

The only significant age-group difference was in use by men of a hospital outpatient department; fewer of the youngest and oldest men used this source. (However, some results should be interpreted with caution due to the small number of participants in the older age groups who reported having sought advice on STIs.)

All participants were asked about their preference for sources of advice about STIs, if all were available in their area and easy to get to. *Figure 11.17* shows that most men (60%) and women (51%) said they would prefer to seek advice from their GP. Clinics (such as Well Woman and family-planning clinics) and other sexual health centres were preferred by a substantial number of men (23%) and women (42%). Only 4% of men and 2% of women preferred hospital outpatient departments. As with their actual source of advice in *Figure 11.16*, more men (6%) than women (2%) preferred to use the internet.

Patterns of preference across age groups are difficult to determine. There were no clear age-group trends in preference for a GP, except that more men and women aged 55-64 said they would prefer to visit a GP. A considerably higher proportion of younger men, and a slightly higher proportion of younger women, preferred an internet site.

Figure 11.17: Preferred source of advice about STIs: by gender and age

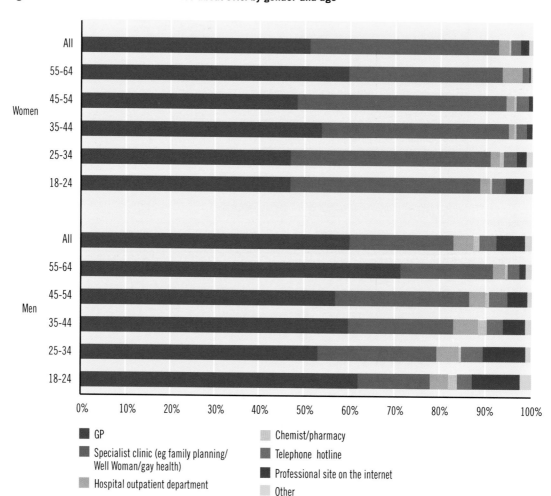

11.7 Summary

THIS chapter has examined the reported prevalence of three negative outcomes of sexual intercourse: crisis pregnancy, abortion and sexually transmitted infections (STIs). As already emphasised, sex and sexuality are a source of tremendous pleasure and well-being for many Irish people, but intercourse can also have negative consequences. It is important within the overall framework of a KAB study to examine the prevalence of these outcomes and the extent to which they are correlated with a range of factors. Such information will be vitally important for the development of policy responses in a number of areas.

The examination of the pattern of crisis pregnancies largely reiterated the findings of the recent ICCP survey by showing that around 28% of women under 46, who have been pregnant, have experienced a crisis pregnancy, but that this varies considerably by age group. Whereas 56% of women under 25 who had been pregnant had experienced a crisis pregnancy, this was true of just 11% of women aged between 55 and 64. This is not a simple statistic. It does not necessarily mean that younger women are more likely to have a crisis pregnancy over their lifetime. However, the large difference in the experience of women under 35 compared to those over 35 might suggest a trend toward greater prevalence. Further evidence of this trend was provided by duration analyses of age at first crisis pregnancy; these showed that women under 35 were not only more likely to have had a crisis pregnancy, but were likely to have it at an earlier age than women over 35.

Education and social class are weakly related to the likelihood of experiencing a crisis pregnancy. Women in casual or steady relationships have a higher probability of experiencing it. The latter association is complex since *current* relationship status is used rather than that at the time of the crisis pregnancy.

Having begun having sex before the age of 17 is also a strong predictor of crisis pregnancy. The association between early sex and various negative outcomes has been found in a number of studies (Rundle *et al* 2004, Johnson *et al* 1994). The reasons for this are complex and still poorly understood, but it seems that some process – perhaps including learning, attitude formation and socio-economic circumstances – leads from early experience to later outcome. Measures of a person's knowledge about fertility and contraception were used but, because of their complexity, it was not possible to infer any process of cause and effect.

This chapter also examined the outcomes of crisis pregnancy. It showed a distinct pattern across age groups that suggests a pattern of change in recent decades. Women who are currently older but had crisis pregnancies in the past were far more likely to become a parent and less likely to have opted for abortion. Among women who are currently younger, abortion has become a more frequent option. It is also striking that the probability of a mother offering her child for adoption after crisis pregnancy has plummeted in recent decades.

The third section examined the prevalence of abortion. Figures from the British ONS show increasing numbers of abortions for Irish nationals travelling to Britain over recent decades, but a decline in the last five years. Our analyses showed some factors that may be implicated in this. Unlike with crisis pregnancy, age was not a major predictor of experiencing an abortion but relationship status was; younger women and those in casual or non-formalised relationships were most likely to report having an abortion.

Turning to the analysis of reported STIs, it was found that the peak ages for men are between 25 and 44 while those for women are under 35. Men who were not in a relationship or those in a casual relationship also had the highest risk. Age of first intercourse emerged as a strong predictor of reporting an STI among both men and women. Having had a same-sex partner was significant among men. The association of same-sex experience and reporting an STI is very large; the risk increases eightfold.

The last section of the chapter examined the use of and preferences for sexual health services. The results showed no significant difference between men and women in levels of seeking advice about STIs, but younger people and those with higher levels of education were more likely to have done so. Importantly, results also showed that living in a city was associated with a higher probability of seeking advice; this may suggest that availability of services outside large urban areas is a problem.

GPs are both the most frequently cited source of advice about STIs and the preferred source, although specialist clinics are also frequently cited as a preferred source. The proportion preferring to use specialist clinics is significantly higher than that actually using them; this again may indicate a mismatch between the demand for and supply of services.

11.8 Reference list

1   Rundle K, Leigh C, McGee H, Layte R. *Irish Contraception and Crisis Pregnancy (ICCP) Study. A Survey of the General Population.* Dublin: Crisis Pregnancy Agency report no. 7, 2004.

2   Crisis Pregnancy Agency. *Towards a Strategy to Address the Issue of Crisis Pregnancy.* Dublin: Crisis Pregnancy Agency, 2003.

3   Crowley P. 'Pre-pregnancy Care'. In: Prendiville W, Scott JR, editors. *Clinical Management of Early Pregnancy.* London: Arnold, 1999.

4   Mahon E, Conlon C, Dillon L. *Women and Crisis Pregnancy.* Dublin: The Stationery Office, 1998.

5   Layte R, Whelan CT. 'Class Transformation and Trends in Social Fluidity in the Republic of Ireland 1973 to 1994'. In: Breen R, editor. *Social Mobility in Europe.* Oxford: Oxford University Press, 2004.

6   Johnson A, Wadsworth J, Wellings K, Field J. *Sexual Attitudes and Lifestyles.* Oxford: Basil Blackwell, 1994.

7   Smith AM, Rissel CE, Richters J, Grulich AE, de Visser RO. 'Sex in Australia: reproductive experiences and reproductive health among a representative sample of women'. *Australian and New Zealand Journal of Public Health* 2003; 27(2):204-209.

8   Rundle K, Leigh C, McGee H, Layte R. 'Irish Contraception and Crisis Pregnancy (ICCP) Study: A Survey of the General Population'. Dublin: Crisis Pregnancy Agency, 2004.

9   Henshaw SK, Singh S, Haas T. 'Recent Trends in Abortion Rates Worldwide'. *International Family Planning Perspectives* 1999; 25(2):44-48.

10 Grulich AE, de Visser RO, Smith AM, Rissel CE, Richters J. 'Sex in Australia: sexually transmissible infection and blood-borne virus history in a representative sample of adults'. *Australian and New Zealand Journal of Public Health* 2003; 27(2):234-241.

11 Warszawski J. 'Self-Reported Sexually Transmitted Diseases and At-Risk Sexual Behaviour'. In: Hubert M, Bajos N, Sandfort T, editors. *Sexual Behaviour and HIV/AIDS in Europe.* London: UCL Press, 1998.

12 Fenton K, Korovessis C, Johnson A. 'Sexual Behaviour in Britain: Reported Sexually Transmitted Infections and Prevalent Chlamydia Trachomatis Infection'. *Lancet* 2001; 358:1851-1854.

13 Grulich AE, de Visser RO, Smith AM, Rissel CE, Richters J. 'Sex in Australia: sexually transmissible infection and blood-borne virus history in a representative sample of adults'. *Australian and New Zealand Journal of Public Health* 2003; 27(2):234-241.

Chapter 12:
Conclusions

12.1 Introduction

THIS chapter draws together the evidence and discussion of the last 11 chapters to derive conclusions about the important dimensions of sexual knowledge, attitudes and behaviours in Irish society and their implications for the development of policy.

Rather than trying to summarise all the material in the report, a task better achieved in the chapters themselves, this chapter focuses on specific issues. When outlining each issue and recommending the possible policy response, it draws on material from the whole report and beyond.

The following sections concentrate on specific issues and sub-groups. It is important to state that the Irish population overall has a very positive and responsible attitude to sex and sexuality, and that the vast majority of individuals surveyed reported high levels of physical and emotional satisfaction. However, it is also important to recognise that the Irish population is not homogenous; behaviours vary enormously across sub-groups. Because of this, sexual health services and policy responses need to be tailored to the preferences and circumstances of specific groups and individuals, if they are to be effective.

The conclusions given here do not fully address the nature of current sexual health services and their possible development. This is the subject of ISSHR Sub-Report 2: 'Sexual Health Challenges and Related Service Provision'.

12.2 Social and cultural change in Ireland

THE current patterns of sexual knowledge, attitudes and behaviours in Ireland can only be fully understood in the light of Irish economic, social and cultural history. Most Irish adults learnt about and experienced sex and sexual relations in a society still deeply influenced by a Roman Catholic moral framework, but this influence has weakened considerably over the last four decades or so. The changes have intensified in recent years as Ireland has become an increasingly multinational, multicultural and multi-faith society.

As discussed and explained extensively in chapters one and four, sexual *attitudes* are still more conservative in Ireland (north and south of the Irish border) than in other Western European states. However, as chapter four also showed by comparing ISSHR results to previous surveys, there has been enormous change.

Attitudes have become increasingly liberal on issues such as sex outside marriage, homosexuality and abortion. Present trends suggest, as with many other aspects of Irish life, that sexual culture in Ireland is moving closer to that of the UK and continental Europe. Depending on the observer, this could be viewed as a positive or negative development, but it is undeniable that Irish attitudes to sex and sexual relations are changing, and changing quickest among younger people. Across the age range, Irish people are now more accepting of a greater range of sexual behaviours and orientations.

Such large-scale social and cultural change is likely to have been accompanied by changes in sexual behaviour, although this relationship is not simple. The chapters of this report have provided ample evidence that younger generations of Irish people have significantly different behaviours to those of older people. Chapter five showed that younger age groups, and younger women in particular, are much more likely to report at least some attraction to the same gender, and young women are much more likely than older women to report a homosexual experience. Along with the attitudinal change, this suggests that a far more open and accepting attitude to same-sex relationships has become established in Ireland.

Similarly, chapter six showed that the age of sexual initiation has decreased progressively over the last half century. Younger Irish people are far more likely than older generations to have experienced vaginal sexual intercourse before the age of 17.

Lastly, chapter seven showed that, to a large extent, young people in Ireland now have as many sexual partners as young people elsewhere in Europe.

Together, these and other changes show that there has been behavioural as well as attitudinal change in Ireland. In the sections below we reflect upon the implications that these changes may have for Irish society.

12.3 First sexual experiences

THERE has been a clear and steady trend, across age cohorts, toward younger age at first sex. Young men currently under 25 have intercourse an average of five years earlier than did men aged between 55 and 64. The difference among young women is even more pronounced; the gap between the oldest and youngest age groups is six years. This trend means that an increasing proportion of young people in Ireland are having their first sexual intercourse before age 17. Just 11% of men aged 55 to 64 and 2% of women of the same age had intercourse before their 17th birthday; this is now true of 31% of men and 22% of women under 25.

The gap here between behaviour and the legal situation is a concern, but perhaps of more concern is the association between early sexual intercourse and poorer sexual health profiles, both at the time and later in life. The ISSHR data show, for instance, that those who had sex before 17 were significantly:

- less likely to use contraception on that first occasion
- more likely to regret that sex happened at that point
- among women, less likely to be fully consenting or as willing as the other partner

In later life, early sexual intercourse was associated with:

- lower probability of using contraception when not wanting to conceive
- lower likelihood of consistent use of condoms
- higher likelihood of experiencing crisis pregnancy, abortion and an STI

International research suggests that a skills-based sex-education programme aimed at developing competence, self-esteem and confidence can have the dual effect of delaying the age of sexual debut and reducing the level of adverse outcomes, whatever the age of debut. The negative sexual health outcomes of early sex appear to arise more from the lack of sexual competence of young people than their age *per se*. There is no reason why competence, self-esteem and confidence could not be improved among younger Irish people also. However, encouraging young people to wait until a later age and giving them the confidence to do so might be just as effective in improving sexual health outcomes.

Since 2003, Relationships and Sexuality Education (RSE) has been mandatory in Irish schools for Junior Cycle pupils. Also, the current Rules and Programmes for Secondary Schools require that RSE be taught to all Senior Cycle pupils. The RSE programme guidelines include information on both the negotiation of sexual partnerships and the use of contraception and protection. However, this programme has not yet been fully implemented.

In an evaluation of sex education in Irish schools in 2000, Morgan (2000) found that:

- 42% of primary and 34% of post-primary schools had not drafted an RSE policy document
- around a quarter of both primary (26%) and post-primary (28%) schools had not established an RSE policy committee

However, a more recent survey of the implementation of SPHE at Junior Cycle carried out by the University of Limerick found substantially higher rates:

- RSE was available to 73% of first-year students, 69% of second-year and 63% of third-year

The authors suggested that, while fewer students received RSE as they moved into adolescence, it is probable that their need for education in RSE was likely to increase over these school years.[1]
The results from the University of Limerick study suggest that many younger people surveyed (the 18 to 24-year-olds) are still not receiving an adequate grounding in sex education. A recent detailed study of the implementation of RSE by post-primary schools, commissioned by the Crisis Pregnancy Agency and the Department of Education and Science, is due to be published in 2006.

12.3.1 The socio-economic context of first intercourse

SURVEYS of sexual behaviour in a number of countries have shown that young men and women from lower social-class backgrounds and those with lower educational qualifications are both more likely to have earlier sexual intercourse and less likely to use contraception when they do so. Results from the ISSHR survey (see chapter six) show that the pattern in Ireland is similar.

International academic and policy research has found that these behaviours are embedded in complex socio-economic processes that are difficult both to unravel and alter. However, it is clear that coming from a poorer social group can have direct effects on behaviour. The ISSHR results showed, for instance, that the cost of contraception and protection is a real issue for young people and those with lower levels of education. If so, reducing this cost or providing protection for free might have a significant affect on behaviour (we discuss this in more detail below).

Other processes are not as simple and amenable to intervention. Chapters three and four showed that lower education and social class are associated with lower levels of sexual knowledge and poorer parent-child communication about the subject of sex. If these two findings are related, targeting interventions to increase communication in these households might be beneficial, although this might not be an easy task.

International research also suggests an even more complex and nuanced relationship between socio-economic status and protective behaviour. It has shown that social deprivation and limited lifetime opportunities for advancement are associated with increased fatalism among young people from lower socio-economic backgrounds. This may mean that they do not protect themselves against future risks because they perceive that they have fewer opportunities than young people who come from more advantaged backgrounds.

If true in the Irish context, such an explanation suggests that attempts should be made to tailor RSE to the needs of young people from disadvantaged backgrounds and those who leave school before upper-secondary education. However, a truly effective response would require a more structural intervention, such as an increase in the proportion of young people getting higher levels of education plus increased social mobility. Of course these actions are not mutually exclusive. A combination of targeted and improved sex education plus a changed opportunity structure would be most effective.

Such structural changes are difficult to bring about. The National Anti-Poverty Strategy (NAPS 2003) has targets for increasing social-welfare rates and lowering the proportions of the population in poverty and of young people leaving school early. This should bear fruit in future years. However, such policies are a first step. They need to be augmented by long-term societal and government commitment to reducing social inequalities.

Overall, both the ISSHR project and research from further afield show that simple explanations that 'blame' lower socio-economic groups and view their behaviours as reckless are naïve and less than helpful.

12.4 The role of sexual health knowledge

A SOUND understanding of the biological, interpersonal and emotional dimensions of sexual relationships is a prerequisite to good sexual health. The Republic of Ireland did not, however, have a systematic and consistent approach to the sex education of young people until the late 1990s. Evidence suggests that many Irish people gained from formal sex education only a rudimentary understanding of sex and sexual relationships, while almost half received no formal sex education at all (see chapter three).

The introduction of the Relationships and Sexuality Education programme (RSE) in 1997 has gone a long way toward ensuring that young people now receive a reliable and systematic understanding of sexual health and relationships, but sex education should not be confined solely to school. Parents have an important responsibility to educate their children about sexual matters. However, the ISSHR study indicates that only a minority of people ever spoke to their parents about sexual issues, although this has changed for younger generations (more on this issue in the next section), and there is now wide acceptance that sex education should occur both in the home and at school.

Finally, it should be emphasised that sex education should not be confined to childhood or teenage years alone, as sex education is a life-long process. Both societies and personal circumstances change through time, sometimes dramatically; this may require individuals to reassess their behaviour and actively seek good sexual health information. By definition, though, individuals cannot know what they do not know; state and other agencies should thus identify knowledge deficits in the population, in particular among sub-groups, and target resources and health promotion accordingly. This may require innovative measures. One way of providing information is through appropriately promoted web-based learning sites. It may also be possible to offer courses within community colleges and through VEC networks.

Accurate targeting of sexual health services and messages is imperative. In the area of contraception, for instance, the ISSHR project shows that consistent use of contraception depends upon a person finding the method best suited to preferences and circumstances, and that these vary widely across the population. The provision of tailored sexual health advice on an ongoing basis to men and women would go far toward reducing levels of crisis pregnancy and sexually transmitted infection.

It is difficult to measure levels of knowledge in a structured social survey and our questions covered only a small number of issues. The results, however, indicate serious gaps in the sexual knowledge of quite large proportions of the Irish adult population. The ISSHR survey showed, for instance, that 44% of women could not correctly identify their most fertile period in the monthly cycle; this increased to 57% among women under 25 (see chapter four). Comparisons with previous studies suggest that knowledge about fertility has worsened since the early 1990s. It could be argued that modern contraception removes the need to understand the details of a woman's cycle, and the fall in knowledge may be a direct result of the increasing use of the contraceptive pill, among younger women in particular. However, the lack of knowledge about fertility may indicate wider deficits.

The ISSHR survey also showed that just over half of men and around three-quarters of women had heard of the STI Chlamydia but, of those that had, substantial proportions (30% of men and 18% of women) had 'poor' knowledge (see chapter four). Knowledge of HIV/AIDS was also limited; around a third of men and women had 'incorrect knowledge'. Even among respondents under 25, who are most likely to have received sex education on the issue of STIs and HIV/AIDS, 28% of men and 25% of women had 'incorrect knowledge' of HIV/AIDS.

Steps need to be taken to improve sexual health knowledge among both the school-going and the adult population. RSE includes a module on human growth and development that includes material on fertility and family planning, plus modules on STIs and protection, but, as noted, not all schools have implemented the RSE programme.

The information deficits revealed in the adult population also suggest that public campaigns and programmes to improve levels of knowledge may be required, particularly among lower-educated/disadvantaged groups where larger knowledge deficits were found. The ISSHR results showed that a substantial minority of respondents were positive about learning more about contraception and safer sex. This desire for more knowledge could be tapped through innovative public-education campaigns on specific health risks.

These low levels of sexual health knowledge were particularly marked among respondents with lower levels of educational qualifications or in manual social classes. These groups are not only more likely to have early sexual intercourse and less likely to use contraception, but also significantly less likely to have good knowledge of fertility, emergency contraception, STIs and HIV/AIDS (see chapter four). This knowledge deficit may be one of the reasons why there are higher levels of risk behaviours among these groups. Analyses of the knowledge variables did not find any strong relationship between knowledge and behaviours across the sample at large, but more research is needed on the impact of knowledge deficits among lower socio-economic groups. It is worrying that the group with the highest risk behaviours are also those who seem to have the lowest levels of knowledge.

12.5 The role of parents in sex education

THE ISSHR study provides evidence that few Irish men and women received sex education at home. Overall, just 11% of men and 21% of women did so. This proportion was higher among younger respondents but, even among under-25s, the proportions were still just 21% of men and 38% of women. These figures suggest that a large majority of young Irish men and women are not receiving sex education at home. The reason seems to be evident in the proportions who found it difficult to speak to their parents about sex. Even among the youngest age cohort, nearly two-thirds of men and almost half of women under 25 did not find this easy. The proportions who found it difficult to talk to their father about sex were considerably higher.

A simplistic solution would be to argue that school should be the primary educator of young people about sex. However, extensive research shows that parental involvement in sex education can have an extremely positive impact on the subsequent behaviour of young people, encouraging later sexual initiation, higher prevalence of protective behaviours and greater confidence in negotiating sexual relationships.

The ISSHR study also found evidence of these relationships. Men who found it easy to talk to their father and women who found it easy to talk to their mother about sex were significantly more likely to use contraception than those who did not find it easy. This suggests that parents have a positive role to play in the sex education of their children. Unfortunately, this is not a role that many feel able to fulfil. Such findings tend to contradict the self-reports of parents themselves, as found in the ICCP survey where most parents reported that they had spoken to their children about sex and felt confident in their ability to do so. A more detailed evaluation of the barriers to and enablers of sexual education of children by their parents is needed to understand this dynamic, so that intervention can most effectively support parents.

The survey found, even after controlling for factors such as age, that people with less education or in a manual social-class position received sex education less often than middle-class people. It might be inferred from such results that schools in more disadvantaged areas were less likely to teach sex education, but analysis showed that the differential was largely accounted for by differences in the probability of receiving sex education at home. People with primary education alone were also less likely to have received sex education. Whereas 26% of respondents under 30 with a third-level qualification had received sex education at home (itself a low proportion), this was true of only 12% of respondents with primary education alone.

The particular challenges of sexuality education for parents in lower socio-economic groups need to be understood and addressed. Intervention to support them needs, of course, to be made in a way that is sensitive to their wishes and concerns.

12.6 Risk behaviours in the Irish population

THE ISSHR survey is the first Irish study of sexual knowledge, attitudes and behaviours. Thus it is not possible to say with certainty that the levels of sexual risk behaviours have increased over time. There is much evidence indicating that sexual attitudes in Ireland have changed substantially in the last three decades (see chapter four). Successive social-attitude surveys make it clear that attitudes toward sexual behaviour have significantly liberalised across the Irish population. In the 1970s, a large majority of Irish people would have stated that sex before marriage, casual sex and homosexual relationships were wrong. By the time of the ISSHR survey in 2004/5, people seeing these behaviours as wrong were in the minority. Perhaps more importantly, the rate of liberalisation has been quicker among younger age groups; this means that the gap in sexual attitudes between generations of Irish people has grown over time.

It would be simplistic and misguided to suggest that this liberalising trend would translate directly into a higher rate of risky behaviours. As we have seen throughout this report, sexual attitudes are often a poor predictor of actual behaviours. The relationship between attitude and behaviour is complex (see chapter four). However, the separation of sex from the context of marriage and the weakening force of moral obstacles to sex with casual partners is likely to have at least contributed to an increase in the average number of partners among Irish men and women. The changing pattern of sexual attitudes across age groups is closely aligned with cohort change in the average number of sexual partners. Whereas older Irish people were less likely than their peers in other countries to have had a high number of partners, the behaviour of younger age groups in Ireland has largely converged with that of their peers in other countries (although the sexual attitudes measured among younger age groups in Ireland were still significantly more conservative than those in other European countries).

This cohort change means that younger age groups in Ireland are beginning their sexual lives at a younger age than was the case for earlier generations. As well, their first sexual experience is much more likely to be with a casual partner or someone with whom they were not having a relationship before sex began. Within sexual relationships, younger age groups are more likely to practise anal sex and to report concurrent sexual relationships. There is some evidence that use of commercial sex has increased among younger men. Each of these behaviours is associated with a higher risk of STIs.

On the positive side, results showed that younger age groups were more likely to use contraception at first intercourse and to use both contraception and protection in later relationships, particularly where the relationship was casual or short-lived. This suggests that younger age groups are more aware of safe-sex messages. There is added evidence of this in higher levels of knowledge among younger age groups about sexual health issues. However, a significant proportion – around 10% of young people – are still not using contraception even when they want to avoid pregnancy. A similar proportion fails to consistently use a condom for contraception and/or protection.

12.7 Planning for sex

A SUBSTANTIAL minority of ISSHR respondents reported that they did not consistently use contraception and protection. As also found in the 2004 ICCP survey, ISSHR showed that a principal reason why both men and women had not used contraception and protection at their most recent sexual intercourse was a lack of planning and preparation. Being able to negotiate safe-sex practices (including abstinence) is of crucial importance. If consistently protected sexual encounters are to be achieved, aspects of self-efficacy (believing that one can do something) need to be combined with attitudes about risk (believing that it is important to do so).

The Crisis Pregnancy Agency already funds a public education campaign on the need to anticipate unplanned sexual encounters. However, the impact of this campaign may be limited by sexual attitudes among at least some men and women. The ICCP survey in 2004 found strong agreement, even among younger Irish people, that a woman carrying condoms was judged negatively. Given this, there is a clear need to develop more positive attitudes toward taking responsibility for contraception and protection in sexual encounters. Public campaigns undertaken in other countries that focus on the irresponsibility of unprotected sex (risking conception and possible STIs) could be considered. These could parallel current Irish campaigns on the irresponsibility of risky behaviours such as drink-driving.

12.7.1 Alcohol and non-use of contraception and condoms

PLANNING for safe sex needs to take into account the fact that the context within which an encounter occurs may not be conducive to responsible behaviour. Of particular concern is the role of alcohol and illicit drugs in shaping behaviour. In the ISSHR survey, intoxication from alcohol and/or illicit drugs was one of the major reasons given for not using contraception and condoms (see chapter 10). Reducing the negative impact of alcohol and drugs on contraceptive and safe-sex practices needs a stronger, clearer policy focus across all sectors that provide education, information and services relating to sexual health and contraception.

Any national alcohol policy should take account of the clear link between alcohol and unprotected sexual behaviour. Similarly, the life-skills programmes provided as part of the RSE and SPHE programmes in schools (which include an exploration of the impact of alcohol on sexual behaviour and particularly risk-taking behaviour) need to be reconsidered, to determine how best to address the challenges that alcohol and/or drugs present in sexual situations.

The ISSHR research has examined knowledge, attitudes and behaviour among people who did not complete second-level education. It is clear that young people who leave school early have sex-education needs that are not being met. Thus it is essential to develop strategies that ensure that this most vulnerable group receive messages concerning contraception and safe sex generally, including the issue of how alcohol and drugs influence sexual behaviour.

12.8 Contraceptive choice and sexual lifestyle

The ISSHR survey shows that the choice of mode of contraception varies significantly according to age group and relationship status. Young people and those in casual or short-lived relationships were more likely to use condoms; older women or those in more settled relationships were more likely to use the pill (see chapter 10). After age 34, other methods such as the coil/IUD/Mirena and sterilisation become more common. As well, most women across all age groups agreed that the medical side-effects of the oral contraceptive pill discouraged their use of it (see chapter four). Around one in 10 women, particularly those with lower educational qualifications, said the role of the pill in weight gain discouraged their use of it.

Such evidence builds on that found in the ICCP survey where about half of the women surveyed felt that the pill had dangerous side-effects and that taking a break from the pill was a good idea. The ICCP survey also showed that a considerable proportion of respondents had reservations about using condoms; men and older respondents agreed that condoms reduced sexual pleasure.

In the ISSHR survey, negative beliefs about the side-effects of the pill were associated with a higher risk of crisis pregnancy (see chapter 11).

The above results combine to underline the need for contraceptive choices that suit the sexual lifestyle and beliefs of individuals, if we are to reduce the overall prevalence of crisis pregnancy. Health professionals should explore contraceptive choices that suit people's lifestyle choices. To do this, some professionals may need additional training or support.

12.8.1 Knowledge of emergency contraception

THE ICCP survey (2004) found that a considerable proportion of women who had had a crisis pregnancy reported that contraceptive pill and condom failure were the primary reason why conception had occurred.

Emergency contraception provides an additional protection against unplanned conception. Building on ICCP, the ISSHR survey showed that awareness of how and when to use emergency contraception was limited; 58% of women and 79% of men were unable to identify the correct time limit (72 hours) for the use of emergency contraception (see chapter four). Even among the youngest age group of women, where knowledge of emergency contraception was highest, 37% could not correctly identify the time limit. Those who were wrong were more likely to underestimate the period in which it could be effectively used. This suggests that emergency contraception may often not be used even when it would be effective. Knowledge of emergency contraception was substantially lower among men and women with lower levels of education and/or from manual social classes.

The general level of knowledge and the distribution of poor knowledge across socio-economic groups suggest that targeted health-promotion strategies are required.

12.8.2   The assumption by older women of their low risk of pregnancy

THE ISSHR survey showed that a substantial proportion of older women had not used contraception consistently even when they did not wish to become pregnant (see chapter 10). Follow-up questions showed that many assumed they had a negligible risk of conception and thus did not use contraception as they felt it was not necessary. Yet many of these women were in their late 30s and 40s. Very few women are infertile before age 45. Although fertility falls in the 30s and particularly after 40, a not insubstantial 14% of women in the ISSHR survey who reported a crisis pregnancy were over 35, and 4% were over 40. This suggests that many women take a greater risk of unplanned and perhaps crisis pregnancy than they realise.

12.9 The cost of contraception and protection

THE individual and societal costs of unplanned pregnancy and infection with STIs and HIV are substantial. Yet the ISSHR results showed that the cost of contraception and protection may lessen the impact of sexual health promotion. For instance, a third of women agreed that the cost of the contraceptive pill discouraged their use of it. This proportion rose to almost 43% among women with lower levels of education, who are also most likely to have less income (see chapter four). Although a smaller proportion agreed that the cost of condoms would discourage their use of them, the proportion was still substantial, at nearly 20% of men and women. The proportion seeing cost as an issue was higher among younger men and women and those with lower levels of education and/or in a manual occupation, exactly the groups that have less income.

This evidence alone suggests that the cost of contraception and protection is a serious issue that should be examined more closely by the Government. But analyses in this report and ISSHR Sub-Report 3: 'Contemporary Sexual Knowledge, Attitudes and Behaviours in Ireland' also show that people who said the cost of condoms discouraged their use of them were also less likely to consistently use them. Analyses also found a link between the issue of cost and greater risk of STI infection. People who believed that the cost of condoms would discourage their use were almost twice as likely as those who did not agree that cost was an issue to report being diagnosed with STI.

Since a pack of three condoms cost around seven euros in 2005, it is not surprising that cost may be a disincentive to people on low incomes when deciding whether or not to buy protection. Given the increasing incidence of STIs in Ireland, particularly among young people, it seems imperative that the Government investigate ways in which the cost of condoms could be reduced substantially or condoms made freely available. For instance, since treating increasing numbers of individuals with STIs is costly, it does not make sense to levy value-added tax on condoms, as if they were a luxury.

12.10 Developing a sexual health strategy

THE ISSHR survey provides a wealth of data on current challenges in sexual health. One reason why the Republic of Ireland lacks a national sexual health strategy is the absence of reliable and representative data. It is now imperative that a strategy be developed.

A number of landmark developments towards a national sexual heath strategy have occurred in Ireland since 1990:

- The Department of Health's previous health strategy document – *Shaping a Healthier Future* (1994) - formed a general basis for the current level of sexual health activity. Among its initiatives was the development of a Women's Health Strategy. This strategy, developed through extensive consultation, gives a prominent place to reproductive and sexual health issues.
- The Department of Health and Children launched its current National Health Strategy, *Quality and Fairness: a Health System for You*, in 2001. It signalled sexual health as an important focus for attention. Action number 16 of 121 in the action plan states: "Measures will be taken to promote sexual health and safer sexual practices." In terms of deliverables, an action plan was to be prepared by 2003. The Department of Health and Children was the responsible agent.
- Following this, the Crisis Pregnancy Agency was established and its first strategy was launched in 2003.
- A 2003 progress report on the National Health Strategy reported that the Sexual Health Action Plan would be developed by late 2004. While this is not yet available, a number of significant components of the plan are in place.
- As regards regional strategies, in October 2001 the then Southern Health Board announced that it was developing a sexual health promotion strategy and, in July 2005, the Health Service Executive (HSE) published a sexual health strategy for the Eastern Region. This aims to "promote sexual health, prevent and manage infections and prevent unintended teen pregnancies". The HSE said it would place more emphasis on primary care services and aspire to providing services "in the right place delivered by the right people and at the right time". However, these regional strategies are no substitute for a national sexual health strategy which would be able to set priorities and targets and produce a more consistent response to sexual health challenges.

Since 2000, many countries have developed or have been developing a national sexual health strategy. Examples are:

- In 2001, the UK Department of Health launched a strategy for England, *Better Prevention. Better Services. Better Sexual Health – The national strategy for sexual heath and HIV*. This was a consultation document which invited feedback. A 27-point action plan was published a year later. Since then a range of reports have been produced, setting quality standards, milestones, and training and best-practice guidelines. Initiatives include the establishment of a national Chlamydia screening programme in 2003 and the development of a toolkit on sexual health and HIV prevention for focused groups (young people, parents, people with learning difficulties, prisoners and intravenous drug users). There has also been a focus on teenage pregnancy (rates in the UK generally are notably higher than those in other European countries). The English strategy involves a 10-year plan.
- A Scottish strategy, *Enhancing Sexual Wellbeing in Scotland: A Sexual Health and Relationships Strategy*, was launched in 2003. Its vision is to have a society "that accepts sex as a normal and healthy aspect of life, in which people understand the value of their own sexual health, the

importance of responsibility and respect for others and have the capacity and means to protect themselves from unwanted outcomes of sexual activity".

- In Northern Ireland, a consultation document – *A Five-Year Sexual Health Promotion Strategy and Action Plan* – was circulated in late 2003. Four priority groups were identified for attention: people under 20 (teen pregnancy and STIs); people under 35 (STIs); gay and bisexual men; and commercial sex workers. This funded plan is now under way.

12.11 The importance of protection as well as contraception

IN recent years, and particularly since the Crisis Pregnancy Agency was established in 2001, there has been a concerted attempt to highlight the need for people to be prepared for sexual intercourse, in terms of having contraception available. This crucially important campaign may well be working; the ISSHR survey showed that the overwhelming majority of Irish people report using contraception when they do not intend to conceive (see chapter 10). However, the findings of the ISSHR study highlight the need to also address the importance of barrier protection during sex.

As well as an apparent increase in crisis pregnancies, there has been a steep rise in the incidence of STIs in Ireland over the last decade or so, particularly among younger age groups (see chapter one). This rise is due to a number of factors; chief among them is the absence or inconsistent use of barrier methods such as condoms. For example, around a quarter of ISSHR respondents whose last sexual intercourse had been with someone they did not know beforehand did not use a condom (see chapter 10). Respondents gave various reasons for not using condoms, including lack of preparedness and having consumed alcohol/drugs. Among those who had just met their partner, around 15% cited 'trust' in their partner as the main reason, even though their partner might not have been aware of their own STI/HIV status. In this situation, 'trust' in one's partner is misplaced and barrier protection essential.

These patterns suggest that a concerted effort should be made to inform people of the risks of unprotected sex in general and, more specifically, that health promotion should balance its message by emphasising the need for protection against *both* conception and infection.

12.12 Information needs into the future

A PREREQUISITE for effective policy and planning is access to up-to-date and valid information. The ISSHR survey provides a much-improved data base of information on sexual knowledge, attitudes and behaviours among the Irish population. However, it raises as many questions as it answers. The large-scale research provided in the ISSHR volumes needs to be followed up with more detailed research.

In particular, more detailed research is needed on sub-groups such as lower socio-economic groups. Among these, the prevalence of risk factors was shown to be higher but, in large-scale research of this type, the reasons for this could not be clarified.

It was also impossible, within a national survey such as ISSHR, to gather enough information on other groups such as non-nationals, gay, lesbian and bisexual individuals, and those with a disability.

Urgent attention should be given to developing data on these groups and examining their sexual health needs. Future research on these and other groups should attempt, where possible, to use compatible concepts and build on the ISSHR research and other recent research such as the ICCP survey.

The ISSHR survey should be seen as providing the baseline data for future research on sexual knowledge, attitudes and behaviours in Ireland. We found that both sexual attitudes and behaviour are rapidly changing, particularly among young people. It is imperative that we build on the work of the ISSHR study by regularly collecting evidence of trends. This will provide the evidence necessary to develop and amend policies for maximum effectiveness.

The extent of change found across age cohorts in the Irish population underlines the general pace of change in sexual knowledge, attitudes and behaviours. Among ISSHR respondents, early sexual experiences were strongly associated with poor sexual health outcomes, both at the time and later in life. Effective sexual health intervention among young people requires a base of evidence. Yet we still have no national source of information on the sexual knowledge, attitudes and behaviours of people under 18. This is a major gap. It is essential that a national survey, along the lines of the ISSHR study but designed with their needs in mind, be carried out among young people.

12.13 Reference list

1   Geary T, McNamara PM. *Implementation of Social, Personal and Health Education at Junior Cycle: National Survey Report*. Limerick: University of Limerick, 2002.

Recommendations

1. Parents need to be acknowledged as the primary relationships and sexuality educators of their children, and to be supported in that role. They need supports provided through a range of initiatives. These supports should particularly address the needs of parents who most need assistance in sex education, such as those in lower socio-economic groups.

2. Sex education needs to be tailored to the needs of all groups, and to those of disadvantaged groups in particular.

3. More generally, health and education policymakers need to work with the wider policy community and government to improve both the educational attainment and perceived opportunities of disadvantaged groups.

4. Innovative methods of providing adult education on sexual health generally should be developed to improve levels of sexual health knowledge across all groups. Specific attention should be directed at vulnerable groups, particularly those in lower socio-economic groups.

5. A holistic programme of relationships and sexuality education needs to be fully implemented as appropriate in all primary and secondary schools nationally. The capacity of these programmes to increase sexual knowledge and competence should be evaluated and augmented where necessary.

6. Public education campaigns should be used to alert all groups, but particularly younger people, that unprotected sex carries with it the double risks of unintended pregnancy and sexually transmitted infections including HIV.

7. Health promotion strategies need to foster more responsible public behaviour concerning the use of alcohol and illicit drugs, given their role in unprotected sexual encounters.

8. Health promotion strategies need to foster more responsible public attitudes to individual planning for safe sex, including consistent use of effective methods of both contraception and protection.

9. Health promotion strategies need to take account of the need for contraceptive choices that suit the sexual lifestyle and beliefs of individuals. Professionals may need training to be able to assist individuals to select from the range of options available.

10. Knowledge of emergency contraception should be made widely available, especially to people in lower socio-economic groups.

11. Public education campaigns should alert older women and their sexual partners about the risks of assuming they have low fertility.

12. Serious attention should be given to reducing the cost of contraception and protection, especially the cost of condoms.

13. Research on sexual knowledge, attitudes, behaviours and health in Ireland should be integrated to ensure best use of public resources in developing a knowledge base capable of informing policy and practice.

14. More detailed research needs to be carried out on the sexual knowledge, attitudes and behaviours of lower socio-economic groups.

15. A national survey of sexual knowledge, attitudes and behaviours should be carried out among young people in Ireland.

The recommendations as outlined form separate but overlapping and complementary components of what needs to be an integrated approach to the overall challenge of promoting sexual health in Ireland. Much is already being done in a variety of setitings towards this agenda. To ensure that the issues outlined can be addressed in a comprehensive, effective and efficient manner, leadership and coordination is now needed. That leadership is best provided through the development of a National Sexual Health Strategy. We now have a timely and comprehensive Irish evidence base from which to develop such a Strategy.

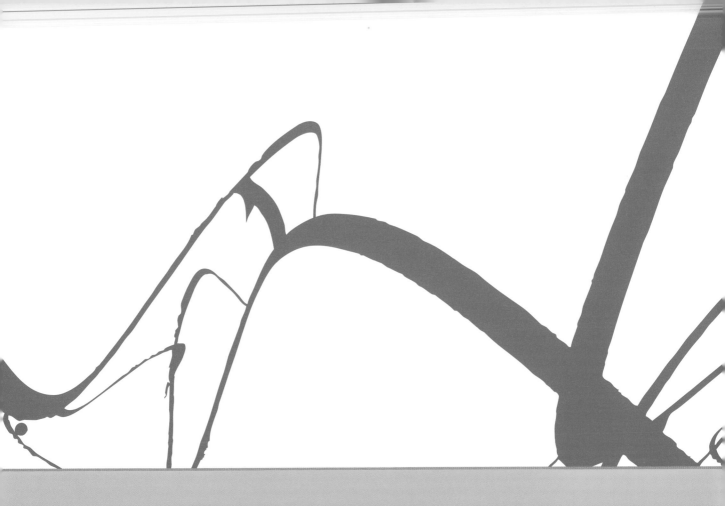

Appendices

APPENDICES 1 to 9 provide additional detail to the information within the chapters of this report.

A guide to the interpretation of these tables is available in chapter two (section 2.13)

List of Appendix tables

Appendix 1

Table 1.1: Proportion who received sex education: by socio-demographic characteristics

	Men		Women	
	%	N	%	N
All	52.7	3,188	60.2	4,253
Current age (years)				
18-24 years	87.9c	759	93.0c	908
25-34 years	73.2***	701	77.7***	966
35-44 years	49.1***	647	59.9***	1,014
45-54 years	29.4***	574	38.0***	755
55-64 years	11.5***	507	18.5***	610
Education (highest level attained)				
Primary	15.3***	263	21.0***	305
Lower secondary	45.4***	544	48.8***	657
Upper secondary	62.0***	1,198	67.7**	1,780
Tertiary	70.7c	1,183	77.0c	1,511
Social class				
Higher professional	57.2	790	70.8	642
Lower professional	55.5	731	65.0	1,097
Administrative/clerical	54.2	428	57.9	978
Skilled manual	46.8	611	68.8	296
Semi/unskilled manual	49.3	492	52.8	892

Significance key: ns = not significant; *=P<0.05;**=P<0.01;***=P<0.001
c = reference group to which all other groups are compared.
NOTE: Significance given adjusting for all variables in the table, except social class.

Table 1.2: Proportion who reported it was easy to talk about sexual matters with their mother when they were growing up: by socio-demographic characteristics

	Men		Women	
	Easy (%)	N	Easy (%)	N
All	17.2	3,188	28.9	4,253
Current age (years)				
18-24 years	35.1c	759	55.9c	908
25-34 years	19.9***	701	38.7***	966
35-44 years	13.9***	647	19.6***	1,014
45-54 years	7.6***	574	15.3***	755
55-64 years	6.4***	507	10.5***	610
Education (highest level attained)				
Primary	5.0***	263	15.5ns	305
Lower secondary	12.9**	544	22.8ns	657
Upper secondary	21.0ns	1,198	32.0ns	1,780
Tertiary	23.7c	1,183	35.7c	1,511
Social class				
Higher professional	19.8ns	790	33.9ns	642
Lower professional	19.7ns	731	32.1ns	1,097
Administrative/clerical	15.3ns	428	25.9ns	978
Skilled manual	14.3ns	611	38.0ns	296
Semi/unskilled manual	16.9c	492	26.9c	892

Significance key: ns = not significant; *=P<0.05;**=P<0.01;***=P<0.001

c = reference group to which all other groups are compared.

NOTE: Significance given adjusting for all variables in the table.

Table 1.3: Proportion who reported it was easy to talk about sexual matters with their father when they were growing up: by socio-demographic characteristics

	Men		Women	
	Easy (%)	N	Easy (%)	N
All	12.5	3,188	8.5	4,253
Current age (years)				
18-24 years	28.0c	759	15.4c	908
25-34 years	14.4***	701	11.7ns	966
35-44 years	9.0***	647	6.9***	1,014
45-54 years	4.1***	547	3.3***	755
55-64 years	4.4***	507	3.7***	610
Education (highest level attained)				
Primary	2.3**	263	4.9ns	305
Lower secondary	11.3ns	544	5.3ns	657
Upper secondary	15.8ns	1,198	10.0ns	1,780
Tertiary	14.9c	1,183	10.5c	1,511
Social class				
Higher professional	13.5ns	790	8.7ns	642
Lower professional	13.3ns	731	9.0ns	1,097
Administrative/clerical	12.7ns	428	7.9ns	978
Skilled manual	11.3ns	611	12.1ns	296
Semi/unskilled manual	12.3c	492	8.2c	892

Significance key: ns = not significant; *=P<0.05;**=P<0.01;***=P<0.001
c = reference group to which all other groups are compared.
NOTE: Significance given adjusting for all variables in the table.

Table 1.4: Perceived helpfulness of sex education received: by socio-demographic characteristics

	Men			Women		
	Helpful (%)	Not helpful† (%)	N	Helpful (%)	Not helpful (%)	
All	49.0	51.0	1,839	53.8	46.2	2,679
Current age (years)						
18-24 years	58.3c	41.7	671	65.6c	34.4	842
25-34 years	47.1**	52.9	545	51.2***	48.8	771
35-44 years	44.0***	56.0	339	45.1***	54.9	628
45-54 years	37.4***	62.6	198	47.9***	52.1	304
55-64 years	37.7***	62.3	86	47.9***	52.1	134
Education (highest level attained)						
Primary	50.4ns	49.6	37	42.3ns	57.7	63
Lower secondary	42.6*	57.4	232	56.7ns	43.3	310
Higher secondary	49.4ns	50.6	742	54.4ns	45.6	1,151
Third level	52.6c	47.4	828	52.7c	47.3	1,155
Social class						
Higher professional	51.5ns	48.5	488	57.1ns	42.9	480
Lower professional	50.7ns	49.3	441	54.4ns	45.6	721
Administrative/clerical	44.7ns	55.3	237	48.6*	51.4	583
Skilled manual	49.7ns	50.3	321	53.0*	47.1	207
Semi/unskilled manual	50.2c	49.8	266	56.8c	43.2	494

† Includes all participants who reported thinking that their sex education had been 'very unhelpful', 'unhelpful', or 'neither'.

Significance key: ns = not significant; *=P<0.05;**=P<0.01;***=P<0.001

c = reference group to which all other groups are compared.

NOTE: Significance given adjusting for all variables in the table, except social class.

Table 1.5: Proportion of men who think young people today should receive sex education, on 5 topics: by socio-demographic characteristics

	Sexual intercourse (%)	Sexual feelings (%)	Contra-ception (%)	Safer sex (%)	Homo-sexuality (%)
Current age (years)					
18-24 years	96.9	94.8	99.1	99.2	90.8
25-34 years	95.4	93.5	98.1	98.7	94.4
35-44 years	96.1	95.7	98.0	98.3	91.7
45-54 years	94.6	95.3	97.8	99.0	93.5
55-64 years	89.2	93.0	96.5	96.8	91.1
Education (highest level attained)					
Primary	90.1	92.2	96.2	97.4	90.3
Lower secondary	93.8	93.9	97.5	98.3	92.0
Upper secondary	95.7	95.6	98.4	98.6	92.6
Tertiary	97.5	95.1	98.8	99.3	93.6
Social class					
Higher professional	95.6	93.9	98.7	99.0	92.3
Lower professional	93.9	95.7	97.0	98.6	93.2
Administrative/clerical	95.3	95.3	98.4	98.0	92.0
Skilled manual	94.3	93.6	97.9	97.9	93.1
Semi/unskilled manual	93.8	94.8	97.7	98.7	91.5
Religiosity					
Not at all	95.0	94.7	98.0	98.8	92.7
A little	95.6	95.5	98.6	98.9	94.1
Quite	94.7	94.2	98.4	98.4	91.5
Very	90.2	91.7	94.3	96.6	89.0
Extremely	95.1	92.7	95.0	95.1	68.3

Table 1.6: Proportion of women who think young people today should receive sex education, on 5 topics: by socio-demographic characteristics

	Sexual intercourse (%)	Sexual feelings (%)	Contra-ception (%)	Safer sex (%)	Homo-sexuality (%)
Current age (years)					
18-24 years	98.3	97.8	99.4	99.4	97.1
25-34 years	98.5	98.3	99.1	99.7	97.5
35-44 years	97.5	97.7	98.7	99.8	96.4
45-54 years	96.1	95.8	97.7	98.4	95.8
55-64 years	91.8	92.0	94.5	96.7	91.8
Education (highest level attained)					
Primary	91.2	94.6	97.4	99.1	94.8
Lower secondary	96.4	95.2	97.4	98.4	94.9
Upper secondary	97.4	97.1	98.2	99.0	96.0
Tertiary	98.8	98.2	99.0	99.3	97.3
Social class					
Higher professional	95.9	94.4	97.3	99.0	94.8
Lower professional	97.3	97.4	98.4	98.4	96.0
Administrative/clerical	97.5	97.5	98.2	99.3	96.1
Skilled manual	96.3	97.4	97.4	98.9	96.3
Semi/unskilled manual	96.6	96.7	98.8	99.3	97.3
Religiosity					
Not at all	99.0	97.9	99.2	99.5	96.8
A little	97.3	97.2	98.7	99.3	97.1
Quite	95.9	96.5	98.1	99.2	95.5
Very	94.6	94.2	95.9	97.1	94.8
Extremely	91.7	91.2	89.8	93.3	75.9

Table 1.7: Participants who would like more information about contraception:by socio-demographic variables

	Men		Women	
	Would like more information (%)	Base	Would like more information (%)	Base
All participants	8.3	3,182	8.7	4,250
Current age (years)				
18-24 years	9.2c	758	15.4c	907
25-34 years	7.6ns	701	7.9***	966
35-44 years	9.2ns	645	5.9***	1,014
45-54 years	8.8ns	572	8.1**	753
55-64 years	6.2ns	506	5.8***	610
Education (highest level attained)				
Primary	8.8ns	263	6.0c	304
Lower secondary	8.6ns	544	8.8ns	656
Higher secondary	8.7ns	1,196	9.6ns	1,779
Third level	6.7c	1,179	8.3ns	1,511
Social class				
Higher professional	6.5ns	787	8.6ns	642
Lower professional	8.0ns	731	8.3ns	1,097
Administrative/clerical	9.2ns	426	8.5ns	978
Skilled manual	8.8ns	611	10.0ns	295
Semi-skilled/unskilled manual	9.7c	492	8.0c	891
Current relationship status				
Not in a relationship	10.2ns	851	10.4ns	960
Married	7.5c	1,500	6.5c	2,359
Cohabiting	3.3ns	239	10.0ns	270
Steady relationship	8.7ns	370	11.0ns	520
Casual relationship	10.2ns	222	17.3*	141

Significance key: ns = not significant; *=P<0.05;**=P<0.01;***=P<0.001
c = reference group to which all other groups are compared.
NOTE: Significance given adjusting for all variables in the table.

Table 1.8: Participants who would like more information about how to have a satisfying sex life: by socio-demographic variables

	Men		Women	
	Would like more information (%)	Base	Would like more information (%)	Base
All participants	20.1	3,177	17.9	4,232
Current age (years)				
18-24 years	22.1c	755	27.4c	900
25-34 years	19.7ns	700	20.2*	964
35-44 years	21.4ns	644	13.2***	1,012
45-54 years	22.5ns	572	15.7**	749
55-64 years	13.3*	506	12.1***	607
Education (highest level attained)				
Primary	16.5ns	263	15.8	303
Lower secondary	21.9ns	542	15.4ns	652
Higher secondary	21.1ns	1,197	18.9ns	1,774
Third level	18.8c	1,175	19.2c	1,503
Social class				
Higher professional	17.8ns	786	20.3 ns	638
Lower professional	22.6ns	730	17.0 ns	1,095
Administrative/clerical	19.0ns	426	18.6*	971
Skilled manual	22.4ns	610	22.0ns	293
Semi-skilled/unskilled manual	19.1c	490	14.8c	891
Current relationship status				
Married	18.7c	1,499	13.8c	2,354
Cohabiting	16.3ns	239	22.2ns	269
Steady relationship	19.3ns	369	20.1ns	518
Casual relationship	21.6ns	222	33.0**	141
Not in a relationship	23.4*	848	21.7ns	950

Significance key: ns = not significant; *=P<0.05;**=P<0.01;***=P<0.001
c = reference group to which all other groups are compared.
NOTE: Significance given adjusting for all variables in the table.

Table 1.9: Participants who would like more information about safe sex/STIs/VD: by socio-demographic variables

	Men		Women	
	Would like more information (%)	Base	Would like more information (%)	Base
All participants	21.4	3,186	21.8	4,248
Current age (years)				
18-24 years	25.1c	759	31.5c	907
25-34 years	22.3ns	701	23.2**	966
35-44 years	21.0ns	647	18.7***	1,013
45-54 years	23.0ns	572	17.9***	753
55-64 years	14.1**	507	16.4***	609
Education (highest level attained)				
Primary	18.9ns	262	20.3	305
Lower secondary	23.5**	544	20.4ns	654
Higher secondary	22.7**	1,197	22.6ns	1,778
Third level	18.4c	1,183	22.3c	1,511
Social class				
Higher professional	21.6ns	789	25.0ns	642
Lower professional	20.8ns	731	19.1*	1,097
Administrative/clerical	19.9ns	427	22.1ns	975
Skilled manual	24.6ns	611	23.1ns	295
Semi-skilled/unskilled manual	19.8c	492	23.0c	892
Current relationship status				
Married	19.6c	1,501	18.2c	2,359
Cohabiting	18.0ns	239	22.2ns	270
Steady relationship	23.0ns	371	30.8ns	520
Casual relationship	21.8ns	222	29.0ns	141
Not in a relationship	24.7ns	853	23.6ns	958

Significance key: ns = not significant; *=P<0.05;**=P<0.01;***=P<0.001
c = reference group to which all other groups are compared.
NOTE: Significance given adjusting for all variables in the table.

Appendix 2

Table 2.1: Proportion with incorrect fertility knowledge: by socio-demographic characteristics

	Men (%)	N	Women (%)	N
All	68.7	3,184	44.0	4,252
Current age (years)				
18-24 years	75.0ns	758	56.5c	908
25-34 years	72.0ns	701	44.1***	965
35-44 years	64.5ns	647	35.5***	1,014
45-54 years	60.3ns	574	42.3***	755
55-64 years	71.8c	504	42.7***	610
Education (highest level attained)				
Primary	77.3***	262	54.5***	305
Lower secondary	70.8***	544	48.7***	657
Upper secondary	68.3***	1,197	42.2*	1,779
Third level	60.4c	1,181	37.4c	1,511
Relationship status				
Not in a relationship	80.8***	852	55.9***	961
Married	60.9c	1,500	37.0c	2,360
Cohabiting	66.5ns	239	46.5ns	270
Steady relationship	65.7ns	371	46.1ns	520
Casual relationship	81.4***	222	46.8ns	141
Social class				
Higher professional	63.8	789	40.6***	642
Lower professional	64.4	730	37.3***	1,097
Administrative/clerical	72.5	427	37.3***	978
Skilled manual	70.9	610	54.1ns	296
Semi/unskilled manual	73.1	492	52.2c	892

Significance key: ns = not significant; *=P<0.05;**=P<0.01;***=P<0.001

c = reference group to which all other groups are compared.

NOTE: Significance given adjusting for all variables in the table, except for social class among men.

Table 2.2: Proportion who correctly identified 72-hour time-limit for emergency contraception: by socio-demographic characteristics

	Men (%)	N	Women (%)	N
All	21.4	3,186	41.8	4,245
Current age (years)				
18-24 years	27.4c	758	63.5c	905
25-34 years	27.9ns	701	55.8ns	963
35-44 years	20.5ns	647	39.6ns	1,013
45-54 years	17.2*	573	25.8**	755
55-64 years	11.1***	507	15.8***	609
Education (highest level attained)				
Primary	12.3**	263	19.3	305
Lower secondary	17.6**	544	31.6ns	657
Upper secondary	23.1ns	1,198	44.3*	1,776
Third level	27.1c	1,181	58.3c	1,507
Relationship status				
Not in a relationship	19.8ns	853	43.8ns	959
Married	18.4c	1502	31.8c	2357
Cohabiting	25.8ns	239	64.4ns	270
Steady relationship	35.7**	370	63.7*	518
Casual relationship	24.0ns	222	55.7ns	141
Social class				
Higher professional	25.7	789	53.7*	642
Lower professional	20.5	731	47.1ns	1095
Administrative/clerical	23.8	428	40.3ns	974
Skilled manual	20.1	611	47.3ns	296
Semi/unskilled manual	18.4	492	34.3c	892

Significance key: ns = not significant; *=P<0.05;**=P<0.01;***=P<0.001

c = reference group to which all other groups are compared.

NOTE: Significance given adjusting for all variables in the table, except for social class among men.

Table 2.3: Proportion with 'good' knowledge (score 3+) of Chlamydia: by selected characteristics

	Men (%)	N	Women (%)	N
All	37.4	3,188	59.7	4,253
Current age (years)				
18-24 years	48.8c	759	75.9c	908
25-34 years	43.4ns	701	67.8*	966
35-44 years	34.1**	647	60.8*	1,014
45-54 years	32.3***	574	51.9**	755
55-64 years	25.7***	507	33.8***	610
Education (highest level attained)				
Primary	19.2	263	31.0***	305
Lower secondary	30.8	544	44.8***	657
Upper secondary	39.7	1,198	63.7***	1,780
Third level	54.1	1,183	80.9c	1,511
Relationship status				
Not in a relationship	40.4ns	854	61.2ns	961
Married	31.6c	1,502	52.8c	2,361
Cohabiting	45.2ns	239	72.4*	270
Steady relationship	49.6ns	371	75.9*	520
Casual relationship	41.3ns	222	71.5ns	141
Social class				
Higher professional	44.2***	790	71.2	642
Lower professional	36.5*	731	69.2	1,097
Administrative/clerical	43.7***	428	59.9	978
Skilled manual	31.4ns	611	57.6	296
Semi/unskilled manual	30.4c	492	50.5c	892

Significance key: ns = not significant; *=P<0.05;**=P<0.01;***=P<0.001

c = reference group to which all other groups are compared.

NOTE 1: Significance given adjusting for all variables in the table, except for education among men and social class among women.

NOTE 2: Individuals who had not heard of Chlamydia are counted as having 'poor' knowledge of Chlamydia and so are included in the analysis as part of the denominator.

Table 2.4: Proportion with correct knowledge (score=3) of HIV and AIDS: by socio-demographic characteristics

	Men (%)	N	Women (%)	N
All	71.3	3168	68.9	4,231
Current age (years)				
18-24 years	72.0c	749	75.1c	908
25-34 years	77.4ns	700	77.2ns	963
35-44 years	72.5ns	645	71.3ns	1,004
45-54 years	72.2ns	570	62.1**	753
55-64 years	59.6ns	504	53.3***	603
Education (highest level attained)				
Primary	57.4***	262	50.8***	303
Lower secondary	66.6***	541	60.4***	653
Upper secondary	74.3**	1189	71.4***	1,768
Third level	81.3c	1176	81.5c	1,507
Relationship status				
Not in a relationship	70.1ns	846	65.6*	957
Married	71.7c	1493	67.0c	2343
Cohabiting	72.0ns	239	78.9ns	270
Steady relationship	77.5ns	370	77.8ns	520
Casual relationship	64.9*	220	72.1ns	141
Social class				
Higher professional	75.1	785	73.8	639
Lower professional	74.4	729	75.3	1091
Administrative/clerical	72.6	427	72.6	971
Skilled manual	69.7	611	69.2	295
Semi/unskilled manual	65.0	487	62.7	892

Significance key: ns = not significant; *=P<0.05;**=P<0.01;***=P<0.001
c = reference group to which all other groups are compared.
NOTE: Significance given adjusting for all variables in the table, except for social class.

Table 2.5: Proportion agreeing that sex before marriage is never wrong: by socio-demographic characteristics

	Men (%)	N	Women (%)	N
All	70.1	3,173	63.7	4,232
Current age (years)				
18-24 years	79.3c	759	78.8c	907
25-34 years	80.4ns	699	76.8ns	963
35-44 years	74.8ns	640	65.3*	1,009
45-54 years	62.1*	572	50.4***	747
55-64 years	46.5***	503	37.8***	606
Education (highest level attained)				
Primary	59.8ns	262	50.7ns	301
Lower secondary	69.7ns	543	61.1ns	651
Upper secondary	74.1*	1,193	65.8ns	1,775
Third level	70.3c	1,175	68.7c	1,505
Relationship status				
Not in a relationship	70.6ns	850	67.4*	958
Married	63.3c	1,491	55.3c	2,344
Cohabiting	85.9***	239	77.9*	270
Steady relationship	83.8***	371	79.3**	519
Casual relationship	81.0***	222	78.6*	141
Social class				
Higher professional	72.5*	787	66.5ns	640
Lower professional	65.1ns	727	62.4ns	1,096
Administrative/clerical	71.2ns	427	65.4ns	972
Skilled manual	75.0***	607	70.5ns	295
Semi/unskilled manual	66.1c	490	62.5c	887
Religiosity				
Not at all	85.4c	808	83.9c	699
A little	73.7***	1,162	67.0***	1,613
Quite	60.7***	882	56.4***	1,381
Very much	45.4***	277	42.0***	468
Extremely	39.3***	39	22.0***	66

Significance key: ns = not significant; *=P<0.05;**=P<0.01;***=P<0.001
c = reference group to which all other groups are compared.
NOTE: Significance given adjusting for all variables in the table.

Table 2.6: Proportion agreeing that 'one-night stands' are always wrong: by socio-demographic characteristics

	Men (%)	N	Women (%)	N
All	30.8	3,170	49.9	4,239
Current age (years)				
18-24 years	14.6c	757	29.2c	904
25-34 years	21.2ns	700	34.3*	963
35-44 years	26.3ns	641	50.3ns	1,012
45-54 years	44.8**	568	62.4ns	751
55-64 years	56.1*	504	84.2**	609
Education (highest level attained)				
Primary	55.7ns	259	78.5**	301
Lower secondary	34.2ns	542	61.9**	657
Upper secondary	23.7ns	1,195	46.0ns	1,777
Third level	22.6c	1,174	31.3c	1,504
Relationship status				
Not in a relationship	23.7**	848	42.4***	957
Married	42.4c	1,493	61.2c	2,354
Cohabiting	11.7*	239	33.0ns	270
Steady relationship	19.6ns	370	35.1ns	517
Casual relationship	12.3***	220	21.7ns	141
Social class				
Higher professional	26.6ns	785	40.8ns	642
Lower professional	29.6ns	724	44.7ns	1,094
Administrative/clerical	31.1ns	427	50.6ns	976
Skilled manual	32.1ns	611	45.7ns	296
Semi/unskilled manual	35.8c	488	55.8c	889
Religiosity				
Not at all	15.4c	806	33.1c	698
A little	25.1***	1,161	43.9***	1,618
Quite	43.5***	880	58.0***	1,384
Very much	55.0***	279	66.9***	469
Extremely	59.3**	39	86.4*	66

Significance key: ns = not significant; *=P<0.05;**=P<0.01;***=P<0.001
c = reference group to which all other groups are compared.
NOTE: Significance given adjusting for all variables in the table.

Table 2.7: Proportion agreeing that homosexual sex is never wrong: by socio-demographic characteristics

	Men (%)	N	Women (%)	N
All	47.4	3,133	58.6	4,125
Current age (years)				
18-24 years	57.1c	750	77.0c	884
25-34 years	59.1ns	692	68.3*	954
35-44 years	49.6ns	637	58.1***	989
45-54 years	36.8**	558	48.0***	719
55-64 years	27.8***	496	32.5***	579
Education (highest level attained)				
Primary	32.6**	260	44.5ns	294
Lower secondary	46.2*	537	53.0*	635
Upper secondary	50.0*	1,181	59.8**	1,727
Third level	55.3c	1,155	68.8c	1,469
Relationship status				
Not in a relationship	50.3ns	840	63.1ns	940
Married	41.1c	1,469	50.1c	2,275
Cohabiting	64.0***	239	73.7**	265
Steady relationship	59.4ns	365	74.0*	506
Casual relationship	47.7ns	220	67.9ns	139
Social class				
Higher professional	48.3ns	776	66.5ns	631
Lower professional	42.9ns	715	57.3ns	1,058
Administrative/clerical	49.2ns	424	58.0ns	954
Skilled manual	50.6*	601	61.1ns	286
Semi/unskilled manual	43.9c	487	57.3c	863
Religiosity				
Not at all	63.4c	797	75.0c	690
A little	45.9***	1,152	61.6***	1,574
Quite	41.2***	863	54.4***	1,337
Very much	33.6***	277	40.8***	456
Extremely	14.3***	39	22.8***	63

Significance key: ns = not significant; *=P<0.05;**=P<0.01;***=P<0.001
c = reference group to which all other groups are compared.
NOTE: Significance given adjusting for all variables in the table.

Table 2.8: Proportion agreeing that abortion is always wrong: by socio-demographic characteristics

	Men (%)	N	Women (%)	N
All	34.7	3,145	37.0	4,202
Current age (years)				
18-24 years	31.8c	742	30.5c	895
25-34 years	31.1ns	689	29.6ns	953
35-44 years	31.0ns	642	36.9ns	1,004
45-54 years	37.9ns	570	39.4ns	746
55-64 years	44.7ns	502	53.7ns	604
Education (highest level attained)				
Primary	46.3***	262	52.3***	304
Lower secondary	37.6***	540	42.8***	646
Upper secondary	33.0***	1,182	35.9***	1,763
Third level	25.7c	1,161	25.5c	1,489
Relationship status				
Not in a relationship	38.7ns	841	37.2ns	947
Married	35.9c	1,490	40.9c	2,337
Cohabiting	24.8ns	234	27.6ns	269
Steady relationship	24.6ns	362	28.4ns	510
Casual relationship	33.7ns	218	26.1ns	139
Social class				
Higher professional	30.0*	780	28.9ns	633
Lower professional	34.8ns	718	32.8ns	1,091
Administrative/clerical	35.3ns	422	35.7ns	967
Skilled manual	31.4**	605	45.7*	291
Semi/unskilled manual	43.1c	485	41.5c	880
Religiosity				
Not at all	20.7c	791	23.2c	689
A little	31.2***	1,150	30.6***	1,606
Quite	43.8***	881	42.9***	1,373
Very much	53.2***	280	57.1***	464
Extremely	73.0***	39	76.1***	65

Significance key: ns = not significant; *=P<0.05;**=P<0.01;***=P<0.001
c = reference group to which all other groups are compared.
NOTE: Significance given adjusting for all variables in the table.

Table 2.9: Proportion stating that use of the 'morning after pill' is never wrong: by socio-demographic characteristics

	Men (%)	N	Women (%)	N
All	52.6	3,140	48.1	4,193
Age group				
18-24 years	60.8c	753	56.3c	896
25-34 years	57.3ns	694	57.2***	953
35-44 years	48.5ns	633	42.5ns	1,000
45-54 years	47.5 ns	561	45.2ns	746
55-64 years	47.3	499	37.5	598
Education (highest level attained)				
Primary	43.6	257	42.6	300
Lower secondary	54.9*	535	46.8ns	641
Upper secondary	54.0ns	1,186	47.9ns	1,752
Third level	54.0c	1,162	52.8c	1,500
Relationship status				
Not in a relationship	56.3ns	843	49.8ns	948
Married	47.0c	1,472	42.8c	2,325
Cohabiting	58.3ns	237	60.8*	269
Steady relationship	56.7ns	368	59.5*	511
Casual relationship	64.8**	220	51.4ns	140
Social class				
Higher professional	54.4ns	782	51.0ns	636
Lower professional	50.4ns	717	49.7ns	1,086
Administrative/clerical	52.4ns	425	47.3ns	960
Skilled manual	53.8ns	599	52.2ns	290
Semi/unskilled manual	48.5c	486	45.1c	884
Religiosity				
Not at all	65.6c	795	65.2c	695
A little	51.3***	1,154	49.9***	1,594
Quite	47.3***	873	44.4***	1,372
Very much	41.9***	275	31.7***	462
Extremely	26.2***	38	16.8***	65

Significance key: ns = not significant; *=$P<0.05$;**=$P<0.01$;***=$P<0.001$
c = reference group to which all other groups are compared.
NOTE: Significance given adjusting for all variables in the table.

Table 2.10: Beliefs about the cost, medical side-effects and potential weight gain from the contraceptive pill: among women, by socio-demographic factors

	Cost would discourage use[1]		*Proportion agreeing that:* Medical side-effects would discourage use[2]		Weight gain would discourage use[3]	
	%	N	%	N	%	N
All women	31.8	4,252	58.6	4,252	12.3	4,252
Current age (years)						
18-24 years	30.5c	908	50.8c	908c	12.4c	908
25-34 years	31.1ns	966	53.1ns	966	13.3ns	966
35-44 years	31.5ns	1,014	65.4***	1,014	10.3ns	1,014
45-54 years	35.4ns	754	65.1***	754	13.1ns	754
55-64 years	30.3ns	610	57.7ns	610	13.1ns	610
Education (highest level attained)						
Primary	35.2ns	305	59.6	305	15.9**	305
Lower secondary	33.1ns	657	58.6	657	13.5**	657
Upper secondary	31.6ns	1,780	57.6	1,780	11.8ns	1,780
Third level	28.9c	1,510	60.2	1,510c	10.0c	1,510
Social class						
Higher professional	29.3	642	54.8ns	960	13.5ns	642
Lower professional	30.6	1,097	63.3**	2,361	10.4ns	1,097
Administrative/clerical	33.8	978	53.7ns	270	12.5ns	978
Skilled manual	31.8	296	49.3ns	520	11.9ns	296
Semi/non-skilled manual	32.2	892	60.0ns	141	12.3c	892
Relationship status						
Not in a relationship	30.8ns	960	58.1ns	642	13.1ns	960
Married	33.4c	2,361	63.2c	1,097	12.2c	2,361
Cohabiting	29.0ns	270	59.3ns	978	13.3ns	270
Steady relationship	29.0ns	520	53.2*	296	11.0ns	520
Casual relationship	28.9ns	141	57.8ns	892	9.3ns	141

Significance key: ns = not significant; *=P<0.05;**=P<0.01;***=P<0.001
c = reference group to which all other groups are compared.
[1] Significance given adjusting for all variables in the table except social class.
[2] Significance given adjusting for all variables in the table except education.
[3] Significance given adjusting for all variables in the table.

Table 2.11: Proportion believing that the cost of condoms would discourage use: by socio-demographic factors

	Men		Women	
	%	N	%	N
All	15.2	3,188	14.2	4,253
Current age (years)				
18-24 years	19.4c	759	16.9c	908
25-34 years	18.4ns	701	19.1ns	966
35-44 years	16.5ns	647	11.7***	1,014
45-54 years	10.5**	574	11.3***	755
55-64 years	8.9***	507	11.4***	610
Education (highest level attained)				
Primary	16.6**	263	16.4*	305
Lower secondary	16.8**	544	14.8ns	657
Upper secondary	15.1ns	1,198	13.9ns	1,780
Third level	12.6c	1,183	12.8c	1,511
Social class				
Higher professional	16.4ns	790	13.5ns	642
Lower professional	11.3*	731	12.3*	1,097
Administrative/clerical	16.7ns	428	13.1ns	978
Skilled manual	13.7ns	611	13.2*	296
Semi/unskilled manual	18.4c	492	17.0c	892
Relationship status				
Not in a relationship	15.2ns	854	13.5ns	961
Married	12.3c	1,502	13.5c	2,361
Cohabiting	23.9*	239	20.5ns	270
Steady relationship	20.4ns	371	16.4ns	520
Casual relationship	20.3ns	222	10.2*	141

Significance key: ns = not significant; *=P<0.05;**=P<0.01;***=P<0.001
c = reference group to which all other groups are compared.
NOTE: Significance given adjusting for all variables in the table.

Table 2.12: Beliefs about whether emergency contraception should be available in Ireland, and how: among men, by socio-demographic factors

	Provided through prescription (%)	Provided over the counter (%)	Should not be available (%)	N
All men	41.1	52.1	6.8	3,120
Current age (years)				
18-24 years	43.7	53.3c	3.0	748
25-34 years	41.6	54.1ns	4.3	691
35-44 years	40.3	52.8ns	6.9	631
45-54 years	39.6	52.0*	8.3	557
55-64 years	40.0	47.0ns	13.0	493
Education (highest level attained)				
Primary	41.7	46.0ns	12.4	258
Lower secondary	39.8	55.1ns	5.1	532
Upper secondary	41.4	52.8ns	5.9	1,175
Third level	41.6	52.3c	6.1	1,155
Social class				
Higher professional	41.1	54.4ns	4.4	777
Lower professional	39.7	52.2ns	8.1	711
Administrative/clerical	40.3	52.0ns	7.7	416
Skilled manual	40.3	52.4ns	7.3	602
Semi/unskilled manual	44.3	48.2c	7.5	483
Relationship status				
Not in a relationship	38.7	54.3**	7.0	833
Married	42.9	48.3c	8.8	1,465
Cohabiting	34.1	63.2**	2.7	236
Steady relationship	46.7	50.4ns	2.8	365
Casual relationship	36.2	62.0***	1.8	221
Religiosity				
Not at all	37.1	60.0c	2.9	788
A little	41.8	54.0*	4.2	1,147
Quite	43.4	46.8***	9.9	869
Very much	39.7	43.0***	17.3	272
Extremely	63.8	17.9***	18.4	39

Significance key: ns = not significant; *=P<0.05;**=P<0.01;***=P<0.001

c = reference group to which all other groups are compared.

NOTE: Model is of the log probability of reporting that EC should be available over the counter where those stating that it should not be available in Ireland are included in the denominator. Significance given adjusting for all variables in the table, except education.

Table 2.13: Beliefs about whether emergency contraception should be available in Ireland, and how: among women, by socio-demographic factors

	Provided through prescription (%)	Provided over the counter (%)	Should not be available (%)	N
All women	51.5	41.6	6.9	4,157
Current age (years)				
18-24 years	48.2	49.2c	2.6	895
25-34 years	50.9	46.0ns	3.1	945
35-44 years	58.8	35.2**	6.0	991
45-54 years	50.3	39.8ns	9.9	732
55-64 years	46.2	38.0ns	15.8	594
Education (highest level attained)				
Primary	48.5	40.7	10.8	297
Lower secondary	49.0	41.7	9.3	645
Upper secondary	53.3	40.9	5.8	1,740
Third level	51.8	43.4	4.8	1,475
Social class				
Higher professional	53.8	40.9 ns	5.3	631
Lower professional	55.5	38.3*	6.2	1,070
Administrative/clerical	53.7	38.9 ns	7.4	955
Skilled manual	47.5	46.3 ns	6.3	288
Semi/unskilled manual	49.4	43.6c	7.1	874
Relationship status				
Not in a relationship	47.3	46.0*	6.7	950
Married	54.1	37.0c	8.9	2,299
Cohabiting	51.0	48.4 ns	0.6	262
Steady relationship	51.5	45.3 ns	3.2	507
Casual relationship	45.6	52.2 ns	2.2	139
Religiosity				
Not at all	43.4	53.2c	3.4	684
A little	51.0	45.0**	4.0	1,589
Quite	56.8	35.9***	7.3	1,361
Very much	50.9	32.3***	16.8	454
Extremely	46.0	17.9***	36.1	64

Significance key: ns = not significant; *=P<0.05;**=P<0.01;***=P<0.001

c = reference group to which all other groups are compared.

NOTE: Model is of the log probability of reporting that EC should be available over the counter where those stating that it should not be available in Ireland are included in the denominator. Significance given adjusting for all variables in the table, except education.

Appendix 3

Table 3.1: Proportion of men with a genital same-sex sexual experience over different periods: by selected characteristics

	Ever (%)	Last 5 years (%)	In last year (%)	Base
All	4.4	3.0	2.7	3,188
Current age (years)				
18-24 years	2.5c	2.4c	1.9c	759
25-34 years	3.8ns	3.5ns	3.3*	701
35-44 years	5.5***	4.3***	3.8***	647
45-54 years	6.8***	3.0*	2.4*	574
55-64 years	3.3*	1.4ns	1.4ns	507
Social class				
Higher professional	4.7	3.2	2.9	790
Lower professional	3.8	2.0	1.7	731
Clerical/administrative	3.0	2.4	2.0	428
Skilled manual	3.6	2.8	2.5	611
Semi/unskilled manual	4.9	3.2	3.0	492
Relationship status				
Not in a relationship	5.8***	5.3***	4.4***	854
Married	3.3c	1.2c	1.1c	1,502
Cohabiting	7.3**	6.3***	6.0***	239
Steady relationship	3.9ns	2.8*	2.8*	371
Casual relationship	4.8*	4.0**	3.3*	222
Location				
Outside city	3.4c	2.1c	1.8c	2,038
Other city	6.3*	5.1**	4.5**	372
Dublin	6.2**	4.6**	4.2**	777
Education (highest level attained)				
Primary	3.8ns	2.3ns	1.8ns	263
Lower secondary	4.5ns	2.6ns	2.1ns	544
Higher secondary	3.7*	3.0ns	2.7ns	1,198
Third level	6.3c	4.1c	3.8c	1,183

Significance key: ns = not significant; *=P<0.05;**=P<0.01;***=P<0.001
c = reference group to which all other groups are compared.
NOTE: Significance given adjusting for all variables in the table, except social class.

TABLE 3.2: Proportion of women with a genital same-sex sexual experience over different periods: by selected characteristics

	Ever (%)	Last 5 years (%)	In last year (%)	Base
All	1.4	1.1	0.9	4,253
Current age (years)				
18-24 years	1.4c	1.4c	0.8c	908
25-34 years	2.0ns	1.6ns	1.1ns	966
35-44 years	1.7ns	1.5ns	1.3*	1,014
45-54 years	1.1*	0.8ns	0.7ns	755
55-64 years	0.2ns	0.0ns	0.0ns	610
Social class				
Higher professional	1.9	1.4	0.9	642
Lower professional	2.5	2.1	1.3	1,097
Clerical/administrative	1.3	1.1	1.0	978
Skilled manual	1.5	1.5	1.2	296
Semi/unskilled manual	0.4	0.4	0.4	892
Relationship status				
Not in a relationship	2.3***	2.0***	2.0***	961
Married	0.4c	0.3c	0.1c	2,361
Cohabiting	3.7***	2.7***	2.1***	270
Steady relationship	2.1*	1.9*	1.2**	520
Casual relationship	1.5ns	1.5*	0.0ns	141
Location				
Outside city	1.2c	1.0c	0.8c	2,920
Other city	1.2ns	1.1ns	0.7ns	444
Dublin	1.9ns	1.4ns	0.9ns	885
Education (highest level attained)				
Primary	3.8ns	0.0ns	0.0ns	305
Lower secondary	4.5*	0.5ns	0.3ns	657
Higher secondary	3.7ns	1.3ns	0.9ns	1,780
Third level	6.3c	2.0c	1.6c	1,511

Significance key: ns = not significant; *=P<0.05;**=P<0.01;***=P<0.001
c = reference group to which all other groups are compared.
NOTE: Significance given adjusting for all variables in the table, except social class.

Appendix 4

Table 4.1: Proportions having sex before age 17: by selected characteristics				
	Men		**Women**	
	%	N	%	N
All	21.3	3,188	12.0	4,253
Current age (years)				
18-24 years	31.3c	759	22.3c	908
25-34 years	26.6*	701	18.7**	966
35-44 years	20.2***	647	8.3***	1,014
45-54 years	14.5***	574	5.7***	755
55-64 years	10.8***	507	2.2***	610
Education (highest level attained)				
Primary	21.4***	263	11.0***	305
Lower secondary	29.0***	544	13.9***	657
Higher secondary	19.9**	1,198	13.1***	1,780
Third level	15.8c	1,183	8.5c	1,511
Social class				
Higher professional	18.4	790	14.6c	642
Lower professional	15.2	731	8.9ns	1,097
Clerical/administrative	19.1	428	11.3ns	978
Skilled manual	25.7	611	15.1ns	296
Semi/unskilled manual	26.4	492	14.0ns	892
Age at menarche				
≥13 Years	-	-	8.6c	2,705
<13 Years	-	-	18.1***	1,532

Significance key: ns = not significant; *=P<0.05;**=P<0.01;***=P<0.001
c = reference group to which all other groups are compared.
NOTE: Significance given adjusting for all variables in the table, except social class and age of menarche for men.

Table 4.2: Socio-demographic determinants of contraceptive use at first vaginal intercourse: by selected characteristics

	Men		Women	
	%	N	%	N
All	66.7	2,752	74.1	3,522
Current age (years)				
18-24 years	87.8c	625	94.1c	730
25-34 years	77.4***	654	86.0***	905
35-44 years	66.6***	601	73.4***	918
45-54 years	50.7***	511	57.9***	614
55-64 years	38.8***	361	39.8***	355
Educational level (highest level attained)				
Primary	42.7***	206	42.1***	207
Lower secondary	60.1**	471	66.0**	506
Higher secondary	72.7ns	1,035	78.6*	1,497
Third level	78.7c	1,040	85.8c	1,312
Social class				
Higher professional	74.5ns	696	79.7ns	545
Lower professional	69.6ns	608	80.5*	913
Clerical/administrative	64.2ns	362	76.5*	830
Skilled manual	61.1ns	543	79.4ns	246
Semi/unskilled manual	64.3c	428	66.0c	729
Relationship with first sexual partner				
Just met/didn't know each other	53.3***	239	77.0ns	45
Knew each other but not in steady relationship	60.3***	819	70.3***	460
Steady relationship/cohabiting/engaged	72.6c	1,563	77.5c	2,587
Married	61.1ns	121	58.8ns	427
Age at first intercourse				
<17 years	58.3***	626	73.8***	443
≥17 years	69.4c	2,126	74.2c	3,079

Significance key: ns = not significant; *=P<0.05;**=P<0.01;***=P<0.001
c = reference group to which all other groups are compared.
NOTE: Significance given adjusting for all variables in the table.

Table 4.3: Level of planning, willingness and regret over first sexual intercourse

	<25 Men	<25 Women	25-34 Men	25-34 Women	35-44 Men	35-44 Women	45-54 Men	45-54 Women	55-64 Men	55-64 Women	ALL Men	ALL Women
	%		%		%		%		%		%	
Planning												
Respondent or partner planned sex	3.0	2.5	4.3	2.3	2.9	4.4	3.3	4.0	5.2	6.2	3.7	3.8
Both planned sex	32.9	49.4	30.5	46.0	29.9	47.6	33.9	47.5	37.2	54.5	32.5	48.6
Neither planned sex	7.5	6.5	9.8	5.7	7.8	7.7	8.5	7.4	11.1	9.1	8.8	7.2
Happened on spur of the moment	56.6	41.5	55.5	46.1	59.4	40.4	54.3	41.2	46.4	30.2	55.0	40.4
N	625	736	659	911	614	970	539	723	459	554	2,896	3,894
Regret												
Should have waited longer before having sex with anyone	16.5	24.4	17.4	28.0	12.1	16.3	11.7	14.5	10.7	10.0	13.8	19.0
Should not have waited so long	1.7	1.4	4.2	1.0	7.7	3.3	7.6	3.7	9.9	4.7	6.1	2.7
It was about the right time	81.9	74.2	78.4	71.1	80.2	80.4	80.7	81.8	79.4	85.3	80.1	78.3
N	626	733	658	915	617	977	540	727	467	556	2,908	3,908
Willingness												
Both equally willing	91.8	87.6	91.1	85.7	91.9	85.3	92.3	85.8	91.7	85.2	91.8	85.9
Respondent more willing	3.1	0.8	3.2	0.9	3.7	0.6	5.0	0.3	4.2	0.4	3.8	0.6
Partner more willing	4.3	11.3	4.3	12.6	3.7	13.4	1.5	12.5	3.4	13.1	3.5	12.6
Can't remember	0.8	0.3	1.4	0.8	0.8	0.7	1.1	1.4	0.6	1.4	1.0	0.9
N	631	738	662	927	626	990	545	734	470	572	2,934	3,961
Contextual factors												
Curious about what it would be like	96.7	93.7	94.3	88.3	91.4	86.6	88.6	76.7	87.0	73.5	91.8	84.4
Carried away by feelings	61.4	46.3	67.7	61.4	70.8	70.0	76.2	68.3	78.8	68.0	70.6	63.2
Most people of same age seemed to be doing it	68.5	53.0	67.8	58.1	61.0	50.1	50.3	42.3	51.9	41.4	60.5	49.5
Seemed like a natural 'follow-on' in the relationship	80.8	83.06	81.8	85.9	86.3	92.4	88.1	92.8	89.9	97.4	85.2	90.2
Self or partner had been drinking or taking drugs	35.8	20.7	37.2	21.8	27.9	16.5	19.2	15.0	12.2	5.8	27.4	16.5
Wanted to lose virginity	62.5	34.8	64.6	41.5	58.6	30.2	43.8	29.5	45.1	41.2	55.8	34.9
In love	47.0	68.4	53.9	76.6	62.4	90.7	71.9	92.7	75.9	98.0	61.6	85.1
To please partner	61.1	36.2	63.5	44.4	72.4	57.69	72.3	68.49	78.6	79.6	69.3	56.3
Felt ready, that it was the right time	82.7	86.6	80.1	87.9	87.1	93.6	89.7	93.4	90.8	96.7	85.8	91.6
N	629	735	655	911	618	975	543	727	461	554	2906	3902

Appendix 5

Table 5.1: Distribution of number of heterosexual partners over lifetime: by age group and gender

	Men (%)						Women (%)					
	18-24	25-34	35-44	45-54	55-64	ALL	18-24	25-34	35-44	45-54	55-64	ALL
0	11.9	4.3	2.9	5.5	7.3	6.3	15.3	3.1	2.8	2.2	5.6	5.8
1	22.6	17.7	27.2	37.3	45.8	29.0	34.5	32.7	53.7	65.2	75.6	50.8
2	7.2	6.7	7.1	5.2	7.6	6.8	12.2	12.9	11.0	7.7	7.3	10.5
3-4	18.0	12.8	15.1	11.6	8.9	13.6	17.6	20.3	14.6	10.6	6.9	14.5
5-9	19.3	25.3	19.5	19.2	13.2	19.6	12.4	20.4	12.5	10.0	3.4	12.3
10+	21.0	33.2	28.3	21.2	17.1	24.8	8.1	10.6	5.5	4.4	1.2	6.2
Median	3	5	4	3	1	4	2	3	1	1	1	1
Mean	6.0	11.0	11.4	8.8	7.2	9.05	3.6	4.2	2.9	2.4	1.5	3
99th centile	45	100	300	70	100	75	30	25	20	15	10	20
Base	759	701	647	574	507	3,188	908	966	1,014	755	610	4,253

Table 5.2: Distribution of number of heterosexual partners in last 5 years: by age group and gender

	Men (%)						Women (%)					
	18-24	25-34	35-44	45-54	55-64	ALL	18-24	25-34	35-44	45-54	55-64	ALL
0	12.2	6.7	6.4	9.9	16.4	9.9	15.8	5.0	9.2	14.1	27.1	13.3
1	24.7	46.8	71.7	76.5	75.4	58.1	36.6	66.7	82.1	81.1	71.6	67.7
2	7.6	10.8	6.2	5.7	3.7	7.0	12.8	11.2	4.6	3.1	0.7	6.8
3-4	18.7	16.4	8.1	4.8	2.8	10.6	17.9	11.0	2.8	1.4	0.6	7.0
5-9	18.7	10.9	4.3	2.0	1.5	7.8	11.2	5.0	1.3	0.2	0.0	3.7
10+	18.1	8.5	3.4	1.1	0.2	6.6	5.7	1.2	0.0	0.0	0.0	1.4
Median	3	1	1	1	1	1	1	1	1	1	1	1
Mean	5.2	3.5	2.3	1.7	1.1	2.9	2.8	1.7	1.1	0.9	0.8	1.5
99th centile	34	30	15	10	6	24	16	10	5	3	2	10
Base	758	700	645	573	506	3,182	908	965	1,014	753	610	4,250

Table 5.3: Distribution of number of heterosexual partners in last year: by age group and gender

	Men (%)						Women (%)					
	18-24	25-34	35-44	45-54	55-64	ALL	18-24	25-34	35-44	45-54	55-64	ALL
0	17.3	13.6	9.8	15.3	23.8	15.4	22.2	11.1	14.9	21.0	34.5	19.7
1	45.6	71.0	82.0	80.8	72.2	70.3	61.5	82.9	82.8	78.14	65.4	74.9
2	15.7	7.2	2.6	2.1	2.5	6.2	9.0	4.5	1.2	0.9	0.2	3.3
3-4	12.5	5.7	3.6	1.5	1.2	5.1	5.1	0.8	1.2	0.0	0.0	1.5
5-9	6.5	1.4	2.0	0.1	0.3	2.2	1.9	0.6	0.0	0.0	0.0	0.5
10+	2.5	1.1	0.0	0.2	0.0	0.8	0.4	0.0	0.0	0.0	0.0	0.1
Median	1	1	1	1	1	1	1	1	1	1	1	1
Mean	1.9	1.3	1.1	1.0	0.8	1.3	1.1	1.0	0.9	0.8	0.7	0.9
99th centile	15	10	6	3	3	7	7	3	3	1	1	3
Base	758	700	644	573	506	3181	908	965	1014	753	610	4250

Table 5.4: Number of heterosexual partners over different periods: by country

	Over lifetime (%)				
	0	**1**	**2-4**	**5+**	**N**
Men					
Ireland - ISSHR	6.3	29.0	20.4	44.3	3,188
GB – NATSAL 1990	6.6	20.6	29.0	43.8	8,384
GB – NATSAL 2000	7.2	11.0	22.1	59.8	4,661
US – NHSLS	3.4	19.5	20.9	56.2	1,394
France – ACSF	4.5	21.4	29.1	45.0	8,772
Australia - ASHR	6.4	10.3	83.3		9,728
Women					
Ireland – ISSHR	5.8	50.8	25.0	18.5	4,253
GB – NATSAL 1990	5.7	39.3	35.1	19.8	10,492
GB – NATSAL 2000	5.3	18.3	30.5	45.9	6,275
US – NHSLS	2.6	31.4	36.4	29.6	1,732
France – ACSF	5.7	46.1	34.4	13.7	10,449
Australia - ASHR	7.2	22.9	69.9		9,578

	Over the last year (%)				
	0	**1**	**2-4**	**5+**	**N**
Men					
Ireland – ISSHR	15.4	70.3	11.3	3.0	3,181
GB – NATSAL 1990	13.1	73.0	12.3	1.5	8,384
GB – NATSAL 2000	-	-	-	-	-
US – NHSLS	9.9	66.8	18.3	5.1	1,408
France – ACSF	11.1	77.5	10.3	1.0	8,942
Australia - ASHR	12.1	74.6	13.3		9,728
Women					
Ireland – ISSHR	19.7	74.9	4.8	0.6	4,250
GB – NATSAL 1990	13.9	79.4	6.4	0.0	10,492
GB – NATSAL 2000	-	-	-	-	-
US – NHSLS	13.6	74.6	10.0	1.7	1,747
France – ACSF	17.3	78.0	4.5	0.2	11,104
Australia - ASHR	13.5	79.1	7.4		9,578

Table 5.5: Proportion with two or more partners in last year: by socio-demographic characteristics

	Men		Women	
	%	N	%	N
All	14.5	3,188	5.5	4,253
Current age (years)				
18-24 years	37.2c	759	16.4c	908
25-34 years	15.6***	701	6.3ns	966
35-44 years	8.5**	647	2.3ns	1,014
45-54 years	4.1***	574	1.1*	755
55-64 years	4.3***	507	0.2**	610
Relationship status				
Not in a relationship	30.3**	854	12.3**	961
Married	2.2c	1,502	0.2c	2,361
Cohabiting	5.4***	239	2.3***	270
Steady relationship	14.3***	371	8.4***	520
Casual relationship	45.5***	222	29.3***	141
Social class				
Higher professional	16.2c	790	9.7c	642
Lower professional	15.2ns	731	5.4ns	1,097
Clerical/administrative	11.8ns	428	4.5ns	978
Skilled manual	14.0ns	611	9.2ns	296
Semi/unskilled manual	12.9*	492	3.7*	892
Education (highest level attained)				
Primary	6.2	263	0.5	305
Lower secondary	12.9	544	3.2	657
Higher secondary	17.2	1,198	6.8	1,780
Third level	17.0	1,183	7.8	1,511
Age of first intercourse				
Sex after 17	10.4c	2,552	4.2c	3,791
Sex before 17	29.7***	636	15.1***	462

Significance key: ns = not significant; *=P<0.05;**=P<0.01;***=P<0.001
c = reference group to which all other groups are compared.
NOTE: Significance given adjusting for all variables in the table, except education.

Table 5.6: Proportion having concurrent sexual relationships in the last year by number of heterosexual and all partners

	Heterosexual partnerships				All partnerships			
	Men		Women		Men		Women	
	%	N	%	N	%	N	%	N
2	19.4	207	12.8	139	17.9	205	13.6	136
3-4	26.0	170	21.4	62	26.6	181	21.5	67
5/9	43.9	68	33.1	23	43.5	70	26.6	21
10+	60.6	30	12.0	3	61.4	38	36.5	4
χ^2	31.32***		9.17		39.13***		4.91	

Significance key: *=p<0.05; **=P<0.01; ***=P<0.001

Table 5.7: Proportions of men who have paid a woman for sex: by selected characteristics

	Ever (&)	In last 5 years (&)	Base
All men	6.4	3.3	3,096
Current age (years)			
18-24 years	3.7c	3.7.0c	721
25-34 years	7.3*	5.8*	687
35-44 years	6.7*	3.4ns	629
45-54 years	5.9*	1.6ns	562
55-64 years	8.4***	0.9ns	497
Relationship status			
Single	8.2c	5.8c	804
Married	5.6**	1.5**	1,483
Cohabiting	5.9*	4.8ns	231
Steady relationship	4.4ns	2.5 *	366
Casual relationship	7.8ns	6.1ns	212
Education (highest level attained)			
Primary	5.2ns	0.6ns	256
Lower secondary	6.8ns	3.6ns	535
Higher secondary	6.8ns	3.9ns	1,159
Third level	5.8c	3.6c	1,146
Social class			
Higher professional	7.6*	4.5*	765
Lower professional	5.3ns	3.9ns	710
Clerical/administrative	5.6ns	1.8ns	411
Skilled manual	6.7ns	2.7ns	603
Semi/unskilled manual	5.1c	2.1c	479
Age of first intercourse			
Sex after 17	5.5c	3.0c	2,460
Sex before 17	9.4ns	4.3ns	636
Homosexual partner ever			
No	5.6c	2.8c	2,984
Yes	28.1***	14.6***	112
Number of unpaid partners ever			
1 or fewer	4.3c	2.3c	1,305
2	5.6ns	3.8ns	247
3 to 9	4.9ns	2.9ns	962
10 or more	13.6***	5.8*	580

Significance key: ns = not significant; *=P<0.05;**=P<0.01;***=P<0.001
c = reference group to which all other groups are compared.
NOTE: Significance given adjusting for all variables in the table.

Table 5.8: Proportion of men who have ever paid for sex with a woman: by number of heterosexual & homosexual partners in lifetime

	All unpaid heterosexual partners		All heterosexual partners		All heterosexual & homosexual partners	
	%	Base	%	Base	%	Base
0	3.6	189	0.0	186	0.0	152
1	0.5	891	0.5	892	0.4	872
2	5.9	218	1.9	210	1.8	214
3-4	4.7	435	4.5	431	4.0	428
5-9	5.4	655	5.3	659	5.4	654
10+	15.3	769	17.2	784	15.9	795
All	6.2	3,157	6.2	3,162	6.0	3,115
X^2	164.46***		237.80***		210.84***	

Significance key: *=P<0.05; **=P<0.01; ***=P<0.001

Appendix 6

Table 6.1: Last occasion of different sexual practices – men (%)

	Vaginal	Cunnilingus	Fellatio	Anal	Any oral
Last 7 days	47.7	15.8	16.7	0.5	19.5
Last 4 weeks	20.3	18.2	19.0	1.1	19.6
Last 3 months	8.7	10.6	11.5	1.2	11.2
Last 6 months	3.7	5.8	6.3	1.4	5.5
Last year	3.9	6.0	6.8	1.7	6.4
Last 5 years	5.4	7.5	9.0	3.5	8.3
Ever	3.3	4.6	5.3	2.0	5.3
Total	93.1	68.5	74.6	11.4	75.8
N	3,152	3,122	2,986	3,147	3,123

Table 6.2: Last occasion of different sexual practices – women (%)

	Vaginal	Cunnilingus	Fellatio	Anal	Any oral
Last 7 days	51.1	13.4	13.4	0.5	15.5
Last 4 weeks	16.6	13.0	13.1	0.7	13.9
Last 3 months	6.0	9.1	9.4	0.7	9.4
Last 6 months	3.8	5.6	5.3	0.8	5.6
Last year	3.5	5.6	5.6	0.8	5.3
Last 5 years	6.5	6.7	6.5	2.3	6.5
Ever	6.0	4.6	4.7	2.3	4.6
Total	93.7	58.0	58.0	8.1	61.0
N	4,154	4,146	3,859	4,193	4,149

Table 6.3: Prevalence of different practices in the last year and ever: by 10-year age group – men

	Vaginal			Oral			Anal		
	Last year (%)	Ever (%)	N	Last year (%)	Ever (%)	N	Last year (%)	Ever (%)	N
<25	79.3	84.2	752	75.5	82.2	744	9.2	11.9	749
25-34	86.2	95.2	700	75.5	87.4	691	8.5	18.3	693
35-44	91.4	97.7	636	71.8	82.4	634	5.6	11.5	640
45-54	85.8	94.7	563	49.6	70.9	557	3.2	7.7	564
55-64	76.3	93.2	501	26.6	47.7	497	1.6	5.6	501
All	84.4	93.1	3,152	62.2	75.8	3,123	5.9	11.4	3,147

Table 6.4: Prevalence of different practices in the last year and ever: by 10-year age group – women

	Vaginal			Oral			Anal		
	Last year (%)	Ever (%)	N	Last year (%)	Ever (%)	N	Last year (%)	Ever (%)	N N
<25	76.0	81.7	897	63.8	71.0	896	5.7	9.2	901
25-34	88.9	96.1	954	67.4	77.4	946	6.1	12.9	955
35-44	86.5	97.8	990	55.4	68.0	980	2.1	6.6	996
45-54	81.4	98.1	729	38.2	51.5	737	2.1	6.6	744
55-64	68.2	94.9	584	11.0	24.4	590	0.6	4.1	597
All	81.2	93.7	4,154	49.9	61.0	4,149	3.5	8.1	4,193

Table 6.5: Sexual practices at most recent event – men (%)

	18-24	25-34	35-44	45-54	55-64	All
Vaginal sex alone	41.8	50.8	63.9	77.1	82.9	62.3
Vaginal + oral	44.4	42.9	29.9	16.9	11.1	30.1
Mutual masturbation alone	1.6	0.8	2.2	3.5	3.6	2.3
Oral sex alone	9.5	3.4	2.9	1.2	1.7	3.8
Vaginal, oral and anal sex	1.1	1.3	0.4	0.1	0.5	0.7
Anal + oral sex	0.3	0.2	0.0	0.4	0.0	0.2
Vaginal + anal sex	1.0	0.4	0.5	0.7	0.2	0.6
Anal alone	0.3	0.2	0.2	0.2	0.0	0.2
Total	100	100	100	100	100	100
N	650	583	463	365	275	2,336

Table 6.6: Sexual practices at most recent event – women (%)

	18-24	25-34	35-44	45-54	55-64	All
Vaginal sex alone	56.0	62.6	74.1	82.6	89.9	72.3
Vaginal + oral	35.7	31.5	21.4	13.0	3.4	21.9
Mutual masturbation alone	1.5	1.8	3.3	3.3	5.9	3.0
Oral sex alone	5.3	2.6	0.8	0.4	0.7	1.9
Vaginal, oral and anal sex	1.4	1.1	0.2	0.5	0.0	0.7
Anal + oral sex	0.1	0.0	0.0	0.0	0.2	0.1
Vaginal + anal sex	0.0	0.5	0.1	0.2	0.0	0.2
Anal alone	0.0	0.0	0.0	0.0	0.0	0.0
Total	100	100	100	100	100	100
N	736	680	480	290	218	2,404

Table 6.7: Proportion having vaginal sex in last year: by selected socio-demographic characteristics

	Men		Women	
	%	N	%	N
All	84.4	3,152	81.2	4,154
Current age (years)				
18-24 years	79.3c	752	76.0c	897
25-34 years	86.2ns	700	88.9*	954
35-44 years	91.4ns	636	86.5***	990
45-54 years	85.8*	563	81.4***	729
55-64 years	76.3***	501	68.2c	584
Relationship status				
Not in a relationship	55.8***	844	40.8***	939
Married	96.0c	1,480	96.3c	2,292
Cohabiting	94.1**	239	93.9***	266
Steady relationship	94.6**	369	94.1***	516
Casual relationship	90.3***	220	88.4***	141
Education (highest level attained)				
Primary	81.1ns	260	67.3**	296
Lower secondary	84.8ns	541	81.2ns	641
Higher secondary	85.3ns	1,184	85.0ns	1,734
Third level	84.5c	1,167	81.1c	1,483
Social class				
Higher professional	86.0ns	780	82.2ns	631
Lower professional	84.6ns	722	82.3ns	1,073
Clerical/administrative	83.7ns	426	84.3ns	955
Skilled manual	85.7ns	607	81.3ns	291
Semi/unskilled manual	82.8c	487	79.4c	870
Number of partners				
1 or fewer partners in the last year	82.1c	2,665	80.3c	3,924
2+ partners in the last year	97.7***	487	95.6***	230

Significance key: ns = not significant; *=P<0.05;**=P<0.01;***=P<0.001
c = reference group to which all other groups are compared.
NOTE: Significance given adjusting for all variables in the table.

Table 6.8: Proportion having oral sex in last year: by selected socio-demographic characteristics

	Men		Women	
	%	N	%	N
All	62.2	3,123	49.9	4,149
Current age (years)				
18-24 years	75.5c	744	63.8c	896
25-34 years	75.5ns	691	67.4ns	946
35-44 years	71.8ns	634	55.4***	980
45-54 years	49.6***	557	38.2***	737
55-64 years	26.6***	497	11.0***	590
Relationship status				
Not in a relationship	47.8***	828	31.4***	942
Married	59.8c	1,476	47.9c	2,291
Cohabiting	85.5**	233	78.2**	264
Steady relationship	88.0*	367	76.4ns	511
Casual relationship	75.5*	219	70.9ns	141
Education (highest level attained)				
Primary	36.4***	257	22.3***	299
Lower secondary	62.7ns	540	39.3***	644
Higher secondary	67.8ns	1,177	54.7***	1,738
Third level	70.1c	1,149	64.9c	1,468
Social class				
Higher professional	68.1	777	60.0	630
Lower professional	59.8	717	53.9	1,067
Clerical/administrative	59.6	419	49.6	957
Skilled manual	62.2	604	53.2	292
Semi/unskilled manual	59.7	481	45.4	872
Number of partners				
1 or fewer partners in the last year	57.2c	2,637	47.5c	3,922
2+ partners in the last year	91.3***	486	89.9***	227

Significance key: ns = not significant; *=P<0.05;**=P<0.01;***=P<0.001

c = reference group to which all other groups are compared.

NOTE: Significance given adjusting for all variables in the table, except social class.

Table 6.9: Proportion having anal sex in last year: by selected socio-demographic characteristics

	Men		Women	
	%	N	%	N
All	5.9	3,147	3.5	4,193
Current age (years)				
18-24 years	9.2c	749	5.7c	901
25-34 years	8.5ns	693	6.1ns	955
35-44 years	5.6ns	640	2.1**	996
45-54 years	3.2*	564	2.1*	744
55-64 years	1.6***	501	0.6**	597
Relationship status				
Not in a relationship	4.6**	839	2.7**	949
Married	4.0c	1,488	2.7c	2,321
Cohabiting	16.7**	232	5.5ns	268
Steady relationship	9.0ns	368	5.8ns	514
Casual relationship	9.9ns	220	8.2ns	141
Education (highest level attained)				
Primary	3.8ns	258	0.3ns	302
Lower secondary	4.6ns	542	3.7ns	650
Higher secondary	7.4ns	1,186	4.0ns	1,757
Third level	5.9c	1,161	4.0c	1,484
Social class				
Higher professional	6.7ns	783	4.9ns	633
Lower professional	5.7ns	725	3.8ns	1,081
Clerical/administrative	4.6ns	419	2.5ns	967
Skilled manual	6.0ns	607	4.6ns	294
Semi/unskilled manual	6.2c	484	2.9c	882
Number of partners				
1 or fewer partners in the last year	4.9c	2,661	2.9c	3,964
2+ partners in the last year	11.6***	486	12.7***	229

Significance key: ns = not significant; *=P<0.05;**=P<0.01;***=P<0.001
c = reference group to which all other groups are compared.
NOTE: Significance given adjusting for all variables in the table.

Table 6.10: Total frequency of genital sexual events: by selected characteristics – men (%)

	Less than twice a year	Less than monthly	Less than weekly	Once or twice a week	2 to 3 times a week	4 to 6 times a week	Daily	Signif.#	Total	N
All men	13.6	14.0	30.8	27.9	10.2	2.9	0.6		100	2,954
Current age (years)										
18-24 years	9.9	27.9	27.3	20.2	10.1	3.7	1.0	c	100	663
25-34 years	14.7	13.6	24.0	28.0	14.6	4.1	1.0	***	100	665
35-44 years	11.6	7.6	29.7	35.5	12.2	3.0	0.4	***	100	619
45-54 years	13.1	8.4	36.7	31.4	7.5	2.7	0.4	***	100	538
55-64 years	20.7	14.0	39.2	21.4	4.1	0.7	0.0	***	100	469
Education (highest level attained)										
Primary	16.7	13.5	36.6	23.5	7.6	1.5	0.6	ns	100	234
Lower secondary	15.0	11.7	30.5	29.6	9.8	3.2	0.2	ns	100	513
Higher secondary	12.7	15.0	29.4	28.1	11.3	3.0	1.0	ns	100	1,113
Third level	11.8	15.0	29.5	29.1	10.1	3.7	1.0	c	100	1,094
Social class										
Higher professional	12.1	15.0	29.7	27.9	10.5	4.2	0.7	ns	100	740
Lower professional	10.1	14.6	33.5	30.5	9.5	1.3	0.5	ns	100	673
Clerical/administrative	16.7	14.1	31.8	23.8	9.1	4.4	0.1	ns	100	394
Skilled manual	14.0	11.6	31.6	29.6	10.2	2.4	0.6	ns	100	571
Semi/unskilled manual	15.6	14.5	30.1	26.6	10.2	2.6	0.4	c	100	459
Relationship status										
Not in a relationship	41.4	33.1	18.3	4.2	2.0	0.9	0.2	***	100	702
Married	4.5	7.3	38.3	36.9	10.7	2.0	0.0	c	100	1,450
Living together	3.5	2.4	22.0	39.2	21.1	10.5	1.2	ns	100	234
Steady relationship	3.4	6.1	29.6	34.3	18.4	5.3	2.9	***	100	363
Casual relationship	9.8	19.8	29.2	24.4	11.1	5.6	0.2	***	100	205

Significance key: ns = not significant; *=P<0.05;**=P<0.01;***=P<0.001; c = reference group to which all other groups are compared.
NOTE: Significance given adjusting for all variables in the table.
Significance is based on the results of OLS models of the log of the frequency of sex, imputing values on a per week basis.

Table 6.11: Total frequency of genital sexual events: by selected characteristics – women (%)

	Less than twice a year	Less than monthly	Less than weekly	Once or twice a week	2 to 3 times a week	4 to 6 times a week	Daily	Signif.#	Total	N
All women	17.2	11.1	29.1	30.3	10.1	1.7	0.5		100	3,906
Current age (years)										
18-24 years	14.6	22.4	21.0	25.1	13.2	3.2	0.6	c	100	763
25-34 years	12.3	10.8	25.6	33.9	13.9	2.5	1.0	***	100	920
35-44 years	13.9	7.3	30.7	35.2	11.1	1.6	0.3	***	100	966
45-54 years	17.2	5.9	33.0	35.5	7.6	0.4	0.4	***	100	704
55-64 years	33.4	10.6	36.6	16.6	2.2	0.6	0.1	***	100	553
Education (highest level attained)										
Primary	34.2	7.3	32.2	22.3	3.4	0.6	0.0	**	100	283
Lower secondary	15.9	9.0	31.6	30.8	10.6	1.3	0.9	ns	100	603
Higher secondary	12.6	11.3	29.2	32.9	11.5	1.9	0.5	**	100	1,620
Third level	17.9	14.8	24.9	29.3	10.6	2.3	0.3	c	100	1,400
Social class										
Higher professional	15.2	13.5	28.9	28.8	10.8	2.0	0.8	ns	100	587
Lower professional	17.1	12.4	27.9	29.1	10.9	2.2	0.3	ns	100	1,011
Clerical/administrative	14.5	9.9	28.9	35.1	9.7	1.6	0.4	ns	100	910
Skilled manual	14.6	15.0	24.5	32.2	12.5	0.8	0.5	ns	100	262
Semi/unskilled manual	18.9	10.3	31.0	28.7	9.3	1.4	0.5	c	100	818
Relationship status										
Not in a relationship	60.0	26.9	8.1	4.1	0.8	0.2	0.0	***	100	770
Married	4.7	6.6	38.8	37.7	11.0	1.3	0.3	c	100	2,253
Living together	4.3	2.8	31.3	40.2	16.1	3.0	2.3	***	100	255
Steady relationship	2.7	4.8	23.5	41.2	21.7	5.2	0.9	***	100	498
Casual relationship	6.2	16.9	33.2	29.8	9.7	3.5	0.7	***	100	130

Significance key: ns = not significant; *=P<0.05; **=P<0.01; ***=P<0.001; c = reference group to which all other groups are compared.

NOTE: Significance given adjusting for all variables in the table.

Significance is based on the results of OLS models of the log of the frequency of sex, imputing values on a per week basis.

Table 6.12: Frequency and desired frequency of sex – men

	Desired frequency				
	More (%)	About right (%)	Less (%)	Total (%)	N
Less than twice a year	60.2	36.3	3.5	100	336
Less than monthly	63.7	33.9	2.5	100	424
Less than once a week	38.8	59.8	1.4	100	889
Once or twice a week	30.4	69.0	0.6	100	840
Twice or three times a week	29.9	69.3	0.9	100	304
Four to six times a week	34.3	65.7	0.0	100	92
At least once a day	40.7	57.3	2.1	100	19
All	41.6	56.9	1.5	100	2,904

Table 6.13: Frequency and desired frequency of sex – women

	Desired frequency				
	More (%)	About right (%)	Less (%)	Total (%)	N
Less than twice a year	37.7	53.5	8.9	100	511
Less than monthly	39.2	51.9	9.0	100	433
Less than once a week	23.6	71.2	5.3	100	1,144
Once or twice a week	19.3	77.8	3.0	100	1,232
Twice or three times a week	15.3	82.4	2.3	100	407
Four to six times a week	6.9	91.6	1.5	100	74
At least once a day	0.0	100.0	0.0	100	20
All	25.0	69.9	5.1	100	3,821

Appendix 7

Table 7.1: Distribution of number of same-sex partners over three periods: by gender

Men	Ever (%)	N	Last 5 years (%)	N	Last year (%)	N
0	-	-	1.3	2	1.5	2
1	41.4	39	59.6	49	76.2	59
2	11.7	12	11.8	11	5.1	6
3 or 4	8.7	12	8.1	7	6.2	7
5 to 9	5.3	7	4.6	6	3.5	4
10+	31.8	34	14.6	20	7.4	8
	100	104	100	95	100	86
Women						
0	-	-	4.0	1	5.3	1
1	47.1	25	62.4	25	76.9	22
2	19.0	7	22.3	6	13.4	3
3 or 4	24.8	8	11.4	5	4.4	1
5 to 9	2.1	1	0.0	0	0.0	0
10+	3.6	2	0.0	0	0.0	0
	100	43	100	36	100	26

NOTE: Only those who have ever had a genital same-sex partner are included.

Table 7.2: Last occasion of different sexual practices for men who report same-sex genital experience in lifetime (%)

	Received oral sex	Gave oral sex	Received anal sex	Gave anal sex	Any oral	Any anal
Last 7 days	8.3	8.0	3.1	2.8	8.3	3.1
Last 4 weeks	13.5	13.5	4.4	4.1	13.5	5.2
Last 3 months	3.0	3.7	2.0	1.2	3.7	2.5
Last 6 months	3.6	2.5	2.2	2.5	4.1	2.2
Last year	3.4	4.7	2.7	3.0	3.8	3.7
Last 5 years	9.7	11.2	7.0	6.7	11.2	7.0
Before last 5 years	24.0	21.0	8.7	7.5	28.9	8.7
Never	34.6	35.3	69.9	72.1	26.7	67.7
N	140	141	144	144	141	144

Table 7.3: Last occasion of different sexual practices: for women who report same-sex genital experience in lifetime (%)

	Received oral sex	Gave oral sex	Any oral
Last 7 days	2.7	2.7	2.7
Last 4 weeks	0.0	0.0	0.0
Last 3 months	4.5	5.2	5.2
Last 6 months	0.0	0.0	0.0
Last year	20.9	19.8	22.5
Last 5 years	23.9	23.2	23.2
Before last 5 years	26.8	23.5	26.8
Never	21.2	25.6	19.6
N	56.0	56.0	56.0

Table 7.4: Experience of homosexual anal sex in the last year*

	Men (%)
Received only	17.8
Gave only	13.9
Both	68.3
Total	100
N	31

*for men having anal sex in last year

Appendix 8

Table 8.1: Proportion using contraception at most recent sexual intercourse: by socio-demographic characteristics

	Men (%)	N	Women (%)	N
All	73.7	2,477	69.1	3,314
Current age (years)				
18-24 years	93.0c	586	94.3c	698
25-34 years	90.8ns	567	90.9ns	756
35-44 years	82.4ns	486	81.3***	765
45-54 years	63.3***	442	50.2***	593
55-64 years	24.4***	396	9.9***	502
Education (highest level attained)				
Primary	51.5ns	200	30.4***	226
Lower secondary	72.0ns	416	62.4ns	526
Upper secondary	78.8ns	928	76.0ns	1,384
Third level	82.2c	933	82.0c	1,178
Social class				
Higher professional	75.7ns	639	75.7ns	500
Lower professional	75.0ns	553	71.6ns	849
Administrative/clerical	70.8ns	331	71.2ns	775
Skilled manual	72.1ns	469	73.9ns	231
Semi/unskilled	71.7c	377	63.8c	680
Relationship status (at time of intercourse)				
Just met/didn't know partner	84.9ns	113	79.7ns	35
Knew partner but not steady	85.4*	369	81.3ns	221
Steady	89.8***	650	89.3**	892
Cohabiting	89.3**	125	90.2*	159
Engaged	89.0ns	31	76.8ns	50
Married	59.2c	1,175	55.6c	1,947

Significance key: ns = not significant; *=P<0.05;**=P<0.01;***=P<0.001
c = reference group to which all other groups are compared.
NOTE: Significance given adjusting for all variables in the table.

Table 9.2: Proportion experiencing an abortion (of women who have experienced a pregnancy): by socio-demographic characteristics

	%	N
All	4.0	2,595
Current age (years)		
18-24 years	10.9c	111
25-34 years	7.7ns	547
35-44 years	4.1ns	823
45-54 years	1.6ns	624
55-64 years	1.5ns	490
Education (highest level attained)		
Primary	0.7*	251
Lower secondary	3.3**	508
Upper secondary	4.1**	1,125
Third level	8.3c	711
Social class		
Higher professional	5.3	285
Lower professional	6.9	663
Administrative/clerical	3.7	650
Skilled manual	3.6	139
Semi/unskilled	2.1	621
Relationship status		
Not in a relationship	6.5***	292
Married	1.6c	2,020
Cohabiting	12.0***	142
Steady relationship	17.7***	111
Casual relationship	15.1***	30
Age of first intercourse		
After 17	3.3c	2,329
Before 17	9.3***	266

Significance key: ns = not significant; *=P<0.05;**=P<0.01;***=P<0.001
c = reference group to which all other groups are compared.
NOTE: Significance given adjusting for all variables in the table, except social class

Appendix 9

Table 9.1: Proportion experiencing a crisis pregnancy: by socio-demographic characteristics of women who have experienced pregnancy	%	N
All	20.7	2,595
Current age (years)		
18-24 years	55.6***	111
25-34 years	34.7***	547
35-44 years	16.8ns	823
45-54 years	16.1*	624
55-64 years	11.0c	490
Education (highest level attained)		
Primary	15.1	251
Lower secondary	20.1	508
Upper secondary	21.2	1,126
Third level	26.1	710
Social class		
Higher professional	22.4ns	285
Lower professional	23.8*	663
Administrative/clerical	18.5ns	650
Skilled manual	29.0ns	139
Semi/unskilled	19.4c	621
Relationship status		
Not in a relationship	32.4***	292
Married	13.6c	2,020
Cohabiting	41.6***	142
Steady relationship	56.7***	111
Casual relationship	31.1ns	30
Age of first intercourse		
After 17	18.2c	2,329
Before 17	40.0**	266

Significance key: ns = not significant; *=P<0.05;**=P<0.01;***=P<0.001
c = reference group to which all other groups are compared.
NOTE: Significance given adjusting for all variables in the table, except education.

Table 8.5: Proportion using a condom at most recent sexual intercourse: by socio-demographic characteristics

	Men (%)	N	Women (%)	N
All	37.3	2,784	31.4	3,833
Current age (years)				
18-24 years	75.5c	592	67.6c	716
25-34 years	47.3***	639	38.7***	901
35-44 years	30.2***	588	26.4***	953
45-54 years	22.1***	518	17.0***	714
55-64 years	8.2***	447	4.0***	549
Education (highest level attained)				
Primary	17.9ns	228	11.0*	268
Lower secondary	31.5*	485	22.8ns	597
Upper secondary	43.6ns	1,033	35.1ns	1,586
Third level	46.1c	1,035	43.2c	1,356
Social class				
Higher professional	40.4	696	39.6	570
Lower professional	40.3	624	31.4	992
Administrative/clerical	36.7	374	30.6	904
Skilled manual	32.2	545	45.6	255
Semi/unskilled	34.9	433	25.9	801
Relationship status (at time of intercourse)				
Just met/didn't know partner	78.2***	113	71.2***	35
Knew partner but not steady	69.4***	373	71.3***	229
Steady relationship	58.7***	673	55.2***	925
Cohabiting	33.6ns	140	41.0***	182
Engaged	37.4ns	35	30.6ns	61
Married	17.0c	1,436	15.7c	2,390

Significance key: ns = not significant; *=P<0.05;**=P<0.01;***=P<0.001

c = reference group to which all other groups are compared.

NOTE: Significance given adjusting for all variables in the table, except social class.

Table 8.4: Proportion consistently using a condom in the last year: by socio-demographic characteristics

	Men (%)	N	Women (%)	N
All	27.6	2,682	23.1	3,530
Current age (years)				
18-24 years	57.3c	596	50.9c	687
25-34 years	33.1**	625	27.3**	867
35-44 years	20.9***	587	15.3***	914
45-54 years	14.5***	492	13.0***	636
55-64 years	7.5***	382	3.1***	426
Education (highest level attained)				
Primary	17.6ns	206	9.0ns	210
Lower secondary	23.2ns	461	14.0*	539
Upper secondary	31.7ns	1,004	26.6ns	1,510
Third level	31.5c	1,011	30.0c	1,271
Social class				
Higher professional	30.8ns	684	29.4ns	536
Lower professional	28.0ns	614	22.0ns	925
Administrative/clerical	28.4ns	355	22.6ns	843
Skilled manual	23.1ns	516	34.9ns	244
Semi/unskilled	25.5c	409	18.4c	719
Relationship status				
Not in a relationship	61.0***	488	58.2***	415
Married	12.7c	1,422	11.4c	2,249
Cohabiting	22.7ns	223	25.2*	250
Steady relationship	37.0**	350	34.4***	491
Casual relationship	46.5***	199	45.2***	125

Significance key: ns = not significant; *=P<0.05;**=P<0.01;***=P<0.001
c = reference group to which all other groups are compared.
NOTE: Significance given adjusting for all variables in the table.

Table 8.3: Reasons for not using contraception at most recent sexual intercourse

	18-24	25-34	35-44	45-54	55-64	All
Sex not planned/ unexpected	16.1	10.2	6.9	4.3	2.0	4.6
Drinking alcohol/taking drugs	19.7	1.4	4.6	1.1	0.9	2.3
Couldn't be bothered	0.0	0.9	0.3	0.6	0.0	0.3
Didn't think to use	15.2	12.0	7.0	5.8	2.3	5.2
Took a chance/got carried away	0.0	7.4	4.3	0.0	0.0	1.2
Young/naïve/stupid/careless	4.6	0.0	0.0	0.2	0.0	0.3
No contraception available	18.1	4.8	4.2	1.6	0.9	2.6
Doesn't like/allergic to contraceptives	5.2	3.7	2.1	1.7	0.5	1.5
Against beliefs/religion	0.0	1.9	1.4	0.4	1.5	1.1
Thought partner was using contraception	0.0	0.7	0.0	0.0	0.4	0.3
Not my responsibility	0.0	0.0	0.6	0.0	0.0	0.1
Forgot contraception	4.4	4.3	0.0	0.0	0.0	0.5
Too difficult to discuss contraception	0.0	0.0	0.0	0.0	0.0	0.0
Didn't understand risks	0.0	1.8	0.0	0.2	0.0	0.2
Didn't mind if became pregnant	0.5	12.1	18.3	6.1	4.8	7.5
Didn't care if (partner) became pregnant	0.0	0.0	0.0	0.0	0.0	0.0
Post-menopausal/unlikely to conceive	1.4	1.2	14.6	58.9	77.1	54.0
Can't remember	16.6	15.5	8.5	3.7	1.5	4.8
N	67	117	220	465	742	1,611

Table 8.2: Contraception and precautions (as a proportion of those reporting contraceptive use) on most recent occasion of sexual intercourse (%)

	18-24	25-34	35-44	45-54	55-64	All
Men						
Condom/male-female sheath	82.1	59.0	44.1	40.3	38.0	57.0
Contraceptive pill	30.1	35.9	29.1	13.6	23.2	28.5
Coil/IUD/Mirena	0.2	3.5	5.5	4.7	2.9	3.3
Cap/diaphragm	0.0	0.0	0.1	0.4	0.4	0.1
Spermicides (gels, sprays or pessaries)	0.2	0.0	0.1	0.0	0.0	0.1
Persona	0.0	0.0	0.0	0.0	0.0	0.0
Safe period/rhythm/Billings	0.2	1.0	3.8	6.7	1.4	2.4
Withdrawal	0.5	2.9	3.1	3.4	6.4	2.6
Injections/implants/patches/ring	2.2	1.0	0.9	0.8	1.9	1.3
Sterilisation	0.0	2.4	14.3	31.5	25.3	10.6
Emergency contraception	0.3	0.4	0.5	0.0	0.0	0.3
N	551	522	405	275	97	1,850
Women						
Condom/male-female sheath	73.7	49.6	39.7	40.5	44.5	52.1
Contraceptive pill	45.7	42.1	20.8	10.1	31.2	32.4
Coil/IUD/Mirena	0.4	8.1	12.7	9.4	1.5	7.3
Cap/diaphragm	0.0	0.1	0.0	0.7	0.0	0.1
Spermicides (gels, sprays or pessaries)	0.2	0.1	0.0	0.0	0.0	0.1
Persona	0.1	0.1	0.3	0.0	0.0	0.1
Safe period/rhythm/Billings	0.2	1.1	5.1	6.5	7.2	2.9
Withdrawal	0.4	2.1	3.2	7.8	5.3	2.8
Injections/implants/patches/ring	3.1	2.8	1.6	0.7	0.0	2.2
Sterilisation	0.0	4.6	18.8	25.3	14.1	10.5
Emergency contraception	0.2	0.2	0.2	0.0	0.0	0.2
N	662	686	624	295	54	2,321

Table 9.4: Proportion ever seeking advice about sexually transmitted infections: by socio-demographic characteristics

	Men		Women	
	%	N	%	N
All	9.4	3176	8.3	4240
Current age (years)				
18-24 years	13.1c	754	16.1c	908
25-34 years	12.7ns	700	12.8ns	964
35-44 years	11.0ns	645	5.1ns	1007
45-54 years	5.2ns	571	3.8**	755
55-64 years	2.4**	506	2.2**	606
Education (highest level attained)				
Primary	2.0**	263	3.4*	304
Lower secondary	9.7*	544	4.7ns	656
Upper secondary	9.2**	1190	7.7ns	1771
Third level	15.1c	1179	15.3c	1509
Social class				
Higher professional	11.7ns	788	13.0ns	638
Lower professional	9.6ns	729	9.2ns	1093
Administrative/clerical	9.5ns	427	6.2ns	975
Skilled manual	7.2ns	611	11.2ns	296
Semi/unskilled	9.4c	490	6.8c	891
Relationship status				
Married	5.6c	1496	3.2c	2351
Cohabiting	12.6*	239	18.0***	270
Steady relationship	16.8***	370	17.9***	520
Casual relationship	12.7*	221	22.9***	141
Not in a relationship	11.8***	850	9.5***	958
Area of residence				
City	12.4**	1144	10.7**	1323
Rural/town	7.7c	2031	7.0c	2913

Significance key: ns = not significant; *=P<0.05;**=P<0.01;***=P<0.001
c = reference group to which all other groups are compared.
NOTE: Significance given adjusting for all variables in the table.

Table 9.3: Experience of sexually transmitted infections: by socio-demographic characteristics

	Men		Women	
	%	N	%	N
All	3.4	3,176	1.8	4,238
Current age (years)				
18-24 years	2.0c	755	2.6c	908
25-34 years	4.8***	700	3.6*	964
35-44 years	4.8***	645	1.1ns	1,006
45-54 years	2.1**	571	1.4ns	755
55-64 years	2.5**	505	0.1*	605
Education (highest level attained)				
Primary	3.3	263	0.4	303
Lower secondary	4.1	544	0.8	656
Upper secondary	2.7	1,192	1.9	1,772
Third level	3.9	1,177	3.4	1,507
Social class				
Higher professional	3.2c	786	3.3c	639
Lower professional	2.9ns	730	2.2ns	1,092
Administrative/clerical	3.7ns	427	2.0ns	974
Skilled manual	5.0ns	611	0.6**	296
Semi/unskilled	2.1ns	491	1.1*	891
Relationship status				
Not in a relationship	4.9***	852	2.2*	957
Married	1.8c	1,495	1.0c	2,350
Cohabiting	3.4	239	3.4ns	270
Steady relationship	4.7***	370	2.6ns	520
Casual relationship	6.5***	220	5.8**	141
Age of first intercourse				
After age 17	2.5c	2,540	1.5c	3,778
Before age 17	6.6***	636	4.5*	460

Significance key: ns = not significant; *=P<0.05;**=P<0.01;***=P<0.001
c = reference group to which all other groups are compared.
NOTE: Significance given adjusting for all variables in the table, except education.

Table 9.5: Sources of advice about STIs: by gender and current age (%)

	18-24	25-34	35-44	45-54	55-64	All
Men						
GP	24.5	37.2	34.5	31.5	41.1	32.3
Family planning/Well Woman clinic	6.5	5.1	0.7	2.6	3.6	4.0
Hospital outpatient department	5.3	16.0	21.7	15.6	6.1	14.1
Other sexual health centre	9.3	15.9	20.4	11.0	9.7	14.5
Chemist/pharmacy	0.0	1.4	1.6	0.0	0.0	0.9
Telephone helpline	0.0	0.0	0.0	0.0	0.0	0.0
Obtained leaflets	25.5	10.9	14.9	22.7	32.6	18.4
Visited an internet site	23.8	11.4	8.7	13.8	6.9	14.3
Other	11.1	7.2	1.3	6.1	0.0	6.2
N	107.0	102.0	67.0	33.0	19.0	328.0
Women						
GP	41.0	46.9	41.3	44.0	24.7	42.5
Family planning/Well Woman clinic	19.3	27.9	21.4	13.5	29.2	22.2
Hospital outpatient department	6.7	7.1	9.7	16.3	24.1	8.8
Other sexual health centre	3.2	13.2	10.6	17.3	0.0	8.6
Chemist/pharmacy	0.7	0.0	0.0	0.0	0.0	0.3
Telephone helpline	0.0	0.0	0.0	0.0	0.0	0.0
Obtained leaflets	16.7	7.5	14.3	5.1	21.9	12.7
Visited an internet site	6.3	1.3	0.0	4.7	0.0	3.4
Other	13.5	4.6	6.0	9.9	0.0	8.7
N	144.0	129.0	51.0	34.0	14.0	372.0